Lecture Notes in Computer Scien

Commenced Publication in 1973
Founding and Former Series Editors:
Gerhard Goos, Juris Hartmanis, and Jan van Leeuwen

Ole Fogh Olsen   Luc Florack
Arjan Kuijper (Eds.)

Deep Structure, Singularities, and Computer Vision

First International Workshop, DSSCV 2005
Maastricht, The Netherlands, June 9-10, 2005
Revised Selected Papers

 Springer

Volume Editors

Ole Fogh Olsen
IT University of Copenhagen, Department of Innovation
Rued Langgaards Vej 7, 2300 Copenhagen S, Denmark
E-mail: fogh@itu.dk

Luc Florack
Technical University of Einhoven
Department of Biomedical Engineering
Den Dolech 2, Postbus 513, 5600 MB Eindhoven, The Netherlands
E-mail: L.M.J.Florack@tue.nl

Arjan Kuijper
IT University of Copenhagen, Department of Innovation
Rued Langgaards Vej 7, 2300 Copenhagen, Denmark
E-mail: arjan@itu.dk

Library of Congress Control Number: 2005935534

CR Subject Classification (1998): I.4, I.5, I.3.5, I.2.10, I.2.6, F.2.2

ISSN   0302-9743
ISBN-10   3-540-29836-3 Springer Berlin Heidelberg New York
ISBN-13   978-3-540-29836-6 Springer Berlin Heidelberg New York

Springer is a part of Springer Science+Business Media

springeronline.com

© Springer-Verlag Berlin Heidelberg 2005
Printed in Germany

Typesetting: Camera-ready by author, data conversion by Scientific Publishing Services, Chennai, India
Printed on acid-free paper   SPIN: 11577812   06/3142   5 4 3 2 1 0

Preface

What is actually the information directly represented in the scale-space? I started to wonder about this shortly after Peter Johansen, 15 years ago, showed me his intriguing paper on how uniquely to reconstruct a band-limited 1D signal from its scale-space toppoints. Still, I have not fully understood its implications. Merely recording where structure vanishes under blurring is sufficient to fully reconstruct the details. Of course, technicalities exist, for example, you must also know negative scale toppoints. Nevertheless, I find it surprising that we may trade the metric properties of a signal with the positions of its inherent structure. The result has been generalized to analytic signals, shown also for the zero crossings of the Laplacean, but has not yet been generalized to 2D. This remains an open problem.

In 2003, Peter Giblin, Liverpool University, Luc Florack, Eindhoven University of Technology, Jon Sporring, University of Copenhagen, my colleague Ole Fogh Olsen, and several others started the project collaboration *Deep Structure and Singularities in Computer Vision* under the European Union, IST, Future and Emerging Technologies program, trying to obtain further knowledge about what information is actually carried by the singularities of shapes and gray-scale images. In this project, we probed from several directions the question of how much of the metric information is actually encoded in the structure of shapes and images. We, and many others, have given hints in this direction. We have shown that—to a very large degree—you may reconstruct 2D images from their toppoints, and—to a very large degree—you may identify images in a database based solely on the toppoints. Likewise, we have shown that—to a very large degree—you may index shapes based on their singularities, as was shown earlier by Benjamin Kimia and colleagues. Hence, the structure may be useful. But still, we do not really know its limitations.

This current volume of LNCS is the proceedings from the workshop held in Maastricht, June 10–11, 2005. This workshop was based on invited speakers and contributed papers subjected to peer review. From these, 22 papers were selected for this volume. They represent the year 2005 state of the art in understanding the relation between structural, topological information represented by singularities and metric information of signals, shapes, images, and colors. The concise results like "the toppoints encode all metric information" still remain, but progress and insight have been gained over the last 15 years. In this volume, the reader will find papers by many of the people who have contributed to the discussion in the past: Does structure matter?

Mads Nielsen
The IT University of Copenhagen

Organization

Organizing Committee

Luc Florack
Mads Nielsen
Arjan Kuijper

Ole Fogh Olsen
Camilla Jørgensen

Technical Committee

Bram Platel
Frans Kanters

Mac Wendelboe

Program Chairs

Ole Fogh Olsen

Luc Florack

Program Committee

Mads Nielsen
Kim Steenstrup Pedersen
Martin Lillholm
Arjan Kuijper
Anna Pagh
Philip Bille
Jon Sporring
Kerawit Somchaipeng

Frans Kanters
Bram Platel
Peter Giblin
Andre Diatta
Ali Shokoufandeh
Benjamin B. Kimia
James Damon

Referees

Remco Duits
Marco Loog

Evguenia Balmachnova

Invited Speakers

James Damon (University of North Carolina)
Ali Shokoufandeh (Drexel University)
Benjamin B. Kimia (Brown University)

Sponsoring Organizations

NWO, the Netherlands Organisation for Scientific Research, and the IST Programme of the European Union are gratefully acknowledged for financial support.

Table of Contents

Oral Presentations

Poster Presentations

Blurred Correlation Versus Correlation Blur

Jan J. Koenderink and Andrea van Doorn

Universiteit Utrecht
j.j.koenderink@phys.uu.nl

Abstract. We discuss the topic of correlation in a scale space setting. Correlation involves two distinct scales. The "outer scale" is the scale of the region over which the correlation will be calculated. Classically this is the whole space of interest, but in many cases one desires the correlation over some region of interest. The "inner scale" is the scale at which the signals to be correlated are represented. Classically this means infinite precision. For our purposes we define "correlation" as the point–wise product of two signals, "blurred correlation" as the integration of this correlation over the region of interest, and "correlation blur" as this point–wise correlation applied to the signals represented at the inner scale. For generic purposes we are interested in "blurred correlation blur". We discuss a well known (and practically important) example of blurred correlation for essentially zero inner scale. Such a situation leads to apparently paradoxical results. We then discuss correlation blur, which can be understood as a form of "regularized" correlation, leading to intuitively acceptable results even for the case of point sets (*e.g.*, temporal events or point sets in space). We develop the formal structure and present a number of examples.

1   Blurred Correlation

We will speak of a "correlation" $r(s)$ of two signals $f(r)$ and $g(r)$ if $r(s)$ is a blurred version of the product of blurred versions of $f(r)$ and $g(r)$. This is a slight generalization of the usual concept where the correlation is the fully blurred product of the unblurred functions. Notice that there exist two essential scale parameters here, namely the "outer scale", which is the scale of the blurring of the product, and the "inner scale", which is the scale of the blurring of the components.

First we will consider the case of very small inner scale, *i.e.*, the components are *fully resolved* at the point where they enter the multiplication process. Such cases are comparatively rare.

A key instance of this "blurred correlation" occurs in human vision[10]. The causal chain in vision goes as follows: An illuminant causes an illumination spectrum $f(\lambda)$ on a surface with spectral reflectance $g(\lambda)$, causing a beam to be scattered to the eye whose luminance—apart from an inessential constant factor—has a spectrum that equals the product $f(\lambda)g(\lambda)$. The product is blurred in the retinal transduction process and gives rise to the blurred correlation $k(\lambda; \sigma) \circ (f(\lambda)g(\lambda))$ of which three point samples enter the optic nerve. The

O.F. Olsen et al. (Eds.): DSSCV 2005, LNCS 3753, pp. 1–11, 2005.

blurring kernel $k(\lambda; \sigma)$ is approximately a gaussian of spectral width σ, it is due to the action spectra of the retinal photoreceptor cells. The point samples are taken at spectral locations such that the kernels centered at these locations have significant overlap. The vector of samples is an element of the three–dimensional colorimetric space, which is a linear projection of the infinitely dimensional Hilbert space of spectra of beams that enter the pupil. One consequently says that the human visual system is "trichromatic".

In the simplest setting the observer has some default assumption concerning the spectrum of the illuminant (for instance that it corresponds to the "average daylight spectrum") and thus can perform low resolution spectroscopy on the spectral reflectances (often called "spectral signatures"). Obviously this inference is rather ambiguous, a fact known as "metamerism". Yet human observers generally manage to distinguish between lemons and oranges on the basis of their "color".

It is easy to prove that surfaces and lightsources may be designed such that surface samples $\{a, b\}$ say will lead to colors $\{\mathcal{P}, \mathcal{Q}\}$ under source A and $\{\mathcal{Q}, \mathcal{P}\}$ under source B. Here $\mathcal{P}$ and $\mathcal{Q}$ may be *any* color you fancy. This fact (it is indeed a fact though we are not aware of a published proof) has led philosophers[4] to state that color vision is impossible! (As the saying goes "colors are mere mental paint".) Thus this fact has very important (and counterintuitive) consequences. Yet it is true. Here is a constructive proof:

Proof: Let $\Delta\lambda$ be a spectral bin width that is *much* narrower than σ, as small as you wish. We partition the spectrum in non–overlapping, contiguous bins of width $\Delta\lambda$. We sample the source spectrum and spectral signatures (as is in fact commonly done in colorimetry). Now we split each bin into two equal sub–bins, say the "left" and "right" sub–bins. We define source A to be the spectrum of a truly white source (say average daylight) in the left bins and zero in the right bins. Similarly, we define source B as zero in the left bins and the same truly white source in the right bins. We double the illuminance to keep the total illuminance equal to that of the proper white source W (which has equal value in both the left and right bin). A piece of white paper (constant reflectance equal to unity) will look the identical white under these three sources. (In fact, virtually *all* surfaces you may encounter in daily life will look identical under these sources.) Next we sample the spectral signatures for the selected beams that will yield the colors $\mathcal{P}$ and $\mathcal{Q}$. Then we prepare the sample a such that the spectrum for $\mathcal{P}$ goes in the left and the spectrum for $\mathcal{Q}$ in the right bins. For the sample b we do the same, except that we interchange the two spectra. As a result source A will produce color $\mathcal{P}$ from sample a and color $\mathcal{Q}$ from sample b, whereas source B will produce color $\mathcal{Q}$ from sample a and color $\mathcal{P}$ from sample b. (Source W will show the color of the equal mixture.) Notice that the same trick allows us to construct a surface and any number of sources n such that the surface will look any predetermined color for source $i \in (1 \ldots n)$. ∎ Q.E.D.

Consider a simple example. A trichromatic vision system has the spectral "fundamental response curves" shown in figure 1. Here we have abstracted the spectral range as the interval $(0, 1)$, and the system simply finds the average radiant power in three subranges of length $1/3$ each, thus the result of a measurement is a color vector $\{r, g, b\}$ where we refer to the coordinates (arbitrarily) as "red", "green" and "blue", for ease of reference.

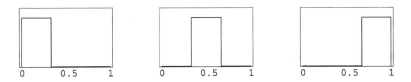

Fig. 1. The fundamental response curves of a color system

We consider a "standard illuminant" with a flat spectrum, and two "special illuminants" A, and B, as shown in figure 2. Notice that the special illuminants have mutually exclusive support, and that both "cover the spectral range uniformly", albeit with frequent minor gaps. These illuminants can be thought of as "multiplexing" the spectrum.

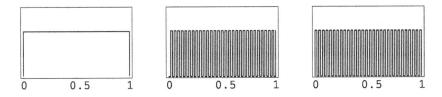

Fig. 2. The powerspectrum of the standard illuminant (left) and the "special illuminants" A and B (center and right respectively)

We consider two samples with spectral signatures shown in figure 3. The "gray" sample has a flat spectral signature, whereas the "special" sample has a rather complicated spectral signature, whose transitions occur at the same positions as those of the special illuminants.

In figure 4 we show the radiant power spectra of the beams that are scattered towards the eye by various combinations of illuminants and samples. These beams lead to *colors* generated by the visual mechanism illustrated in figure 1. We assume that all this "observer" does is report these colors, which we will describe in terms of the conventional color names.

The way a magician might try to fool the observer (who is supposed to be unaware of the way the magician prepared the illuminants and samples) might run as follows

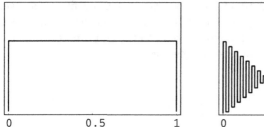
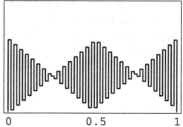

Fig. 3. The spectral signatures of the gray sample (left) and the special sample (right)

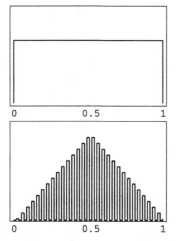
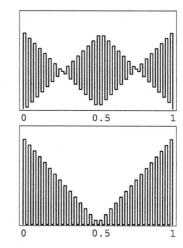

Fig. 4. The beams scattered towards the eye from the gray sample (top left) and special sample (top right), as illuminated by the standard illuminant. The bottom row shows the beams scattered towards the eye from the special sample as illuminated by the special beam A (left) and B (right).

1. The magician takes the gray sample and holds it under each illuminant in turn. The observer reports "white" (that is $\alpha\{1,1,1\}$) in all three cases. The magician does this in order to let the observer believe that the three illuminants are the same.
2. In order to strengthen this (false!) impression the magician might show samples with smooth spectral signatures like $\beta\lambda$, (looks blue) $\beta(1-\lambda)$ (looks red), $4\beta(\lambda-0.5)^2$ (looks purple), $\beta[1-4(\lambda-0.5)^2]$ (looks green). They look identical under all three illuminants.
3. The magician selects one illuminant (the *standard* illuminant!) in order to let the observer compare the samples, perhaps remarking that the "illuminants are the same anyway". Both the gray sample and the special sample look the same to the observer (both $\gamma\{1,1,1\}$, that is "white"). The magician does

this in order to let the observer believe (falsely again!) that the samples are the same.

4. In order to strengthen this (false!) impression the magician might show the samples under a number of illuminants with simple spectra like $\delta\lambda$, (looks blue) $\delta(1-\lambda)$ (looks red), $4\delta(\lambda-0.5)^2$ (looks purple), $\delta[1-4(\lambda-0.5)^2]$ (looks green). The two samples look identical under all such illuminants.

5. Now the magician has prepared the observer for his "magic": The magician takes the special sample (white paper!) and places it under the special illuminants (white lights!) in turn. Under the special illuminant A the special sample looks *green* (that is $\varepsilon\{2,5,2\}$), and under the special illuminant B the special sample looks *purple* (that is $\varphi\{4,1,4\}$)!

The observer is suitably impressed by this true magic! How can a piece of white paper become *colored* when illuminated by a white source? If this is possible anything goes! As many philosophers have it: "Color is mere mental paint".

In principle there is nothing that would prevent one from preparing such a trick, no principle of physics is violated by the magician. Yet the observer has no way to predict the outcome of any case on the basis of mere color observations.

Although this is all true, and one has to grant the philosophers that color vision is indeed impossible(!), the result should be highly *counterintuitive*. It is indeed counterintuitive because cases like this appear as sheer "magic", since such cases simply *never* occur (to such an extent) in real life. Indeed the setting up of this situation asks for very precise engineering, the way magicians set up their tricks (although not physically impossible, current technology is not up to this feat). Several things are very "non–generic" in the ecological sense:

— actual illuminants and spectral signatures are not that articulated. Most spectra are smooth, even on the scale σ;

— even if the illuminant spectrum and spectral signatures were to be rough on a scale finer than σ, it is *very* unlikely indeed that they would happen to be "in sync" as the example requires. The physical reason is that spectral signatures and illuminant spectra are due to completely independent physical causes.

As a result, in real life colors are far from being "mental paint". Indeed, color vision is much closer to some form of very low resolution spectroscopy. It is not a miracle at all (as many philosophers would have it) that you easily (in normal circumstances) distinguish between lemons and oranges on the basis of their color.

This suggests perhaps that there is something very artificial about the notion of "blurred correlation" in the sense that it allows "miracles": Invisible structures (because not resolved in the signals f and g) may give rise to visible effects in the blurred correlation r. Such effects occur if—behind the scene—some common cause structures the signals at the microlevel. In practice blurred correlation is only useful if you have some independent (we mean not obtained via the observation of the signals f and g) prior knowledge. Examples include "point matching" where you have two point clouds known to differ only by some transformation from a known group.

The "blurred correlation" case occurs frequently in computer vision in problems of image registration, point matching in sparse point clouds, *etc.* Cases like color vision are so interesting because the inner scale pops up in the phenomena though the system itself (the visual system) functions at a completely different (outer) scale. This leads to (from the perspective of the system) "magic" effects that can in no way be accounted for.

2   Correlation Blur

In "correlation blur" it are the *components* that are blurred, *before* they enter into the multiplication process. In most cases we will follow this up by a blurring of the correlation, but in the first instance we will ignore this step. Notice that correlation blur would serve to "regularize" the colorimetric example in the sense that it will make no difference whether the samples are presented under the sources A, B or W. This effect cannot be obtained by blurring the correlation (as happens in color vision), thus "correlation blur" differs essentially from "blurred correlation".

Correlation blur is commonly applied in the correlation of point events[1]. If events are of arbitrarily short duration, then no two physical event trains are likely to show any correlation at all, because there will necessarily be some temporal or spatial uncertainty in the exact moments of occurrence of the events. Notice that this renders the very notion of "correlation" meaningless. Hence it is common practice to compute correlation relative to some (often arbitrarily assigned) "correlation window". Such a window effectively introduces the inner scale. Although the introduction of a "correlation window" is common enough, it is usually considered a mere (trivial) technicality, hardly worth mentioning. Yet the correlation window width will obviously show up in the results. It is much to be preferred to take the introduction of the inner scale in the correlation process serious and frame a formal theory of it.

Cases where correlation blur is perceived to be evidently necessary are abundant in vision. Consider cases like two "intersecting" schools of (different) fish, treetops, and so forth. Of course the fish nor the twigs actually (physically) "overlap" in the sense of sharing a common volume of flesh or wood, yet the schools or the treetops evidently *do* share (distributed) biomass. Human observers spontaneously "see" the degree of overlap in such cases. Visually the schools of fish or treetops *do* share a common volume. One obviously needs to adjust the notion of "geometrical overlap" accordingly.

One way to obtain such effects formally is to blur the component functions before the multiplication takes place[8,9], in other words, to consider "correlation blur". Thus we are led to consider the signal $r = (k_\sigma \circ f) \bullet (k_\sigma \circ g)$ ("$\circ$" denotes convolution, "$\bullet$" correlation—here shift and multiplication), for the kernel k for which we will assume a gaussian. Explicitly we have

$$r(t, s) = \left(\int k_\sigma(\tau) f(t - \tau) \, d\tau \right) \left(\int k_\sigma(\xi) g(t + s - \xi) \, d\xi \right)$$

$$= \int K_\sigma(\tau, \xi) h(t - \tau, t + s - \xi) \, d\tau d\xi,$$

where we have introduced the (isotropic) kernel

$$K(u, v) = k(u) k(v) = K(\sqrt{\|u\|^2 + \|v\|^2}),$$

and the product function $h(u, v) = f(u) g(v)$ in $\{u, v\}$–product space. Thus the correlation $r(t, s)$ is the blurred version (with blur kernel $K(u, v)$) of the product $f(t) g(t + s)$ of the unblurred functions, in the *product image* domain, that is the "raw" ("unblurred") correlation.

The classical correlation is the integral of $r(t, s)$ over t, for $s = 0$ the integral over the diagonal of the product image domain. But due to the width σ of the kernel the blurring of the original signals has the effect of effectively integrating over a diagonal strip of finite width. This is the "correlation window" effect.

The correlation blur of two sets can be understood as the linear superposition of gaussians due to *pairs of points*, one point in the first, the other in the second set. For consider the pair of weighted points

$$f(t) = F\delta(t - t_0)$$
$$g(t) = G\delta(t - t_1),$$

then the autocorrelation is

$$r(t, 0) = FG \, K_\sigma(t - t_0, t - t_1),$$

which reaches a maximum at the average location t_{mean}

$$t_{\text{mean}} = \frac{t_0 + t_1}{2}.$$

depending on the separation Δt

$$FG \, K_\sigma(\sqrt{2}\|\Delta t\|) \qquad \text{where} \qquad \Delta t = \frac{t_0 - t_1}{2},$$

Thus due to the weight $K_\sigma(\sqrt{2}\|\Delta t\|)$ only pairs of points that are close on the inner scale will contribute significantly. Thus we obtain an intuitive representation of the "event windowing" praxis.

In general we will add a blur to the correlation blur. We obtain

$$r(t, s) = \int k_\eta(\zeta) \left[\int K_\sigma(\sqrt{\|\tau\|^2 + \|\xi\|^2}) h(t + \zeta - \tau, t + \zeta + s - \xi) \, d\tau d\xi \right] d\zeta,$$

where $k_\eta(\zeta)$ denotes an isotropic Gaussian kernel of scale parameter η. If the average distance between the fish in a school is large with respect to the inner scale, such an additional blur will serve to smooth away the "fishy" structure

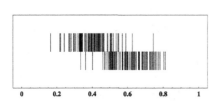 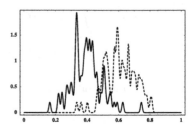

Fig. 5. Left: Two random event trains. The events have been drawn from somewhat staggered gaussian distributions of equal width. The "overlap" is visually evident. Right: Blurring the event trains yields noisy estimates of the p.d.f's used to generate the event trains. These estimates have common support, whereas the original event trains have not.

of the school. Notice that this "blurred correlation blur" depends on two scales, the "inner scale" σ and the "outer scale" η (where typically $\eta \gg \sigma$).

We have obtained a nice, linear "scale space" representation[5,2,3], albeit in the *product space*, and dependent on two scales, rather than just a single scale. One may develop a formal theory of correlation as a special branch of scale space theory.

Correlation blur thus serves to "define correlation where these isn't any" and thus it depends essentially on the current *context* whether the concept makes sense. Both the inner and the outer scale can only be picked if the nature of the problem has been agreed upon. For a single structure (a pair of given images say) one might easily be interested in various aspects of the mutual structure and for each aspect the choice of inner and outer scale would be different. Any pair of images can thus be associated with a two parameter (inner and outer scale) "blurred correlation blur" scale space. Such association structures are clearly of considerable practical interest, yet have (thus far) not been formally studied, at least not in the most general setting.

3   An Example

The simplest case concerns a pair of one–dimensional images. We will consider point clouds that mutually overlap in the obvious *visual* sense, yet have only insignificant classical correlation. *E.g.*, we may assume that no point in one image coincides precisely with any point in the other image. We will consider two point clouds that are defined via random locations drawn from certain p.d.f's. In that case one intuitively expects the (suitably) blurred correlation blur to reflect the product of these (implicit) densities. An example is shown in figure 5.

Blurring the signals produces overlapping distributions, and indeed, the product of the blurred functions reveals the "overlap" (figure 6). A blurring of the product produces a result that is quite similar to the product of the distributions from which the random pulse trains were generated.

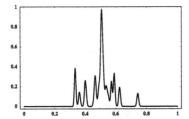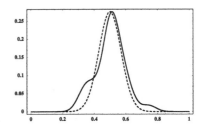

Fig. 6. Left: The product of the blurred event trains (the "correlation blur") yields a noisy estimate of the "overlap" as it is "seen" by the human observer. Right: The "blurred correlation blur" is (for these parameters at least) a reasonable estimate of the product of the original p.d.f.'s. This function is—at least for many purposes—far more informative than the classical correlation function (which is zero!).

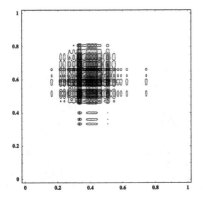

Fig. 7. The two event trains in product space. Blurring this "image" implements "correlation blur". The autocorrelation is found on the diagonal of the space. Pooling over areas "blurs the correlation".

In this case it is possible to display the product space, see figure 7. In most cases the high dimensionality of product space will prohibit its display.

If you have two overlapping or even non–overlapping regions, say two circular discs (figure 8), they develop an overlap in the sense of correlation blur. When the inner scale doesn't allow a clear cut separation of the regions, we obtain a kind of "tunneling" whereby points may change there membership and start to belong to *both* regions. In figure 8 the circles actually overlap. We produced two random point clouds by generating random points for unform distributions in these circular areas. Figure 9 shows the point sets blurred to the inner scale. The correlation blur (figure 10 *left*) reveals the "overlap" that is also visually compelling. The blurred correlation blur (figure 10 *right*) yields a fairly smooth (most of the random point structure has been removed) estimate of the overlap.

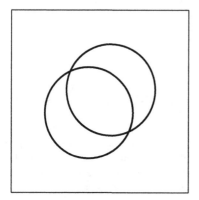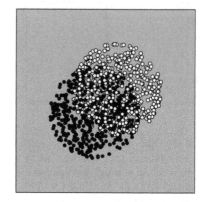

Fig. 8. Left: Two overlapping circular disks in the plane. Right: Two overlapping "circular" point sets in the plane. The overlap is visually compelling, though no point of the first set coincides with any point of the second set: As point sets the overlap is empty.

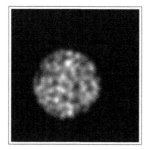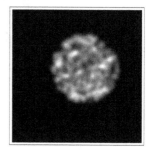

Fig. 9. The blurred point sets

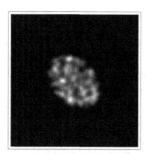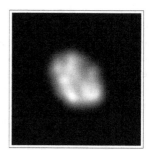

Fig. 10. At left the product of the blurred point sets (the "correlation blur"), at right the "blurred correlation blur". The blurred correlation blur is a good estimate of the "overlap" defined by the "overall shapes" of the point clouds.

The same procedure works in case of two disjoint uniform areas. The blurring at the inner scale "generates fuzzy overlap", although the degree of such overlap is very small unless the regions are rather close on the inner scale. This phenomenon is well known in human visual perception, where it sometimes leads to erroneous observations in unfamiliar visual circumstances as in microscopy or astronomy[6], or is used in the visual arts where the observer may pick a larger than usual inner scale to generate novel (and sometimes unusual) visual connections. In the latter case the observer is aware of different geometrical structures at at least a pair of distinctly different inner scales. Important as such cases are in the arts, there exists hardly any proper psychophysical material on them. Cases like "crowding" may be a case in point[7].

References

1. Aboelela, E., Douligeris, C.: Fuzzy Temporal Reasoning Model for Event Correlation in Network Management, 24th Conference on Local Computer Networks, October 17–20, (1999), Lowell, Massachusetts
2. Florack, M. J.: Image Structure, Vol. **10** of Computational Imaging and Vision Series, Kluwer Academic Publishers: Dordrecht, The Netherlands (1997)
3. Haar Romeny, B. M. ter: Front–End Vision and Multi-Scale Image Analysis, Kluwer Academic Publishers: Dordrecht, The Netherlands (2003)
4. Byrne, A.: The Philosophy of Color, The M.I.T. Press: Cambridge MA (1997)
5. Lindeberg, T.: Scale–Space Theory in Computer Vision, Kluwer Academic Publishers: Dordrecht, The Netherlands (1994)
6. Pasachoff, J. M., Schneider, G., Golub, L. M.: Space Studies of the Black Drop Effect at a Mercury Transit, 25th meeting of the IAU, Joint Discussion 2, 16 July, (2003), Sydney Australia ADS
7. Pelli, D, G.: Crowding is unlike ordinary masking: Distinguishing feature integration from detection. J. of Vision **4** (2004) 1136–1169
8. Robinson, A. H., Bryson, R. A.: A method of describing quantitatively the correspondence of geographical distributions. Annals of the Association of American Geographers, **47** (1957) 379–391
9. Tsin, Y.: Kernel Correlation as an Affinity Measure in Point-Sampled Vision Problems, doctoral dissertation, tech. report CMU–RI–TR–03–36, Robotics Institute, Carnegie Mellon University, (2003)
10. Wyszecki, G., Stiles, W. S.: Color science : concepts and methods, quantitative data and formulae, John Wiley and Sons, 2nd edition: New York (2000)

A Scale Invariant Covariance Structure on Jet Space

Bo Markussen[1], Kim Steenstrup Pedersen[2], and Marco Loog[2]

[1] Department of Computer Science,
University of Copenhagen, Denmark
boma@diku.dk
[2] Image Analysis Group, Department of Innovation,
IT University of Copenhagen, Denmark
{kimstp, marco}@itu.dk

Abstract. This paper considers scale invariance of statistical image models. We study statistical scale invariance of the covariance structure of jet space under scale space blurring and derive the necessary structure and conditions of the jet covariance matrix in order for it to be scale invariant. As part of the derivation, we introduce a blurring operator A_t that acts on jet space contrary to doing spatial filtering and a scaling operator S_s. The stochastic Brownian image model is an example of a class of functions which are scale invariant with respect to the operators A_t and S_s. This paper also includes empirical results where we estimate the scale invariant jet covariance of natural images and show that it resembles that of Brownian images.

1 Introduction

Statistical image models are receiving growing attention, e.g. [1,2,3,4,5,6], especially due to the increasing popularity of Bayesian methods in image analysis and computer vision, where such models are applied as a priori models of natural images.

In this paper we discuss invariance properties of statistical image models. We focus on stationarity and statistical scale invariance. Stationarity has the consequence that there are no preferred positions in images and scale invariance leads to no preferred scales. Both assumptions are generally agreed upon as being reasonable for natural images, and scale invariance is furthermore supported by various empirical findings, e.g. [7,8,4].

We consider the scale space jet representation of images and focus on the second order statistics of the jet, i.e. the covariance structure. Assuming stationary image increments and scale invariance, we derive necessary conditions of the covariance structure of jet space. As part of this derivation we introduce a blurring operator A_t which acts on jet space as well as a scaling operator S_s which acts as a scale normalization of the axes of jet space, i.e. the partial derivatives. We express statistical scale invariance in terms of statistical invariance under the combination of these two operators.

O.F. Olsen et al. (Eds.): DSSCV 2005, LNCS 3753, pp. 12–23, 2005.

As an example of a scale invariant random function having stationary increments we consider Brownian images. Pedersen [4] suggest that natural images are approximately scale invariant and have a covariance structure similar to that of Brownian images. We also give some empirical evidence that supports this claim.

The structure of this paper is as follows: The necessary covariance structure is derived in several steps in sec. 2. We begin in sec. 2.1 by deriving the covariance structure based on the assumption of stationarity. In sec. 2.2, we introduce the blurring operator A_t, and finally the necessary structure of the covariance matrix based on scale invariance is derived in sec. 2.3. We discuss the Brownian image model in sec. 3 and present empirical results on natural images in sec. 4. Finally, we conclude in sec. 5.

2 Statistical Invariance Properties

In this section invariance properties for statistical image models are introduced. Let $f\colon \mathbb{R}^2 \to \mathbb{R}$ be a two-dimensional gray scale image at scale $s = 0$. We assume that f is a random function, and that $f(0) = 0$. The image f_s at scale $s > 0$ is defined through Gaussian blurring

$$f_s(x) = (g_s * f)(x) = \int_{\mathbb{R}^2} g_s(x - y)\, f(y)\, \mathrm{d}y, \qquad g_s(x) = \frac{1}{2\pi s}\, \mathrm{e}^{-\frac{x_1^2 + x_2^2}{2s}}.$$

Observe that the scale is parameterized in terms of the variance of the blurring kernel. The higher order structure is given by the non-trivial derivatives

$$f_s^{(n,m)}(x) = \frac{\partial^{n+m}}{\partial x_1^n\, \partial x_2^m} f_s(x), \qquad (n, m) \in \mathbb{I} \overset{\text{def}}{=} \mathbb{N}_0^2 \setminus \{(0,0)\}.$$

We assume that f, and hence f_s for every $s > 0$, has zero mean, $\mathbb{E}[f(x)] = 0$, and that the partial derivatives $f_s^{(n,m)}(x) = \frac{\partial^{n+m}}{\partial x_1^n\, \partial x_2^m} f_s(x)$ have second moments for every $x \in \mathbb{R}^2$, $s > 0$ and $(n, m) \in \mathbb{I}$.

We make two assumptions on the image structure: stationarity and scale invariance. Stationarity states that the statistical properties of the increments $f(x) - f(y)$ only depends on the difference $x - y$. Formulated in terms of the covariance structure this means that there exists covariance functions $\rho\colon \mathbb{R}^2 \to \mathbb{R}_+$ such that

$$\mathrm{Var}\big(f(x) - f(y)\big) = \rho(x - y). \tag{1}$$

Observe, that we do not assume the image increments to be isotropic, i.e. that the variance function only depend on the distance $|x-y|$. Thus, stationarity is a more general assumption than isotropy. Moreover, we emphasize that stationarity of the image model itself is not assumed, e.g. we have $f(0) = 0$. If the image f at scale $s = 0$ has stationary increments, then the same is true for the images f_s at every scale $s > 0$.

Scale invariance is formulated in terms of blurring, which can be interpreted as zooming away, i.e. only features on the coarser scale are recognizable. In order to fully implement the zooming away, and hence scaling and not merely blurring, the space should also be appropriately scaled. Let $\alpha > 0$ be the exponent connecting blurring scale s to the physical scale. Doing the scaling around the origin $x = 0$, statistical scale invariance can be stated as the equivalence of the probability distributions of the images $f_s(s^\alpha x)$ and $f_t(t^\alpha x)$ for every $s, t > 0$, i.e.

$$\left\{ f_s(s^\alpha x) \right\}_{x \in \mathbb{R}^2} \overset{\mathcal{D}}{=} \left\{ f_t(t^\alpha x) \right\}_{x \in \mathbb{R}^2}.$$

Introducing the jet $\frac{\partial^{n+m}}{\partial x_1^n \partial x_2^m} f_s(s^\alpha x) = s^{\alpha n + \alpha m} f_s^{(n,m)}(s^\alpha x)$ this implies the distributional equivalence

$$\left\{ s^{\alpha n + \alpha m} f_s^{(n,m)}(s^\alpha x) \right\}_{(n,m) \in \mathbb{I}} \overset{\mathcal{D}}{=} \left\{ t^{\alpha n + \alpha m} f_t^{(n,m)}(t^\alpha x) \right\}_{(n,m) \in \mathbb{I}} \tag{2}$$

for every $x \in \mathbb{R}^2$ and $s, t > 0$, i.e. the distribution of the scale normalized derivatives does not depend on the scale.

In the following sections we investigate the implications of the imposed assumptions on the structure of the covariance of the jet, which is given by

$$\Phi_s = \left\{ \mathrm{Cov}\left(f_s^{(j,k)}(x), f_s^{(n,m)}(x) \right) \right\}_{(j,k),(n,m) \in \mathbb{I}} \in \mathbb{R}^{\mathbb{I} \times \mathbb{I}}.$$

As shown in sec. 2.1 stationarity implies that the covariance Φ_s indeed does not depend on the position x. Moreover, defining the anti-diagonals $\Psi_{2n,2m}$ by

$$\Psi_{2n,2m} = \left\{ (-1)^{\frac{i-k}{2} + \frac{j-l}{2}} 1_{i+k=2n, j+l=2m} \right\}_{(i,j),(k,l) \in \mathbb{I}}, \tag{3}$$

there exists positive constants $c_{n,m}(s) > 0$ such that

$$\Phi_s = \sum_{(n,m) \in \mathbb{I}} c_{n,m}(s) \Psi_{2n,2m}. \tag{4}$$

In sec. 2.3 we prove that there exists an image model with stationary increments and being scale invariant in the sense of eq. (2) if and only if $\alpha = \frac{1}{2}$. For $\alpha \neq \frac{1}{2}$ there only exist image models which are scale invariant in an infinitesimal sense. In both cases these invariance properties holds true if and only if the constants $c_{n,m}(s)$ satisfy the condition

$$c_{n+1,m}(s) + c_{n,m+1}(s) = \frac{2\alpha n + 2\alpha m}{s} c_{n,m}(s). \tag{5}$$

Finally, for $\alpha \neq \frac{1}{2}$ we describe exactly how the infinitesimal scale invariant models fail to be strict scale invariant, cf. eq. (11).

2.1   Stationary Image Models

In this section we give a characterization of the covariance structure for the jet under the assumption of stationary image increments, cf. eq. (1). For positions

$x, y \in \mathbb{R}^2$ employing $f(0) = 0$ yields

$$\mathrm{Cov}\big(f(x), f(y)\big) = \mathbb{E}[f(x)\, f(y)]$$

$$= \frac{\mathbb{E}\big[(f(x) - f(0))^2\big] + \mathbb{E}\big[(f(y) - f(0))^2\big] - \mathbb{E}\big[(f(x) - f(y))^2\big]}{2}$$

$$= \frac{\rho(x) + \rho(y) - \rho(x - y)}{2}.$$

Let positions $x, y \in \mathbb{R}^2$, scales $s, t > 0$ and differentiation orders $(j, k), (n, m) \in \mathbb{I}$ be given. Interchanging the blurring integrals and the expectation and using symmetry of the blurring kernel, i.e. $g_s(u) = g_s(-u)$, we have

$$\mathrm{Cov}\big[f_s^{(j,k)}(x), f_t^{(n,m)}(y)\big]$$

$$= \mathrm{Cov}\left[\int_{\mathbb{R}^2} (-1)^{j+k} \frac{\partial^{j+k} g_s(x - u)}{\partial u_1^j \, \partial u_2^k}\, f(u)\, du, \int_{\mathbb{R}^2} (-1)^{n+m} \frac{\partial^{n+m} g_t(y - v)}{\partial v_1^n \, \partial v_2^m}\, f(v)\, dv\right]$$

$$= \int_{\mathbb{R}^2} \int_{\mathbb{R}^2} g_s(x - u)\, g_t(y - v)\, \frac{\partial^{j+k}}{\partial u_1^j \, \partial u_2^k} \frac{\partial^{n+m}}{\partial v_1^n \, \partial v_2^m} \mathrm{Cov}\big[f(u), f(v)\big]\, du\, dv$$

$$= \int_{\mathbb{R}^2} \int_{\mathbb{R}^2} g_s(x - u)\, g_t(y - v)\, \frac{\partial^{j+k+n+m}}{\partial u_1^j \, \partial u_2^k \, \partial v_1^n \, \partial v_2^m} \frac{\rho(u) + \rho(v) - \rho(u - v)}{2}\, du\, dv$$

$$= -\frac{1}{2} \int_{\mathbb{R}^2} \int_{\mathbb{R}^2} g_s(x - u)\, g_t(y - v)\, \frac{\partial^{j+k+n+m}}{\partial u_1^j \, \partial u_2^k \, \partial v_1^n \, \partial v_2^m} \rho(u - v)\, du\, dv$$

$$= \frac{(-1)^{1+j+k}}{2} \int_{\mathbb{R}^2} \int_{\mathbb{R}^2} g_s(x - u)\, g_t(y - v)\, \frac{\partial^{j+k+n+m}}{\partial v_1^{j+n} \, \partial v_2^{k+m}} \rho(u - v)\, du\, dv$$

$$= \frac{(-1)^{1+j+k}}{2} \int_{\mathbb{R}^2} \int_{\mathbb{R}^2} g_s(x - y - u)\, g_t(v)\, \frac{\partial^{j+k+n+m}}{\partial v_1^{j+n} \, \partial v_2^{k+m}} \rho(u - v)\, du\, dv.$$

Modulo the sign $(-1)^{j+k}$ the latter integral only depends on j, k, n, m via the sums $j + n$ and $k + m$. Moreover, since the variance function ρ must be even the integral vanishes unless both $j + n$ and $k + m$ are even. Thus, we have showed that $\mathrm{Cov}\big[f_s^{(j,k)}(x), f_t^{(n,m)}(y)\big]$ for $(j, k), (n, m) \in \mathbb{I}$ equals

$$1_{j+n \text{ even}, \, k+m \text{ even}} \, (-1)^{\frac{j-n}{2} + \frac{k-m}{2}} \, \mathrm{Cov}\big[f_s^{(\frac{j+n}{2}, \frac{k+m}{2})}(x - y), f_t^{(\frac{j+n}{2}, \frac{k+m}{2})}(0)\big].$$

We can recap this in terms of the covariance structure $\Phi_s \in \mathbb{R}^{\mathbb{I} \times \mathbb{I}}$ of the entire jet $\{f_s^{(n,m)}(x)\}_{(n,m) \in \mathbb{I}}$ at position x and scale s,

$$\Phi_s = \Big\{\mathrm{Cov}\big(f_s^{(j,k)}(x), f_s^{(n,m)}(x)\big)\Big\}_{(j,k),(n,m) \in \mathbb{I}}$$

$$= \Big\{\mathrm{Cov}\big(f_s^{(j,k)}(0), f_s^{(n,m)}(0)\big)\Big\}_{(j,k),(n,m) \in \mathbb{I}} \tag{6}$$

$$= \sum_{(n,m) \in \mathbb{I}} c_{n,m}(s)\, \Psi_{2n,2m}.$$

for some positive constants $c_{n,m}(s) > 0$ and where the anti-diagonals $\Psi_{2n,2m}$ are defined by eq. (3)

2.2   Gaussian Blurring in Jet Space

In this section we consider the representation of Gaussian blurring in the jet space domain. We assume that the image f_s at scale $s > 0$ can be represented by its Taylor series around every x, i.e.

$$f_s(y) = \sum_{(n,m)\in\mathbb{N}_0^2} \frac{f_s^{(n,m)}(x)}{n!\,m!}(y_1 - x_1)^n(y_2 - x_2)^m, \quad f_s^{(n,m)}(x) = \frac{\partial^{n+m} f_s(x)}{\partial x_1^n \partial x_2^m}.$$

Consider the operators $\mathcal{J}_x$, $\mathcal{T}_x$ taking the image into the jet space of partial derivatives at x and combining the jet into the Taylor series, respectively,

$$\mathcal{J}_x(f_s) = \left\{ \frac{\partial^{n+m} f_s(x)}{\partial x_1^n \partial x_2^m} \right\}_{(n,m)\in\mathbb{N}_0^2},$$

$$\mathcal{T}_x\big(\{j_{n,m}\}_{(n,m)\in\mathbb{N}_0^2}\big)(y) = \sum_{(n,m)\in\mathbb{N}_0^2} \frac{j_{n,m}}{n!\,m!}(y_1 - x_1)^n(y_2 - x_2)^m.$$

The operators $\mathcal{T}_x \circ \mathcal{J}_x$ and $\mathcal{J}_x \circ \mathcal{T}_x$ take the image and the jet, respectively, into themselves. Gaussian blurring of the jet by scale t is given by

$$f_{t+s}^{(j,k)}(x) = \int_{\mathbb{R}}\int_{\mathbb{R}} \frac{e^{-\frac{(y_1-x_1)^2+(y_2-x_2)^2}{2t}}}{2\pi t} f_s^{(j,k)}(y)\,dy_1\,dy_2$$

$$= \int_{\mathbb{R}}\int_{\mathbb{R}} \frac{e^{-\frac{(y_1-x_1)^2+(y_2-x_2)^2}{2t}}}{2\pi t} \sum_{(n,m)\in\mathbb{N}_0^2} \frac{f_s^{(j+n,k+m)}(x)}{n!\,m!}(y_1 - x_1)^n(y_2 - x_2)^m\,dy_1\,dy_2.$$

Interchanging the integrals and the sum we find

$$f_{t+s}^{(j,k)}(x) = \sum_{(n,m)\in\mathbb{N}_0^2} \frac{f_s^{(j+n,k+m)}(x)}{n!\,m!} \int_{\mathbb{R}}\int_{\mathbb{R}} \frac{e^{-\frac{(y_1-x_1)^2+(y_2-x_2)^2}{2t}}}{2\pi t}(y_1 - x_1)^n(y_2 - x_2)^m\,dy_1\,dy_2$$

$$= \sum_{(n,m)\in\mathbb{N}_0^2} \frac{t^{n+m} f_s^{(j+2n,k+2m)}(x)}{2^{n+m} n!\,m!}.$$

If the $\mathbb{N}_0^2 \times \mathbb{N}_0^2$-matrix A_t is defined by

$$A_t = \left\{ 1_{j\le n, j+n \text{ even}, k\le m, k+m \text{ even}} \frac{(t/2)^{\frac{n-j+m-k}{2}}}{(\frac{n-j}{2})!\,(\frac{m-k}{2})!} \right\}_{(j,k),(n,m)\in\mathbb{N}_0^2}, \tag{7}$$

then the effect of blurring on the jet is given by

$$\mathcal{J}_x(f_{s+t}) = \mathcal{J}_x(g_t * f_s) = A_t\,\mathcal{J}_x(f_s).$$

The matrix A_t is invertible being upper triangular with ones on the diagonal, and the matrix inverse is given by

$$A_t^{-1} = \left\{ 1_{j\le n, k\le m, j+n \text{ even}, k+m \text{ even}} \frac{(-t/2)^{\frac{n-j+m-k}{2}}}{(\frac{n-j}{2})!\,(\frac{m-k}{2})!} \right\}_{(j,k),(n,m)\in\mathbb{N}_0^2}.$$

Thus, the definition of A_t for $t > 0$ in eq. (7) can be extended to $t < 0$ such that $A_t^{-1} = A_{-t}$. Doing this we have the group property $A_s A_t = A_{s+t}$ for every $s, t \in \mathbb{R}$. This explains our choice to parameterize the scale with the variance in the blurring kernel.

Deblurring can be achieved by $f_s = \mathcal{T}_x \big(A_t^{-1} \mathcal{J}_x(f_{t+s}) \big)$, which complies with the work by Florack et al. [9]. Florack et al [9] introduces the multi-scale local jet image representation using not only the spatial derivatives but also including derivatives with respect to scale. They construct polynomial parametric representations of the local image structure based on the multi-scale local jet. This approach allow them, among other things, to do deblurring of images by extrapolation of the given local jet.

In the application in sec. 2.3, we discard the zeroth order structure. For this we introduce the jet

$$\mathcal{J}_{x,\mathbb{I}}(f_s) = \left\{ \frac{\partial^{n+m} f_s(x)}{\partial x_1^n \, \partial x_2^m} \right\}_{(n,m) \in \mathbb{I}}.$$

With a slight abuse of notation the blurring A_t operates on $\mathcal{J}_{x,\mathbb{I}}(f_s)$ by neglecting the zeroth order structure. Doing this we have $\mathcal{J}_{x,\mathbb{I}}(f_{s+t}) = A_t \mathcal{J}_{x,\mathbb{I}}(f_s)$. Moreover, an application of the binomial formula yields that

$$A_t \Psi_{2n,2m} A_t^* = \sum_{(i,j) \in \mathbb{I}: i \leq n, j \leq m} \frac{(-t)^{n-i+m-j}}{(n-i)! \, (m-j)!} \Psi_{2i,2j}, \tag{8}$$

2.3 Scale Invariance in Jet Space

In this section, we investigate the scale invariance property in jet space. For $s > 0$, let the operator S_s on jet space be defined by

$$S_s \big(\{ j_{n,m} \}_{(n,m) \in \mathbb{I}} \big) = \big\{ s^{n+m} \, j_{n,m} \big\}_{(n,m) \in \mathbb{I}}.$$

Then S_s describes the scale normalization going from scale st to scale t. Verification using the matrix representation of the operators shows the commutation relation $A_t S_s = S_s A_{st}$. This identity can also be proven using the interpretations as blurring and scaling, respectively. The scale invariance property eq. (2) can be recapped as

$$S_{(s+t)\alpha} A_t \mathcal{J}_{x,\mathbb{I}}(f_s) = S_{(s+t)\alpha} \mathcal{J}_{x,\mathbb{I}}(f_{s+t}) \overset{\mathcal{D}}{=} S_{s\alpha} \mathcal{J}_{x,\mathbb{I}}(f_s),$$

and hence

$$\mathcal{J}_{x,\mathbb{I}}(f_s) \overset{\mathcal{D}}{=} S_{(\frac{s+t}{s})\alpha} A_t \mathcal{J}_{x,\mathbb{I}}(f_s). \tag{9}$$

An equation for the covariance structure Φ_s of the jet is found by taking the covariance of both sides of eq. (9). For simplicity of the equations we, however, insert the blurring st instead of t. Doing this eq. (9) implies

$$\begin{aligned}
\Phi_s &= \mathrm{Cov}\big(\mathcal{J}_{x,\mathbb{I}}(f_s)\big) = \mathrm{Cov}\big(S_{(1+t)\alpha} A_{st} \mathcal{J}_{x,\mathbb{I}}(f_s)\big) \\
&= (S_{(1+t)\alpha} A_{st}) \, \mathrm{Cov}\big(\mathcal{J}_{0,\mathbb{I}}(f_s)\big) \, (S_{(1+t)\alpha} A_{st})^* \\
&= (S_{(1+t)\alpha} A_{st}) \, \Phi_s \, (S_{(1+t)\alpha} A_{st})^*.
\end{aligned}$$

Thus, a scale invariant covariance structure Φ_s at scale s is an eigenvector under the linear mappings $\Phi \mapsto (S_{(1+t)^\alpha} A_{st}) \Phi (S_{(1+t)^\alpha} A_{st})^*$ with eigenvalue 1 for every relative blurring factor $t > 0$. We search for a solution also satisfying the stationarity assumption eq. (6). Inserting $\Phi_s = \sum_{(n,m)\in\mathbb{I}} c_{n,m}(s) \Psi_{2n,2m}$ the eigenvalue problem reads

$$\sum_{(n,m)\in\mathbb{I}} c_{n,m}(s) \Psi_{2n,2m} = \Phi_s = (S_{(1+t)^\alpha} A_{st}) \Phi_s (S_{(1+t)^\alpha} A_{st})^*$$

$$\overset{(8)}{=} \sum_{(n,m)\in\mathbb{I}} \left((1+t)^{2\alpha n + 2\alpha m} \sum_{i,j\in\mathbb{N}_0} \frac{(-s\,t)^{i+j}}{i!\,j!} c_{n+i,m+j}(s) \right) \Psi_{2n,2m}$$

and hence

$$c_{n,m}(s) = (1+t)^{2\alpha n + 2\alpha m} \sum_{i,j\in\mathbb{N}_0} \frac{(-st)^{i+j}}{i!\,j!} c_{n+i,m+j}(s). \tag{10}$$

A solution to this eigenvector equation should hold true for every $t > 0$. Especially, taking the derivative with respect to t at $t = 0$ we find

$$0 = (2\alpha n + 2\alpha m)\, c_{n,m}(s) - s \left(c_{n+1,m}(s) + c_{n,m+1}(s) \right),$$

which is equivalent to eq. (5). It can now be checked whether a solution to the infinitesimal eigenvector problem, i.e. a vector $c_{n,m}(s)$ satisfying eq. (5), also satisfy eq. (10). In this case the addition formula for binomial coefficients gives

$$(1+t)^{2\alpha n + 2\alpha m} \sum_{i,j\in\mathbb{N}_0} \frac{(-st)^{i+j}}{i!\,j!} c_{n+i,m+j}(s)$$

$$= (1+t)^{2\alpha n + 2\alpha m} \sum_{k\in\mathbb{N}_0} \frac{(-st)^k}{k!} \sum_{j=0}^{k} \frac{k!}{(k-j)!\,j!} c_{n+k-j,m+j}(s)$$

$$\overset{(5)}{=} (1+t)^{2\alpha n + 2\alpha m} \sum_{k\in\mathbb{N}_0} \frac{(-st)^k}{k!} \frac{(2\alpha)^k}{s^k} \frac{(n+m+k-1)!}{(n+m-1)!} c_{n,m}(s)$$

$$= \left(\frac{(1+t)^\alpha}{\sqrt{1+2\alpha t}} \right)^{2n+2m} c_{n,m}(s).$$

This implies that

$$(S_{(1+t)^\alpha} A_{st}) \Phi_s (S_{(1+t)^\alpha} A_{st})^* = S_{\frac{(1+t)^\alpha}{\sqrt{1+2\alpha t}}} \Phi_s S^*_{\frac{(1+t)^\alpha}{\sqrt{1+2\alpha t}}},$$

and hence

$$\Phi_s = (S_{\sqrt{1+2\alpha t}} A_{st}) \Phi_s (S_{\sqrt{1+2\alpha t}} A_{st})^*. \tag{11}$$

Thus, the solution to the infinitesimal eigenvector problem is a solution to the global eigenvector problem if and only if $\alpha = \frac{1}{2}$. For $\alpha \neq \frac{1}{2}$ we have found the solutions to the infinitesimal eigenvector problem, and described exactly how they fail to be solutions to the global eigenvector problem. E.g. for $\alpha = 1$ we have

$$\Phi_s = (S_{\sqrt{1+2t}} A_{st}) \Phi_s (S_{\sqrt{1+2t}} A_{st})^*.$$

Finally, we remark that there is a wide class of solutions to eq. (5). We mention

$$c_{n,m}(s) = \gamma (s/\alpha)^{-n-m} (n+m-1)!,$$
$$c_{n,m}(s) = \gamma (s/\alpha)^{-n-m} \frac{(2n)! (2m)!}{2^{n+m} n! m! (n+m)} \tag{12}$$

with γ being a constant. The latter solution correspond to the covariance structure for the Lévy Brownian motion. More about this in the following section.

3 Brownian Images: A Scale Invariant Model

The Brownian image model, also known as the Lévy Brownian motion, is an example of scale invariant random functions. A Brownian image $B(x)$ is a Gaussian random function with stationary independently identically Gaussian distributed increments $B(x + \Delta x) - B(x)$ having zero mean and variance proportional to the length $|\Delta x|$, i.e. $\{B(x + \Delta x) - B(x)\} \sim \mathcal{N}(0, \sigma_0 |\Delta x|)$.

Notice that the Brownian image $B(x)$ is nowhere differentiable with probability 1. But the scale space of the Brownian model $B_s(x) = (g_s * B)(x)$ is C^∞ differentiable, hence we can compute the scale space jet $\mathcal{J}_x(B_s)$.

The scale space of a Brownian image induces a Gaussian distribution in jet space, $\{\mathcal{J}_{x,\mathbb{I}}(B_s)\} \sim N(0, \Sigma_s)$, where the covariance structure is given by

$$\Sigma_s = \text{Cov}(\mathcal{J}_{x,\mathbb{I}}(B_s)) = \left\{ \text{Cov}\left(B_s^{(i,j)}(x), B_s^{(k,l)}(x) \right) \right\}_{(i,j),(k,l)\in\mathbb{I}}. \tag{13}$$

From sec. 2, we know that the covariance structure of a scale invariant random image with stationary increments is given by eq. (6) and (12). To summarize, for $n = i + k$ and $m = j + l$ both even we have

$$\text{Cov}\left(B_s^{(i,j)}(x), B_s^{(k,l)}(x) \right) = (-1)^{\frac{n-j}{2} + \frac{m-k}{2}} \frac{\gamma s^{-\frac{n+m}{2}} n! m!}{2^{n+m} (n/2)! (m/2)! (n+m)}, \tag{14}$$

and otherwise the covariance vanishes. Here γ acts as a global variance parameter of $B(x)$.

It is interesting to note that this corresponds to the covariance derived by Pedersen [4]. In [4] the jet covariance is stated in terms of the inner product between the two random functions $B_s^{(i,j)}(x)$ and $B_s^{(k,l)}(x)$,

$$\text{Cov}\left(\langle \mathcal{J}_{x,\mathbb{I}}(B_s) \rangle \right) = \left\{ \text{Cov}\left(\left\langle B_s^{(i,j)}(x), B_s^{(k,l)}(x) \right\rangle \right) \right\}_{(i,j),(k,l)\in\mathbb{I}}. \tag{15}$$

Due to the ergodicity of the Brownian model this is equivalent to computing the jet covariance as in eq. (13).

Fig. 1. Examples of the natural images used in the experiments. The resolution of the gray value images in the database is 1024×1536 pixels.

From eq. (14) we observe that the jet covariance structure of a Brownian image is scale invariant under change of scale in the spatial domain, $B_s(x) = (g_s * B)(x)$, if we introduce scale normalized derivatives in the jet operator

$$\mathcal{J}_{x,\mathbb{I}}(B_s) = \left\{ s^{\frac{n+m}{2}} \frac{\partial^{n+m} B_s(x)}{\partial x_1^n \, \partial x_2^m} \right\}_{(n,m) \in \mathbb{I}}.$$

4   Connection with Natural Images

The Brownian image model is one example of a scale invariant random function. Another example of a nearly scale invariant random function is natural images. Pedersen [4] suggest that the covariance structure of natural images is similar to that of Brownian images as defined in sec. 3. Here we give further empirical evidence of this claim.

We use 1126 images from the van Hateren natural stimuli collection [10] for the experiments conducted in this section. Examples of these images can be found in fig. 1. For every image we compute the 4-jet $\left\{ f_s^{(n,m)}(x) \right\}_{(n,m) \in \mathbb{I}:n,m \leq 4}$ at 10 different scales in the range $s \in [4, 4096]$ using scale normalized derivatives $f_s^{(n,m)}(x) = s^{\frac{n+m}{2}} \frac{\partial^{n+m}}{\partial x_1^n \partial x_2^m} f_s(x)$ excluding the zeroth order term. For every image we pick at random the 4-jets at 6000 image points. This leads to a data set of 6.7 million 4-jets per scale. For each scale s, we estimate the covariance matrix C_s of the 4-jet. Notice that this procedure leads to an implicit assumption of stationarity of natural images.

In order to show that the covariance structure of natural images resemble that of Brownian images, we have to verify that the covariance matrix C_s for natural images has the same structure as derived in this paper and given in eq. (13) and (14).

The signs of the 4-jet covariance matrix C_s follows the theoretical alternating signs, as given by $\Psi_{2n,2m}$ defined in eq. (3), up to and including scale $s = 900$.

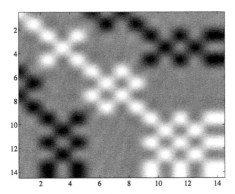

Fig. 2. Signs of the covariance matrix for the 4'th order jet. Black pixels correspond to -1, white pixels to 1, and gray to 0. The numbering of the axes correspond to the usual ordering $L_x, L_y, L_{xx}, L_{xy}, \ldots$.

Beyond this scale, sign errors start to appear. The alternating signs are visualized in fig. 2.

The derivation in sec. 2 leads to a sparse covariance matrix with only a few non-zero elements. These non-zero elements have an intricate proportionality among them. In order to verify whether natural images exhibit this structure, we compute the ratio between the non-zero elements indexed by i of the natural image covariance C_s and the theoretical covariance Φ_s, C_s^i/Φ_s^i. We divide this ratio by the mean $\mu_s = \frac{1}{N}\sum_{i=1}^N C_s^i/\Phi_s^i$ in order to remove the multiplicative contrast factor of the natural images. Fig. 3 shows a plot of $C_s^i/(\Phi_s^i\mu_s)$ for the indices i of non-zero elements at different scales s. The spikes seen, especially at high scales, in fig. 3 corresponds to the following covariances in order of appearance: $E[f_yf_y]$, $E[f_y, f_{yyy}]$, $E[f_{yy}, f_{yy}]$, $E[f_{yy}, f_{yyyy}]$, $E[f_{yyy}, f_y]$, $E[f_{yyy}, f_{yyy}]$, $E[f_{yyyy}, f_{yy}]$, $E[f_{yyyy}, f_{yyyy}]$. This consistent bias along the y direction could be explained by a dominating horizon in the images used in the experiment.

As can be seen in fig. 4, the elements of the covariance matrix C_s, which the theory predicts should be zero for Brownian images, is also close to zero for natural images.

To conclude, natural images appear to have a covariance structure similar to that of Brownian images within a limited range of scales. This scale range is bounded from below and above by the inner and outer scales of the involved images. For the natural images and the sampling of the scale axis used in these experiments, the range appear to be approximately $s \in [4, 169]$. The results are not as clear cut as those presented in [4]. The difference is that Pedersen only considered the eigenvalues of the covariance matrix, contrary to what we do here, namely compare all non-zero elements of the covariance matrix.

A consequence of the similarity between natural and Brownian images is that natural images also have an approximately scale invariant covariance structure within the above mentioned range of scales. Hence, to approximation there are no preferred scale in the visual world (at least within the range of valid scales).

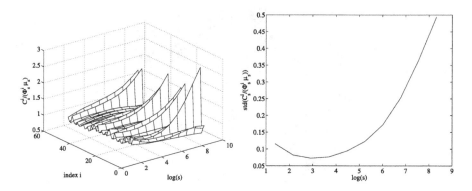

Fig. 3. (Left) The factor $C_s^i/(\Phi_s^i \mu_s)$ of non-zero covariances for the 4'th order jet of natural images. (Right) The standard deviation of the factors as a function of log-scale $\log(s)$.

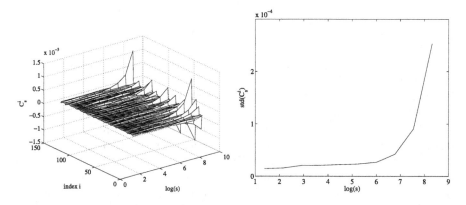

Fig. 4. (Left) Covariances C_s^i for the 4-jet for which $\Phi_s^i = 0$. (Right) The standard deviation of C_s^i as a function of log-scale $\log(s)$.

While conducting the experiments, we assumed both stationarity and isotropy of natural images, i.e. that there are no preferred position or orientation in the visual world. In general, we find this assumption reasonable, but the images in the van Hateren database [10] apparently have a bias towards the y direction, hence violating the isotropy assumption.

5   Conclusion

We studied scale invariance of the covariance structure of jet space, where scale invariance was defined in terms of the jet blurring operator A_t and the jet scaling operator S_s. Under the assumptions of stationary increments and statistical scale invariance defined in terms of the combination of A_t and S_s, we derived the necessary structure of the jet covariance matrix. We then introduced the stochastic Brownian image model as an example of a class of functions that are scale invariant under the operators A_t and S_s. The paper also include empirical results that show that the covariance matrix of natural images is approximately scale invariant with similar structure as derived in sec. 2.

We show that strict scale invariance implies $\alpha = 1/2$, which means that the standard deviation $s^{1/2}$ is consistent with the physical scale. That is, the usual scale normalization based on dimensionality analysis is consistent with scale invariance.

An interesting question for further research is whether there are other models that are stationary and scale invariant as defined in sec. 2 which would be a better model of natural images. We know that natural images are not Gaussian [11,3], hence higher order statistics is needed to fully capture the distribution of images, which means that we should extend the analysis to include higher order moments.

References

1. Mumford, D., Gidas, B.: Stochastic models for generic images. Quarterly of Applied Mathematics **59** (2001) 85–111
2. Lee, A.B., Mumford, D., Huang, J.: Occlusion models for natural images: A statistical study of a scale-invariant dead leaves model. International Journal of Computer Vision **41** (2001) 35–59
3. Grenander, U., Srivastava, A.: Probability models for clutter in natural images. IEEE Transaction on Pattern Analysis and Machine Intelligence **23** (2001) 424–429
4. Pedersen, K.S.: Properties of Brownian image models in scale-space. In Griffin, L.D., Lillholm, M., eds.: Scale Space Methods in Computer Vision: Proceedings of the 4th Scale-Space conference. LNCS 2695, Isle of Skye, Scotland (2003) 281–296
5. Pedersen, K.S., Duits, R., Nielsen, M.: On α kernels, Lévy processes, and natural image statistics. In R. Kimmel, N. Sochen, J.W., ed.: Scale Space and PDE Methods in Computer Vision. Volume LNCS 3459. (2005) 468–479
6. Geusebroek, J.: The stochastic structure of images. In R. Kimmel, N. Sochen, J.W., ed.: Scale Space and PDE Methods in Computer Vision. Volume LNCS 3459. (2005) 327–338
7. Field, D.J.: Relations between the statistics of natural images and the response properties of cortical cells. J. Optic. Soc. of Am. **4** (1987) 2379–2394
8. Ruderman, D.L., Bialek, W.: Statistics of natural images: Scaling in the woods. Physical Review Letters **73** (1994) 814–817
9. Florack, L., ter Haar Romeny, B.M., Viergever, M., Koenderink, J.: The gaussian scale-space paradigm and the multiscale local jet. International Journal of Computer Vision **18** (1996) 61–75
10. van Hateren, J.H., van der Schaaf, A.: Independent component filters of natural images compared with simple cells in primary visual cortex. Proc. R. Soc. Lond. Series B **265** (1998) 359 – 366
11. Huang, J., Mumford, D.: Statistics of natural images and models. In: Proc. of IEEE Conf. on Computer Vision and Pattern Recognition. (1999)

Essential Loops and Their Relevance for Skeletons and Symmetry Sets

Arjan Kuijper and Ole Fogh Olsen

Image Group, IT-University of Copenhagen,
Rued Langgaardsvej 7, DK-2300 Copenhagen, Denmark

Abstract. The Symmetry Set ($\mathcal{SS}$) and its representation in parameter space, the pre-Symmetry Set, can be used to describe a shape with a linear data structure containing strings. As shape descriptor one specific string can be chosen. This string represents not only the major axis of the shape, but it also contains information of the complete shape. The string is augmented with information about the special points along the (pre-) Symmetry Set that it resembles. Changes in this simple line structure are directly related to so-called transitions (topological changes) of the $\mathcal{SS}$ and the Pre-$\mathcal{SS}$. It also carries information about the skeleton, or Medial Axis.

1 Introduction

In shape analysis, much effort has been put into the research on the skeleton, or Medial Axis [1], as a way to represent the shape in a more simplified way. As it was soon realized, the Medial Axis it itself didn't carry enough information [4] and sophisticated extensions were built, like the Shock Graph method [12]. Basically, each point on the Medial Axis is endowed with additional structure related to the distance to the shape itself or related to its neighbours. Next, the potential changes of the Medial Axis were investigated, yielding a set of possible transition [5]. In that way different shapes can be related to each other for shape indexing and retrieval [10,11].

The results on transitions boiled down from the results on the possible transitions of the Symmetry Set. This set, containing the Medial Axis as subset, has been thoroughly studied in [3]. Its transitions are described in [2]. The Symmetry Set has its advantage in being easily described in a mathematical sense, but its spatial visualization not suited to human perception. So most of the research has been focused on the (augmented) Medial Axis [6].

Recently, however, a data structure was presented for the Symmetry Set [9], that can be visualized by a sequence of nodes, that are pair wise joined.

In the pre-Symmetry Set special branches may be present. These branches are spanned by the entire shape and are called essential loops. There are either zero or two essential loops for a closed non self-intersecting curve. If there are two essential loops, each contains information about the complete shape. It then suffices to select only one of these branches instead of taking the complete set

O.F. Olsen et al. (Eds.): DSSCV 2005, LNCS 3753, pp. 24–35, 2005.

as in [9]. This branch can easily be found using the pre-Symmetry Set [7], the Symmetry Set in parameter space. Augmented with special points of the (pre-) Symmetry Set, this branch represents the shape. The branch can be described as a simple line sequence which allows modifications based on known changes of the (pre-) Symmetry Set. We show how this structure can be obtained and describe its relation to the skeleton, or Medial Axis.

2   Symmetry Set

The Symmetry Set is defined as the closure of the loci of the circles tangent to a shape, see Figure 1a. The shape is given by the oval. Inside a circle is tangent to

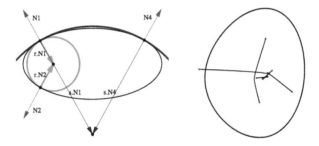

Fig. 1. a) Definition of the Symmetry Set. See text for details. b) A shape and the Symmetry Set.

it at two locations, so the *unit* normals $\mathcal{N}_1$ and $\mathcal{N}_2$ are equal for the shape and the circle. The centre of the circle is found by multiplying minus the radius r with the normals. Note that this is also a Medial Axis point. Next, also outside a circle is tangent to the shape at two locations, where the unit normals $\mathcal{N}_1$ and $\mathcal{N}_4$ are equal for the shape and the circle. From this image it follows immediately that a point on the shape relates to at least two points on the Symmetry Set, in contrast with the Medial Axis.

Another tool that is used in the analysis of the Symmetry Set is the evolute. Let κ be the curvature of a shape $\mathcal{S}$, then the evolute is given by $\mathcal{S} + \mathcal{N}/\kappa$. In Figure 1b an oval, its Medial Axis (vertical line) and Symmetry Set (all line segments) are shown.

2.1   Points on the Symmetry Set

Due to the geometry of the shape and the order of tangency, five distinct types of points are generic on the Symmetry Set [3], see Figure 2. An A_1^2 point is the "common" midpoint of a circle tangent at two distinct points of the shape. An A_3 point is the midpoint of a circle located at the evolute and tangent at the

point of the shape with the local extremal curvature. The endpoint of a branch of
the $\mathcal{SS}$. An A_1A_2 point is the midpoint of a circle tangent at two distinct points
of the shape but located at the evolute. A turning point on the $\mathcal{SS}$. An A_1^3 point
is the midpoint of one circle tangent at three distinct points of the shape. An
intersection of three branches of the $\mathcal{SS}$. An A_1^2/A_1^2 point is the centre of two
circles tangent at two pairs of distinct points of the shape with different radii.
Since this produces only an intersection due to projection on the plane, it is
omitted in what follows.

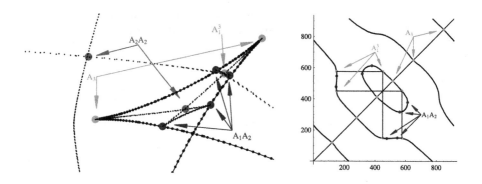

Fig. 2. a) Close up of the Symmetry Set with annotated special points and the evolute
(joined points). b) Visualizing the Pre-Symmetry Set with annotated special points.

2.2   Transitions

In the following we briefly state the possible transitions of the $\mathcal{SS}$. For more
details the reader is referred to [2].

At an A_1^4 transition a collision of A_1^3 points appears. Before and after the
transition six lines, four A_1^3 points occur. The result on the $\mathcal{MA}$ is a reordering
of the connections of two connected Y-parts of the skeleton. For the $\mathcal{SS}$, however,
the Y-parts are the visible parts of $\mathcal{SS}$ branches going through A_1^3 points. So for
the $\mathcal{SS}$ representation nothing changes.

At an A_1A_3 transition, a cusp of the evolute (and thus an end part of a $\mathcal{SS}$
branch including a A_3 point) intersects a branch of the $\mathcal{SS}$ and an A_1^3 point as
well as two A_1A_2 points are created or annihilated. The A_1^3 point lies on the A_3
containing branch, while the other branch contains a "triangle" with the A_1^3 and
the A_1A_2's as corner points.

The A_4 transition corresponds to creation or annihilation of a swallowtail
structure of the evolute and the creation or annihilation of the enclosed $\mathcal{SS}$
branch with two A_3 and two A_1A_2 points.

At an $A_1^2A_2$ transition two non-intersecting A_1A_2-containing branches meet
a third $\mathcal{SS}$ branch at the evolute, creating two times three different branches
intersecting at two A_1^3 points. Or the inverse transition occurs.

The A_2^2 moth transition describes the creation or annihilation of a SS branch containing only four A_1A_2 and no A_3 points. These points lie pair wise on two opposite parts of the evolute. Each point is connected via the SS to the two points on the opposite part of the evolute.

When going through an A_2^2 nib transition, two branches of the SS, each containing an A_1A_2 point, meet and exchange a sub-branch.

3   Pre-symmetry Set

The pre-SS is obtained by visualizing the Symmetry Set in parameter space, so essentially it is visualizing the pairs of points on the shape at which the circl is tangent. This is done in Figure 2b.

On the axis one finds the parameters p_i and p_j. The black curved lines represent the zero crossings. The diagonal is formed by the points (p_i, p_i) and can therefore represent the shape itself.

Firstly, it needs to be remarked that the diagram repeats across its borders: the parameter moves along a closed curve. So the diagram represents a torus. Furthermore, the axis are to be identified, since they both relate to the same parameter along the shape. So the image is symmetric in the diagonal and the plot represents in fact a Moebius strip, with the diagonal as its boundary.

In this Figure, one can see two curves ranging over the entire domain and one closed loop (bottom left with parts bottom right and (the symmetric counterpart) top left).

3.1   Points on the Pre-symmetry Set

Since curves in the pre-SS don't intersect, one easily obtains separate branches. At A_3 points, one has $p_i = p_j$, since they are located at the diagonal and don't concern two different points on the shape. Note that these points arise from local extrema of the curvature on the shape. These extrema alternate being minima and maxima. At A_1A_2 points the SS hits the evolute and is reflected. This implies that one of the two involved points, say p_i, is also reflected. The pre-SS therefore has a horizontal or vertical tangent. At an A_1^3 point three parts of the SS intersect. In the pre-SS these points are detectable as the occurrence of the triple point sets (p_1, p_2), (p_1, p_3), and (p_2, p_3) (and, of course, its diagonal symmetric counterpart). This is visualized by the box-set in Figure 2b. All other points are A_1^2 points.

3.2   Transitions

The list of transitions valid for the SS, also apply to the pre-SS. In the following we state the consequences of these events for the pre-SS, see [8] for details.

At an A_1^4 transition a collision of A_1^3 points appears. This implies that in the pre-SS four box-sets (see Figure 2b), each combining the three positions, coincide. Before and after the transition there are six curves with, each of them two A_1^3. The only thing that changes is the ordering of each pair of A_1^3 points on each curve. This boils down to inverting the order of the four box-sets.

At an $A_1 A_3$ transition, one curve goes through an inflection point and changes from zero to two local extrema (horizontal or vertical tangents) - which are $A_1 A_2$ points. Outside the two extrema two positions of the A_3 are located, the third is located on the curve that represents the other SS-branch involved in the interaction.

The A_4 transition corresponds to creation or annihilation of a closed loop on the diagonal in the pre-SS, thus containing two A_3 points on the diagonal and two $A_1 A_2$ points as the horizontal and vertical tangents (note that the diagonal is a axis of symmetry).

At an $A_1^2 A_2$ transition two branches with each an $A_1 A_2$ point surrounded by two A_1^3 points meet and leave without the A_1^3 points. The $A_1 A_2$ points have the same tangent. On a third branch two A_1^3 points meet and vanish. Or, of course, the opposite (creation) event occurs.

When going through an A_2^2 moth transition, a closed off-diagonal loop is created or annihilated in the Pre-SS. It cannot intersect the diagonal. Note that in the visualization also a loop occurs due to mirroring in the diagonal.

When going through an A_2^2 nib transition, two branches approach with their local $A_1 A_2$ points with the same kind of tangent. They meet, forming an intersection, exchanging connection and afterwards they move away with again the same kind of tangent, but opposite to the one before (horizontal vs. vertical, or vice versa).

4   Essential loops

Observing the pre-SS of Figure 2b, there are exactly 2 curves that are spanned by all points on the shape, i.e. the complete pre-SS diagram domain is needed to represent these curves [7]. They are called *essential loops*.

Recall from section 3.1 that the intersections of the curves (or loops, as they are closed) in the pre-SS diagram with the diagonal represent the local extrema of the shape. They can be numbered sequentially, e.g. starting at the origin. Consequently, the starting point can be chosen such that even numbers relate to maxima, and odd numbers to minima

Each curve that intersects the diagonal, intersects it twice, since a branch with a begin point needs to have an end point. Such curves can be assigned the two numbers of the intersection points.

When tracing such a curve from the first diagonal point to the second one via the upper diagonal part of the diagram, one can note that for essential loops the second point is reached via the lower diagonal part of the diagram, while non-essential loops reach the diagonal via the upper diagonal part. Consequently, on these curves, the number of both horizontal and vertical $A_1 A_2$ points is odd for non-essential loops ("as the curve needs to return"), and even for essential loops. The essential loops cross the boundary an odd number of times, while for the non-essential loops this number is even.

Theorem 1. *Any non-essential loop must have an even and an odd number. Essential loops have to appear pair wise with an even-even and an odd-odd numbered intersection.*

Proof. Consider the allowed transitions and the evolution of an ellipse, with two essential loops, to an arbitrary shape. At this evolution two events are possible: closed loops can be created and swaps may occur. At A_4's closed loops are created with an even and an odd number. In an A_2^2-nib, two branches (and therefore two endpoints) are exchanged. Without loss of generality we can take two curves with intersections $(1, 2), (3, 4)$ that can perform two changes, A: $(1, 3), (2, 4)$ or B: $(1, 4), (2, 3)$. In case B, after the swap again two non-essential loops are present, they have both even-odd numbered intersections with the diagonal, and one loop is encapsulated by the other; In case A, an odd-odd and even-even pair is created. Since the loops may not intersect each other in the pre-SS diagram, this can only be established when the new curves starting in the points 1and 2 in the upper diagonal part do not return to the diagonal in that part, but approach the diagonal in the lower diagonal part. Then, however, they range over the entire diagram and have become essential loops. Obviously, these transitions can also occur in the opposite direction.

In the following, we distinguish between essential loops that connect minima of the curvature (min-min), and those that connect maxima (max-max).

Definition 1. *If at least two essential loops are present, a* maximal *essential loop (MEL) is identified as an essential loop with the two intersections of the diagonal relating to two local maxima of the curvature.*

4.1   On Maximal Essential Loops

Although the situation with two essential loops may seem generic, the transitions do not prohibit the existence of any even number of essential loops. In practice, besides two, the case with zero essential loops has been observed. In order to say more on this, first the following result is needed:

Theorem 2. *Two A_1^3 points can be connected by at most one path along the SS branches.*

Proof. Consider two A_1^3 points that are tangent to the shape at the points (i_1, j_1, k_1) and (i_2, j_2, k_2) with $i_1 < j_1 < k_1$ and $< k_2 < j_2 < i_2$. Assume, without loss of generality, that $k_1 < k_2$. Then the two points can only be connected via SS branches that are spanned by pairs of intervals along the shape that are subsets of the intervals (k_1, k_2) and (i_2, i_1) - one clockwise, the other anti-clockwise (say left and right). For the latter interval it is taken into account that the end and begin point are joined. Each pair of intervals ends when an A_1^3 point is reached. Then a new pair of intervals starts, where at least one of the two intervals has the start point equal to the end point of one of the two old intervals. So at most on one of the two sides of the shape a jump can occur.

Two different paths require two disjoined sets of intervals; there can not be two points on the shape that contribute to both paths. On the contrary, each point on the shape contributes to both paths, since that occurred at each A_1^3 point and the SS branches depend continuous on the shape. Then each interval connects to the same A_1^3 point, i.e. the interval is empty. There cannot be two different paths.

One way to interpret this result is that a closed, non self-intersecting shape cannot generate a SS with a cycle. Then the following holds:

Theorem 3. *A part of the MEL is visible at the Medial Axis.*

Proof. As the MEL starts and ends in locations related to local maxima of the curvature, it starts and ends inside the shape. Regarding the part of the $\mathcal{MA}$ inside the shape, its end points also relate to local maxima of the curvature. Second, to the $\mathcal{MA}$ all points on the shape contribute pair-wise. If the MEL remains within the shape, it must coincide with the $\mathcal{MA}$. If it is also present outside the shape, it must have two A_1^3 points in common one "to get out" and one "to get in". Since cycles cannot occur, the MEL and the $\mathcal{MA}$ share at least the path between these A_1^3 points.

Theorem 4. *A MEL links two A_3 end points of the Medial Axis.*

Proof. The end points of the $\mathcal{MA}$ are due to local maxima of the curvature. On the other hand, not all end points of a SS branch become visible on the $\mathcal{MA}$. When a new branch (a non-essential loop) is created in an A_4, the end point related to the maximal curvature only become part of the $\mathcal{MA}$ after an $A_1 A_3$ transition - when it intersects the $\mathcal{MA}$ [2,8,5]. So if the end points of the MEL are not part of the $\mathcal{MA}$, the entire MEL cannot intersect the $\mathcal{MA}$. This contradicts the previous Theorem.

Theorem 5. *A MEL defines a main axis to the Medial Axis, being the linking two A_3 points along the Medial Axis.*

Proof. This follows directly from the previous two Theorems.

Using these results, we have the following:

Theorem 6. *There is at most one MEL for a closed, non self-intersecting shape.*

Proof. Suppose there are two MELs. They have endpoints (p_1, p_3) and (p_2, p_4) with $p_1 < p_2 < p_3 < p_4$, since they cannot intersect in the pre-SS. Then there is a path along the $\mathcal{MA}$ from the points determined by p_1 and p_3. A second path connects p_2 and p_4. These paths necessarily need to have at least one point in common. If they cross, it occurs at an A_1^4 point, a circle tangent at four points simultaneously, which is non-generic. If they would meet in an A_1^3 point, they need to have a segment of the $\mathcal{MA}$ ranging between two A_1^3 points in common, since they both define $\mathcal{MA}$ parts. But then the two MELs coincide at this segment, which is also non-generic.

Consequently, there are either zero or two essential loops. Since the essential loops are spanned by the entire domain, they contain local symmetry information of the whole shape. So we could say that in the case that there are two essential loops, we can identify two global axes of symmetry, while in the case of no essential loops there are no such axes. Since there are two spatial dimensions, there are generically not more that two global axes of symmetry to be expected.

Theorem 7. *In the case that there is a MEL, each A_1^3 point on the MEL that is part of the Medial Axis is encountered twice, so of the three distinct curves intersecting at this A_1^3 point, two belong to the same SS branch.*

This states that at a fork in the Medial Axis (where three parts meet) two of the parts contribute to the same SS branch and therefore that the begin and end point of the MEL are the begin and end point of a connected part of the Medial Axis.

Proof. This is a direct consequence of the fact that there is exactly one path between two A_1^3 points. As the A_3 points are connected by the MEL, necessarily the A_1^3 points on the $\mathcal{MA}$ connect two $\mathcal{MA}$ parts that belong to the MEL.

As a consequence, the MEL can be divided in two $A_3 - A_1^3$ parts and some $A_1^3 - A_1^3$ parts, with each A_1^3 appearing twice as a begin and end point. The part of a MEL (e.g. in Figure 4) that connects the two A_3 points, contains an even number of $A_1 A_2$ points. When starting at an A_3 point of the MEL and following the MEL, at a certain moment - before an $A_1 A_2$ is encountered - an A_1^3 is met. Here a horizontal or vertical jump in the pre-SS diagram can be taken to an other part of the MEL, skipping an even number of $A_1 A_2$ points, see also Figure 5. Therefore, a subset of the MEL can be taken that doesn't contain $A_1 A_2$ points and consists of two $A_3 - A_1^3$ parts and some $A_1^3 - A_1^3$ parts, with each A_1^3 appearing twice as a begin and end point.

All closed shapes can be obtained from the ellipse by adding perturbations, and similarly their pre-SS diagram are obtained by adding perturbations, i.e. the transitions [8]. For the ellipse the maximal essential loop is simply represented by $A_3 - A_3$, while perturbations of the shape yield a more complicated structure: $A_3 - X - A_3$, where X is solely determined by the transitions of the pre-SS. In general, X will contain several $A_1 A_2$ and A_1^3 points. It therefore remains to investigate the possible structures and changes of X.

4.2   Transitions of an Essential Loop

From the transitions of the pre-SS, the transitions on the essential loop can be derived directly [5,8]. In the following, i and j are indices and X and Y parts of the sequence. Examples will be given in the next section.

At an A_1^4 transition pairs of $A_1^3[i] - A_1^3[i+1]$ points on the pre-SS curve meet (coincide) and continue afterwards.

At an $A_1 A_3$ transition, the curve gets or looses a string $A_1^3[i] - A_1 A_2[j] - A_1 A_2[j+1] - A_1^3[i]$.

The A_4 transition doesn't contribute to an essential loop; it only creates a non-essential loop.

At an $A_1^2 A_2$ transition the sequence $A_1^3[i] - A_1^3[j]$ may be created or annihilated. Note that since $A_1 A_2$ points are required for this transition, it affect a part that doesn't contribute to the $\mathcal{MA}$.

At an A_2^2 moth transition nothing happens on the essential loop.

When going through an A_2^2 nib transition, the structure is either locally expanded or simplified if the pre-$\mathcal{SS}$ transition involves a closed moth loop: from $X_1 - Y - X_2$ to $X_1 - X_2$ or vice versa, with the changes at two $A_1 A_2$ points. It Implies a rotation of information when the pre-$\mathcal{SS}$ transition involves a curve that intersects the diagonal. Then the sequence $A_3[1] - X_1 - A_1^3[j] - X_2 - A_1 A_2[i] - A_1^3[j] - Y$ changes to $A_3[2] - X_3 - A_1^3[j] - X_4 - A_1 A_2[i] - A_1^3[j] - Y$. As this implies a change of end point, it also describes the possibility of pair wise removing or creating essential loops.

5 Example

As an example shape clarifying the theory presented above, we took a fish shape from the data base considered in [10,11]. This fish shape is shown in Figure 3, with its $\mathcal{SS}$ (left) and its pre-$\mathcal{SS}$ (right). As we allowed ourselves no data modification after the parameterization was obtained, the results are non-aligned sets of points.

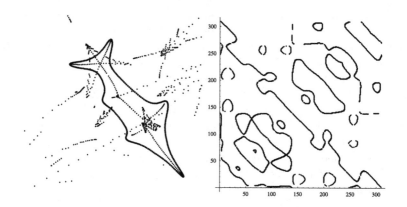

Fig. 3. Left: Fish, with its $\mathcal{SS}$. Right: Pre-$\mathcal{SS}$ of the fish.

Its $\mathcal{MA}$ containing essential loop is the branch ranging from top left to bottom down. It is also depicted in Figure 4. On the right, the $\mathcal{SS}$ branch is shown. It ranges from the top left tail of the fish to its nose. Since the pre-$\mathcal{SS}$ is symmetric, it suffices to investigate on half of the branch in the pre-$\mathcal{SS}$. This is visualized in Figure 5. The branch starts top left (equivalent to the origin of the pre-$\mathcal{SS}$ - at the diagonal) and ends bottom right, again at the diagonal. It

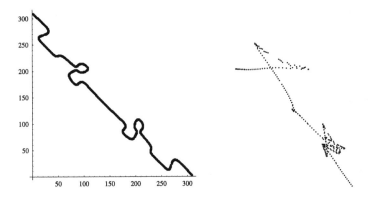

Fig. 4. The maximal essential loop in the Pre-Symmetry Set (left) and its related $\mathcal{SS}$ branch of the fish

traverses several $A_1 A_2$ points, at horizontal and vertical tangents, annotated by numbers, and A_1^3 points, annotated with capitals and connected by vertical or horizontal lines (parts of the boxes).

A simple representation of the string - and the shape - thus boils down to be (let $A_3[1]$ and $A_3[2]$ be the end points) $A_3[1] - I - II - III - IV - A_3[2]$ with

- $I = A - 1 - 2 - A$,
- $II = B - 3 - 4 - B$,
- $III = C - D - 5 - 6 - D - 7 - -E - 8 - 9 - E - 10 - C$, and
- $IV = F - 11 - 12 - F$.

Note that III can be subdivided into

- $III = C - V - 7 - VI - 10 - C$, with
- $V = D - 5 - 6 - D$ and
- $VI = E - 8 - 9 - E$.

So each of these sub parts may have been arisen from $A_1 A_3$ transitions.

Next, we can see what happens at an A_2^2-nib transition. Let the points 5 and 9 meet and exchange branches. Then point 4 would be connected to 10 via point - say - 5, while the other branch is a closed loop with points 6,7,8, and 9. This resembles a simplification of part III with the removal of the parts V and VI and point 5 taking over the role of point 7. The effect of two subsequent $A_1 A_3$ transitions removing these two parts would have the same impact on the essential loop (albeit that then no closed loop remains).

In this figure the dotted segments represent the $\mathcal{MA}$ part of the essential loop, i.e. the $\mathcal{MA}$ lines connecting the top left tail to the nose of the fish. It is easily found as the subset $A_3[1] - A, A - B, B - C, C - F, F - A_3[2]$. The $\mathcal{MA}$ segments in the complete pre-$\mathcal{SS}$ is shown in Figure 6a see [7] for more details on deriving this structure and its left-right ordering.

One can see 4 extra diagonal intersecting part, representing the four other $\mathcal{MA}$ branches, labelled 2,3, 5, and 6. The parts A to C are the $\mathcal{MA}$ parts without

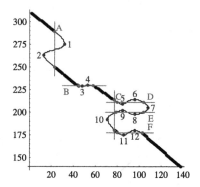

Fig. 5. Top left part of the maximal essential loop of pre-$\mathcal{SS}$ of the fish. See text for explanation of the annotation.

endpoints. One can see that parts 1,6, and A form a junction in an A_1^3 form - one can draw a box structure at these points, just like in Figure 2b.

In Figure 6b the fish with the $\mathcal{MA}$ and the essential $\mathcal{SS}$ branch is shown.

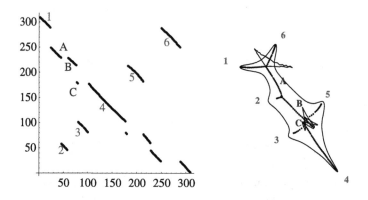

Fig. 6. a: Presence of the $\mathcal{MA}$ in the pre-$\mathcal{SS}$ of the fish. Numbers denote branches with endpoints, capitals interior parts. b: Fish, its $\mathcal{MA}$ (dotted) with annotation of Figure 6 and the $\mathcal{SS}$ branch related to the maximal essential loop.

Here it also clear that these three parts are connected. Furthermore, information about branch 6 is contained in the swallowtail part. arising at the junction, which was labelled before as the segment I, viz. $A - 1 - 2 - A$. When the second type of A_2^2-nib transition occurs, this part swaps (it is mirrored in the line given by part A) and the essential loop ends in point 6 instead of point 1. An A_4 occurs if the order of the two $\mathcal{MA}$ branches 3 and 5 swap their connectivity. In the pre-$\mathcal{SS}$ of Figure 5 this is visual as the coincide of the lines C, D, and F. At the transition four locations are involved and the vertical line C is relocated to the right, close to point 7. The very small $\mathcal{MA}$ part between the lines C and E is then transported to the be somewhere between the points 6 and 7, signalling that first the horizontal jump (corresponding to branch 5 on the left side of the fish, seen from the tail) is taken, and then the vertical jump (corresponding to branch 3 on the right side).

6   Summary and Conclusions

In this paper we investigated essential loops in the pre-Symmetry Set. There are either zero or two of them. If there are two, one relates to two minima of curvature on the shape, the other to two maxima. Selecting the latter one yields a linear structure containing by definition all shape information. It represents part of the $\mathcal{MA}$ directly, that can be regarded as the main $\mathcal{MA}$. Other $\mathcal{MA}$-related information is contained in the remainder of the string. Changes of the string depend on known transitions of the (pre-)$\mathcal{SS}$ and are presented. The procedure is exploited on an example shape, and possible changes are shown. As a result, one ends up with a structure the can be considered as a Simplified Symmetry Set, being in between the Medial Axis and the Symmetry Set.

References

1. H. Blum. Biological shape and visual science (part i). *Journal of Theoretical Biology*, 38:205–287, 1973.
2. J. W. Bruce and P. J. Giblin. Growth, motion and 1-parameter families of symmetry sets. *Proceedings of the Royal Society of Edinburgh*, 104(A):179–204, 1986.
3. J. W. Bruce, P. J. Giblin, and C. Gibson. Symmetry sets. *Proceedings of the Royal Society of Edinburgh*, 101(A):163–186, 1985.
4. P. J. Giblin and B. B. Kimia. On the intrinsic reconstruction of shape from its symmetries. *IEEE Tr. on Pat. Anal. and Mach. Int.*, 25(7):895–911, 2003.
5. P. J. Giblin and B. B. Kimia. On the local form and transitions of symmetry sets, medial axes, and shocks. *International Journal of Computer Vision*, 54(1/2):143–156, 2003.
6. B.B. Kimia. On the role of medial geometry in human vision. *Journal of Physiology - Paris*, 97(2-3):155–190, 2003.
7. A. Kuijper. On data structures from symmetry sets of 2D shapes. Technical Report TR-2004-47, IT University of Copenhagen, 2004.
8. A. Kuijper and O.F. Olsen. Transitions of the pre-symmetry set. In *Proceedings of the 17th ICPR 2004*, volume III, pages 190–193, 2004.
9. A. Kuijper, O.F. Olsen, P.J. Giblin, Ph. Bille, and M. Nielsen. From a 2D shape to a string structure using the symmetry set. In *Proceedings of the 8th ECCV 2004, Part II*, pages 313–326, 2004. LNCS 3022.
10. M. Pelillo, K. Siddiqi, and S. Zucker. Matching hierarchical structures using association graphs. *IEEE Tr. on Pat. Anal. and Mach. Int.*, 21(11):1105–1120, 1999.
11. T.B. Sebastian, P.N. Klein, and B. B. Kimia. Recognition of shapes by editing shock graphs. In *Proceedings of the 8th ICCV (2001)*, pages 755–762, 2001.
12. K. Siddiqi, A. Shokoufandeh, S. Dickinson, and S. Zucker. Shock graphs and shape matching. *International Journal of Computer Vision*, 30:1–22, 1999.

Pre-symmetry Sets of 3D Shapes

André Diatta and Peter Giblin

Department of Mathematical Sciences, University of Liverpool,
Liverpool L69 7ZL, England
adiatta@liv.ac.uk, pjgiblin@liv.ac.uk

Abstract. We show that the pre-symmetry set of a smooth surface in 3-space has the structure of the graph of a function from $\mathbb{R}^2$ to $\mathbb{R}^2$ in many cases of interest, generalising known results for the pre-symmetry set of a curve in the plane. We explain how this function is obtained, and illustrate with examples both on and off the diagonal. There are other cases where the pre-symmetry set is *singular*; we mention some of these cases but leave their investigation to another occasion.

1 Introduction

In this paper, we consider in some detail the structure of pre-symmetry sets in 2D and 3D. Recall that, given M, a smooth closed curve in 2D or surface in 3D, the *pre-symmetry set* $\mathcal{P}$ of M is the closure of the set of pairs of distinct points $(\mathbf{p}, \mathbf{q}) \in M \times M$ for which there exists a circle or sphere tangent to M at $\mathbf{p}$ and at $\mathbf{q}$. From the pre-symmetry set it is not difficult to pass to the *symmetry set* which is the locus of centres of these circles or spheres, together with the centres of the limiting circles. When M is a plane curve, parametrized by the points of a circle S^1, we can consider $\mathcal{P}$ as a subset of the torus $S^1 \times S^1$, represented in the plane by a square with opposite sides identified. Note that in any dimension $\mathcal{P}$ is symmetric: $(\mathbf{p}, \mathbf{q}) \in \mathcal{P}$ if and only if $(\mathbf{q}, \mathbf{p}) \in \mathcal{P}$; it follows that in 2D we can also regard $\mathcal{P}$ as contained in $S^1 \times S^1$ with symmetric pairs identified. This is called the *symmetric product* of two circles and is a Möbius band in which the boundary of the band represents the 'diagonal' points $\mathbf{p} = \mathbf{q}$. In the 3D case, with M say topologically equivalent to a 2-sphere, we could consider $\mathcal{P}$ as a subset of $S^2 \times S^2$, which is topologically a complex quadric surface, or of the symmetric product which is topologically a complex projective plane[1].

However we shall not be concerned here with global models of the pre-symmetry set, but rather with local or multi-local models. Starting from a circle

---

[1] This is a classic result and is proved by regarding S^2 as the Riemann sphere, that is complex numbers together with ∞, and then associating with an unordered pair (z_1, z_2) of elements of S^2 the unique quadratic polynomial $az^2 + bz + c$ with roots z_1 and z_2. The corresponding element of the complex projective plane is then $(a : b : c)$ and the diagonal corresponds to the conic $b^2 = 4ac$. In fact the symmetric product of any closed 2-dimensional manifold with itself is known to be a 2-manifold, a surprising fact since one might imagine that the diagonal would cause singularities.

O.F. Olsen et al. (Eds.): DSSCV 2005, LNCS 3753, pp. 36–48, 2005.

or sphere S_0 having $k \geq 2$ contact points with our curve or surface M, the pre-symmetry set can be partitioned into strata:

• one stratum for each pair of distinct contact points, $\mathbf{p}_i, \mathbf{p}_j$ say, chosen from the k points. Here, we consider circles or spheres tangent to M at points *at or close to* $\mathbf{p}_i$ and $\mathbf{p}_j$ (if $k > 2$ then these circles or spheres 'lose contact' with M close to the other $k - 2$ contact points of S_0 and M).

• one stratum for each contact point $\mathbf{p}_i$ between S_0 and M which is of type A_3 or higher—a vertex and its circle of curvature in 2D, or a ridge point and the corresponding sphere of curvature in 3D. This stratum of $\mathcal{P}$ arises from circles or spheres which are tangent to M at two points both of which are close to $\mathbf{p}_i$.

Note that we are concerned here with the symmetry set and not the medial axis: the circles or spheres do not have to remain inside M (or more generally be maximal with respect to M). We can consider the above strata separately in our investigations. For example, starting with a sphere S_0 having contact A_1 at two points $\mathbf{p}_1, \mathbf{p}_2$ and A_3 at $\mathbf{p}_3$ with a surface M, we will have four strata which correspond to contacts close to $\mathbf{p}_1, \mathbf{p}_3$; $\mathbf{p}_2, \mathbf{p}_3$; $\mathbf{p}_1, \mathbf{p}_2$; and $\mathbf{p}_3, \mathbf{p}_3$.

In what follows we shall concentrate on the strata:

• arising from *two* contact points: *off-diagonal* strata, or
• arising from *one* contact point: *on-diagonal* strata

since the other cases can be reduced as above to these two. We shall argue that the 'correct' way to think of these strata of the pre-symmetry set $\mathcal{P}$ in 2D ($n = 2$) or 3D ($n = 3$), when they are non-singular, is as *the graph of a mapping from $\mathbb{R}^n$ to $\mathbb{R}^n$*. In this way we can capture the structure in a uniform way, both for a single curve or surface and for a 1-parameter family of such. The mapping in question will arise in a slightly different way for the on-diagonal and off-diagonal cases, but the principle is the same for both. Several of the standard examples of mappings from the plane to the plane [6,9]—fold, cusp, lips, beaks, swallowtail—arise naturally in this context. See Figure 3.

The 2D case is relatively well-known [7]; in §2 we summarize some results and interpret one of the cases as the graph of a mapping $\mathbb{R} \to \mathbb{R}$ in order to set the scene for the 3D case. We also take the opportunity to prove a result which explains why only certain singularities of the pre-symmetry set can occur on the diagonal.

In §3 we turn to 3D. The underlying calculations here are rather complicated and we suppress them in favour of giving details of the results. This is part of a larger investigation of all the symmetry sets and pre-symmetry sets in 3D, for surfaces and generic 1-parameter families. Figure 3 summarises the results from §3, Figure 2 treats the example of fold maps.

2   The Pre-symmetry Set in 2D

Given a smooth plane curve M with parametrization $\gamma : S^1 \to \mathbb{R}^2$ the pre-symmetry set is contained in the set of pairs defined by the equations

$$g(s,t) = 0, \text{ where } g(s,t) = (\gamma(s) - \gamma(t)) \cdot (\mathbf{T}(s) \pm \mathbf{T}(t)), \tag{1}$$

where $\mathbf{T}$ stands for the unit tangent vector. The zero set of g also contains diagonal pairs (s, s), and pairs where the tangents are parallel, and these need to be excluded when finding the true pre-symmetry set.

2.1   The Pre-symmetry Set at a Diagonal Point

Let us examine the equation (1) close to a diagonal point, that is, when the curve M has a vertex. We take M in local form having a vertex at the origin:

$$\gamma(x) = (x, y) \text{ where } y = f(x) = a_2 x^2 + a_4 x^4 + a_5 x^5 + \ldots, \quad a_2 \neq 0,$$

with no x^3 term. Expanding (1) with the $+$ sign we find that there are no solutions close to the origin besides $s = t$, and for the $-$ sign the leading terms (of degree 5) factorise as

$$2a_2(a_2^3 - a_4)(s + t)(s - t)^4.$$

For an *ordinary vertex* (contact with the tangent circle of type A_3 exactly), $a_2^3 \neq a_4$ and the local structure of the pre-symmetry set, apart from the diagonal, is a smooth transverse curve $s + t + \text{h.o.t.} = 0$.

For A_4 contact we need to go to the next terms which are

$$-a_2 a_5(3s^2 + 4st + 3t^2)(s - t)^4,$$

where $a_5 \neq 0$. The quadratic form here is positive definite, so apart from the diagonal term there is an *isolated point* at $s = t = 0$. Note that there *cannot* be a pair of real branches of the pre-symmetry set at such a diagonal point. We can also see this by noting that at an A_4 point the curvature κ does not have an extremum (since $\kappa' = \kappa'' = 0, \kappa''' \neq 0$) and on an arc without an extremum of curvature there can be no bitangent circles [10].

The same analysis can be continued to A_5, where the leading term is

$$2a_2(2a_2^5 - a_6)(s + t)(2s^2 + st + 2t^2)(s - t)^4,$$

having a single transverse branch $s + t + \text{h.o.t.} = 0$. The factor $2a_2^5 - a_6$ is zero only for an A_6 singularity. We find:

for k odd, a circle having A_k contact with the curve M results in a single branch of the pre-symmetry set transverse to the diagonal; and for k even it results in an isolated point of the pre-symmetry set on the diagonal.

2.2   Transitions Visible on the Pre-symmetry Set

The transitions which occur on symmetry sets were classified in [1]; some of these are 'visible' on the pre-symmetry set. There has been considerable work on this [7]. We only give examples here, together with an alternative interpretation of one of the cases, in line with our work on 3D pre-symmetry sets below.

- A_4: the pre-symmetry set has an isolated point on the diagonal, growing to a closed loop transverse to the diagonal in two places; compare §2.1.
- A_2^2: two cases (1) moth, with the pre-symmetry set an isolated point growing into a closed loop, and (2) nib, with the pre-symmetry set a transverse crossing of two branches separating two ways. Note that *off* the diagonal, there is the possibility of both isolated point and transverse crossing on the pre-symmetry set, in contrast with the situation *on* the diagonal described in §2.1.
- $A_1 A_3$: The pre-symmetry set has two strata, one on-diagonal and one off-diagonal. The off-diagonal stratum has an inflexion parallel to one parameter axis and the line through the inflexion parallel to the other parameter axis passes through the diagonal point. See Figure 1.

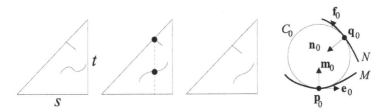

Fig. 1. Left three figures: an $A_1 A_3$ transition seen in the pre-symmetry set; half of $S^1 \times S^1$ is shown, the 45° line being the diagonal $s = t$. The transitional moment is in the centre, with an inflexional tangent parallel to the s parameter axis on one stratum of the pre-symmetry set. There is also a diagonal point on the other stratum for the same value of s. Right: the setup for analysing the $A_1 A_3$ pre-symmetry set. The general bitangent circle under consideration has contact points $\mathbf{p}(s)$ close to $\mathbf{p}_0$ and $\mathbf{q}(t)$ close to $\mathbf{q}_0$. Since A_3 occurs at the 'first' point $\mathbf{p}_0$ and A_1 at the 'second' point $\mathbf{q}_0$ we could also write this as $A_3 A_1$.

We consider in more detail the case of $A_1 A_3$, as a preparation for the 3D case. Let M, N be smooth arcs with arclength parameters s, t, general points $\mathbf{p} = \mathbf{p}(s), \mathbf{q} = \mathbf{q}(s)$ and curvatures $\kappa(s), \lambda(s)$ respectively. Suppose that a circle C_0 is tangent to M with contact A_3 at the point $\mathbf{p}_0 = \mathbf{p}(0)$, and tangent to N with contact A_1 at the point $\mathbf{q}_0 = \mathbf{q}(0)$. Write $\mathbf{e}, \mathbf{m}$ for the unit tangent and normal at $\mathbf{p}$ and $\mathbf{f}, \mathbf{n}$ for the unit tangent and normal at the point $\mathbf{q}$. Finally write r for the radius of a bitangent circle with contact points $\mathbf{p}$ and $\mathbf{q}$. See Figure 1. Since the circle C_0 has A_3 contact with M at $s = 0$, this point is a vertex of M and we have $r\kappa = 1$ and $d\kappa/ds = 0$ at $s = 0$.

We take as the defining equation of the pre-symmetry set $F(s,t) = \mathbf{0}$ where

$$F(s,t) = \mathbf{p} + r\mathbf{m} - \mathbf{q} - r\mathbf{n}. \tag{2}$$

The Jacobian matrix of the mapping $F : \mathbb{R}^3 \to \mathbb{R}^2$ is the 3×2 matrix with columns the vectors $\mathbf{e}(1 - r\kappa)$, $-\mathbf{f}(1 - r\lambda)$, $\mathbf{m} - \mathbf{n}$. Now, using suffix 0 to mean evaluation at $s = 0$ or $t = 0$, $\kappa_0 = 1/r$, $\lambda_0 \neq 1/r$ so at $s = t = 0$ the first of the column vectors is zero and the others are nonzero multiples of $\mathbf{f}_0$, $\mathbf{m}_0 - \mathbf{n}_0$.

The first is tangent to the circle C_0 and the second is parallel to $\mathbf{p}_0 - \mathbf{q}_0$ which is a chord of the circle; hence the two vectors are independent and we deduce from the implicit function theorem that (2) has solution with t and r smooth functions of s near $s = 0$.

Now consider t and s as these functions of s and write t' for dt/ds, etc. Regarding (2) as an *identity* in s we can differentiate with respect to s and get

$$\mathbf{e}(1 - r\kappa) + r'\mathbf{m} - \mathbf{f}(1 - r\lambda)t' - r'\mathbf{n} = 0.$$

At $s = 0$ the first term is zero and again $\mathbf{m} - \mathbf{n}, \mathbf{f}$ are independent so we deduce $r'_0 = t'_0 = 0$. Differentiating again with respect to s, putting $s = 0$ and keeping only the terms which are nonzero at $s = 0$ gives $r''(\mathbf{m} - \mathbf{n}) = \mathbf{f}(1 - r\lambda)t''$, so that $r''_0 = t''_0 = 0$. Thus both r and t, as functions of s, have degenerate critical points. In fact differentiating again shows that for exactly A_3 at $s = 0$ and A_1 at $t = 0$ we have the next derivatives of r and t nonzero. The fact that t has $t'_0 = t''_0 = 0$ is illustrated in Figure 1 where the stratum of the pre-symmetry which is off-diagonal, namely the graph of t, has an *inflexion*. Furthermore with a little more trouble we can show that in a generic family of curves this A_2 *singularity of the function t* is versally unfolded, that is it behaves as shown in Figure 1 with two critical points vanishing in the inflexion.

We conclude:

Proposition 1. *At an A_1A_3 singularity the off-diagonal stratum of the pre-symmetry set has the structure of the graph of a function with a critical point of type A_2, that is a critical point equivalent to $t = s^3$, an ordinary inflexion. In a generic family of curves the pre-symmetry set has two ordinary critical points 'before' the A_1A_3 transition and none 'after'.*

In the 3D situation we shall also identify the pre-symmetry set as the graph of a function of a well-defined type. See illustrations in Figure 2 and Figure 3.

3   The Pre-symmetry Set in 3D

In this section we shall investigate the strata of the pre-symmetry set of a smooth closed surface as in §1. We shall split into the off-diagonal and the on-diagonal cases; the results are strikingly similar but the details are different. In fact we shall suppress most of the underlying mathematical calculations, which are similar to those in §2 but more complicated since we are dealing here with surfaces instead of curves.

There are a great many cases of transitions on the symmetry set in 3D. Bogaevsky [2] has determined the transitions on the 3D medial axis (see also [4]) and in unpublished work has given a list of all possible transitions on the 3D symmetry set, some of which have been investigated by Pollitt [8]. In this paper we shall determine the pre-symmetry set for a small number of representative cases; more mathematical detail and a larger number of cases will appear elsewhere.

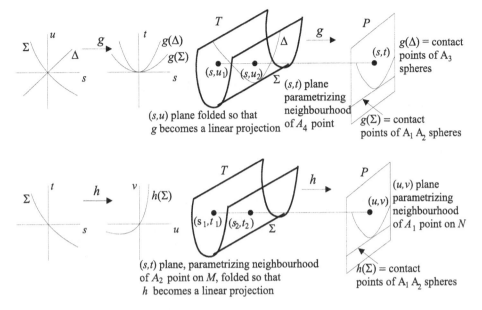

Fig. 2. Schematic diagrams of two of the mappings which we consider, both equivalent to folds. Above, Case A_4: g maps a parameter plane T to a neighbourhood P of the A_4 point. For a point (s,t) 'above' the fold line $g(\Sigma)$ on P, there are two bitangent spheres, with contact at $(s,u_1),(u_1,v(s,u_1))$ and at $(s,u_2),(u_2,v(s,u_2))$. Below, Case A_2A_1: for a point (u,v) 'above' the fold line $h(\Sigma)$ on P = neighbourhood of the A_1 point, there are bitangent spheres with contact at $(s_1,t_1),(u,v)$ and at $(s_2,t_2),(u,v)$.

For the symmetry set of a generic surface M in $\mathbb{R}^3$ we consider here the following singularities:

$$A_3, \quad A_4, \quad A_1A_2, \quad A_1A_3,$$

and for symmetry sets occurring in generic 1-parameter families of surfaces we consider

$$A_1A_3 \text{ transitions}, A_1A_4, A_5.$$

These results can also be used to determine other cases with three contact points, such as $A_1^2A_2$ and $A_1^2A_3$. The cases A_2^2, A_2A_3 can be treated similarly.

3.1 The Off-Diagonal Case

The basic setup is two pieces of smooth surface and a given sphere tangent to both of them at known points. We then seek nearby points such that there is a sphere tangent at these nearby points. To put the matter more precisely, consider two pieces of surface M and N and chosen points $\mathbf{p}_0, \mathbf{q}_0$ such that there is a sphere S_0 tangent to M at $\mathbf{p}_0$ and to N at $\mathbf{q}_0$. The order of tangency at either point might be A_k for k an integer such that the total tangency is consistent with either a single generic surface or a surface in a generic 1-parameter family

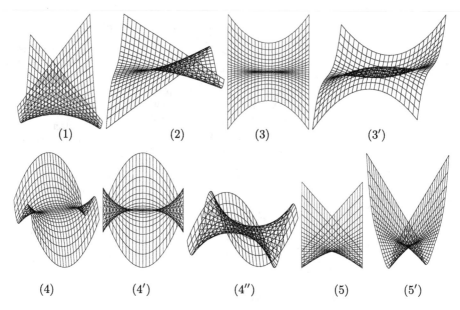

Fig. 3. Standard projections of a curved surface, say T in $\mathbb{R}^3$ to the plane P of the paper. (1) fold; (2) cusp; (3) lips with unfolding (3′); (4′) beaks with unfolding (4) and (4″); and (5) swallowtail with unfolding (5′). These have the following interpretations in the context of this paper. (1) Fold (compare Figure 2): (i) Prop. 3(b), T represents a neighbourhood of an A_2 point on M and P represents a neighbourhood of an A_1 point on N for an A_2A_1 singularity. Points of P 'below' the fold line have no corresponding bitangent spheres on T while points of P 'above' the fold line have two. (ii) Prop. 4(b), A_4. Now, T represents the parameter plane of s and u while P represents the surface M. Thus points of M 'below' the fold line are not contact points for a bitangent sphere while points 'above' are contact points for two such spheres. (2) Cusp: Prop. 3(c), generic A_3A_1 (fin point) only. The two fold lines ending in the cusp give points of M (represented by the curved surface T of the figure) which are contact point of A_2A_1 spheres, as in (1). (3) Lips: (i) Prop. 3(d): one of the A_3A_1 transitional cases; (ii) Prop. 4(c), A_5. (3′) shows the situation immediately 'after' the transition, with two cusps, representing generic A_3A_1 points as in (2). (4) Beaks: the other A_3A_1 transition, Prop. 3(d), only. This time two A_2A_1 curves 'survive' the transition though the A_3A_1 points (cusps as in (2)) are annihilated. (5) Swallowtail: A_4A_1 transition, Prop. 3(e), only.

of surfaces. For example A_3 at $\mathbf{p}_0$ and A_1 at $\mathbf{q}_0$ would be a typical case. (The case of D_4 contact at an umbilic $\mathbf{p}_0$ and A_1 contact elsewhere is also generic in a 1-parameter family, and can be treated similarly.)

We take local parameters (s, t) on M near $\mathbf{p}_0$ and (u, v) on N near $\mathbf{q}_0$, where $s = t = 0$ at $\mathbf{p}_0$ and $u = v = 0$ at $\mathbf{q}_0$, general points on M and N being denoted $\mathbf{p}$ and $\mathbf{q}$. Then the parameter space of points close to the pair $(\mathbf{p}_0, \mathbf{q}_0)$ is $\mathbb{R}^4$, with coordinates (s, t, u, v). We seek the set of such points in $\mathbb{R}^4$ such that there is a sphere tangent to M at the point with parameters (s, t) and tangent to N at the point with parameters (u, v). This set is the local pre-symmetry set for the pair of surfaces M, N. As in §2.2 we shall in many cases identify the pre-symmetry set with the graph of a mapping of known type.

Let r denote the radius function: the radius of the given sphere S_0 is r_0. Further, let $\mathbf{m}$ be the unit normal at $\mathbf{p}$, oriented so that for $\mathbf{p}_0$ the normal passes through the centre of the given sphere, and let $\mathbf{n}$ be the unit normal at $\mathbf{q}$, oriented similarly. Then the condition for a pre-symmetry set point is

$$G(s, t, u, v, r) = 0 \text{ where } G(s, t, u, v, r) = \mathbf{p} + r\mathbf{m} - \mathbf{q} - r\mathbf{n}. \qquad (3)$$

In this equation, which is three scalar equations, there are five 'unknowns' s, t, u, v, r so we expect a two-dimensional solution. Note in particular that, on $G = 0$, the vectors $\mathbf{p} - \mathbf{q}$ and $\mathbf{m} - \mathbf{n}$ are parallel.

For the purpose of calculation we shall assume that neither $\mathbf{p}_0$ nor $\mathbf{q}_0$ is an umbilic point of the corresponding surface. This enables us to use principal directions for our coordinates around these points. Note that umbilics are isolated so we are losing only a finite number of bitangent spheres. Thus we shall assume the $s = $ constant and $t = $ constant curves on M are, near $\mathbf{p}_0$, principal curves, and that for $s = 0$ and for $t = 0$ these curves are unit speed; and similarly for N. Let $\mathbf{e}_1, \mathbf{e}_2$ be principal directions at $\mathbf{p}$ and $\mathbf{f}_1, \mathbf{f}_2$ principal directions at $\mathbf{q}$. Finally we use κ_1, κ_2 for the principal curvatures of M and λ_1, λ_2 for the principal curvatures of N.

The Jacobian matrix of G at $(0, 0, 0, 0, r_0)$ has the following vectors for its columns, using the fact that differentiating the normal in a principal direction $\mathbf{e}$ produces the corresponding principal curvature times $\mathbf{e}$:

$$(1 - r\kappa_1)\mathbf{e}_1, \quad (1 - r\kappa_2)\mathbf{e}_2, \quad -(1 - r\lambda_1)\mathbf{f}_1, \quad -(1 - r\lambda_2)\mathbf{f}_2, \quad \mathbf{m} - \mathbf{n} \qquad (4)$$

Note that $\mathbf{m} - \mathbf{n}$ is parallel to the chord joining $\mathbf{p}$ and $\mathbf{q}$, by (3).

The implicit function theorem gives us:

Proposition 2. *Suppose that the contact at $\mathbf{q}_0$ is of type A_1, which is the same as saying that $r \neq 1/\lambda_1$ and $r \neq 1/\lambda_2$. Then u, v, r are smooth functions of s and t on the set $G = 0$ and in particular the pre-symmetry set*
$$\{(s, t, u, v) : G(s, t, u, v, r) = 0 \text{ for some } r\}$$
is the graph of a smooth function $g : (s, t) \rightarrow (u, v)$.

The following result gives the nature of the mapping g for several cases. The role of g is that, for any point $\mathbf{p}$ near $\mathbf{p}_0$, g gives a point $\mathbf{q}$ near $\mathbf{q}_0$ such that there is a bitangent sphere tangent to M at $\mathbf{p}$ and to N at $\mathbf{q}$. Thus *every* point near $\mathbf{p}_0$ is a possible first point of contact but only points of the image of g are possible second points of contact. Furthermore, a given $\mathbf{q}$ may be the image of several points $\mathbf{p}$ under g. We illustrate these properties in Figure 3 and Figure 2.

We explain the terms used in the Proposition after the statement.

Proposition 3. (a) *In the $A_1 A_1$ case, g is a local diffeomorphism;*
(b) *in the $A_2 A_1$ case[2], g is a fold mapping;*

---

[2] We write $A_2 A_1$ rather than $A_1 A_2$ simply because the 'first' point $\mathbf{p}_0$ is an A_2 and the 'second' point $\mathbf{q}_0$ is an A_1.

(c) *in the generic $A_3 A_1$ case ('fin point' on the medial axis), g is a cusp mapping;*
(d) *in the transitional $A_3 A_1$ cases, g is a lips or beaks mapping;*
(e) *in the $A_4 A_1$ case, g is a swallowtail mapping.*

Part (c) here is to be compared with Proposition 1 where the inflexion on the pre-symmetry set in the $A_1 A_3$ case was interpreted as the graph of a mapping $\mathbb{R} \to \mathbb{R}$ of type A_2. Here we interpret the structure of the pre-symmetry set as the graph of a cusp mapping $\mathbb{R}^2 \to \mathbb{R}^2$. Note the distinction between a *generic* $A_3 A_1$, which occurs on a single smooth surface and a *transitional* $A_3 A_1$ which is one of the two forms identified by Bogaevsky [2] in his classification of transitions on the 3D medial axis.

In the above Proposition, we use the standard names of classes of maps $\mathbb{R}^2 \to \mathbb{R}^2$. These maps have the following 'normal forms' [9] up to smooth changes of coordinates in the two copies of $\mathbb{R}^2$:

(a) local diffeomorphism: $(x,y) \to (x,y)$
(b) fold mapping: $(x,y) \to (x,y^2)$
(c) cusp mapping: $(x,y) \to (x, xy + y^3)$
(d) lips or beaks mapping: $(x,y) \to (x, x^2 y \pm y^3)$ (+ lips, − beaks)
(e) swallowtail mapping: $(x,y) \to (x, xy + y^4)$.

The different cases are separated by examining the critical set Σ of g, that is the set of points (s,t) for which (using suffices to denote partial derivatives) $\det \begin{pmatrix} u_s & u_t \\ v_s & v_t \end{pmatrix} = u_s v_t - u_t v_s = 0$. Standard recognition of singularities gives:

(a) Σ is empty
(b) Σ is a smooth curve and the restriction $g|\Sigma$ of g to Σ is nonsingular
(c) Σ is a smooth curve and $g|\Sigma$ has a cusp of the form $t \to (t^2, t^3)$
(d) Σ is an isolated point for a lips and a pair of transverse curves for a beaks
(e) Σ is a smooth curve and $g|\Sigma$ is of the form $t \to (t^3, t^4)$.

Ideally we would like a direct link between the contact of a sphere and the nature of the mapping g, but as yet we do not know of such a link. Our result is proved on a case by case basis by direct calculation. We give a brief indication of the calculations in §3.2. We shall see in §3.3 that much the same result holds in the on-diagonal case, though the mapping g is replaced by a different one.

3.2   Some Calculations

Starting from the equation $G = 0$ where G is given in (3), we can differentiate with respect to s and t using standard results about the derivatives of tangent vectors and normal vectors along curves on a surface; see for example [6, §6.1] for the relevant formulas. Needless to say the details become complicated by the time the second or third derivatives are reached, and we suppress these details here, merely giving an indication of how the calculations begin.

Differentiating $G = 0$ with respect to s and t, which are arclengths on the principal curve $t = 0$, $s = 0$ respectively, gives

$$\frac{\partial}{\partial s} : \mathbf{e}_1(1 - r\kappa_1) + r_s(\mathbf{m} - \mathbf{n}) = \mathbf{f}_1(1 - r\lambda_1)u_s + \mathbf{f}_2(1 - r\lambda_2)v_s, \qquad (5)$$

$$\frac{\partial}{\partial t} : \mathbf{e}_1(1 - r\kappa_2) + r_t(\mathbf{m} - \mathbf{n}) = \mathbf{f}_1(1 - r\lambda_1)u_t + \mathbf{f}_2(1 - r\lambda_2)v_t, \qquad (6)$$

valid along the curves $t = 0$, $s = 0$ respectively. At points away from these curve we need to allow for the non-unit speed nature of the parameter curves; however these speeds do not affect our calculations when we evaluate at $s = t = 0$.

Consider the $A_1 A_1$ case. Then $1 - r\kappa_1$, $1 - r\kappa_2$, $1 - r\lambda_1$, $1 - r\lambda_2$ are all nonzero at $s = t = 0$. Taking the vector product of the right-hand sides of (5) and (6) then gives $(1 - r\lambda_1)(1 - r\lambda_2)(u_s v_t - v_s u_t)\mathbf{n}$. The mapping $g : (s, t) \to (u, v)$ is a local diffeomorphism at $s = t = 0$ if and only if this is nonzero. However, if the left-hand sides of (5) and (6) are parallel vectors, then $\mathbf{e}_1, \mathbf{e}_2$ and $\mathbf{m} - \mathbf{n}$ are linearly dependent, and this is impossible since $\mathbf{e}_1, \mathbf{e}_2$ are tangent vectors to the sphere S_0, and $\mathbf{m} - \mathbf{n}$ is parallel to the chord $\mathbf{p} - \mathbf{q}$ of the same sphere. Hence in the $A_1 A_1$ case, g is a local diffeomorphism, verifying assertion (a) of Proposition 3.

Keeping the contact at $\mathbf{q}_0$ as A_1, so that $1 - r\lambda_1$, $1 - r\lambda_2$ are nonzero, but moving to A_2 contact at $\mathbf{p}_0$ we have $1 - r\kappa_1 = 0$; note that for A_3 (ridge or crest point) we will have also $\kappa_{1s} = 0$: the derivative of κ_1 in the first principal direction equal to zero [5, p.144]. Using the linear independence of $\mathbf{m} - \mathbf{n}$, $\mathbf{f}_1, \mathbf{f}_2$ (5) now gives r_s, u_s, v_s all equal to 0 at $s = t = 0$, while r_y, u_y, v_y can all be evaluated at $s = t = 0$ from (6). For example, $r_y = -\mathbf{e}_2 \cdot \mathbf{n}(1 - r\kappa_2)/(\mathbf{m} \cdot \mathbf{n} - 1)$, where the denominator cannot be 0 since the points $\mathbf{p}_0, \mathbf{q}_0$ are distinct. We can now check the assertion (b) of Proposition 3. Continuing in this way we find, for $A_3 A_1$, that r_{ss}, u_{ss}, t_{ss} are all zero at $s = t = 0$, and the condition for Σ to be singular comes to $u_{st}v_t - u_t v_{st} = 0$. A very similar argument to that in the $A_1 A_1$ case enables us to express this condition as $\mathbf{e}_2 \cdot \mathbf{n}(1 - r\kappa_2)\kappa_1^2 = \kappa_{1t}(\mathbf{m} \cdot \mathbf{n} - 1)$, and after some manipulation this corresponds precisely to the transitional $A_3 A_1$ condition found by Pollitt [8]: more picturesquely, it means that the osculating plane of the line of curvature on M at $\mathbf{p}_0$ in the direction $\mathbf{e}_1$ passes through $\mathbf{q}_0$. In this way we verify (c) and (d) of Proposition 3.

Unfortunately the criterion which distinguishes the two $A_3 A_1$ transitional cases, and which therefore distinguishes lips from beaks, though computable, is complicated and we do not have a simple geometrical interpretation of it. There is a strong link with the function $R(s, t) = r\kappa_1$: in fact in the transitional $A_3 A_1$ situation, $R_s = R_t = 0$ at $s = t = 0$, and the 'lips' case corresponds to R having a maximum or minimum and the 'beaks' case to R having a saddle point.

3.3   The Local (On-Diagonal) Case

Here we consider the case of the pre-symmetry set of a single surface piece M corresponding to points close to an $A_{\geq 3}$ singularity, at $\mathbf{p}_0$ say, which may be taken as the origin in $\mathbb{R}^3$. This case has the additional difficulty that the points in question intersect the diagonal of the space $\mathbb{R}^4$, that is the set of points (s, t, s, t). This means that, in the notation of (3), $G^{-1}(\mathbf{0})$ will never be smooth and we have to 'eliminate' the diagonal component in some way. It turns out that we can often do this by using a different parametrization from that in §3.1.

We give brief details below. As before, we let (s,t) and (u,v) be the parameters for points of contact of a bitangent sphere, where now all four numbers s,t,u,v are close to 0. In practice we can take M in Monge form $z = f(x,y)$ so that the contact points are $\mathbf{p} = (s,t,f(s,t))$ and $\mathbf{q} = (u,v,f(u,v))$:

$$f(x,y) = \tfrac{1}{2}(\kappa_1 x^2 + \kappa_2 y^2) + b_0 x^3 + b_1 x^2 y + b_2 x y^2 + b_3 y^3$$
$$+ c_0 x^4 + \ldots + c_4 y^4 + d_0 x^5 + \ldots + d_5 y^5 + \ldots. \qquad (7)$$

Instead of having r,u,v expressed as smooth functions of s,t it is much better to use s,u as the parameters and express r,t,v in terms of these. The great advantage of this is that the diagonal points appear as $s = u$, that is, the intersection of the diagonal with the true pre-symmetry set appears as a *curve* $\{(s,t(s,s),s,v(s,s)\}$ on the pre-symmetry set (pre-SS).

The pre-SS is symmetrical about the diagonal in the sense that, for all a,b,c,d, $(a,b,c,d) \in$ pre-SS $\iff (c,d,a,b) \in$ pre-SS. This implies that,

$$\text{for all } (s,u) \in \mathbb{R}^2 \text{ we have } t(s,u) = v(u,s). \qquad (8)$$

We find the following. Let $h : (s,u) \to (s,t(s,u))$ be the mapping determined by t as a function of s and u. The relation between this and the mapping $(s,u) \to (u,v(s,u))$ is completely symmetric so we need consider only h. The role of h is to parametrize the points $\mathbf{p}$ close to the origin which are one point of contact of a bitangent sphere. The other point of contact is parametrized by $(u,v(s,u))$. A simple calculation of the power series expansions for t and v up to order 3 at least, in u and s, allows to get: $r = \frac{1}{\kappa_1} - \frac{\kappa_{1t}\alpha}{\kappa_1^2}(s+u) + \ldots$ where $\kappa_{1t} = 2b_1$.

Proposition 4. (a) A_3: *h is a local diffeomorphism (see note below)*,
(b) A_4: *h is a fold mapping*,
(c) A_5: *h is a lips mapping (beaks mappings do not occur)*.

In all cases the pre-symmetry set is the graph of a smooth function h and is therefore itself smooth. Fig. 3 illustrates these cases (see also Fig. 2).

Note on A_3. There is an exception, which occurs when the tangent to the ridge (crest line) through the origin is in the 'other' principal direction. That is, if the ridge corresponds to the principal direction $\mathbf{e}_1$ then the tangent is in the direction $\mathbf{e}_2$. This is slightly mysterious, but in this case we can use a less satisfactory parametrization, by s and t, instead.

There follow some brief details of the above cases.

$\mathbf{A_3}$: We find

$$t(s,u) = \alpha(s+u) + \text{ h.o.t.}, \quad v(s,u) = \alpha(s+u) + \text{ h.o.t.}, \qquad (9)$$

and $\alpha = \tfrac{1}{4}(\kappa_1^3\kappa_2 - \kappa_1^4 - 8c_0\kappa_2 + 8c_0\kappa_1 + 4b_1^2)/(c_1\kappa_2 - c_1\kappa_1 - 2b_1 b_2)$. The numerator of α is zero precisely when the contact is A_4; see below for this case. The denominator being zero is the exceptional case noted above.

$\mathbf{A_4}$: We find

$$t(s,u) = t_{20}s^2 + t_{11}su + t_{02}u^2 + \ldots; v(s,u) = t_{02}s^2 + t_{11}su + t_{20}u^2 + \ldots, \quad (10)$$

and the constant coefficients t_{ij} are determined by the local geometry of the surface, namely $t_{02} = \dfrac{3(d_0\kappa_1^2 - 2d_0\kappa_1\kappa_2 + b_1c_1\kappa_1 - b_1c_1\kappa_2 + b_1^2b_2 + d_0\kappa_2^2)}{(\kappa_1 - \kappa_2)(c_1\kappa_2 - c_1\kappa_1 - 2b_1b_2)}$

$t_{20} = t_{02} + b_1/(\kappa_1 - \kappa_2)$, $t_{11} = \frac{4}{3}t_{02}$.

The coefficients in v as compared with t are explained by (8). (As with A_3 there is an exceptional case, if the denominator of t_{02} is zero. Here, this means that *the ridge is singular*: this is a transitional A_4 case, where the ridge is undergoing a transition. See [5, p.174].) The coefficient t_{02} of u^2 is zero if and only if the singularity is A_5 or higher; thus for A_4 it is nonzero. From this it is easy to check that the mapping $h : (s, u) \rightarrow (s, t)$ is a fold. The critical set Σ of h is given by $t_{11}s + 2t_{02}u + \ldots = 0$ and has tangent line $2s + 3u = 0$. The fold mapping ensures that, given a point (s_1, u_1) close to the origin, and not on Σ, there is a second distinct point (s_2, u_2) with the same image under γ. This means that $s_1 = s_2 = s$ say, and $t(s, u_1) = t(s, u_2) = t$, say. Then $(s, t, u_1, v(s, u_1))$ and $(s, t, u_2, v(s, u_2))$ both belong to the pre-symmetry set, and the points $(u_1, v(s, u_1))$, $(u_2, v(s, u_2))$ are the distinct points of contact of two spheres, both tangent to M at (s, t). Compare Figure 2.
A_5: We find

$$t = \frac{b_1}{\kappa_1 - \kappa_2}s^2 + t_{30}s^3 + t_{21}s^2u + t_{21}su^2 + \tfrac{2}{3}t_{21}u^3 + \text{h.o.t.} \qquad (11)$$

The critical set of the mapping $(s, u) \mapsto (s, t)$ is now $t_{21}s^2 + 2t_{21}su + 2t_{21}u^2 + $ h.o.t. $= 0$. The discriminant of this quadratic form is $-4t_{21}^2 < 0$ so that the critical set of the mapping has an isolated point at the origin. This means that it can be only 'lips' and not 'beaks'.

4   Conclusion

We have studied pre-symmetry sets of surfaces in 3D, analysing many of them as graphs of functions. This approach brings out the geometry of the pre-symmetry sets and allows one to see them evolving through a generic transition. There are many other interesting cases to study, particularly those where the pre-symmetry set is in fact a singular surface.

Acknowledgements. This work is a part of the DSSCV project supported by the IST Programme of the European Union (IST-2001-35443). The first author was supported by this grant. The authors are also grateful to V. Zakalyukin, A. Pollitt and A. Kuijper for helpful discussions.

References

1. J.W.Bruce and P.J.Giblin 'Growth, motion and one-parameter families of symmetry sets', *Proc. Royal Soc. Edinburgh* 104A (1986), 179–204.
2. I.A.Bogaevsky, 'Perestroikas of shocks and singularities of minimum functions', *Physica D* 173, 1–28, 2002.

3. A. Diatta and P.J. Giblin, 'Geometry of isophote curves', *Scale Space Theory and PDE Methods in Computer Vision, Lecture Notes in Computer Science* 3459 (2005), 50–61.
4. P.J.Giblin, B.B.Kimia and A.J.Pollitt, 'Transitions of the 3D medial axis under a one-parameter family of deformations', *preprint.*
5. P.L.Hallinan, C.G.Gordon, A.L.Yuille, P.J.Giblin and D.Mumford, *Two and Three Dimensional Patterns of the Face*, A.K.Peters 1999.
6. J.J.Koenderink, *Solid Shape*, M.I.T.Press 1990.
7. A. Kuijper, O. Fogh Olsen, 'Transitions of the Pre-Symmetry Set', *17th International Conference on Pattern Recognition* (3) (2004) 190–193.
8. A.J.Pollitt, *Euclidean and Affine Symmetry Sets and Medial Axes*, Ph.D.Thesis, University of Liverpool, 2004. http://www.liv.ac.uk/~pjgiblin
9. Joachim Rieger, 'Families of maps from the plane to the plane', *J. London Math. Soc.* (2) 36 (1987), 351–369.
10. Yuille, A.; Leyton, M. 3D symmetry-curvature duality theorems. *Comput. Vision Graphics Image Process.* 52 (1990), 124–140.

Deep Structure of Images in Populations Via Geometric Models in Populations

Stephen M. Pizer, Ja-Yeon Jeong, Robert E. Broadhurst,
Sean Ho, and Joshua Stough

Medical Image Display & Analysis Group,
University of North Carolina, Chapel Hill, NC, USA

Abstract. We face the question of how to produce a scale space of image intensities relative to a scale space of objects or other characteristic image regions filling up the image space, when both images and objects are understood to come from a population. We argue for a schema combining a multi-scale image representation with a multi-scale representation of objects or regions. The objects or regions at one scale level are produced using soft-edged apertures, which are subdivided into sub-regions. The intensities in the regions are represented using histograms. Relevant probabilities of region shape and inter-relations between region geometry and of histograms are described, and the means is given of inter-relating the intensity probabilities and geometric probabilities by producing the probabilities of intensities conditioned on geometry.

1 Introduction

This workshop focuses largely on finding the essential structure in the 2D images that are input to the human visual system. It marvels that the mature visual system can in 100-200ms make out a complex object, a multi-object complex, or a textured region such as a forest and identify it, and it wonders how such direct image access is possible.

But the immature human visual system has a far more limited capability, and some part of that limitation is that it has not built up the models of the world corresponding to the objects and regions of texture that can be recognized. The models are somehow a very important part of the deep structure. This position applies as well when we are exploring the methods of computer vision, or more generally, of image analysis. This paper therefore explores a model-relative point of view for which the deep structure is found in an image when such models are present.

First, where do the models come from? They must come from multiple instances of the geometric layouts, i.e., using statistics to form probabilistic descriptions. Similarly, the images must come from multiple instances. We therefore expect that the structure we build will involve *probability densities on geometry and probability densities on images*. The model-relative point of view suggests that we will need probabilities on images $\underline{I}$ *conditioned on geometry* $\underline{z}$.

O.F. Olsen et al. (Eds.): DSSCV 2005, LNCS 3753, pp. 49–59, 2005.

For reasons that need not be repeated to attendees of this workshop, the image data need to be understood at multiple scales. However, we argue that this data need to be understood in reference to geometric models that themselves are understood at multiple scales. It is this interaction between image intensity data and geometric models that is the essence of this paper. We do not claim to have solved the problem completely, but we hope to communicate some useful points and to develop some important relations. We have developed these largely in the context of our main application of the analysis of 3D medical images such as CT and MR images, but we suggest that many of the ideas apply in the context of 2D light images of the visible world (e.g., see the work on active appearance models by Cootes et al. [1998]).

Sections 2-4 describe the basic ideas of the geometric descriptions and relations, intensity descriptions, and the probabilistic relations between geometry and intensity that we propose. Section 5 presents the ideas of geometry and its probability with mathematical detail, and section 6 presents the ideas of image intensities conditioned on geometry and its probability. Section 7 describes evidence for the usefulness of the proposed representation, and section 8 closes this paper with a discussion of issues yet to be faced and work yet to be done.

2   Objects, Object-Based Coordinates, and Neighbors

In images, objects or named real world regions are typically characterized by a uniform color or color mixture or texture that may vary in a predictable way across the object, or they are made up of a small collection of such regions. Thus the regions are formed, to first approximation, by successive subdivision. A major point is that one needs a coordinate system *relative to the object or region* to describe this intensity information in the context of a collection of objects or real world regions that vary in shape across the population of such objects. To save space, henceforth we will call this an "object-based coordinate system". With such a coordinate system $\mathbf{u}$, intensity properties $\underline{I}$ can be transformed from the Euclidean coordinates $\mathbf{x}$ in which they arrive to the camera to the object-based coordinates, producing an intensity distribution $I(\mathbf{u})$ that can be the subject of statistical analysis. Similarly, objects, named regions, *and their inter-relations* have a statistical geometry that is coupled with the image intensities or textures that yield the object percept.

Inter-relations among neighbors are central to geometry and thus images of geometric entities. But these relations occur at many scales: objects and named regions have neighbors that are other objects and named regions; object sections have neighbors that are other object sections; voxels or pixels have neighbors that are other voxels or pixels. This setup is illustrated in Fig. 1.

If describing the inter-relations among the smaller scale entities is not to produce a combinatorially unwieldy representation, these neighborhood relations need to be pretty local *relative to their scale*. Thus, we need multiscale geometry and multiscale image intensity representations, and we need a geometry that understands abutments and region inter-relations at a scale.

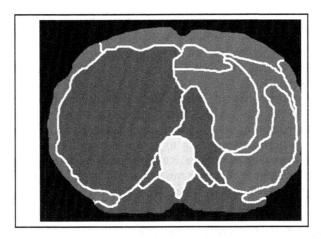

Fig. 1. An abdominal image region made up of sub-regions, showing only one level of subdivision. A region of interest, shown in the lightest shade, can be the whole image domain or a subset of that domain that itself forms a region at some scale. The neighbors of the region of interest are shown in the darkest shade.

For the purposes of this paper we will assume a fixed subdivision topology and a fixed neighborhood relation topology. Variation in this topology is a worthwhile topic but not within the realm of this paper. Maintaining this topology allows slidings of one region along another at the regional scale and these are needed, not just diffeomorphic transformations. Abutting objects or nearby objects can not only change relative shape, but also they can change relative position and orientation, in a way quite possibly correlated with the shape of their neighboring objects and regions. A way of probabilistically measuring a combination of object shape and inter-object geometric relation is discussed in the paper by Pizer, Jeong, Lu, et al. in this volume [2005].

3 Intensity Histograms Via Object-Based Apertures

Regional intensity representations have, we believe, traditionally been far too local, indicating pixel by pixel what the probability distribution of intensity should be. Of course, summarizing intensity over not-too-local regions is the aim of using apertures in the aperture scale space methods of ter Haar Romeny [2003], Florack [2000], Lindeberg [1994], and many others. However, we argue first, that the scale selection should be with respect to the geometry-based coordinate system $\mathbf{u}$ rather than the Euclidean coordinate system $\mathbf{x}$, and second, that the information within the aperture can usefully be more richly summarized as a histogram rather than as a single intensity for the aperture-weighted region. The first point is buttressed by results of Sean Ho's dissertation [2004] that probability distributions on intensities in an along-object-boundary scale space are more generalizable and specific than the more commonly used ones that are local in along-boundary location. The second point, regarding the benefits of the uses of probabilities on regional histograms, is discussed in the companion paper by Broadhurst et al. [2005]. That paper gives some early results on the method for computing statistics of intensity histograms and the advantages not only of that choice but of doing this across multiple regions chosen in object-relative coordinates. Of course, histogram probabilities are only useful if the image intensities are somehow normalized to remove intensity non-calibration effects, but this is true for any analysis of intensities across different images.

The regional, histogram-based approach, of course, begs the question of region size, and this is a matter of scale, i.e., aperture. Because the regions have tolerance at any scale, the aperture corresponding to a region needs to be soft with a falloff distance that increases with region size, but on the other hand, the aperture needs to be determined by the statistics of the intensity distribution in the region, and this may have a rather harder or rather softer edge. We discuss this further in section 4.

4 Geometric and Histogram Statistics

The geometric relations that we have been discussing, of the formation of object-based coordinates, are most economically understood in terms of local orientation at least as much as position. Indeed, the early human vision system has orientation, position, and scale as its three major coordinates. Together, these spaces, or the abstract spaces of the corresponding geometric transformations of rotation, translation, and magnification, are curved. Therefore, if we are to do probabilistic analysis in these terms, our Euclidean feature spaces will not do. Linear spaces may provide the best engineering mechanisms for statistics, and nonlinear transformations such as the rotations involved in local twisting and bending may have their mathematical underpinnings in tangent planes (linear spaces) on curved manifolds. Nevertheless, probabilities defined on the non-Euclidean feature spaces must be the essential basis for our geometric statistics, and these have been provided by the methods of Fletcher [2004] and Pennec [1999] that have been built on statistical approaches pioneered by Kendall [1989] and Grenander [1976, 1978]. Based on these ideas, we use probability distributions based on Fréchet means on curved manifolds and principal geodesics defined via manifold tangent planes at the mean.

Since we need a discrete scale space via successive subdivision, we need a means of producing probabilities at any scale. For this we use the method of residues described in [Lu 2005]. The idea is to describe the probability distribution for the global region first and define the residue at the global scale level for each training sample to be the representation of the training sample itself. Then successively, large scale to small (increasing j in Fig. 2), we remove from the residue of each training sample at a scale level j the projection onto the manifold forming the domain of the probability at scale level j-1. This leaves residues at each scale level that describe only information at that scale level, i.e., an analogy to the Laplacian pyramid. Probabilities can then be done scale level by scale level on the corresponding residues.

Histogram statistics need to be provided in a feature space in which straight lines (geodesics) between histograms produce valid interpolations. In the companion paper by Broadhurst et al. [2005], a histogram representation in terms of average quantile values of the histogram is described that has the desired property: moving along geodesics according to an Earth Mover's distance. Thus, principal component analysis in this space is a useful way of forming probability distributions on histograms.

5 Mathematics and Probability of Multiscale Geometry

Let us put this in mathematical and probabilistic terms. Fig. 2 will schematize our results.

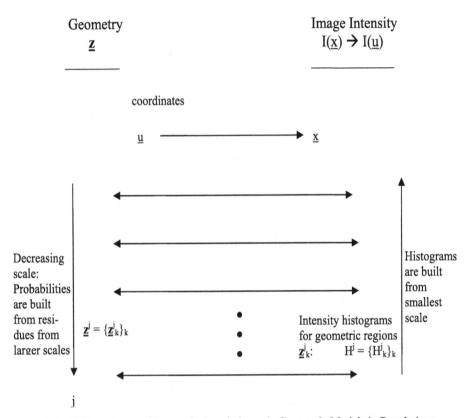

Fig. 2. The schema of Images in Populations via Geometric Models in Populations

Let $\underline{z}$ stand for one's geometric representation of a region of space densely filled with subregions. These subregions form objects and regions in the interstitium between objects, but we will use the word "region" to refer to either. We use m-reps for object representations at large and moderate scales because they enable parts, provide economical descriptions of all of the local geometric transformations needed, are able to provide the object-based coordinate system of objects' interiors, and allow inter-object and inter-part relations also to be represented economically. We use diffeomorphic displacements at small scales. But the discussions below are intended to apply to whichever representation you might use, as long as that representation provides region-based coordinates.

Statistical analyses of intensities requires that intensities be compared at corresponding positions across training cases. Similarly, subdivision of regions must be done with appropriate spatial correspondence. These correspondences are implied by the geometry, i.e., by the layout and shape of the regions, perhaps via statistics of the training cases. We characterize this correspondence via the object-based coordinate system named $\mathbf{u}$.

Let $\underline{I}$ describe a discrete image, i.e., a tuple made up of a scalar value for each pixel or voxel. The object-based coordinates of a region allow us to designate those pixels or voxels within the region and thus allow the formation of histograms of objects or other connected image regions. These objects or regions have a neighborhood relation with abutting regions. If histograms are to be the region descriptors, probably the smallest size regions should still have many pixels or voxels.

If the space described by $\underline{z}$ is to be divided into subregions, each subregion can be described as an aperture, i.e., a weighting function in $\mathbf{u}$. We see the ideal aperture as representing the certainty a pixel or voxel is in the region. Thus the aperture would have the value of 1 well interior to the region "boundary", have the value of 0 well exterior to the region "boundary", and fall smoothly from 1 to 0. These spatial subdivisions forming the regions need to get successively smaller as the level of detail increases. The need for discrete subdivision suggests that the levels of detail be discrete and that the process is subdivision, i.e., decreasing aperture size or scale. Thus we index level by j, and we take the inverse point of view of many at this workshop and let j increase as the level of detail, i.e., the spatial scale decreases. Let $\underline{z}^j_k$ indicate the aperture describing the kth region at the jth scale level. And let $\mathbf{u}^j_k$ describe the object-based coordinate system implied by $\underline{z}^j_k$.

We need to describe the intensities within the aperture (region) $\underline{z}^j_k$. These can be described by histograms of $I(\mathbf{u}^j_k)$, with aperture weighted counts. We use the symbol H^j_k for the histogram for the kth region at scale level j. Notice that, rather than being described directly in $\mathbf{x}$, $\underline{z}^j_k$ needs to be described by apertures in $\mathbf{u}^{j-1}_m$, where m designates the parent region of region k,j. Each object-based coordinate must then be transferred to Euclidean coordinates $\mathbf{x}$.

Because regions not only have soft apertures but also have level surfaces of aperture weight that are smoother, the larger the scale (lower the scale index j), we can expect object regions to contains a small contribution from pixels or voxels in neighboring regions. Indeed, it is possible that we may wish to train histograms excluding these neighbor-region voxels and even possible that we might train boundary region histograms that explicitly have a nearly half-and-half mixture of the two neighboring histograms.

Just as regions have soft apertures in space, histograms need soft apertures in intensity. These apertures should increase as the spatial scale increases. In effect, this means that the bin sizes of the histograms should increase with spatial scale and that the bins should overlap, having soft edges. This might be done directly, but it is probably preferable to do it on the Earth Mover's features of histograms produced by Gaussian-weighted average quantile values of histograms [Broadhurst 2005].

The regional geometric representations need to be described over a population of cases, and the regional intensity distributions need to be described over that population of cases, so we need probability densities on multiscale geometric histograms. The means of doing statistics on histograms is described in detail in the companion paper by Broadhurst et al. [2005].

As for statistics on geometry, besides understanding that statistics on geodesic manifolds will be necessary if twisting and bending is to be described and that these statistics will be on residues at the respective scales, it is important to understand that a region's geometry does not simply involve its own shape but also that of its neighbors. One of the major functions of having various scales is to allow neighbors to be local at that scale. Indeed, our picture is that a neighbor of a region includes all and only abutting regions at the same scale as the region. Thus denote by $N(j,k)$ the set of regions that are neighbors of region j,k: $\{j,m \mid$ region j,m abuts region $j,k\}$. Of course, this definition can be loosened to include second-order abutments or even higher order abutments. Since objects can slide along each other in these populations, we have another orientational relation that must be described using geodesic manifolds.

The importance of relationships with neighbors means that a Markov Random Field is the appropriate model of geometry. That is, we need to focus on $p(\underline{z}^j_k \mid \underline{z}_{N(j,k)})$, where we use the notation $\underline{z}_{N(j,k)}$ as a shorthand for $\{\underline{z}^j_m \mid (j,m) \in N(j,k)\}$. This density involves two factors, the shape of the region and its inter-relation with its neighbors: $p(\underline{z}^j_k \mid \underline{z}_{N(j,k)}) = p(\text{shape of } \underline{z}^j_k, \text{inter-relationship of } \underline{z}^j_k \text{ and } \underline{z}_{N(j,k)})$.

This suggests handling object shape and inter-object relations together: one way to do this is via the region augmentation and prediction method described in the companion paper by Pizer, Lu, Jeong, et al. That paper shows how to train the shape plus neighbor probabilities. Also, [Han 2005] shows how to use this same approach for the relation between protrusion and indentation subfigures and their host figures. Rather than using these conditional probabilities to compute $p(\underline{z}^j)$, this latter probability density is never evaluated, but rather one can find the mode of $p(\underline{z}^j)$ by the Iterative Conditional Modes algorithm using the conditional probabilities $p(\underline{z}^j_k \mid \underline{z}_{N(j,k)})$.

As shown by the down-pointing arrow in the "Geometry" column in Fig. 2, we create the geometric statistics from large scale to small. In contrast, histograms are created from the original image, i.e., from the smallest scale, so the vertical arrow in the "Image Intensity" column is shown pointing upward. As described earlier, we use residues to create geometric probabilities for scale j based on removing the larger scale changes at scale $j-1$ from the training cases. We have thereby implicitly assumed the conditional independence of the probabilities of the geometry of a parent region with each of its subregions. But we have found empirically that this property does not hold. Thus we either must include parent regions and children regions as neighbors, or we must adjust the principal geodesic analysis forming the probabilities to iteratively adjust the respective probabilities to obtain the desired property.

6   Mathematics and Probability of Coupled Image Histograms and Multiscale Geometry

We now move on to combining the intensity histogram statistics and the geometric statistics. As shown in Fig. 2, we believe it is appropriate to combine these scale level by scale level. Let us take segmentation, i.e., region designation in a particular target case, as our driving problem. From the Bayesian point of view we wish to compute the posterior optimum, i.e. arg $\max_z$ p($\underline{z}$ | $\underline{I}$). Doing this scale by scale means optimizing p($\underline{z}^j$|$\underline{I}$). Moreover, we do not optimize p($\underline{z}^j$|$\underline{I}$) directly but rather apply the Iterative Conditional Modes algorithm to   p($\underline{z}^j_k$ | $\underline{z}_{N(j,k)}$, $\underline{I}$). But p($\underline{z}^j_k$ | $\underline{z}_{N(j,k)}$, $\underline{I}$) = p($\underline{I}$ | $\underline{z}^j_{k \cup N(j,k)}$) p($\underline{z}^j_k$ | $\underline{z}_{N(j,k)}$) × a constant with respect to $\underline{z}^j_k$.

The density p($\underline{I}$ | $\underline{z}^j_{k \cup N(j,k)}$) is related to the joint density p($\underline{z}^j_{k \cup N(j,k)}$, $\underline{I}$) by p($\underline{z}^j_{k \cup N(j,k)}$, $\underline{I}$) = p($\underline{I}$ | $\underline{z}^j_{k \cup N(j,k)}$) p($\underline{z}^j_{k \cup N(j,k)}$). The latter factor is a subset of the characterization of the geometry of the j,kth region and its inter-relation with its neighbors. Therefore, the intensity information, given the geometry can be considered to be fully independent of the geometry, once the intensity information is analyzed in object-relative coordinates. More precisely, this will be true except for the small effects of overlapping skirts of the apertures for adjacent regions. This proposition may well not hold for regions of just a few pixels or voxels, and for these the more common Gaussian aperture-based single intensity value might be the preferred basis for probabilities.

From the independence proposition it follows that p($\underline{I}$ | $\underline{z}^j_{k \cup N(j,k)}$) can be given as a product of histograms relevant to scale j. Which histograms are these? Consider j=1, the scale level at which information global to the whole domain of the image is summarized. At that scale level, there is only one region, and histograms of each of its sub regions is needed, i.e., p($\underline{I}$ | $\underline{z}^1$) = $\Pi_{i \in \text{ regions at scale 2}}$ p(H^2_i).

A similar argument applies for smaller (larger index) scale levels. p($\underline{I}$ | $\underline{z}^j_{k \cup N(j,k)}$) requires the histograms of all sub-regions of $\underline{z}^j_k$, H^{j+1}_m for m a child of j,k, but as well it requires histograms of regions just exterior to $\underline{z}^j_k$. These may be N(j,k) or sub-regions of these neighbors. Call these exterior regions N'(j,k). Thus we have concluded that   p($\underline{I}$ | $\underline{z}^j_{k \cup N(j,k)}$) = $\Pi_{m \text{ a subregion of } (j,k)}$ p(H^{j+1}_m) $\Pi_{i \in N'(j,k)}$ p($H^{j \text{ or } j+1}_i$).

7   Results Using Proposed Statistical Framework

We have created quite a complex structure. While we have argued each of its steps and might find the structure elegant, what other evidence can we adduce for its validity? As described in the following, object and histogram statistics in our examples have desirable properties. Tries at segmentation by posterior optimization of deformable m-reps using major parts of this structure are showing success. But far more validation is needed. In particular, we do not have results using all of the proposed framework together, but we have the following results, each using many of its components.

In the companion paper by Pizer, Jeong, Lu, et al. [2005] we have shown that at an object scale level, using a set of three 3D objects $\{\underline{z}^j_k\}_k$ in the male pelvis without interstitial regions and using a way to describe p(shape of $\underline{z}^j_k$, inter-relationship of $\underline{z}^j_k$ and $\underline{z}_{N(j,k)}$) that is explained in that paper, we find that samples from the generated probability distributions are nearly geometrically proper and that the probability distributions have intuitively reasonable means and principal modes of variation.

We have carried out segmentation experiments using a three-scale structure on m-rep models of the three objects: bladder, prostate, and rectum in CT images from a population over many days from the same patient. In these experiments the three scale levels are the global scale, the object scale, and the medial atom, i.e. through-object-subsection, scale. The image contrasts at the boundary of the prostate are extremely low at large portions of its boundary (see Fig. 3). The log likelihood, i.e., log $p(\underline{I} \mid \underline{\mathbf{z}}^j_{k \cup N(j,k)})$ values used were based on normalized intensity correlations rather than our proposed histogram-based probabilities. As illustrated in Fig. 3, on trials on multiple days of one patient, the segmentation appeared to be clinically acceptable [Chaney 2004].

Studies reported in the companion paper by Broadhurst et al. [2005] produced segmentation results of the bladder, prostate, and rectum on the aforementioned patient's CTs for the global scale level only. The results from a variety of methods for evaluating log $p(\underline{I} \mid \underline{\mathbf{z}}^j_{k \cup N(j,k)})$ were compared. These included a variety of means of determing the structure and size of the regions over which histograms were computed. A method using histogram statistics showed improvements over the method using normalized correlation to measure log $p(\underline{I} \mid \underline{\mathbf{z}}^j_{k \cup N(j,k)})$.

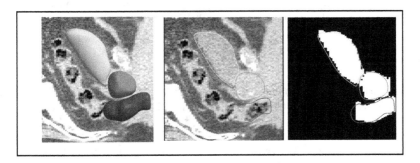

Fig. 3. Slice of CT of male pelvis and 3D segmentation result using a multi-scale posterior optimization of an m-rep, largely according to the schema described in this paper. Shown in white is a cross section of a manual segmentation, for comparison with the computer segmentation shown in color.

8 Discussion

The method of histogram probabilities has already been extended to populations $\underline{I}$ describing a collection of values at each pixel or voxel, where the values may be separate such as luminance and two chromanences, or they may be derived from $\underline{I}$, such as a collection of derivatives of $\underline{I}$ or a collection texture features, e.g., obtained by Gabor filtering with different filters [Broadhurst 2004].

We have much work left to do. The details of many of the stages of this schema are left to be designed, implemented and evaluated. Among the open questions are how precisely should the regions be formed; what is the best way to represent inter-region geometric relationships; what is the best way to produce statistics on these inter-region geometric relationships; how precisely do we transition from the large and moderate scales at which m-reps seem a particularly attractive object representation to the scale of the individual voxel; how do we transition from histograms at these large and moderate scales to Gaussian scale space at the scale of the individual voxel.

Yet the initial results are quite attractive. They certainly overcome the problem associated with regional summaries into a single intensity, that intensities are located more precisely than their scale would suggest, when generating probabilities on image intensities. This problem is found in not only Gaussian scale spaces but also those produced from geometry-limited diffusion. We think our multiscale schema for working with deep structure of images in populations via geometric models in populations is worth following and recommend it to others for consideration and improvement.

Acknowledgements

We are grateful to Sarang Joshi and Edward Chaney for scientific discussions and to Delphine Bull for help in preparing this paper. The work described in this paper was done under the partial support of NIH grant P01 EB02779.

References

Broadhurst, RE (2004). Simplifying Texture Classification. Univ. of N.C. Dept. of Computer Science technical report TR05-009. http://midag.cs.unc.edu/pubs/tech-rpts/ Broadhurst_ TR05_9.pdf

Broadhurst, RE, J Stough, SM Pizer, E Chaney (2005). Histogram Statistics of Local Model-Relative Image Regions. In this volume, *International Workshop on Deep Structure, Singularities and Computer Vision.*

Chaney, E, S Pizer, S Joshi, R Broadhurst, T Fletcher, G Gash, Q Han, JY Jeong, C Lu, D Merck, J Stough, G Tracton, MD J Bechtel, J Rosenman, YY Chi, and K Muller (2004). Automatic Male Pelvis Segmentation from CT Images via Statistically Trained Multi-Object Deformable M-rep Models, Presented at American Society for Therapeutic Radiology and Oncology (ASTRO).

Cootes, TF, GJ Edwards and CJ Taylor (1998). Active Appearance Models. *Proc. European Conference on Computer Vision* 1998 (H.Burkhardt & B. Neumann Ed.s). **2**: 484-498, Springer.

Fletcher, PT, C Lu, SM Pizer, S Joshi (2004). Principal Geodesic Analysis for the Study of Nonlinear Statistics of Shape. *IEEE Transactions on Medical Imaging*, **23**(8): 995-1005.

Florack, L, A Kuijper (2000). The Topological Structure of Scale-Space Images. *J. Mathematical Imaging and Vision*, **12**(1): 65-79.

Grenander, U (1976). *Pattern Synthesis: Lectures in Pattern Theory*, volume I. Springer-Verlag.

Grenander, U (1978). *Pattern Synthesis: Lectures in Pattern Theory*, volume II. Springer-Verlag.

Han, Q, SM Pizer, D Merck, S Joshi, JY Jeong (2005). Multi-figure Anatomical Objects for Shape Statistics. To appear, *Information Processing in Medical Imaging* (IPMI). Springer LNCS.

Ho, S. (2004). Profile Scale Spaces for Statistical Image Match in Bayesian Segmentation. Dissertation, Univ. of N.C. Dept. of Computer Science, http://midag.cs.unc.edu/pubs/phd-thesis/SHo04.pdf

Kendall, DG (1989). A survey of the statistical theory of shape. *Statistical Science*, **4**(2): 87–120.

Lindeberg, T (1994). Scale-space theory: a basic tool for analyzing structures at different scales. *Journal of Applied Statistics*: Special issue on Statistics and Images, **21**(2): 223-261.

Lu, C, SM Pizer, S Joshi, JY Jeong (2004). Statistical Multi-object Shape Models. In preparation. http://midag.cs.unc.edu/LuC2004.pdf

Pennec, X (1999). Probabilities and statistics on Riemannian manifolds: basic tools for geometric measurements. In *IEEE Workshop on Nonlinear Signal and Image Processing*.

Pizer, SM, JY Jeong, C Lu, K Muller, S Joshi (2005). Estimating the Statistics of Multi-Object Anatomic Geometry Using Inter-Object Relationships. In this volume, *International Workshop on Deep Structure, Singularities and Computer Vision*.

ter Haar Romeny, BM (2003). *Front-End Vision and Multi-Scale Image Analysis: Multi-Scale Computer Vision Theory and Applications, written in Mathematica*. Kluwer Academic.

Estimating the Statistics of Multi-object Anatomic Geometry Using Inter-object Relationships

Stephen M. Pizer, Ja-Yeon Jeong, Conglin Lu,
Keith Muller, and Sarang Joshi

Medical Image Display & Analysis Group (MIDAG),
University of North Carolina, Chapel Hill NC 27599, USA

Abstract. We present a methodology for estimating the probability of multi-object anatomic complexes that reflects both the individual objects' variability and the variability of the inter-relationships between objects. The method is based on m-reps and the idea of augmenting medial atoms from one object's m-rep to the set of atoms of an object being described. We describe the training of these probabilities, and we present an example of calculating the statistics of the bladder, prostate, rectum complex in the male pelvis. Via examples from the real world and from Monte-Carlo simulation, we show that this means of representing multi-object statistics yields samples that are nearly geometrically proper and means and principal modes of variations that are intuitively reasonable.

1 Introduction

Since multiple objects form a given anatomic region, there has been a desire to characterize probabilistically populations of multi-object anatomic geometry. Our companion paper [2] makes the case that probabilities on populations of geometric regions are an essential part of multiscale probabilities on geometric-model-based image intensities. In the schema described there regions of space with predictable intensity histograms are placed in a neighbor relationship, and this is done at a number of different discrete scale levels. In another of our papers [5], three scale levels are under consideration: that global to the image, that consisting of only objects without interstitial regions, and that consisting of certain through-object subsections. Here we assume the ability to handle the global scale level and through-object subsection scale level, and we focus on the critical issue of how to produce probability distributions that reflect not only region (object) shape but also inter-object geometric relationships.

The approaches to forming probability distributions on multi-object anatomic geometry that have been tried so far consist of representing the objects and doing global statistics on these representations, as derived from some dozens of training cases. Among the representations to which this approach has been applied are point distribution models [3], diffeomorphisms from atlases [14], distance functions or their levels sets [7], and our own m-reps [1]. We suggest

O.F. Olsen et al. (Eds.): DSSCV 2005, LNCS 3753, pp. 60–71, 2005.

that such global statistics pay inadequate attention to the objects themselves and most especially to the inter-relations among objects. We provide a concrete method that generates probabilities directly on objects and their relationships.

M-reps are representations of object interiors that consist of hierarchies of sheets of medial atoms. They are designed to have the following properties: 1) By medial atom transformations they explicitly capture local bending and twisting (rotation), local magnification, and local elongation, and they separate these from one another. 2) They are based on the subdivision of an object into figures, i.e., main bodies, protrusions, and indentations. Moreover, they provide a fixed topology of such branching for a population of objects and thus allow statistics on this population. 3) They provide a local coordinate system for object interiors that can provide correspondences across instances of an object. 4) They allow neighboring geometric entities to be understood as medial atom transformations of each other. This allows rich characterization of neighbor relationships, for situations internal to a figure, between figures, or between objects.

We use m-reps as the geometric models and statistics using geodesic distance on the curved manifold of a symmetric space [4]. Here we restrict the discussion to objects each of which can be represented by a single sampled sheet of medial atoms (Fig. 1), i.e., "single-figure objects". We show examples describing the variability of the bladder, prostate, and rectum complex in the male pelvis within a patient across a series of treatment days.

We assume that we are given a single-figure m-rep model for multiple objects, for many training cases, and we assume further that the object complexes have already been aligned across the cases and that the medial atoms correspond across the cases.

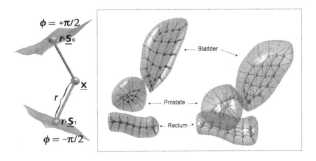

Fig. 1. Medial atom with a section of implied boundary surface (left). An m-rep 3-object complex for the bladder, the prostate, and the rectum of a patient in different view in a box (right).

Limiting ourselves here to the object level of locality, we assume that any truly global variation of the complex has been removed from each object, via the residue technique described in [5]. We do not consider the interstitium between and around objects.

The subject of sections 2-6 is how to express and compute the probabilities of the objects and of the inter-object geometry. In section 2 we overview the approach and then in succession treat its three major components, namely section 3: atom augmentation to simultaneously capture objects and their relations to other objects, section 4: propagation of the inter-object relations to remaining objects, and section 5: inter-object residues to describe the variation remaining after the propagation of effects from other objects. In section 6 we explain how to train probabilities for objects by successive PGA's on object residues.

We say that a geometric model for a complex of non-interpenetrating objects is *proper* if a) the topology of the objects is retained, b) each object in the model does not have singularities or folds of its boundary or interior, and c) the non-interpenetration of objects is retained within the tolerances appropriate for the scale of the description. Many previous methods for estimating inter-object probability distributions have produced samples some of which are decidedly improper. In section 7 we test our method by illustrating that models sampled from our probability distributions on intra-patient bladder, prostate, and rectum deformations are nearly proper and that the means and principal modes of variation of these distributions are intuitively reasonable. We also briefly discuss application of these ideas to segmentation by posterior optimization. Section 8 discusses further opportunities for evaluation, and extensions and alternatives to the proposed methods.

2   Overview of the Approach

We assume that in each case we have n objects, with m-reps $\underline{\mathbf{z}}^2 = \{M_k\}_{k=1}^n$ where M_k is an ordered set of medial atoms and $\underline{\mathbf{z}}^2$ describes the geometric representation of objects at the second scale level as in [2]. Each interior medial atom requires an 8-tuple to represent, describing a hub and two equal-length spokes (Fig. 1), and each grid-edge medial atom requires a 9-tuple to represent, describing a hub, two equal-length spokes, and a third spoke formed from their bisector, which may be of a different length. In our present approach we assume that the objects will be provided in an order of decreasing stability, i.e., whose posterior probability, based on both geometric and intensity variability and edge sharpness, are in decreasing levels of tightness. In this work we provide object statistics in this order, treating each object once. The details of dealing with these objects' statistics in sequence are described in section 6. In section 8 we discuss the extension to a form of a Markov process described in [2].

The main new idea of this paper (Fig. 2) is that while estimating the statistics of a particular object M_k we deal with that object's inter-relation with other atoms by augmenting highly correlated atoms A_k in the remaining objects $R_k = \cup_{i>k}(M_i)$ to M_k to produce "augmented" representations $U_k = M_k \cup A_k$. We can write $p(\underline{\mathbf{z}}^2) = p(U_k, R_k) = p(U_k)p(R_k|U_k)$. In specifying $p(R_k|U_k)$, we divide the effect into a deterministic prediction from U_k and an U_k-independent probability on the residue of R_k from that prediction. When comparing this to the equation in the companion paper [2], $p(\underline{\mathbf{z}}_k^2 \mid \underline{\mathbf{z}}_{N(2,k)}) =$

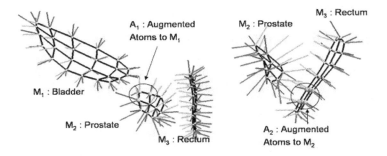

Fig. 2. A discrete m-rep for the bladder (M_1), the prostate (M_2), the rectum (M_3) 3-object complex of a patient. The augmented atoms in the prostate forming A_1 are shown with their hub enlarged (left). The prostate (M_2), the rectum (M_3) of the same patient the enlarged atoms in the rectum form A_2 (right).

$p(\text{shape of } \underline{\mathbf{z}}_k^2, \text{ inter-relation of } \underline{\mathbf{z}}_k^2, \text{ and } \underline{\mathbf{z}}_{N(2,k)})$, we see that in effect we are describing the shape of R_k by its residue and the interrelation with M_k via U_k.

We now describe the other aspect of our new idea, the deterministic propagation of augmenting atoms' movement in the statistics of one augmented object to the remainder of the objects to be processed. The idea is that if an object changes position, pose, size, or shape, its neighboring objects will change sympathetically. In particular (Fig. 3), let all of the atoms in these other objects whose statistics are yet to be determined be R_k. The changes in A_k will be reflected in sympathetic changes in $R_k \setminus A_k$ [1] before the statistics on $R_k \setminus A_k$ are calculated. The details of this propagation are discussed in section 4.

We synthesize these probability distributions via principal geodesic analysis (PGA)[4]. This method of augmentation is discussed further in section 3.

Fig. 3. Assuming we have produced statistics for the augmented bladder U_1, which has augmenting atoms A_1 in the prostate (M_2), we illustrate the sympathetic change of $R_1 \setminus A_1$ caused by A_1

---

[1] Recall that the notation $A \setminus B$ means the set difference A minus B.

3   Objects Inter-relation by Augmentation

Because we have evidence that atoms in one object that are near another object are most highly correlated with that other object, we describe the inter-relation of a multi-object using these nearby atoms for augmentation. In the male-pelvis example of Fig. 2, medial atoms in bladder M_1 should be more highly correlated with medial atoms nearby in prostate A_1 than those in the rest of the prostate or in the rectum $R_1 \setminus A_1$. Thus we let the nearby prostate atoms form A_1, producing the representation of the augmented bladder U_1. We study the effect of the deformation of the bladder on the augmenting atoms and then study the relation of changes in the augmenting atoms A_1 to that of rest of the prostate and the rectum, $R_1 \setminus A_1$. We use the latter results in a stage we call prediction, which is explained next.

4   Prediction of Movements from Augmentation by Using the Shape Space of the Remaining Objects

In prediction we reflect a change in M_k in the statistics of R_k by predicting how $R_k \setminus A_k$ bends, twists or warps from the change of M_k through augmenting atoms A_k. In doing so, we take account of the shape space of the remainder objects R_k as suggested in [6], but using PGA in a nonlinear symmetric space rather than the principal component analysis used in [6].

Recall that PGA involves first finding the mean μ of m-reps $\{\mathbf{M}_i \in \mathcal{M}\}_{i=1}^N$, where $\mathcal{M}$ is the symmetric space of an m-rep $\mathbf{M}_i$ and N is the number of training cases; projecting $\{\mathbf{M}_i\}_{i=1}^N$ to the tangent space $T_\mu \mathcal{M}$ at μ by the log map[2] $(\log_\mu : \mathcal{M} \to T_\mu \mathcal{M})$; and then doing PCA in the tangent space, which yields a set of principal directions $\{v_l\}_{l=1}^h$ in $T_\mu \mathcal{M}$. Taking the exponential map $(\exp_\mu : T_\mu \mathcal{M} \to \mathcal{M})$ of $\{v_l\}_{l=1}^h$ gives a set of principal geodesics in $\mathcal{M}$, which in turn generates a submanifold $\mathcal{H}$ of $\mathcal{M}$. $\mathcal{H}$ is the shape space in which different modes of variations restricted to $\mathcal{H}$ of $\{\mathbf{M}_i\}_{i=1}^N$ are described via principal geodesics. The projection of $\mathbf{M}_i$ onto the shape space $\mathcal{H}$, $Proj_\mathcal{H}(\mathbf{M}_i)$[3], describes the unique variation within $\mathcal{H}$ nearest in geodesic distance to $\mathbf{M}_i$.

Now consider the augmented m-rep object $U_k = (M_k \cup A_k)$ and R_k $(A_k \subset R_k)$. Let μ_r and H_r be the mean and the shape space generated by principal geodesics in the symmetric space $\mathcal{M}_r$ of R_k, which we can obtain by performing PGA on training cases of R_k. If we know how U_k deforms, i.e., how M_k and A_k change together, $Proj_{H_r}(A_k)$ predicts how the remaining object R_k changes sympathetically through A_k in the shape space H_r:

$$Proj_{\mathcal{H}_r}(A_k) = \exp_{\mu_r} \left(\sum_{l=1}^{h_r} \langle \log_{\mu_r}(A_k), v_l \rangle \cdot v_l \right), \qquad (1)$$

---

[2] Refer to [4] for detailed explanation of the log map and the exponential map.

[3] More precisely, the projection operator $Proj_\mathcal{H} : \mathcal{M} \to \mathcal{H}$ is approximated by $Proj_\mathcal{H}(\mathcal{M}) = \exp_\mu \left(\sum_{l=1}^h \langle \log_\mu(\mathcal{M}), v_l \rangle \cdot v_l \right)$. For detailed explanation, refer to [4].

where $\{v_l\}_{l=1}^{h_r}$ are principal directions in the tangent space at μ_r corresponding to the principal geodesics in H_r and the dimension of $\log_{\mu_r}(A_k)$ is adjusted to match with that of v_l by adding zeros to $\log_{\mu_r}(A_k)$ for parameters corresponding to $R_k \setminus A_k$. Then the prediction for the remainder R_k can be defined as

$$Pred(R_k; A_k) := Proj_{\mathcal{H}_r}(A_k) \ . \tag{2}$$

Notice that $Pred(R_k; A_k)$ is also an m-rep.

5   Residues of Objects in Order

If we describe the changes in U_k and the sympathetic changes in $R_k \setminus A_k$, all that is left to describe statistically is the remaining changes in R_k after the sympathetic changes have been removed. If the objects are treated in order and each object has augmenting atoms only in the next object, this will mean that n probability distributions will need to be trained, namely, for U_1, for U_2 after the sympathetic changes from U_1 have been removed, ... , for U_n after the sympathetic changes from $U_1, U_2 \ldots$, and U_{n-1} have been removed. The removal of sympathetic changes is accomplished via the residue idea described in [5]. Next we explain how such residues are calculated between a predicted remainder $\mathbf{N}^0$ and the actual value $\mathbf{M}$ of that remainder.

5.1   Difference of Medial Atoms

A medial atom $\mathbf{m} = (\mathbf{x}, r, \mathbf{u}, \mathbf{v})$ is defined as an element of the symmetric space $G = R^3 \times R^+ \times S^2 \times S^2$ where the position $\mathbf{x} \in R^3$, the spoke length $r \in R^+$, and two unit spoke directions $\mathbf{u}, \mathbf{v} \in S^2$ (S^2 is a unit sphere). If an m-rep has d medial atoms, the m-rep parameter space becomes $\mathcal{M} = G^d$. Let $\mathbf{R_w}$ represent the rotation along the geodesics in S^2 that moves a point $\mathbf{w} \in S^2$ to the north pole $\mathbf{p} = (0, 0, 1) \in S^2$. For given any two medial atoms $\mathbf{m}_1, \mathbf{m}_2 \in G$ where $\mathbf{m}_i = (\mathbf{x}_i, r_i, \mathbf{u}_i, \mathbf{v}_i)$, $i = 1, 2$, the difference between them can be described as follows:

$$\ominus : G \times G \longrightarrow G$$
$$\mathbf{m}_1 \ominus \mathbf{m}_2 := (\mathbf{x}_1 - \mathbf{x}_2, \tfrac{r_1}{r_2}, \mathbf{R_{u_2}}(\mathbf{u}_1) \, \mathbf{R_{v_2}}(\mathbf{v}_1)) \ . \tag{3}$$

$\mathbf{m}_1 \ominus \mathbf{m}_2$ is the difference between $\mathbf{m}_1, \mathbf{m}_2$ relative to $\mathbf{m}_2$ coordinates. Like $\mathbf{m}_1$ and $\mathbf{m}_2$, $\mathbf{m}_1 \ominus \mathbf{m}_2 \in G$.

Corresponding to the difference operator $\ominus$, the addition operator $\oplus$ can be defined as:

$$\oplus : G \times G \longrightarrow G$$
$$\mathbf{m} \oplus \Delta\mathbf{m} := (\mathbf{x} + \Delta\mathbf{x}, r \cdot \Delta r, \mathbf{R_u}^{-1}(\Delta\mathbf{u}), \mathbf{R_v}^{-1}(\Delta\mathbf{v})) \tag{4}$$

for given $\mathbf{m} = (\mathbf{x}, r, \mathbf{u}, \mathbf{v})$ and the difference $\Delta\mathbf{m} = (\Delta\mathbf{x}, \Delta r, \Delta\mathbf{u}, \Delta\mathbf{v})$. This operation is neither commutative nor associative. As an m-rep object is a collection of medial atoms, these operations can be individually applied to each atom of the object.

5.2   Residues in an Object Stage

Our probabilistic analysis proceeds object by object in order. After some object has been described probabilistically and its sympathetic effect has been applied to its remainder, there is a further change in the remaining objects to be described. We call that further change the residue of the remainder objects with respect to the probability distribution on the first. More precisely, let $\mathbf{M} \in \mathcal{M}$ be an m-rep or an m-rep residue of one object fitting a particular training case where $\mathcal{M}$ is a symmetric space of $\mathbf{M}$ and let $p(\mathbf{N})$ be a probability distribution on $\mathbf{N} \in \mathcal{M}$ describing part of the variation of $\mathbf{M}$. Notice that if $D(p)$ represents the domain of p, then $D(p)$ is a submanifold of $\mathcal{M}$. Relative to the probability distribution p, $\mathbf{N}^0$, the closest m-rep to $\mathbf{M}$ in $D(p)$, is

$$\mathbf{N}^0 = \arg \min_{\mathbf{N} \in D(p)} d(\mathbf{M}, \mathbf{N}), \tag{5}$$

where $d(\mathbf{M}, \mathbf{N})$ is the geodesic distance on $\mathcal{M}$. Then the residue $\Delta\mathbf{M}$ of $\mathbf{M}$ with respect to p can be defined as

$$\Delta\mathbf{M} := \mathbf{M} \ominus \mathbf{N}^0 . \tag{6}$$

In the method we are describing, we use the prediction $Pred(\mathbf{M}; \mathbf{A})$ from a set of augmented atoms $\mathbf{A}$ in $\mathbf{M}$ to $\mathbf{M}$'s previous object (of which movements have an effect on $\mathbf{M}$) as an approximation to $\mathbf{N}^0$ because the prediction is made on the shape space of $\mathbf{M}$ and the augmentation can give a good estimation to the overall effect of $\mathbf{M}$'s previous object. We expect the prediction $Pred(\mathbf{M}; \mathbf{A})$ to be close to $\mathbf{N}^0$. Thus we compute $\Delta\mathbf{M} := \mathbf{M} \ominus Pred(\mathbf{M}; \mathbf{A})$.

6   Training the Probabilities for Objects

Training the probabilities for the object is done via successive PGA's on the object residues. Using the notation from Sec. 2, let O^i be a multi-object m-rep residue in case i from which any truly global variations are removed from $\{M_k^i\}_{k \in K}$, where $I = \{1, \ldots, N\}, K = \{1, \ldots, n\}$ are index sets for N training cases and n objects. Then $O^i = \{\Delta M_k^i\}_{k \in K}$ forms a multi-object m-rep residue of the ith training case.

The residues $\{O^i\}_{i \in I}$ are treated in the order of objects M_k from $k = 1$ to n. First we apply PGA on $\{\Delta U_1^i\}_{i \in I}$, the residue of the first object, to get the mean μ_1 and a set of principal variances and associated principal geodesics $\{\exp_{\mu_1}(v_1^l)\}_{l=1}^{n_1}$, where $v_1^l \in T_{\mu_1}\mathcal{M}_1$. This mean, principal variances, and principal geodesics provide our estimate of the probability distribution of ΔU_1. Let $\mathcal{H}_1$ be a submanifold of $\mathcal{M}_1$, where $\mathcal{M}_1$ is the symmetric space for ΔU_1. The projection of ΔU_1^i onto the geodesic submanifold $\mathcal{H}_1$, $Proj_{\mathcal{H}_1}(\Delta U_1^i)$, describes the variation unique to ΔU_1^i in $\mathcal{H}_1$. Now we need to update the residue $\{\Delta R_1^i\}_{i \in I}$ to reflect the sympathetic effect from ΔM_1 on ΔR_1 by ΔA_1. That is done using the prediction $Pred(\Delta R_1^i; \Delta A_1^i)$ as described in Sec. 4.

So the residue for the next object (the second object) that we use to apply PGA is no longer $\{O^i\}_{i \in I}$. The updated residue of the remainder to the first object becomes

$$\Delta^2 R_1^i = \Delta R_1^i \ominus Pred(\Delta R_1^i; \Delta A_1^i) \quad i \in I . \tag{7}$$

Once we have the new updated residue $\Delta^{k-1} U_k^i \subset \Delta^{k-1} R_k^i$ for the kth object, $k = 2, \ldots, n$, we repeat the same steps 1) applying PGA on $\Delta^{k-1} U_k^i$ and 2) updating the residue of the remainder, which produces a set of means $\{\mu_k\}_{k \in K}$ and sets of principal geodesics $\{\{\exp_{\mu_k}(v_k^l)\}_{l=1}^{n_k}\}_{k \in K}$ on object residues.

7 Geometrically Proper Objects in Probability Distributions in the Male Pelvis

Samples being geometrically improper has been a problem for other methods such as PCA on distance functions or on dense PDMs. Examples of what we mean by geometrically improper is wrong topology, interpenetration of separated objects, folding, and singularities such as unwanted corners and cusps. There are two reasons why we would expect that our methods would avoid geometrically improper samples from their probability distributions.

1) M-reps are founded on the idea that using primitive transformations including local twisting and bending of objects will yield an economical representation of the single and multi-object transformations of anatomy between individuals or within an individual over time. When using such transformations in the representation methods and in particular in the methods of description of object inter-relations via augmentation and prediction, nonlinear PGA is necessary to produce sample object complexes that are geometrically proper.

2) The regular grids of medial atoms that we generate from training binary images of objects [9] are designed to have large geodesic distance to improper entities on the manifold $\mathcal{M}$. Thus we might hope that objects within $[-2, +2]$ standard deviations will also be proper. Analysis of our objects using a criterion based on the radial shape operator of [8] could be used to avoid improper models, but this criterion has not been applied in the work described in this paper.

The most basic test of our probability distributions is to visually judge whether those generated samples are proper and whether the principal geodesic directions derived from real patient data explain variations we see in the training samples. Because our training set is just a particular sample subset of a population of m-reps, we wish to know how our method would fare on other training sample subsets. We can accomplish this by generating new random samples from our probability distributions and test whether training from these samples produces a probability distribution whose samples are proper.

We generate the new samples by assuming that each tangent plane principal component from the original training follows the standard normal distribution once we scale the principal directions by the square root of corresponding eigenvalues in the tangent space. Thus, for each object residue we randomly sample

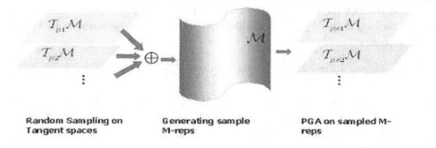

Random Sampling on   Generating sample   PGA on sampled M-
Tangent spaces   M-reps   reps

Fig. 4. Left: tangent spaces at object residue means from real patient data. Middle: m-rep parameter space. Right: object residue means from generated training data. The movie of 100 sampled m-reps from patient 1 and patient 2 data is at http://midag.cs.unc.edu/pubs/papers/movies/100SamplesPat1and2.avi. In the movie the point of view changes from time to time.

each principal component following the standard normal distribution to generate random points on each tangent space about the mean $\{\mu^k\}_{k \in J}$. By taking exponential maps of those points, we generate m-reps and residues that can be combined by $\oplus$ to produce new training sample m-reps. PGA on such a new sampled training set yields a new mean and set of principal directions and variances, whose samples we can judge as to how proper they are.

We applied our new method to obtain the probability distributions from two training sets, each of which are obtained from bone-aligned male-pelvis CT images of a real patient over several days. A single-figure m-rep was fit to each organ: 4x6 grids of medial atoms for the bladder, 3x4 grids for the prostate, and 3x7 grids for the rectum. The total number of medial atoms is 57, so the dimension of the m-rep parameter space is 456. Our software to fit the single figure m-reps to binary image of each organ provides reasonable correspondence of medial atoms across cases by penalizing irregularity and rewarding correspondence to one case [9]. Inter-penetrations among m-reps of the three objects were restricted in the fitting [9] of each training case. We have 11 cases (m-reps) of one patient (patient 1) and 17 cases of another patient (patient 2).

Figure. 5 displays the first modes of variation of patient 1 and 2 at PGA coefficients -2, -1, 1, 2 standard deviations of bladder with prediction, prostate with prediction and rectum in Fig. 5 from the top row to the bottom row.

In these movies, as well as the ones seen in fig. 4, we see the following behaviors: 1) The m-reps produced as samples or chosen along principal geodesics yield limited inter-object penetration, as desired since the training samples have small inter-object penetration. 2) The surfaces of the m-rep sample implied objects are smooth, with few exceptions. Folding is not observed, and the introduction of sharp ridges happens seldom, only at crest positions which are sharp in some of the training cases. 3) The principal geodesics seem to correspond to anatomically observed changes. For example, we see strong growth in the bladder correspond-

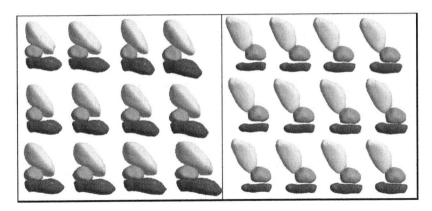

Fig. 5. Illustration of first modes of variation of patient 1 in the box on the left and that of patient 2 in the box on the right. The movie that shows the first modes of variations of patient 1 and then patient 2 is at `http://midag.cs.unc.edu/pubs/papers/movies/VariationsPat1and2.avi`.

ing to filling and strong bulging of the rectum corresponding to the introduction of bowel gas. Also, the prostate residue shows only modest shape changes, a behavior expected from the fact that the prostate is typically quite hard.

It is in this sense that we say that our statistical method provides samples that are "nearly geometrically proper and means and principal modes of variations that are intuitively reasonable."

In addition to the evaluation of m-rep probabilities just described, we can also judge the probabilities A) on the ability of the PGA to extract known independent random deformations in simulations and B) by their usefulness in segmentation. A) In simulations with compositions of independent random bendings, twistings, and magnifications of an ellipsoid, PGA extracted these basic deformations very well. B) PGA m-rep probabilities trained from images of a given patient on a variety of days were used as the prior in segmentation by posterior optimization of m-reps of the bladder, prostate, rectum complex in target images of the same patient on different days. The details of the application to segmentation are given in [2] and [12], object segmentation using histogram statistics is described in [15], and the results on a few cases, agreeing well with human segmentations, have been reported in [13]. Briefly, the results are anecdotal but encouraging.

8   Discussion and Conclusion

We presented new ideas in estimating the probability distribution of multi-object anatomic objects via augmentation and prediction with principal geodesic analysis suggested in [4]. As described in our companion paper [2], a schema involving neighboring regions at multiple scales has much to recommend it. At each scale level in this schema, except the global level, a means is needed to produce statistics reflecting region shape and inter-region relations for neighboring regions. This paper has shown the viability of a particular method for producing these statistics.

We have also applied our approach of augmentation and prediction to compute statistics of m-reps of multi-figure objects, the structure of which is described in [10]. We take hinge atoms as augmented atoms and predict the sympathetic change of a subfigure from the change of its host figure [11].

In this paper, we have limited the residue to the object level of locality. But we can compute finer residues at the medial atom level of locality and do further analysis as described in [5].

Other evaluations of the sample probability distributions generated using Monte Carlo approaches to generate new sample training sets are in progress. These involve measuring the bias and reliability of the resulting probability distributions and determining the number of training samples required.

We can avoid ordering the objects by considering the mutual neighbor relation in augmentation. This extension from the present approach to the Markov Random Field approach as discussed in [2] is suggested by real situations such as male-pelvis example that we used: not only can the bladder induce a change in the prostate and rectum but also the change of a prostate can induce sympathetic change in the bladder and rectum, etc.

We have chosen the augmented atoms based on the distance between atoms in one object and the other because we have preliminary evidence done by [5] that those nearby atoms are highly correlated. Another test needed is whether the remaining atoms are independent of the primary object when conditioned on the augmenting atoms. In addition, attention is needed to defining the global statistics so that the object probabilities and the global probabilities are conditionally independent of each other. In this way the global probabilities will not simply involve principal geodesic analysis of $\cup_{k=1}^{n} M_k$.

The success of geodesic statistics depends on the initial alignment of the training cases. In the example used in this paper, a global alignment of the cases was accomplished using a rigid object, the pelvic bones. In multi-patient cases, however, the alignment needs to be accomplished by the Procrustes algorithm using the geodesic distance metric [4]. Once the global statistics have been computed, it may be desirable to realign for each object, before the residue for that object is analyzed.

Finally, a possible measure to explain the inter-object relation is canonical correlation. Canonical correlation explains the relation of two sets of variables each in a linear space. Here we wish to relate M_k and its neighbors. Because the principal geodesics are defined in tangent spaces to the symmetric space $\mathcal{M}$, we speculate that we can incorporate this canonical correlation directly as an alternative to the method described in this paper.

We thank Edward Chaney, Gregg Tracton, and Derek Merck for pelvis models. This work was done under the partial support of NIH grant P01 EB02779.

References

1. S.M. Pizer, T. Fletcher, Y. Fridman, D.S. Fritsch, A.G. Gash, J.M. Glotzer, S. Joshi, A. Thall, G Tracton, P. Yushkevich, and E.L. Chaney, "Deformable M-Reps for 3D Medical Image Segmentation," *International Journal of Computer Vision - Special UNC-MIDAG issue*, (O Faugeras, K Ikeuchi, and J Ponce, eds.), vol. 55, no. 2, pp. 85-106, Kluwer Academic, November-December 2003
2. S.M. Pizer, JY. Jeong, R. Broadhurst, S. Ho, and J. Stough, "Deep Structure of Images in Populations via Geometric Models in Population," in *this volume, International Workshop on Deep Structure, Singularities and Computer Vision (DSSCV)*, 2005.
3. T.F. Cootes, C.J. Taylor, D.H. Cooper, and J. Graham, "Active Shape Models Their Training and Application," *Computer Vision and Image Understanding*, Elsevier, Vol. 61 (1995), No. 1, pp.38-59.
4. P.T. Fletcher, C. Lu, S.M. Pizer, and S. Joshi, "Principal Geodesic Analysis for the Study of Nonlinear Statistics of Shape," *IEEE Transactions on Medical Imaging*, vol. 23, no. 8, pp. 995-1005, IEEE, Aug. 2004.
5. C. Lu, S.M. Pizer, and S. Joshi, "Statistical Multi-object Shape Models," *in preparation*.
6. K. Rajamani, S. Joshi, and M. Styner, "Bone model morphing for enhanced surgical visualization," in *International Symposium on Biomedical Imaging*, pp.1255-1258, Apr. 2004.
7. A. Tsai, A. Yezzi, W. Wells, C. Tempany, D. Tucker, A. Fan, E. Grimson, and A. Willsky, "A Shape-Based Approach to Curve Evolution for Segmentation of Medical Imagery," *IEEE Transactions on Medical Imaging*, Vol. 22, No. 2, 137-154, February 2003.
8. J. Damon, "Determining the Geometry of Boundaries of Objects from Medial Data," To appear, *International Journal of Computer Vision*, 2005.
9. D. Merck, S. Joshi, G. Tracton, and S.M. Pizer, "On Single Figure Statistical M-Rep Model Construction," *in preparation*.
10. Q. Han, C. Lu, G. Liu, S.M. Pizer, S. Joshi, and A. Thall, "Representing Multi-Figure Anatomical Objects," in *International Symposium on Biomedical Imaging*, pp. 1251-1254, Apr. 2004.
11. Q. Han, S.M. Pizer, D. Merck, S. Joshi, and JY. Jeong, "Multi-figure Anatomical Objects for Shape Statistics," To appear, *Information Processing in Medical Imaging (IPMI)*, 2005.
12. S.M. Pizer, P.T. Fletcher, S. Joshi, A.G. Gash, J. Stough, A. Thall, G. Tracton, and E.L. Chaney, "A Method and Software for Segmentation of Anatomic Object Ensembles by Deformable M-Reps," To appear, *Medical Physics*, 2005.
13. E. Chaney, S.M. Pizer, S. Joshi, R. Broadhurst, P.T. Fletcher, G. Gash, Q. Han, JY. Jeong, C. Lu, D. Merck, J. Stough, G. Tracton, MD J. Bechtel, J. Rosenman, YY. Chi, and K. Muller. "Automatic Male Pelvis Segmentation from CT Images via Statistically Trained Multi-Object Deformable M-rep Models," *Presented at American Society for Therapeutic Radiology and Oncology*, 2004.
14. S. Joshi, "Large Deformation Diffeomorphisms and Gaussian Random Fields for Statistical Characterization of Brain SubManifolds," PhD Thesis, Dept. of Electrical Engineering, Sever Institute of Technology, Washington Univ., Aug. 1997.
15. R.E. Broadhurst, J. Stough, S.M. Pizer, and E.L. Chaney, "Histogram Statistics of Local Image Regions for Object Segmentation," in *this volume, International Workshop on Deep Structure, Singularities and Computer Vision (DSSCV)*, 2005.

Histogram Statistics of Local Model-Relative Image Regions

Robert E. Broadhurst, Joshua Stough,
Stephen M. Pizer, and Edward L. Chaney

Medical Image Display & Analysis Group (MIDAG),
University of North Carolina, Chapel Hill NC 27599, USA
`reb@cs.unc.edu`

Abstract. We present a novel approach to statistically characterize histograms of model-relative image regions. A multiscale model is used as
an aperture to define image regions at multiple scales. We use this image
description to define an appearance model for deformable model segmentation. Appearance models measure the likelihood of an object given a
target image. To determine this likelihood we compute pixel intensity
histograms of local model-relative image regions from a 3D image volume near the object boundary. We use a Gaussian model to statistically
characterize the variation of non-parametric histograms mapped to Euclidean space using the Earth Mover's distance.

The new method is illustrated and evaluated in a deformable model
segmentation study on CT images of the human bladder, prostate, and
rectum. Results show improvement over a previous profile based appearance model, out-performance of statistically modeled histograms over
simple histogram measurements, and advantages of regional histograms
at a fixed local scale over a fixed global scale.

1 Introduction

Multiscale image descriptors are important for understanding and segmenting
deep structures in images. Deformable geometric models have also been shown to
be a powerful tool for segmentation. Geometric models generate model-relative
image descriptors, which are often used in the human visual system and whose
importance is argued in the companion paper by Pizer et al [11]. In this paper, we use a multiscale model-relative image description for the segmentation
of 3D deformable objects in medical images. Automatic segmentation methods
that statistically learn the likelihood of an object given an image have several
desirable qualities. We define an image likelihood measure using non-parametric
histograms as our basic image measurement and describe a new method to statistically learn their variation. These histograms are measured in model-relative
regions defined at a particular scale using the geometric model as an aperture.

Appearance models at extremely local scale levels are based on the correlation
of pixel intensities. Intensities are acquired along profiles normal to the object
boundary [4,15] or from entire model-relative image regions [3,6]. These methods

O.F. Olsen et al. (Eds.): DSSCV 2005, LNCS 3753, pp. 72–83, 2005.
© Springer-Verlag Berlin Heidelberg 2005

can be used in conjunction with image filters to summarize information at a larger spatial scale and to measure image structure such as texture, gradients, or corner strength [14]. Local methods, however, have difficulty capturing the inter-relations among pixel intensities in a region.

Region based methods, which are at larger spatial scales, are better than local methods at capturing pixel inter-relations. This is accomplished by aggregating pixel intensities over global image regions such as object interior or exterior, in one of two ways. In the first, region statistics, such as mean and variance, are computed. These statistics are either learned during training or functions of them are defined to be minimized [2,16]. Although the variation of region statistics can be learned during training, the statistics themselves capture limited information. In the second, each region is represented by a histogram, and a distance to a learned reference histogram is defined. Histograms provide a rich estimate of a region's intensity distribution but previous work only specifies a reference histogram and not its expected variation [5].

In this paper, we use a region based method that defines several model-relative regions. This allows a multiscale image description that can be used at a large scale level with one or two global regions defined per object, or at more local scale levels with many smaller regions per object. We segment images using this image description at three fixed scale levels. First, we use global image regions as in previous methods. Then, we describe two approaches to define increasingly local regions. These novel local region approaches have the advantage of histogram measurements with increased locality and tighter distributions, which help drive our segmentation algorithm to a more clearly defined optimum. In order to define these local regions we need a shape model that specifies a voxel to voxel correspondence near the object boundary; for this we use m-reps (see section 3.1) [9,10]. To form a statistical description of each region, we map non-parametric histograms to points in Euclidean space using the Earth Mover's distance (EMD) [1,7,13]. Then, we apply standard statistical tools to model histogram variation. Straight-line paths between histograms in the resulting space provide interpolated histograms representing plausible distributions. The lack of distribution assumptions allow inhomogeneous regions to be modeled, though this typically results in loose distributions. In this case, we define local regions to reduce distribution variability. Therefore, we have an image descriptor that can model any intensity distribution while maintaining tightness using regions at an appropriate scale.

Appearance models allow two simplifying assumptions when defining the probability of an image given a model. Image dependence on a model can be decomposed into describing the image relative to the model and further correlations between the image and object shape. Appearance models can reasonably assume that model-relative images have intensities with no further probabilistic dependence on object shape. The probability of a model-relative image is determined using several image measurements, which are also often assumed to be independent. However, local measurements are highly interrelated due to their small scale so it is inaccurate to consider them as independent. It is also difficult to model local measurement inter-relations, since this requires a global high dimensional appearance representation with a complicated and hard to train covariance [3]. On the other hand, as argued in the companion paper [11] we can reasonably assume that larger scale regional measurements of a model-relative image are independent, if the image is divided into anatomically based local regions and geometric variation is entirely captured by the shape prior.

Thus, we assume regional image measurements relative to object shape are conditionally independent. This defines image likelihood as the product of the probability densities derived from each region.

In section 2 we introduce our histogram methodology and construct a statistically learned histogram likelihood measure. In section 3 we overview our segmentation framework and give segmentation results using global image regions. In section 4 we extend this work to local image regions.

2   Statistical Modeling of Non-parametric Histograms

We fully train a non-parametric histogram based appearance model. To do this we map histograms to points in Euclidean space in such a way that straight-line paths between two points produce a natural interpolation between the corresponding histograms. This mapping allows us to use standard statistical tools, such as Principal Component Analysis (PCA) and Gaussian modeling.

In section 2.1 we construct this mapping and consider properties of the resulting space. In section 2.2 we define the likelihood of a histogram. In section 2.3 we provide an example.

2.1   Mapping Histograms to Euclidean Space

Our mapping can be understood by considering the similarity measure defined between two histograms that will correspond to Euclidean distance. We use the EMD, which was introduced by Rubner et al. for image retrieval [13] and has since been shown to be equivalent to the Mallows distance [8]. The EMD representation we use is described for texture classification in [7] and used to build statistical models in [1].

The EMD, and the Mallows distance for discrete distributions, can be thought of as measuring the work required to change one distribution into another, by moving probability mass. The position, as well as frequency, of probability mass is therefore taken into account yielding two major benefits. First, over-binning a histogram, or even using its empirical distribution, has no additional consequences other than measuring any noise present in the distribution estimate. Second, this distance measure to some extent mimics human understanding [13].

The Mallows distance between continuous one-dimensional distributions q and r, with cumulative distribution functions Q and R, respectively, is defined as

$$M_p(q,r) = \left(\int_0^1 |Q^{-1}(t) - R^{-1}(t)|^p dt \right)^{1/p}.$$

For example, consider the Mallows distance between two Gaussian distributions $N(\mu_1, \sigma_1^2)$ and $N(\mu_2, \sigma_2^2)$. For $p = 2$, this distance can be shown to be $\sqrt{(\mu_1 - \mu_2)^2 + (\sigma_1 - \sigma_2)^2}$.

For discrete one-dimensional distributions, consider two distributions x and y represented by empirical distributions with n observations, or equi-count histograms with n bins and the average value of each bin stored. Considering these values in sorted order, x and y can be represented as vectors $\bar{x} = n^{-1/p} * (x_1, \ldots, x_n) = (x_1', \ldots, x_n')$ and $\bar{y} = n^{-1/p} * (y_1, \ldots, y_n) = (y_1', \ldots, y_n')$ with $x_1 \leq \ldots \leq x_n$ and $y_1 \leq \ldots \leq y_n$. The Mallows distance between x and y is then defined as the L_p vector norm between $\bar{x}$ and $\bar{y}$

$$M_p(x, y) = \left(\frac{1}{n} \sum_{i=1}^n \|x_i - y_i\|^p \right)^{1/p} = \left(\sum_{i=1}^n \|x_i' - y_i'\|^p \right)^{1/p}.$$

Therefore, this representation maps histograms to points in n-dimensional Euclidean space in which distances are understood as M_2 histogram distances. In this space, there is a particular straight line path of interest. The mean of any histogram can be changed by an arbitrary amount by adding this amount to every bin in the histogram. Since the mean of a histogram represents its position, changes in histogram position are orthogonal to changes in shape.

Another property of this space is that Gaussian distributions exist in a linear two-dimensional subspace. As for general distributions, one axis of this space represents the Gaussian's mean. As shown above, the remaining orthogonal direction is linear in the Gaussian's standard deviation.

Points in a convex portion of this space represent valid histograms. That is, a point $\bar{x}$ is a valid histogram if and only if $x_1 \leq \ldots \leq x_n$. Therefore, the mean of a set of histograms, or any interpolated histogram, will always be valid. In the next section, the likelihood of a histogram is computed assuming that the mean of a set of histograms and straight-line paths from the mean are representative of the input set. In section 2.3 we demonstrate this with an example.

2.2   Histogram Likelihood

In this section, we statistically define a histogram's likelihood. We can use standard statistical tools for this task since we have sensibly mapped histograms to Euclidean space. For each region, we construct a multi-variate Gaussian model as a parametric estimate of a histogram's likelihood. Gaussian models stretch space, modifying the M_2 metric, to account for the variability in the training data. Thus, Gaussian models naturally enhance the M_2 metric even though they are not proper in the sense that points representing invalid histograms are assigned a non-zero probability.

When constructing a multi-variate Gaussian model, we cannot estimate a full covariance matrix since we are in a high dimension low sample size situation. This is a standard problem in medical imaging since large training sets are often unavailable, which are required to accurately estimate the covariance of a model

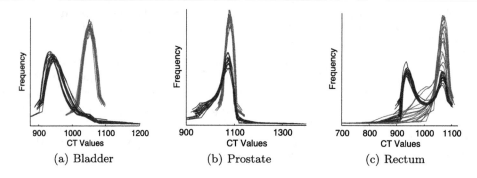

(a) Bladder   (b) Prostate   (c) Rectum

Fig. 1. Histograms from interior (red) and exterior (blue) bladder, prostate, and rectum regions in 17 images of the same patient

containing a desirable number of histogram bins. Therefore, we estimate a non-singular covariance of the form

$$k = \sum_{i=1}^{m} U_i U_i^T + \sigma I$$

where each U_i is a vector and I is the identity matrix. We compute the maximum likelihood estimate of k for a fixed m given the training histograms in each region. This estimate can be computing using PCA. The U_i vectors correspond to the principal directions with the m largest eigenvalues, λ_i. These vectors are scaled by $\lambda_i - \sigma$. σ corresponds to the average squared projection error normalized by the number of remaining dimensions.

As discussed in the companion paper [11], regions contain incorrectly labeled voxels as a consequence of the object model having its own scale. When collecting training histograms for each region, we remove such voxels. This allows us to model the true variability in each region and to define a more accurate optimum for segmentation. This approach does not, however, take into account the expected variation of the actual training segmentations. This can result in a covariance estimate that biases segmentations towards either the object interior or exterior. Therefore, we create an unbiased covariance estimate by normalizing each covariance matrix such that the average Mahalanobis distance of the training histograms is the same in each region.

2.3 Global Regions Example

We present the following example to demonstrate the construction of a histogram's likelihood. We use 17 CT images of the pelvic region from a single patient. The interior and exterior of the bladder, prostate, and rectum, within 1 cm of each boundary, define six global regions. For each region, figure 1 shows the 17 25 bin histograms. In general, the interior of the bladder, which consists of bladder wall and urine, has higher CT values than its exterior. The bladder

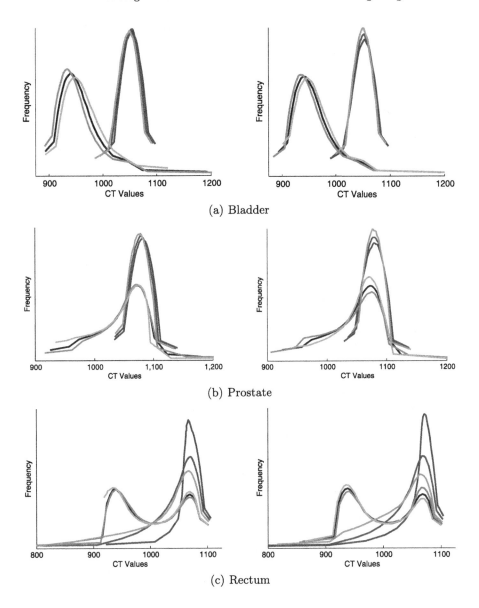

(a) Bladder

(b) Prostate

(c) Rectum

Fig. 2. Histograms representing the mean of 17 interior and exterior regions. Shown along with each mean is ±1.5 standard deviations along the first (left) or second (right) principal direction from the mean (slightly smoothed). The first mode often contains more tail and less peak movement than the second mode. Some of these tail movements have been cropped out of the graphs.

exterior consists of fatty and prostate tissue, with the heavy tail representing the latter. We only model a portion of the rectum and hence its exterior contains interior rectum intensities, making the exterior rectum histogram bimodal.

For each region, we compute the mean of the 17 histograms, $m = 2$ principal directions of variation, and σ. Figure 2 shows each region's mean and ± 1.5 standard deviations along each principal direction from the mean. The mean and each mode appear representative of the training data.

3   Segmentation Using Global Regions

In this section we use global regions, as defined in section 2.3, for segmentation. To do this we first discuss in section 3.1 our shape model and segmentation framework. In section 3.2 we then present segmentation results using these global image regions.

3.1   The Segmentation Framework

Our goal is to automatically segment the bladder, prostate, and rectum in CT images. We use the m-rep model of single 3D figures, as in [10], to describe the shape of these deformable objects. As detailed in the companion paper [12], the object representation is a sheet of medial atoms, where each atom consists of a hub and two equal-length spokes. The representation implies a boundary that passes orthogonally through the spoke ends. Medial atoms are sampled in a discrete grid and their properties, like spoke length and orientation, are interpolated between grid vertices. The model defines a coordinate system which dictates surface normals and an explicit correspondence between deformations of the same m-rep model and the 3D volume in the object boundary region. This allows us to capture image information from corresponding regions.

M-reps are used for segmentation by optimizing the posterior of the geometric parameters given the image data. This is equivalent to optimizing the sum of the log prior and the log likelihood, which measure geometric typicality and image match, respectively. Geometric typicality is based on the statistics of m-rep deformation over a training set, described in the companion paper [12]. We use the method described in section 2 for the image match.

In this paper, our primary concern is to determine the quality of the image likelihood optimum defined by our appearance model. We evaluate this by segmenting the bladder, prostate, and rectum from an intra-patient dataset consisting of 17 images. Each image is from the same CT scanner and has a resolution of $512 \times 512 \times 81$ with voxel dimensions of $0.977 \times 0.977 \times 3.0$ millimeters. These images are acquired sequentially during the course of the patient's treatment for prostate cancer. As an initial test of our framework, we segment each image using a leave-one-out strategy, which supplies sufficient training data to estimate adequate and stable statistics. We estimate the model prior and likelihood using m-reps fit to manual segmentations of the training images. We gather shape statistics for the combined bladder, prostate, and rectum object ensemble and define a shape space using six principal geodesics, which captures approximately 94% of the shape variance. We ignore the model prior and perform a maximum likelihood segmentation within the shape space.

We compare our segmentation results to a profile based method. This profile method uses normalized correlation with profiles from the first image and is described in [15]. All other aspects of these segmentation algorithms are identical, including the shape space and automatic rigid body initialization. Comparisons are made relative to manual segmentations and put into context by showing our shape model's ability to represent the manual segmentations during training. Training performance serves as a baseline for the best expected performance of our appearance model.

3.2   Segmentation Results Using Global Regions

We now evaluate the performance of three versions of our appearance model. For all three, we use two global regions for each object, defined as the object interior and exterior within a fixed 1 cm collar region of the boundary. We represent each region using a 25 bin equi-count histogram.

The three versions of our appearance model learn increasingly more information during training. The *Simple Global* model creates a reference histogram for each region from the first image. The image match is the sum of M_2 distances to each reference histogram. This model can be directly compared with the profile approach, since only the first image is supplied to both. The *Mean Global* model calculates the average histogram for each region using all the other images. In this case, the image match is the sum of M_2 distances to each average histogram. The last model, *Gaussian Global*, uses the fully trained likelihood measure introduced in section 2.2. The image match for this model is the sum of Mahalanobis distances in each Gaussian model. Each model independently learns two principal directions of variation and σ.

Table 1 reports volume overlap, defined as intersection over union, and average surface distance, defined as the average shortest distance of a boundary point on one object to the boundary of the other object. Results show segmentation accuracy improves with increased statistical training. Table 1 also shows a significant improvement of the global histogram based appearance models over the previous profile based model. Directly comparing the profile and histogram

Table 1. Segmentation results of our appearance model using global image regions. Results are measured against manual contours, and compared against a previous profile based method and the ideal of our shape model attained during training.

Appearance Model	Volume Overlap			Ave. Surface Dist. (mm)		
	Bladder	Prostate	Rectum	Bladder	Prostate	Rectum
Training	88.6%	87.8%	82.8%	1.11	1.05	1.15
Profile	79.8%	76.0%	64.8%	2.07	2.20	2.72
Simple Global	80.7%	78.4%	67.1%	1.97	1.94	2.47
Mean Global	81.8%	79.4%	68.0%	1.84	1.86	2.42
Gaussian Global	84.8%	79.6%	72.1%	1.53	1.86	2.00

based methods, *Simple Global* achieves better results for all three objects. In the next section we further improve these results using local image regions.

4   Defining Local Image Regions

Next, we use the appearance model described in section 2 with local model-relative image regions. Local regions have tighter intensity distributions than global regions since intensities are more locally correlated. This results in an image likelihood measure with a more clearly defined optimum, especially when global regions consist of multiple homogeneous tissue regions. Since smaller regions are summarized, however, local regions provide less accurate distribution estimates. They also require a shape model that defines a voxel correspondence near the object boundary.

Our dataset contains at least two examples of global region inhomogeneity. First, the exterior bladder region consists of both prostate and fatty tissue. The bowel can also be present, though this is not the case in this dataset. A second example is the exterior rectum region. We only model the portion of the rectum near the prostate, so there are two arbitrary cutoff regions with exterior distributions matching those of the rectum's interior.

We describe two approaches to define local regions. In section 4.1 we manually partition the global interior and exterior regions. In section 4.2 we define overlapping regions centered around many boundary points. In section 4.3 we give results using both methods.

4.1   Partitioning Global Image Regions

Local regions can be defined by partitioning an object's surface, and hence the 3D image volume near the surface, into local homogeneous tissue regions. Such a partitioning can either be specified automatically, based on distribution estimates from a training set (see future directions), or manually delineated using anatomic knowledge.

In this section, we manually define several interior and exterior local regions for the bladder, prostate, and rectum using limited anatomic knowledge. We used several heuristics to create our manual partitions, which are shown in figure 3. First, more exterior regions are defined since there is more localized variability in the object exterior. For the bladder model a local exterior region is defined near the prostate. A local region is also defined for the portion of the bladder opposite the prostate since this region experiences the most shape variability between images. Lastly, for the rectum model a local exterior region is defined in each arbitrary cutoff region.

4.2   Local Image Regions

An alternative method to define local regions is to consider a set of boundary points that each describe the center of a region. Define an interior and exterior

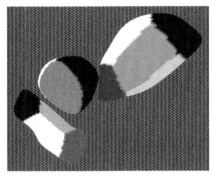
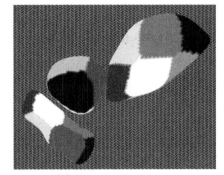

(a) Interior Partitions   (b) Exterior Partitions

Fig. 3. Manual surface partitions of the bladder, prostate, and rectum defining local interior (a) and exterior (b) regions. For the bladder, prostate, and rectum we define 6, 3, and 4 interior regions, and 8, 5, and 8 exterior regions, respectively.

Table 2. Segmentation results using local image regions. The Gaussian appearance model using the two local region methods is compared to the global region method.

Appearance Model	Volume Overlap			Ave. Surface Dist. (mm)		
	Bladder	Prostate	Rectum	Bladder	Prostate	Rectum
Training	88.6%	87.8%	82.8%	1.11	1.05	1.15
Gaussian Global	84.8%	79.6%	72.1%	1.53	1.86	2.00
Gaussian Partition	83.0%	80.5%	72.1%	1.74	1.77	2.01
Gaussian Local	83.2%	80.5%	73.0%	1.67	1.78	1.95

region for each point by first finding the portion of the surface within a radius of each point. Then, each region consists of all the voxels within a certain distance to the boundary that have model-relative coordinates associated with the region's corresponding surface patch. This approach can define overlapping image regions at any scale and locality, and learning boundaries between local regions is unnecessary.

For the bladder, prostate, and rectum we use 64, 34, and 58 boundary points, respectively. Each region is set to a radius of 1.25 cm and the collar region is kept at ± 1 cm, as in previous results.

4.3   Results

Table 2 gives segmentation results using the Gaussian appearance model from section 2 for both local region approaches. The *Partition* method refers to the approach described in section 4.1, and the *Local* method refers to the approach described in section 4.2. Both methods use 25 histogram bins and Gaussian models restricted to 2 principal directions of variation. These results show that both the *Local* and *Partition* methods are roughly equivalent to the *Global* method. However, there is a consistent improvement by the *Local* method in the segmentation of the rectum.

5   Conclusions

In this paper we defined a novel multiscale appearance model for deformable objects. We have shown that our histogram based appearance model outperforms a profile based appearance model for a segmentation task when only one training image is available. We also described a method to statistically train histogram variation when multiple training images are available and demonstrated its improved segmentation accuracy. Finally, we considered regions at different scales and showed that local image regions have some benefits over global regions, especially for rectum segmentation.

6   Future Directions

We only present initial segmentation results in this paper. Our next step is to validate these findings in a more comprehensive intra-patient study of the pelvic region. Then, we plan to consider other anatomical objects including the kidneys.

In the pelvic region, gas and bone produce outlying CT values. When there is a significant amount of these extreme values our mapping can produce unnatural interpolations. Therefore, we will investigate a technique to identify these intensities in advance and compute a separate estimate of their variation.

As described in [11], we plan to do a multiscale optimization. Such an approach could use the three region scales described in this paper. Furthermore, we will use geometric models to describe soft instead of hard apertures. For example, a voxel's contribution to a measurement could be weighted by a Gaussian, based on its distance to the object's boundary. Using multiscale regions and soft apertures should smooth the segmentation objective function, resulting in a more robust optimization.

We desire a more principled approach considering tissue composition for defining regions in the *Partition* method. We hope to characterize the intensity distributions of particular tissue types, to estimate the tissue mixtures over image regions using mixture modeling, and finally to optimize the regions for maximum homogeneity. In addition, we may train on the model-relative position of these regions, to help capture inter-object geometric statistics.

We only considered histograms of pixel intensities in this paper. We will extend this framework to estimate the distribution of additional features, such as texture filter responses or Markov Random Field estimates. Although the EMD defines a distance measure between multi-dimensional distributions, we plan to assume the independence of these features and then apply the same techniques described in this paper.

Acknowledgements

We thank J. Stephen Marron for discussions on histogram statistics, Sarang Joshi for discussions on Gaussian parameter estimation, and the rest of the MIDAG team for the development of the m-rep segmentation framework. The work reported here was done under the partial support of NIH grant P01 EB02779.

References

1. R. E. Broadhurst. Simplifying texture classification. Technical report, University of North Carolina, http://midag.cs.unc.edu, 2004.
2. T. Chan and L. Vese. Active contours without edges. In *IEEE Trans. Image Processing*, volume 10, pages 266–277, Feb. 2001.
3. T. F. Cootes, G. J. Edwards, and C. J. Taylor. Active appearance models. In *ECCV*, 1998.
4. T. F. Cootes, C. J. Taylor, D. H. Cooper, and J. Graham. Active shape models their training and application. In *Computer Vision and Image Understanding*, volume 61, pages 38–59, 1995.
5. D. Freedman, R. J. Radke, T. Zhang, Y. Jeong, D. M. Lovelock, and G. T. Y. Chen. Model-based segmentation of medical imagery by matching distributions. In *IEEE Trans. on Medical Imaging*, volume 24, pages 281–292, Mar. 2005.
6. S. Joshi. *Large Deformation Diffeomorphisms and Gaussian Random Fields for Statistical Characterization of Brain Submanifolds*. PhD thesis, 1997.
7. E. Levina. *Statistical Issues in Texture Analysis*. PhD thesis, 2002.
8. E. Levina and P. Bickel. The earth movers distance is the mallows distance: Some insights from statistics. In *ICCV*, pages 251–256, 2001.
9. S. M. Pizer, P. T. Fletcher, S. Joshi, A. G. Gash, J. Stough, A. Thall, G. Tracton, and E. L. Chaney. A method & software for segmentation of anatomic object ensembles by deformable m-reps. *Medical Physics*, To appear.
10. S. M. Pizer, T. Fletcher, Y. Fridman, D. S. Fritsch, A. G. Gash, J. M. Glotzer, S. Joshi, A. Thall, G. Tracton, P. Yushkevich, and E. L. Chaney. Deformable m-reps for 3d medical image segmentation. *IJCV*, 55(2):85–106, 2003.
11. S. M. Pizer, J. Y. Jeong, R. E. Broadhurst, S. Ho, and J. Stough. Deep structure of images in populations via geometric models in populations. In *DSSCV*, 2005.
12. S. M. Pizer, J. Y. Jeong, C. Lu, K. Muller, and S. Joshi. Estimating the statistics of multi-object anatomic geometry using inter-object relationships. In *DSSCV*, 2005.
13. Y. Rubner, C. Tomasi, and L. J. Guibas. A metric for distributions with applications to image databases. In *ICCV*, pages 59–66, 1998.
14. I. M. Scott, T. F. Cootes, and C. J. Taylor. Improving appearance model matching using local image structure. In *IPMI*, 2003.
15. J. Stough, S. M. Pizer, E. L. Chaney, and M. Rao. Clustering on image boundary regions for deformable model segmentation. In *ISBI*, pages 436–439, Apr. 2004.
16. A. Tsai, A. Yezzi, W. Wells, C. Tempany, D. Tucker, A. Fan, W. E. Grimson, and A. Willsky. A shape-based approach to the segmentation of medical imagery using level sets. In *IEEE Trans. Medical Imaging*, volume 22, Feb. 2003.

The Bessel Scale-Space

Bernhard Burgeth, Stephan Didas, and Joachim Weickert

Mathematical Image Analysis Group,
Faculty of Mathematics and Computer Science, Bldg. 27,
Saarland University, 66041 Saarbrücken, Germany
{burgeth, didas, weickert}@mia.uni-saarland.de
http://www.mia.uni-saarland.de

Abstract. In this paper we propose a novel type of scales-spaces which is emerging from the family of inhomogeneous pseudodifferential equations $(I - \tau\Delta)^{\frac{t}{2}} u = f$ with $\tau \geq 0$ and scale parameter $t \geq 0$. Since they are connected to the convolution semi-group of Bessel potentials we call the associated operators $\{R_{t,\tau}^n \mid 0 \leq \tau, t\}$ either Bessel scale-space ($\tau = 1$), R_t^n for short, or scaled Bessel scale-space ($\tau \neq 1$). This is the first concrete example of a family of scale-spaces that is **not** originating from a PDE of parabolic type and where the Fourier transforms $\mathcal{F}(R_{t,\tau}^n)$ do **not** have exponential form. These properties make them different from other scale-spaces considered so far in the literature in this field.

In contrast to the α-scale-spaces the integral kernels for $R_{t,\tau}^n$ can be given in explicit form for any $t, \tau \geq 0$ involving the modified Bessel functions of third kind K_ν. In theoretical investigations and numerical experiments on 1D and 2D data we compare this new scale-space with the classical Gaussian one.

Keywords: Bessel potential, Bessel-functions, α-scale-space, convolution, semi-group, pseudodifferential operator,co-histogram.

1 Introduction

In retrospect modern scale-space theory began with the pioneering work of Taizo Iijima [17] in the late fifties. Although his work was not noticed by the western scientific community for decades the vivid research on scale-space methodologies has resulted in a large amount of techniques valuable for image processing and computer vision. This is documented in numerous articles and books, see [12,31,21,29,33] and the literature cited therein.

The Gaussian scale-space is the archetype of a linear scale-space. Its relation to linear diffusion processes was first pointed out to the image processing community by Iijima [18].

However, scale-space properties can also be spotted in non-linear diffusion processes, a field inspired by the path-breaking work of Perona and Malik [26]. These non-linear theories embrace anisotropic diffusion processes [33,27], morphological operations [32,6,19] as well as the evolution of level curves [2,24,28,20].

O.F. Olsen et al. (Eds.): DSSCV 2005, LNCS 3753, pp. 84–95, 2005.

Highly non-linear, sometimes even degenerated differential equations are the mathematical language to describe these theories [31,33,15,3,13,8].

Be that as it may, the linear setting, meaning the assumed validity of the superposition principle, and the exploration of underlying axiomatic theory was and is an active field of research, [4,2,33,12,22,25,34] and [10].

In this linear setting the importance of the Gaussian scale-space cannot be overestimated, although in recent years other concrete examples of linear scale-space concepts have received considerable attention:

- First the Poisson scale-space arising from the Laplace equation in potential theory has been introduced by Felsberg and Sommer [11] to image processing. It allows an explicit analytical integral representation with the Poisson kernel.
- After that the so-called α-scale-spaces with $\alpha \in]0, 1]$ have been proposed as the continuous link between the trivial ($\alpha = 0$), the Poissonian ($\alpha = \frac{1}{2}$) and the Gaussian ($\alpha = 1$) scale-space. They are ruled by an pseudodifferential equations, and unfortunately no exact integral representation formulas for their solutions are known. See [10] for a very comprehensive exposition about theory and history of this scale-space family.
- Very recently the relativistic scale-spaces [7] instigated by a Schroedinger pseudodifferential equation from theoretical physics have been shown to bridge the gap between Poisson ('zero-mass-limit') and the trivial scale-space ('infinite-mass-limit'). Explicit integral formulas involving kernels with Bessel functions of the third kind have been given in [7].

All these examples have in common that they emanate from (pseudo-) differential equations of parabolic type, such as the $\alpha-$scale-spaces:

$$\partial_t u = -(-\Delta)^\alpha u$$

with initial condition $u(x,0) = f(x)$.

The goal of this paper is to investigate the scale-space that arise from the following inhomogeneous elliptic PDE involving arbitrary positive powers $t \geq 0$ of the Laplacian and the identity operator I:

$$(I - \Delta)^{\frac{t}{2}} := \left(I - \sum_{i=1}^{n} \frac{\partial^2 u}{\partial x_i^2} \right)^{\frac{t}{2}} = f, \tag{1}$$

with a suitable function $f : \mathbb{R}^n \longrightarrow \mathbb{R}$.

The parameter t should be interpreted as a smoothing parameter: The application of an partial differential operator to a function u roughens it. Intuitively, if u is to fulfill (1) (even in the distributional sense) it must be smooth enough to produce f, and the larger t is the smoother the function u has to be. Hence, solving (1) for u means in effect calculating smoother versions of f.

However, equation (1) is *not* an evolution equation of parabolic type. Although it is not done in this article, one has the opportunity to tackle this equation with the highly developed numerical methods for elliptic PDEs. Furthermore, inhomogeneous PDEs might be the starting point for a fruitful nonlinear and anisotropic theory, just as it was the case for the Gaussian scale-space. We will examine the smoothing procedure ruled by (1), establish the associated convolution semi-group properties by spectral methods. In contrast to the scale-space examples mentioned above this semi-group is not of exponential type.

The associated integral representation kernels are explicitly known as Bessel potentials, a generalisation of Riesz potentials. Hence, the properties of this scale-space can be explored also with methods from real analysis.

The paper is structured as follows: In the following section we use the Fourier transform a function $f \in L^2(\mathbb{R}^n)$ given by

$$\mathcal{F}(f)(k) = \int_{\mathbb{R}^n} e^{-2\pi i k \cdot x} f(x) \, dx \, .$$

to study (1). This will lead directly to the definition of the Bessel scale-space. After a study of its properties we will also present scaled versions of the Bessel scale-space. Experiments illustrating the potential and limitations of the novel scale-spaces are described in Section 3. A summary and an outlook for ongoing in Section 4 complete the paper.

2   Bessel Scale-Space

We recall that the action of the differential operator Δ is multiplication by $-4\pi|k|^2$, implying that (1) Fourier transforms into

$$(1 + 4\pi^2|k|^2)^{\frac{t}{2}} \hat{u} = \hat{f} \, .$$

According to theory of spectral methods for PDEs this entails that formally the solutions to (1) are computed via convolution with the integral kernel $G_n(\cdot, t)$ which appears as the inverse Fourier transform of

$$\mathcal{F}(G_n)(\cdot, t) := \frac{1}{(1 + 4\pi^2|k|^2)^{\frac{t}{2}}} \, ,$$

that is,

$$G_n(x, t) = \int_{\mathbb{R}^n} \frac{1}{(1 + 4\pi^2|k|^2)^{\frac{t}{2}}} e^{2\pi i k \cdot (x-y)} \, dk \, .$$

This integral can be evaluated in every dimension n yielding the known explicit formula for the Bessel kernels [23,9]

$$G_n(x, t) = \frac{1}{\sqrt{\pi}^n \sqrt{2}^{\,n+t-2} \Gamma(\frac{t}{2})} \frac{K_{\frac{n-t}{2}}(|x|)}{|x|^{\frac{n-t}{2}}} \, ,$$

Γ denotes the Gamma function and K_ν stands for the modified Bessel function of third kind with index ν.

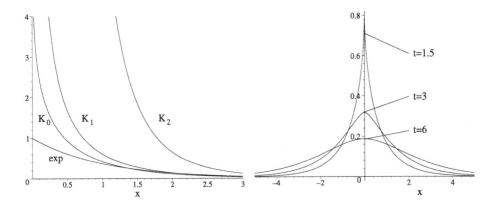

Fig. 1. *Left:* Comparison of the exponential and Bessel functions K_0, K_1 and K_2. *Right:* Examples of the Bessel kernel for $n = 1$ with $t = 1.5$, 3, 6.

The Bessel functions K_ν can be evaluated via fast converging series expansions and three-term recursive formulas. For more details see [1]. Figure 1 compares the exponential function e^{-x} with some Bessel functions. The Bessel functions are exponentially decaying for large x.

Using formulas in [1] for K_ν one can derive explicit expressions of Bessel kernels for special values of t:

$$G_n(x, n + 1) := \frac{1}{\pi^{\frac{n}{2}} 2^n \Gamma(\frac{n+1}{2})} e^{-|x|},$$

which is a continuous function, not differentiable at $x = 0$, and

$$G_n(x, n + 3) := \frac{1}{\pi^{\frac{n}{2}} 2^{n+1} \Gamma(\frac{n+3}{2})} (1 + |x|) e^{-|x|},$$

which is in fact twice continuous differentiable in $\mathbb{R}^n$.

This has an interesting effect: a merely continuous function convolved with $G_n(x, n + k)$ produces only a C^{k-1}-smoothed version. This behaviour is different from Gaussian, Poissonian, or relativistic scale-spaces, where the filtered functions are even analytical for every scale parameter $t > 0$.

Figure 2 displays the Bessel kernel for various values of t and also its comparison with a Poisson and a Gaussian kernel.

For notational convenience we define the operator R_t^n on $L^2(\mathbb{R}^n)$ via the convolution

$$R_t^n f(x) := (G_n(\cdot, t) * f)(x) = \int_{\mathbb{R}^n} G_n(x - y, t) f(y) \, dy. \tag{2}$$

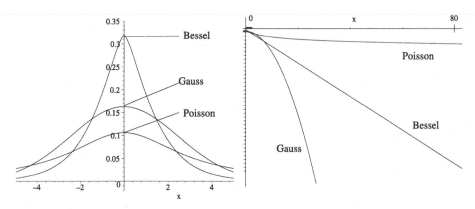

Fig. 2. *Left:* Comparison between different kernels including Bessel ($\tau = 1$), Gaussian, and Poisson kernel in 1D centered at the origin with $t = 3$. *Right:* Comparison of the asymptotic behaviour of the same kernels for large values of x (logarithmic scale on y-axis).

2.1 Behaviour of $G_n(\cdot, t)$ in the Limit $t \downarrow 0$

According to a theorem of P. Levi [5] stating the continuity of the (inverse) Fourier transform the relation

$$\mathcal{F}(R_t^n)(k) = \frac{1}{(1 + 4\pi|k|^2)^{\frac{t}{2}}} \longrightarrow 1 \quad \text{if } t \downarrow 0$$

confirms that R_t^n approximates the identity operator I in the distributional sense if t is small. This can also be shown by methods from real analysis based on the explicit knowledge of the Bessel potentials.

2.2 Semigroup Properties

From the theory of contraction semi-groups [16] we infer that the operator R_t^n determines a contraction semi-group on $L^2(\mathbb{R}^n)$. Indeed, in view of Plancherel's theorem, it is enough to verify that the Fourier transforms $\mathcal{F}(R_t^n)$ of the family $\{R_t^n\}$ satisfy the conditions

1. $\mathcal{F}(R_{s+t}^n)\mathcal{F}(f) = \mathcal{F}(R)_s^n\mathcal{F}(R_t^n)\mathcal{F}(f) = \mathcal{F}(R_t^n)\mathcal{F}(R_s^n)\mathcal{F}(f)$ for all $s, t \geq 0$,

2. $\|\mathcal{F}(R_t^n)\mathcal{F}(f) - \mathcal{F}(R_s^n)\mathcal{F}(f)\|_2 \longrightarrow 0 \quad$ for $\quad t \longrightarrow s$,

3. $\mathcal{F}(R_0^n) = 1$, expressing the fact that $R_0^n = I$, the identity,

4. $\|\mathcal{F}(R_t^n)\mathcal{F}(f)\|_2 \leq \|\mathcal{F}(f)\|_2$, the contraction property.

Due to the properties of the elementary functions $\frac{1}{(\sqrt{1+c})^t}$ with $c > 0$ it is not difficult to check that the operator R_t^n indeed fulfills these conditions.

2.3 Regularity

We define the Sobolev spaces $H^s(\mathbb{R}^n)$ as in [30] (with $2\pi k$ instead of k) by

$$H^s(\mathbb{R}^n) := \left\{ u \in L^2(\mathbb{R}^n) \mid \left(1 + 4\pi^2 |k|^2\right)^{\frac{s}{2}} \mathcal{F}(u) \in L^2(\mathbb{R}^n) \right\}$$

for all functions in $L^2(\mathbb{R}^n)$ and $s \in \mathbb{R}$.

Then it follows without difficulty that R_t^n increases the regularity:

$$R_t^n : H^s(\mathbb{R}^n) \longrightarrow H^{s+t}(\mathbb{R}^n)$$

In this sense the operator indeed produces smoother versions $\tilde{u}^t = R_t^n f$ of a given $f \in L^2(\mathbb{R}^n)$. Summarising the analysis above we state

Proposition 2.1. *1. The families of operators $\{R_t^n \mid t \geq 0\}$ form an additive semi-group for any fixed $n \geq 0$.*
  2. For every $t \geq 0$ the average grey-value is preserved under the action of R_t^n.
  3. The operators R_t^n are translational invariant.

However, it is not difficult to see that the Bessel scale-space is not scale invariant. As already indicated before, the scale parameter t plays also the role of a smoothing parameter; roughly speaking, the smoothness is increased by t. This is not the case for the standard linear scale spaces, where the smoothness of the filtered signal immediately jumps to its highest level, analyticity.

2.4 Scaled Bessel Scale-Spaces

The following generalisation of the Bessel kernel is close at hand: we introduce a scaling parameter $\tau \geq 0$ via

$$G_{t,\tau}^n(x) := \tau^n G_t^n(\tau x).$$

Then we have

$$\mathcal{F}(G_{t,\tau}^n)(k) = \frac{1}{\left(1 + 4\pi^2 \tau^2 |k|^2\right)^{\frac{t}{2}}},$$

furthermore, all the properties of G_t^n mentioned above carry over, essentially verbatim, to $G_{t,\tau}^n$, including semi-group, contraction and limit properties. $R_{t,\tau}^n$ denotes the corresponding convolution operator. For $\tau = 0$ the operator degenerates to the identity, $R_{t,0}^n = I$, while for $\tau = 1$ we obtain the Bessel scale-space, $R_{t,1}^n = R_t^n$.

Numerical examples for these scaled versions of the Bessel scale-space are presented in the following experimental section.

3 Numerical Experiments

In this section we display some results of numerical experiments to visualise the properties of the Bessel and the scaled Bessel scale-spaces. We contrast the novel

Bessel with the Gaussian scale-space. First we take a look at the Bessel and Gaussian scale-space in 1D. The results are captured in a 3D-plot in Fig. 3. We have chosen a signal with discontinuities to visualise the regularising properties of the Bessel scale-space. The differences are not dramatic, especially since the weaker regularity of the Bessel-filtered signals is not discernable from the analyticity of the Gaussian filtered results. In order to compare the effect of Gauss and Bessel filtering of 2D-images we utilised so-called co-histograms [14]. Co-histograms $h_{f,g}(m, n)$ are 2D-histograms encoding the frequency of *ordered pairs* of grey values (m, n) of an image pair (f, g). They are constructed via the formula

$$h_{f,g}(k, l) = \frac{1}{MN} \sum_{i=1}^{M} \sum_{j=1}^{N} \delta(f_{i,j}, k) \cdot \delta(g_{i,j}, l) \,,$$

where δ stands for the Kronecker symbol and $M \times N$ is the size of the images f, g. Figure 4 depicts the co-histogram as a grey value image. Differences in the images f and g result in asymmetry of the co-histogram and its departure from being diagonal. At the very beginning Gauss and Bessel filtering of the office image without noise do not yet have a strong effect ($t = 0.1$), hence the diagonal dominant form of the co-histogram. The appearance changes with increasing scale t, furthermore, in the limit $t \rightarrow \infty$ the co-histogram will tend towards one bright spot on the diagonal marking the average grey value common to both filter processes. For larger times there is no visible difference in the ability of removing (Gaussian) noise between the two scale-space concepts. Only for very small times there is a discrepancy indicated by the spread of the corresponding co-histogram (Fig. 4, middle column, second row).

The situation is different for a binary image (last column of Fig. 4); in this case the co-histograms indicate a clearly discernable difference between the two types of filtering throughout the evolution processes.

We remark that fixing the parameter t and using τ as parameter also leads to a scale-space structure, referred to as the scaled Bessel scale-space in the previous chapter. Fig. 5 contrasts a scaled version (right column) with the non-scaled version of the Bessel scale-space. One may notice the convergence towards the mean value for increasing values of t or τ, respectively.

4   Conclusion

The goal of this paper is to introduce the novel two-parameter family of Bessel scale-spaces. In proposing this peculiar example we hope to convey our opinion that not only parabolic (pseudo-)differential equations can serve as a birthplace for scale-spaces. The underlying Bessel convolution semi-group turned out to possess a non-exponential Fourier transform. The degree of smoothness of the filtered data grows steadily (in terms of Sobolev exponents) for increasing scale parameter t, in contrast to other common scale-spaces. Nevertheless, opposite to the α-scale-spaces these new scale-spaces admit integral representations with

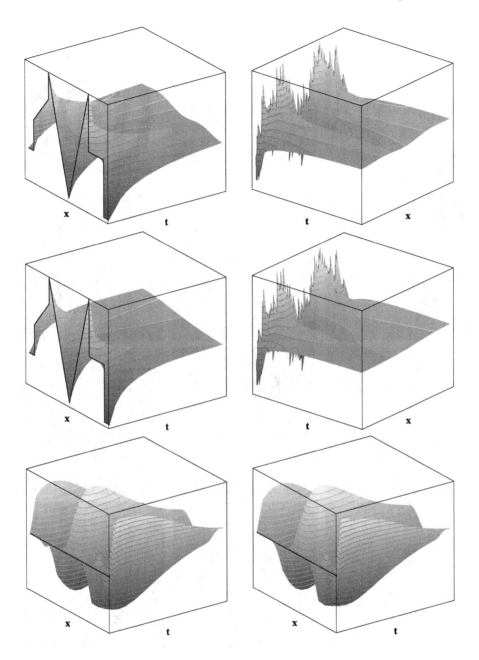

Fig. 3. Bessel scale-space in 1D. *Left column, top* : Smoothing of a signal in Bessel scale-space. *Left column, middle* : Smoothing of this signal in Gaussian scale-space. *Left column, bottom* : Difference in signal evolution w.r.t. scale-spaces above. Note that the scale on the z-axis has been stretched by the factor 7 in comparison with the images above. *Right column:* The same with noisy signal (Gaussian noise added to the original signal on the left).

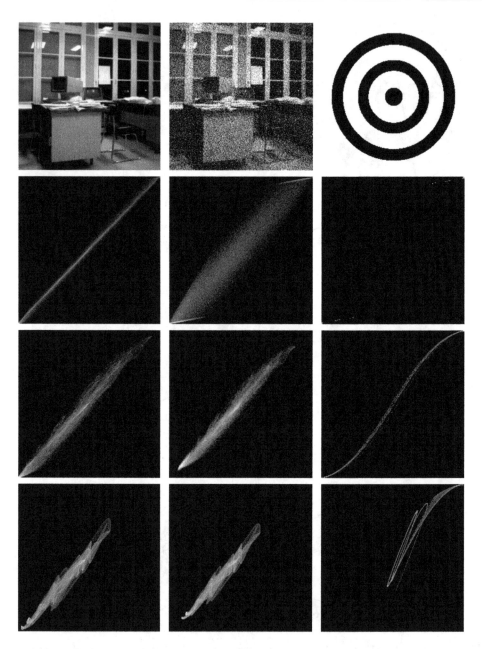

Fig. 4. Co-histograms: Comparison of Gaussian and Bessel scale-space in 2D. *Top row:*
Original images. *Second row:* Co-histograms comparing Gauss and Bessel filtering of
the corresponding images of the first row with $t = 0.1$. *Third row:* The same with
$t = 10$. *Fourth row:* The same with $t = 100$.

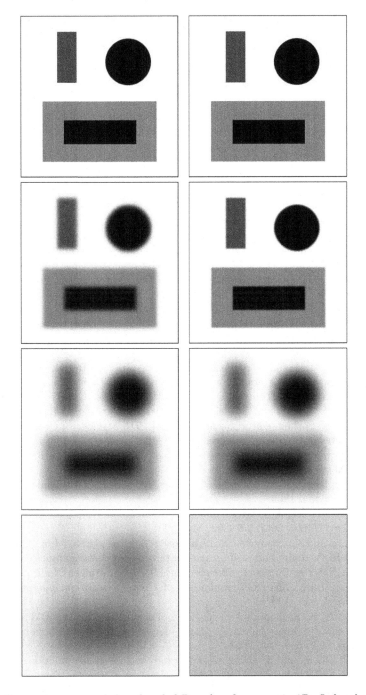

Fig. 5. Comparing non-scaled and scaled Bessel scale-spaces in 2D. *Left column:* Non-scaled Bessel scale-space, $\tau = 1$. *Left column, from top to bottom:* $t = 0$, 10, 100, 1000. *Right column:* Scaled Bessel scale-space, with fixed $t = 100$. *Right column, from top to bottom:* $\tau = 0$, 0.1, 1, 10.

explicitly known kernels. They involve modified Bessel functions K_ν of the third kind and hence bear some resemblance to the relativistic scale-spaces.

Ongoing research on Bessel scale-spaces encompasses studies of variational formulations, special features as well as non-linear extensions and their numerical treatment.

Acknowledgements. We gratefully acknowledge partly funding by the *Deutsche Forschungsgemeinschaft (DFG)*, project WE 2602/2-2.

References

1. M. Abramowitz and I.A. Stegun, editors. *Handbook of Mathematical Functions.* Dover Publications,Inc., New York, 9 edition, 1972.
2. L. Alvarez, F. Guichard, P.-L. Lions, and J.-M. Morel. Axioms and fundamental equations in image processing. *Archive for Rational Mechanics and Analysis*, 123:199–257, 1993.
3. G. Aubert and P. Kornprobst. *Mathematical Problems in Image Processing: Partial Differential Equations and the Calculus of Variations*, volume 147 of *Applied Mathematical Sciences*. Springer, New York, 2002.
4. J. Babaud, A. P. Witkin, M. Baudin, and R. O. Duda. Uniqueness of the Gaussian kernel for scale space filtering. *IEEE Transactions on Pattern Analysis and Machine Intelligence*, 8:26–33, 1986.
5. H. Bauer. *Wahrscheinlichkeitstheorie*. Walter de Gruyter, Berlin, 1991.
6. R. W. Brockett and P. Maragos. Evolution equations for continuous-scale morphological filtering. *IEEE Transactions on Signal Processing*, 42:3377–3386, 1994.
7. B. Burgeth, S. Didas, and J. Weickert. Relativistic scale-spaces. In J. Weickert R. Kimmel, N. Sochen, editor, *Scale-Space and PDE Methods in Computer Vision*, Lecture Notes in Computer Science, pages 1–12. Springer, 2005.
8. F. Cao. *Geometric Curve Evolution and Image Processing*, volume 1805 of *Lecture Notes in Mathematics*. Springer, Berlin, 2003.
9. W.F. Donoghue. *Distributions and Fourier Tarnsforms*. Academic Press, New York and London, 1969.
10. R. Duits, L. Florack, J. de Graaf, and B. ter Haar Romeny. On the axioms of scale space theory. *JMIV*, 20(3):267–298, May 2004.
11. M. Felsberg and G. Sommer. Scale-adaptive filtering derived from the Laplace equation. In B. Radig and S. Florczyk, editors, *Pattern Recognition*, volume 2032 of *Lecture Notes in Computer Science*, pages 95–106. Springer, Berlin, 2001.
12. L. Florack. *Image Structure*, volume 10 of *Computational Imaging and Vision*. Kluwer, Dordrecht, 1997.
13. G. Gilboa, N. A. Sochen, and Y. Y. Zeevi. Forward-and-backward diffusion processes for adaptive image enhancement and denoising. *IEEE Transactions on Image Processing*, 11(7):689–703, 2002.
14. P. Hao, C. Zhang, and A. Dang. Co-histogram and image degradation evaluation. In *ICIAR 2004*, volume 3211 of *Lecture Notes in Computer Science*. Springer, Berlin, 2004.
15. H. J. A. M. Heijmans. Scale-spaces, PDEs and scale-invariance. In M. Kerckhove, editor, *Scale-Space and Morphology in Computer Vision*, volume 2106 of *Lecture Notes in Computer Science*, pages 215–226. Springer, Berlin, 2001.

16. E. Hille and R. S. Philips. *Functional Analysis and Semi-Groups*. American Mathematical Society, Providence, 1957.
17. T. Iijima. Basic theory of pattern observation. In *Papers of Technical Group on Automata and Automatic Control*. IECE, Japan, December 1959. In Japanese.
18. T. Iijima. Basic theory on the construction of figure space. *Systems, Computers, Controls*, 2(5):51–57, 1971. In English.
19. P. T. Jackway and M. Deriche. Scale-space properties of the multiscale morphological dilation–erosion. *IEEE Transactions on Pattern Analysis and Machine Intelligence*, 18:38–51, 1996.
20. R. Kimmel. *Numerical Geometry of Images: Theory, Algorithms, and Applications*. Springer, New York, 2003.
21. T. Lindeberg. *Scale-Space Theory in Computer Vision*. Kluwer, Boston, 1994.
22. T. Lindeberg. On the axiomatic formulations of linear scale-space. In J. Sporring, M. Nielsen, L. Florack, and P. Johansen, editors, *Gaussian Scale-Space Theory*, volume 8 of *Computational Imaging and Vision*, pages 75–97. Kluwer, Dordrecht, 1997.
23. N.Aronszajn and K.T. Smith. Theory of bessel potentials. *Ann. Inst. Fourier (Grenoble)*, 11:385–475, 1961.
24. P. J. Olver, G. Sapiro, and A. Tannenbaum. Classification and uniqueness of invariant geometric flows. *Comptes Rendus de l'Académie des Sciences de Paris, Série I*, 319:339–344, 1994.
25. E. J. Pauwels, L. J. Van Gool, P. Fiddelaers, and T. Moons. An extended class of scale-invariant and recursive scale space filters. *IEEE Transactions on Pattern Analysis and Machine Intelligence*, 17:691–701, 1995.
26. P. Perona and J. Malik. Scale space and edge detection using anisotropic diffusion. *IEEE Transactions on Pattern Analysis and Machine Intelligence*, 12:629–639, 1990.
27. A. H. Salden. *Dynamic Scale-Space Paradigms*. PhD thesis, Faculty of Medicine, Utrecht University, The Netherlands, November 1996.
28. G. Sapiro and A. Tannenbaum. Affine invariant scale-space. *International Journal of Computer Vision*, 11:25–44, 1993.
29. J. Sporring, M. Nielsen, L. Florack, and P. Johansen, editors. *Gaussian Scale-Space Theory*, volume 8 of *Computational Imaging and Vision*. Kluwer, Dordrecht, 1997.
30. M. E. Taylor. *Partial Differential Equations I – Basic Theory*. Springer, New York, 1996.
31. B. M. ter Haar Romeny, editor. *Geometry-Driven Diffusion in Computer Vision*, volume 1 of *Computational Imaging and Vision*. Kluwer, Dordrecht, 1994.
32. R. van den Boomgaard. The morphological equivalent of the Gauss convolution. *Nieuw Archief Voor Wiskunde*, 10(3):219–236, November 1992.
33. J. Weickert. *Anisotropic Diffusion in Image Processing*. Teubner, Stuttgart, 1998.
34. J. Weickert, S. Ishikawa, and A. Imiya. Linear scale-space has first been proposed in Japan. *Journal of Mathematical Imaging and Vision*, 10(3):237–252, May 1999.

Linear Image Reconstruction from a Sparse Set of α-Scale Space Features by Means of Inner Products of Sobolev Type*

Remco Duits, Bart Janssen, Frans Kanters, and Luc Florack

Eindhoven University of Technology, Den Dolech 2,
NL-5600 MD Eindhoven, The Netherlands
{R.Duits, B.J.Janssen, F.M.W.Kanters, L.M.J.Florack}@tue.nl
http://www.bmi2.bmt.tue.nl/image-analysis/people/rduits

Abstract. Inner products of Sobolev type are extremely useful for image reconstruction of images from a sparse set of α-scale space features. The common (non)-linear reconstruction frameworks, follow an Euler Lagrange minimization. If the Lagrangian (prior) is a norm induced by an inner product of a Hilbert space, this Euler Lagrange minimization boils down to a simple orthogonal projection within the corresponding Hilbert space. This basic observation has been overlooked in image analysis for the cases where the Lagrangian equals a norm of Sobolev type, resulting in iterative (non-linear) numerical methods, where already an exact solution with non-iterative linear algorithm is at hand. Therefore we provide a general theory on linear image reconstructions and metameric classes of images. By applying this theory we obtain visually more attractive reconstructions than the previously proposed linear methods and we find connected curves in the metameric class of images, determined by a fixed set of linear features, with a monotonic increase of smoothness. Although the theory can be applied to any linear feature reconstruction or principle component analysis, we mainly focus on reconstructions from so-called topological features (such as top-points and grey-value flux) in scale space, obtained from geometrical observations in the deep structure of a scale space.

Keywords: Scale Space, Sobolev Spaces, Gelfand Triples, Tikhonov Regularization, Top Point Reconstruction, Deep Structure, Flux Features.

1   Introduction

In linear scale space theory one obtains a so-called α-scale space representation $u_f^\alpha : \mathbb{R}^d \times \mathbb{R}^+ \to \mathbb{R}$ of a grey value image image $f \in \mathbb{L}_2(\mathbb{R}^d)$ by means of a

---

* The Netherlands Organization for Scientific Research is gratefully acknowledged for financial support.

O.F. Olsen et al. (Eds.): DSSCV 2005, LNCS 3753, pp. 96–111, 2005.

holomorphic semi group generated by $-(-\Delta)^{\alpha}$, $0 < \alpha \leq 1$. Such a scale space is obtained by means of a convolution

$$u_f^{\alpha}(\mathbf{x}, s) = (K_s^{\alpha} * f)(\mathbf{x}), s > 0, \mathbf{x} \in \mathbb{R}^d,$$

where $K_s^{\alpha} = \mathcal{F}^{-1}[\boldsymbol{\omega} \mapsto e^{-s\|\boldsymbol{\omega}\|^{2\alpha}}]$. These isotropic linear scale space representations follow from a list of fundamental axioms, cf.[1] and the most common cases are $\alpha = 1$ and $\alpha = \frac{1}{2}$ leading to respectively a diffusion system and $\alpha = 1/2$ a potential system on the upper space $s > 0$. In these cases the convolution kernel equals respectively the Gaussian kernel and the Poisson kernel:

$$K_s^1(\mathbf{x}) = \frac{1}{(4\pi s)^{d/2}} e^{-\frac{\|\mathbf{x}\|^2}{4s}} \quad \text{and} \quad K_s^{\frac{1}{2}}(\mathbf{x}) = \frac{2}{\sigma_{d+1}} \frac{s}{(s^2 + \|\mathbf{x}\|^2)^{\frac{d+1}{2}}}. \quad (1)$$

In α-scale space one can use all kinds of differential invariants to detect local structure such as corners and lines. These differential invariants $\Phi : C^{\infty}(\mathbb{R}^d) \to C^{\infty}(\mathbb{R}^d)$ are algebraic (not necessarily linear) combinations of so-called α-derivatives of $f \in \mathbb{L}_2(\mathbb{R}^d)$, given by

$$D_s^{\mathbf{n}} f := D^{\mathbf{n}}(K_s^{\alpha} * f) = (D^{\mathbf{n}} K_s^{\alpha}) * f , \quad s > 0, \alpha \in (0, 1], \mathbf{n} = (n^1, \dots, n^d) \in \mathbb{N}^d, \quad (2)$$

such that they are Euclidean invariant, i.e. $\Phi \circ \mathcal{U}_g = \mathcal{U}_g \circ \Phi$, for all g within the Euclidean motion group $G = \mathbb{R}^d \rtimes SO(d)$, where $\mathcal{U} : G \mapsto \mathcal{B}(\mathbb{L}_2(\mathbb{R}^d))$ is given by $\mathcal{U}_g \psi(\mathbf{x}) = \psi(R^{-1}(\mathbf{x} - \mathbf{b})), g = (\mathbf{b}, R) \in G$.

Notice that the α-derivatives given by (2) are *bounded* (and thereby well-posed) operators on $\mathbb{L}_2(\mathbb{R}^d)$, which is clearly not the case for the usual derivative operators. This statement directly follows from the Plancherel Theorem and the fact that $\omega \mapsto \omega^p e^{-s|\omega|^{2\alpha}}$ is uniformly bounded on $\mathbb{R}$ for all $p \in \mathbb{N}$. In case $d = 2$ a complete set of functionally independent differential invariants up to second order is given by $\{u, u_x^2 + u_y^2, u_{xx} + u_{yy}, u_{xx} u_y^2 - 2u_{xy} u_x u_y + u_{yy} u_x^2, u_x u_y u_{xx} - u_x^2 u_{xy} + u_y^2 u_{xy} - u_x u_y u_{yy}\}$. By introducing Gauge coordinates w, v, where w is along the gradient of $u = u_f^{\alpha}$ and v orthogonal to it, i.e. $\mathbf{e}_w(\mathbf{x}) = \frac{\nabla_{\mathbf{x}} u}{\|\nabla_{\mathbf{x}} u\|}$ and $\mathbf{e}_v(\mathbf{x}) = R_{\frac{\pi}{2}} \mathbf{e}_w$, these differential invariants are simply expressed as $\{u, u_w, u_{ww} + u_{vv}, u_{vv}, u_{vw}\}$. Beyond Euclidean invariance, there is affine invariance. A differential invariant $\Phi : C^{\infty}(\mathbb{R}^d) \to C^{\infty}(\mathbb{R}^d)$ is called affine invariant if $\mathcal{U}_g \Phi = \Phi \mathcal{U}_g$, for all $g \in \mathbb{R}^d \rtimes A(d)$, where $A(d) = \{M \in GL(d) : \det M = 1\}$. In the case $d = 2$, we have that every element in $A(2)$ is a composite of a rotation, shearing and an axis-rescaling. The respective matrix representations of these linear mappings are given by

$$R_\theta = \begin{pmatrix} \cos\theta & -\sin\theta \\ \sin\theta & \cos\theta \end{pmatrix}, \quad S_c = \begin{pmatrix} 1 & c \\ 0 & 1 \end{pmatrix}, \quad L_\lambda = \begin{pmatrix} \lambda & 0 \\ 0 & \lambda^{-1} \end{pmatrix}, \quad (3)$$

$\theta \in [0, 2\pi), c \in \mathbb{R}$ and $\lambda \in \mathbb{R}$. Consequently, a differential invariant which is also invariant under (the left regular actions of) the subgroups $\{S_c \mid c \in \mathbb{R}\}$ and $\{L_\lambda \mid \lambda \in \mathbb{R}\}$ is affine invariant. The affine invariants up to second order are given by $\{u, \det H_{\mathbf{x}}(u), (R_{\pi/2} \nabla_{\mathbf{x}} u)^T H_{\mathbf{x}}(u) R_{\pi/2} \nabla u\}$ or equivalently in

Gauge-coordinates $\{u, u_{vv}u_{ww} - u_{vw}^2, u_w^2 u_{vv}\}$. With respect to affine invariants on $u_f^\alpha(\cdot, s)$ it should be noticed that they do not correspond to affine features on the original image f, since in general for $g = (A, \mathbf{b})$ and $u_{\mathcal{U}_g f}^\alpha(\cdot, s) = \mathcal{U}_g\, u_f^\alpha(\cdot, s)$ holds for all $f \in \mathbb{L}_2(\mathbb{R}^2)$ if and only if A is orthogonal.

In this article we focus on the question:
" *Given a sparse set of linear scale space features can we obtain an approximate reconstruction of the original image f in a fast operational and linear method ?* ".

A Euclidean invariant way of obtaining features from an image f is by means of differential invariants (on u_f^α) as described above, but they are mostly non-linear with respect to f. Therefore we select points where certain differential invariants vanish and compute the n-th order jet at these points, where n equals the order of the differential invariant, which are linear features of the type given by equality (2), so-called α-derivatives. Notice to this end that this does not affect Euclidean invariance of the reconstruction algorithm we will present.

It is a well known problem that the construction of f from $u_f(\cdot, s)$ for any $s > 0$ fixed is extremely ill-posed, as it requires an inverse convolution of the low-pass filter K_s^α. By considering multiple orientations (leading to a so-called orientation score) and proper directed wavelets one can get around this problem, as is shown in [2], but here we will consider multiple scale representations rather than multiple orientation representations of images. In theory an α-scale space is analytic in (x, y, s), but again computing an image reconstruction by means of Taylor expansion of (in)finite order from a single point in scale space is highly ill-posed. Nevertheless, it *is* possible to give an approximate reconstruction of f from a sparse set of linear features obtained by means of α-derivatives, which should be considered as an interpolation rather than an inverse convolution. But first we will study the topological structure of a scale space, also known as *deep structure*, as it seems most reasonable that the features should *at least* capture the topological structure of the scale space.

2   Deep Structure

The topological structure in a scale space and in particular the change of topological structure of $u(\cdot, s)$ over $s > 0$, reflects the hierarchical structure of objects (like blobs) in an image. As the resolution increases extrema disappear until at finite scale $S > 0$ only one extremum is left, cf.[3]. Points in scale space where a saddle and extremum annihilate or points where an extremum and a saddle are created are called top-points. The set of top-points is given by

$$\{(\mathbf{x}, s) \mid (\det H_{\mathbf{x}} u(\cdot, s))(\mathbf{x}) = 0 \text{ and } (\nabla_{\mathbf{x}} u(\cdot, s))(\mathbf{x}) = \mathbf{0}\}.$$

Notice that in a top point all affine differential invariants vanish.[1] At these points the topological structure changes. Other interesting points in scale space

---

[1] The other way around need not be true: $u_{vv}u_w = 0$ and $\det Hu(\cdot, s) = 0$ is equivalent to $u_w = \det Hu(\cdot, s) = 0$ or $u_{vv} = u_{vw} = 0$. In the latter case the isophote curvature and the flowline curvature vanish, i.e. the isophotes and flowlines are straight lines.

are scale space saddles[2], these are exactly those points were $\nabla_{\mathbf{x},s} u(\mathbf{x}, s) = (\mathbf{0}, 0)$, cf. [4]. For investigation on the stability of top-points we refer to Balmachnova et al.[5].

Another important geometrical quantity is the *grey-value flow* within an α scale space u_f^α of image f. This multi-scale vector field is given by

$$\mathbf{F}_\alpha[u_f^\alpha](\mathbf{x}, s) = (\mathbf{f}_s^\alpha * f)(\mathbf{x}), \qquad (4)$$

where $\mathbf{f}_s^\alpha(\mathbf{x}) = \mathcal{F}^{-1}[\boldsymbol{\omega} \mapsto i\frac{1}{\|\boldsymbol{\omega}\|^{2(1-\alpha)}}\boldsymbol{\omega}\, e^{-s\|\boldsymbol{\omega}\|^{2\alpha}}](\mathbf{x})$. To this end we notice that

$$\frac{\partial}{\partial s}[u_f^\alpha] = -(-\Delta)^\alpha u_f^\alpha = \operatorname{div} \mathbf{F}_\alpha[u_f],$$

which is easily verified in the Fourier domain: $-\|\boldsymbol{\omega}\|^{2\alpha} = i\boldsymbol{\omega} \cdot i\frac{1}{\|\boldsymbol{\omega}\|^{2(1-\alpha)}}\boldsymbol{\omega}$. The grey-value flow tells us how the grey-value particles flow within the scale space representation and reveals the interaction between extremal paths in scale space. We will use this flux vector field to compute so-called flux features. For the special case of a Gaussian scale space $\alpha = 1$ the grey-value flow is obtained by means of the gradient as we have $\mathbf{F}_{\alpha=1}[u_f](\mathbf{x}, s) = \nabla_{\mathbf{x}} u_f(\mathbf{x}, s)$ and $\mathbf{f}_s^{\alpha=1} = \nabla_{\mathbf{x}} K_s^1(\mathbf{x})$. For the special case of a Poisson scale space $\alpha = \frac{1}{2}$ the grey value flow is obtained by means of the Riesz transform $\mathbf{F}_{\alpha=\frac{1}{2}}[u_f](\mathbf{x}, s) = \mathbf{R}_{\mathbf{x}} u_f(\mathbf{x}, s)$ and $\mathbf{f}_s^{\alpha=\frac{1}{2}}$ equals the vector-valued conjugate Poisson kernel: $\mathbf{f}_s^{\alpha=\frac{1}{2}}(\mathbf{x}) = \mathbf{R}_{\mathbf{x}} K_s^{1/2}(\mathbf{x}) = \frac{2}{\sigma_{d+1}}\frac{\mathbf{x}}{(s^2+\|\mathbf{x}\|^2)^{\frac{d+1}{2}}}$. By extending a scale space with its flow, one obtains a vector scale space which equals the first order jet of a Gaussian scale space if $\alpha = 1$ and which equals the monogenic scale space, cf.[6], if $\alpha = 1/2$.

3   Linear Image Reconstruction Schemes

In this section we will generalize the standard linear reconstruction scheme from the usual case where the space of images is modelled as $\mathbb{L}_2(\mathbb{R}^2)$ to the more general case of an arbitrary Hilbert space H. Later we consider the case where H is a Hilbert space of Sobolev-type.

Let $\{\tilde{\psi}_k\}_{k=1}^n$ be a set of n continuous linear functionals (features) on a Hilbert space H, which are linearly independent. Then by the Riesz representation theorem there exist unique $\{\psi_k\}_{k=1}^n$ in H such that $\langle \tilde{\psi}_k, f \rangle = (\psi_k, f)_H$, for all $f \in H$. The values $(\psi_k, f)_H$, $k = 1, \ldots, n$ are called features. Let V be the span of $\{\psi_k\}_{k=1}^n$. Two images $f, g \in H$ have the same features iff $f - g \in V^\perp$. This defines an equivalence relation on H and the equivalence classes are given by

$$[f] = \{g \in H \mid g \sim f\} = f + V^\perp .$$

---

[2] As is shown in [1], there do not exist interior extrema (with respect to scale and position) in α-scale spaces.

Theorem 1. *Inside the metameric class of images, the unique element with minimal H-norm equals the orthogonal projection of f onto V:*

$$\mathcal{P}_V f = \sum_{k=1}^{n} (\psi^k, f)\psi_k, \tag{5}$$

where the reciprocal base vectors are given by $\psi^k = \sum_{l=1}^{n} G^{kl}\psi_l$, *where* $\sum_{k=1}^{n} G^{ik}G_{kj} = \delta_j^i$, *with Gramm-matrix:* $G = [G_{kj}] = [(\psi_k, \psi_j)_H]$.

Proof. By the Pythagoras theorem we have

$$\min_{g\in[f]} \|g\|^2 = \min_{g\in[f]} \|g - \mathcal{P}_V f + \mathcal{P}_V f\|^2 = \min_{g\in[f]} \|g - \mathcal{P}_V f\|^2 + \|\mathcal{P}_V f\|^2 \tag{6}$$

and this equals $\|\mathcal{P}_V f\|^2$ only in the case $g = \mathcal{P}_V f$. Finally we notice that a closed[3] linear subspace of a Hilbert space is again a Hilbert space and thereby the orthogonal projection is unique. □

The special case $H = \mathbb{L}_2(\mathbb{R}^2)$ in Theorem 1, is a standard linear reconstruction scheme in image analysis, see for example [7] and later [8], [9]. In image analysis this reconstruction theory is usually put in a more indirect Euler-Lagrange framework. For example in the work of Nielsen and Lillholm, cf. [7], [8], where it is already mentioned that the prior need not be an $\mathbb{L}_2$-norm and that there exist much better priors (in the sense that one clearly obtains visually more appealing image reconstructions), such as minimal entropy and a first order Sobolev-norm. But they were unaware of Theorem 1 and thereby they used iterative non-linear schemes to approximate the global minimum. In case of a minimum entropy based prior, which is not[4] a norm induced by an inner product, this is plausible (and probably the best you can get). However, in the case where the prior equals a norm of Sobolev type the exact minimum is given by $P_V f$. Lemma 1 shows that if the prior is a norm on a Hilbert space this boils down to the same result as in Theorem 1 (*as it should*).

Lemma 1. *In the Euler Lagrange framework, the unique solution of the minimization of the convex positive energy* $E(g) = \frac{1}{2}(g, g)_H$, *under the conditions* $(\psi_i, g)_H = c_i \in \mathbb{C}$ *(fixed) for* $i = 1, \ldots, n$, *where* $\{\psi_i\}$ *are linearly independent in H, satisfies*

$$< DE(g), f >= (g, f) = \sum_{i=1}^{n} \lambda^i(\psi_i, f)_H, \quad \text{for all } f \in H \tag{7}$$

and is given by the orthogonal projection $g = \mathcal{P}_V f$, *given by (5), of the original image f on the linear span V of the filters* ψ_i.

---

[3] A finite dimensional subspace is always closed, but this statement reveals how to deal with the case $n \to \infty$.

[4] A norm on a vector space V is induced by an inner product iff the parallelogram law $\|x + y\|^2 + \|x - y\|^2 = 2(\|x\|^2 + \|y\|^2)$ holds for all $x, y \in V$. In this case the inner product is given by $(x, y) = \frac{1}{4}\{\|x + y\|^2 - \|x - y\|^2 + i\|x - iy\|^2 - i\|x + iy\|^2\}$.

Proof. The uniqueness and last part of the proof is already given by Theorem 1. With respect to the first part we only mention that the Gateaux variation of the energy at g in the direction of f is given by

$$< DE(g), f >= \lim_{\lambda \to 0} \frac{E(g + \lambda f) - E(f)}{\lambda} = (g, f), \text{ for all } f \in H$$

and the Lagrange multipliers must be equal to $\lambda^i = (\psi^i, g)$, where $\{\psi^i\}_{i=1}^n$ denotes the reciprocal basis.   □

Instead of iterative schemes we use directly compute the exact solution $P_V f$, for the cases (recall the example in section 4.1) where the Hilbert space H equals a space of Sobolev-type, for example $\mathbb{H}_\gamma^{k,2}(\mathbb{R}^2) = \{f \in \mathbb{L}_2(\mathbb{R}^2) \mid (Rf, Rf) = (R^2 f, f) < \infty\}$, where $R = (I + \gamma^{2k}|\Delta|^k)^{\frac{1}{2}}$, $k = 1, 2, \ldots$, $\gamma > 0$, as explained in Corollary 1. In the next chapter we will deal with some important theoretical issues that inevitably arise when working with spaces of Sobolev type, but it is not necessary to understand all details to understand the algorithm from a practical point of view. At this point, if the reader is not interested in these more theoretical aspects, we directly refer to Figures 2 and 1 and Corollaries 1, 2.

4   Gelfand Triples

Let H be a complex Hilbert space and $\mathcal{R}$ an unbounded, positive and selfadjoint operator on H, for which the inverse $\mathcal{R}^{-1}$ is bounded. Note that the boundedness of $\mathcal{R}^{-1}$ implies that the domain $D(\mathcal{R}) = \{f \in H \mid \mathcal{R}f \in H\}$ equals $D(\mathcal{R}) = \mathcal{R}^{-1}(H)$.

Definition 1. *Define the space H^I as the linear space $D(\mathcal{R})$ equipped with the inner product $(f, g)_I = (\mathcal{R}f, \mathcal{R}g)_H$ for all $f, g \in H$.*

Notice that H^I is again a Hilbert space: Let f_n be a Cauchy sequence in H^I. Then $\mathcal{R}f_n$ is a Cauchy sequence in H. H is a Hilbert space, so $\mathcal{R}f_n \to g$ in H, for some $g \in H$. But then, since $\mathcal{R}^{-1}$ is bounded, it follows that f_n is also a Cauchy sequence in H: $\|f_n - f_m\| \le \|\mathcal{R}^{-1}\|\|\mathcal{R}f_n - \mathcal{R}f_m\|$. So $f_n \to f$ in H, for some $f \in H$. Now $\mathcal{R}$ is self adjoint and therefore closed, so $f \in D(\mathcal{R})$ and $\mathcal{R}f = g$. Now we have $\mathcal{R}f_n \to \mathcal{R}f$ in H, so $f_n \to f$ in H^I and $f \in H^I$.

Definition 2. *Define the Hilbert space H^{-I} as the completion of H equipped with the inner product $(f, g)_{-I} = (\mathcal{R}^{-1}f, \mathcal{R}^{-1}g)_H$.*

The operator $\mathcal{R}$ on H induces the map $\tilde{\mathcal{R}} : H^I \to H$ by $\tilde{\mathcal{R}}f = \mathcal{R}f$ for all $f \in H^I = D(\mathcal{R})$. Since $\|\tilde{\mathcal{R}}f\|_H = \|f\|_I$ for all $f \in H^I$, the map $\tilde{\mathcal{R}}$ is an isometry. By boundedness of R^{-1}, it follows that $\tilde{R}$ is also surjective and hence a unitary map.

Define $\check{\mathcal{R}} : D(\mathcal{R}) \to H^{-I}$ by $\check{\mathcal{R}}f = \mathcal{R}f$ for all $f \in D(\mathcal{R})$. Since $\|\check{\mathcal{R}}f\|_{-I} = \|f\|_H$ for all $f \in D(\mathcal{R})$, the map $\check{\mathcal{R}}$ is closable and its extension is an isometry. Since $\mathcal{R}(D(\mathcal{R})) = H$ and H is dense in H^{-I} the closure is also surjective, hence a unitary map. Write $\tilde{\tilde{\mathcal{R}}}$ for the closure of $\check{\mathcal{R}}$. Hence the following triple (known as Gelfand Triple) is obtained

$$H^I \overset{\tilde{\mathcal{R}}}{\hookrightarrow} H \overset{\tilde{\tilde{\mathcal{R}}}}{\hookrightarrow} H^{-I}. \tag{8}$$

It follows by the Riesz representation theorem and the unitarity of $\tilde{\mathcal{R}}$ and $\tilde{\tilde{\mathcal{R}}}$ that the space H^{-I} is naturally isomorphic to the anti-dual space of H^I under the pairing $\langle F, f \rangle = (\tilde{\mathcal{R}}^{-1}F, \tilde{\mathcal{R}}f)_H$ for all $F \in H^{-I}$ and $f \in H^I$. Note that by the selfadjoint-ness of $\mathcal{R}$

$$\langle F, f \rangle = (F, f)_H \tag{9}$$

if $F \in H$ for all $f \in H^I$. In this paper $\mathcal{R}$, $\tilde{\mathcal{R}}$ and $\tilde{\tilde{\mathcal{R}}}$ are all denoted by the same symbol $\mathcal{R}$. From the context it is clear which operator is meant by this symbol.

4.1   Spaces of Sobolev Type

By a Theorem of John von Neumann, [10]p.200, we have that for every closed densely defined operator $\mathcal{A}$ in a Hilbert space H the operator $\mathcal{A}^*\mathcal{A}$ is self adjoint and $(I + \mathcal{A}^*\mathcal{A})$ has a bounded inverse. So a particular case of a Gelfand triple is obtained by setting $\mathcal{R} = (I + \mathcal{A}^*\mathcal{A})^{1/2}$, where $\mathcal{A}$ is a closed densely defined operator. In that case we have

$$(f, g)_I = (\mathcal{R}f, \mathcal{R}g)_H = (f, g)_H + (\mathcal{A}f, \mathcal{A}g)_H . \tag{10}$$

Example 1: Let $k \in \mathbb{N}$. Then it is well-known that the operator $D_k = (1 + \gamma^{2k}|\triangle|^k)^{\frac{1}{2}}$ with domain $\mathbb{H}_\gamma^{k,2}(\mathbb{R}^2)$ is an unbounded, positive and self-adjoint operator on $\mathbb{L}_2(\mathbb{R}^2)$ with bounded inverse. So $\mathcal{A} = \gamma(\sqrt{-\triangle})^k$ and $\mathcal{R} = D_k$ and we obtain the Gelfand triple

$$\mathbb{H}_\gamma^{k,2}(\mathbb{R}^2) \hookrightarrow \mathbb{L}_2(\mathbb{R}^2) \hookrightarrow \mathbb{H}_\gamma^{-k,2}(\mathbb{R}^2). \tag{11}$$

For a detailed discussion on these spaces, in particular $\gamma = 1$, we refer to [10]I.10, pp.56.

Remark: The Gelfand triple structure is interesting for the case that $\mathcal{A}$ is unbounded, since if $\mathcal{A}$ is bounded (and thereby $\mathcal{R}$ is bounded) we have by (10) that :

$$\|f\|_H^2 \le \|f\|_I^2 \le (1 + \|\mathcal{A}\|^2)\|f\|_H^2,$$

so the norms (and the thereby induced topologies) are equivalent. Moreover, if $\mathcal{A}$ is bounded the set $\mathcal{D}(\mathcal{R})$ equals H and the Riesz representant of $f \mapsto (\phi, f)$ in H^I is given by $\mathcal{R}^{-2}\phi = (I + \mathcal{A}^*\mathcal{A})^{-1}\phi$:

$$(\mathcal{R}^{-2}\phi, f)_I = (\mathcal{R}^{-1}\phi, \mathcal{R}f)_H = (\mathcal{R}\mathcal{R}^{-1}\phi, f)_H = (\phi, f)_H.$$

Summarizing, if $\mathcal{A}$ is bounded the sets H^I and H are equal and by the Riesz representation theorem H is unitary equivalent with its dual H', so operator $\mathcal{A}$ only tells us how H is identified with H'.

4.2 Trajectory Spaces

In a Hilbert Space H we consider the general evolution equation $\frac{du}{ds} = \mathcal{A}u$, with $\mathcal{A}$ a negative unbounded self-adjoint operator. $\mathcal{A}$ is the infinitesimal generator of a holomorphic semi-group. Solutions $u(\cdot) : (0, \infty) \to H$ of this equation are called trajectories. Such a trajectory may or may not correspond to an "initial condition at $s = 0$" in H. The set of trajectories is considered as a space of generalized functions. The test function space is defined to be $\mathcal{S}_{H,\mathcal{A}} = \bigcup_{s>0} e^{s\mathcal{A}}(H)$.

Theorem 2. *Let H be a Hilbert space. Let Q be a strongly continuous, holomorphic semigroup, with infinitesimal generator $\mathcal{A} < 0$. Then $\mathcal{S}_{H,\mathcal{A}}$ consists exactly of those $f \in \mathcal{D}(\mathcal{A}^\infty)$ such that*

$$\sum_{k=1}^{\infty} \frac{s^k}{k!} \|\mathcal{A}^k f\| < \infty \qquad \text{for a certain } s > 0 . \tag{12}$$

This is a well-known result in functional analysis and its proof can for example be found in [11] or [1]Appendix, Thm 11. Now by taking $\mathcal{R} = e^{-s\mathcal{A}}$ on H, with bounded inverse $e^{s\mathcal{A}}$ we obtain the following Gelfand-triples:

$$\mathcal{S}_{H,\mathcal{A}} \overset{\mathcal{R}}{\hookrightarrow} H \overset{\mathcal{R}}{\hookrightarrow} \mathcal{S}'_{H,\mathcal{A}}. \tag{13}$$

Example: $H = \mathbb{L}_2(\mathbb{R}^d)$, $\mathcal{A} = \Delta$, then $(\mathcal{R}^{-1}f) = K_s^1 * f$, where K_s^1 is the Gaussian kernel, recall (1), and we obtain the Gelfand triple

$$\mathcal{S} \overset{\mathcal{R}}{\hookrightarrow} \mathbb{L}_2(\mathbb{R}^d) \overset{\mathcal{R}}{\hookrightarrow} \mathcal{S}'. \tag{14}$$

where $\mathcal{S}_{\mathbb{L}_2(\mathbb{R}^d),\Delta} = \mathcal{S} = \{\phi \in C^\infty(\mathbb{R}^d) \mid \forall_{\mathbf{k},\mathbf{q}} \sup_{\mathbf{x}\in\mathbb{R}^d} |\mathbf{x}^\mathbf{k}\phi^{(\mathbf{q})}| < \infty\}$ is the usual Schwarz space.[5]

4.3 A Linear Image Reconstruction Based on Inner Products of Sobolev Type

By taking the space of images H^I (for example $H^I = \mathbb{H}_\gamma^{2k,2}(\mathbb{R}^d)$ or $H^I = \mathcal{S}_{\mathbb{L}_2(\mathbb{R}(d)),-(-\Delta)^\alpha}$) in Theorem 1 we obtain the metameric class

$$[f] = \{g \in H^I \mid (\kappa_k, f)_I = (\kappa_k, g)_I, \text{ for } k = 1, \ldots, n\} , \quad \text{with } \kappa_k = \mathcal{R}^{-2}\psi_k, k = 1, \ldots n,$$

and the optimal solution within this metameric class $\arg\min_{g\in[f]} \|g\|_{H^I}^2$, is given by $g = P_V f$. Notice that $(\kappa_k, g)_I = (\psi_k, g)_{\mathbb{L}_2(\mathbb{R}^2)}$, so the metameric classes still consist of images (within H^I) with the same features. But initially, the space of images was the modeled by $H = \mathbb{L}_2(\mathbb{R}^2)$ space (and not the smooth space H^I), so we want our metameric classes within $\mathbb{L}_2(\mathbb{R}^2)$ rather than H^I. Theorem 3, takes care of this.

---

[5] In case of the Poisson semigroup ($\mathcal{A} = -\sqrt{-\Delta}$) leads to the Gelfand-Shilov space $\mathcal{S}_1$ rather than the Schwarz space, see [1].

Theorem 3. *Let $f \in H$. Let $[f]$ denote the metameric class of all elements $g \in H$ such that*

$$g \sim f \Leftrightarrow (\mathcal{R}^{-1}f, \mathcal{R}\kappa_k)_I = (\mathcal{R}^{-1}g, \mathcal{R}\kappa_k)_I \,, \text{ for all } k = 1, \ldots, n.$$

with $\kappa_k \in H^{II}$, i.e. $\mathcal{R}\kappa_k \in H^I$. Then the unique solution of the minimization problem $\min\limits_{g \in H^I, g \sim f} \|g\|_I$ is given by $g = P_V^{ext} f = \sum\limits_{i=1}^{n} (\mathcal{R}\kappa^i, \mathcal{R}^{-1}f)_I \kappa_i$, with $\kappa^i = \sum\limits_{j=1}^{n} G^{ij} \kappa_j$, where $\sum\limits_{k=1}^{n} G^{ik} G_{kj} = \delta_j^i$, with $G_{kj} = (\kappa_k, \kappa_j)_I$.

Proof. First notice that P_V^{ext} is the natural extension of P_V, i.e. the restriction of P_V^{ext} to H^I equals P_V: $P_V^{ext}|_{H^I} = P_V$, which directly follows by the fact that $\mathcal{R}$ is self adjoint and therefore

$$(\mathcal{R}\psi, \mathcal{R}^{-1}f)_I = (\psi, f)_I \text{ for all } f \in H^I \text{ and } \psi \in H^{II}. \tag{15}$$

Without loss of generality we may assume that $\{\kappa_k\}$ is an orthonormal base in H_I. Then we have $g - P_V^{ext} f \perp P_V^{ext}$, since by $f \sim g$ and (15) it follows that

$$(g - P_V^{ext} f, P_V^{ext})_I = (\mathcal{R}\kappa^j, \mathcal{R}^{-1}f)(g, \kappa_j) - \overline{(\mathcal{R}\kappa^j, \mathcal{R}^{-1}f)}(\mathcal{R}\kappa^j, \mathcal{R}^{-1}f) = 0 \,.$$

So again Pythagoras: $\min\limits_{g \sim f, g \in H_I} \|g\|_I^2 = \min\limits_{g \sim f, g \in H_I} \|g - P_V^{ext}f + P_V^{ext}f\|_I^2 = \min\limits_{g \sim f, g \in H_I} \|g - P_V^{ext}f\|_I^2 + \|P_V^{ext}f\|_I^2$ we conclude that this equals $\min\limits_{g \sim f, g \in H_I} \|g\|_I^2 = \|P_V^{ext}f\|_I^2$ iff $g = P_V^{ext}f$ $\qquad\square$

By taking the respective pairs $H = \mathbb{L}_2(\mathbb{R}^d)$, $\mathcal{R} = (I + \gamma^{2k}|\Delta|^k)^{\frac{1}{2}}$ and $H = \mathbb{L}_2(\mathbb{R}^d)$, $\mathcal{R} = e^{\frac{s}{2}|\Delta|^\alpha}$ in Theorem 3 we obtain the following corollaries:

Corollary 1. *Let $f \in \mathbb{L}_2(\mathbb{R}^d)$. Let $[f]$ denote the equivalence class of all elements $g \in \mathbb{L}_2(\mathbb{R}^d)$ such that*

$$g \sim f \Leftrightarrow (\psi_k, f)_{\mathbb{L}_2(\mathbb{R}^2)} = (\psi_k, g)_{\mathbb{L}_2(\mathbb{R}^2)}, \text{ for all } k = 1, \ldots, n.$$

Then the unique solution of the minimization problem

$$\min\limits_{g \in \mathbb{H}_\gamma^{k,2}(\mathbb{R}^2), g \sim f} \|g\|_{\mathbb{H}_\gamma^{k,2}(\mathbb{R}^2)}^2 = \min\limits_{g \in \mathbb{H}_\gamma^{k,2}(\mathbb{R}^2), g \sim f} (g, g)_{\mathbb{L}_2(\mathbb{R}^2)} + (g, \gamma^{2k}|\Delta|^k g)_{\mathbb{L}_2(\mathbb{R}^2)}$$

is given by $g = P_V^{ext} f$, where $P_V^{ext} f = ((I + \gamma^{2k}|\Delta|^k)^{\frac{1}{2}} \kappa^i, (I + \gamma^{2k}|\Delta|^k)^{-\frac{1}{2}} f)_{\mathbb{H}_\gamma^{k,2}(\mathbb{R}^2)} \kappa_i$, where κ^k are the reciproke vectors of $\kappa_k = (I + \gamma^{2k}|\Delta|^k)^{-1} \psi_k$.

Important: Notice that $\kappa_k = R_{d=2}^{k,\gamma} * \psi_k$, where $R_{d=2}^{k,\gamma,0}(\mathbf{x}) = \mathcal{F}^{-1}(\omega \mapsto \frac{1}{2\pi}(1 + \gamma^{2k}|\omega|^{2k})^{-1})(\mathbf{x})$ is the reproducing kernel (at **0**) of $\mathbb{H}_\gamma^{k,2}(\mathbb{R}^2)$, for $k > 1$, see Appendix. The reproducing kernels are needed to project $\mathbb{L}_2$-linear onto linear Sobolev-features, which is the basic reason for the succes of our approach to feature reconstruction: The features themselves do not change, but the projection basis is subject to a Tikhonov regularization. In this way " the reconstructed Lena gets rid of her smallpox ", see fig 1.

Corollary 2. *Let $f \in \mathbb{L}_2(\mathbb{R}^d)$. Let $[f]$ denote the equivalence class of all elements $g \in \mathbb{L}_2(\mathbb{R}^d)$ such that*

$$g \sim f \Leftrightarrow (\psi_k, f)_{\mathbb{L}_2(\mathbb{R}^2)} = (\psi_k, g)_{\mathbb{L}_2(\mathbb{R}^2)}, \text{ for all } k = 1, \dots, n.$$

Then the unique solution of the minimization problem

$$\min_{g \in S_{\mathbb{L}_2(\mathbb{R}^2), -|\Delta|^\alpha}, g \sim f} (g, g)_{\mathbb{L}_2(\mathbb{R}^2)} + \sum_{k=1}^{\infty} (g, s^{2k} |\Delta|^{\alpha k} g)_{\mathbb{L}_2(\mathbb{R}^2)} \qquad (16)$$

is given by $g = P_V^{ext} f$, where $P_V^{ext} f = (e^{\frac{s}{2}|\Delta|^\alpha} \kappa^i, e^{-\frac{s}{2}|\Delta|^\alpha} f)_{S_{\mathbb{L}_2(\mathbb{R}^2), -|\Delta|^\alpha}} \kappa_i$, where κ^i are the reciproke vectors of $\kappa_i = \left(e^{\frac{s}{2}|\Delta|^\alpha}\right)^{-2} \psi_i = K_{s/2}^\alpha * K_{s/2}^\alpha * \psi_i = K_s^\alpha * \psi_i$.

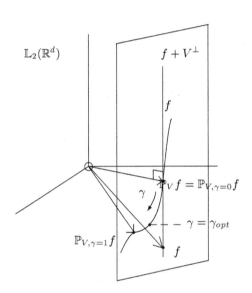

Fig. 1. Illustration of metameric class $f + V^\perp$ of images with equal features. For $\gamma = 0$ we have a orthogonal projection. For $\gamma > 0$ this projection is orthogonal in $\mathbb{H}_\gamma^{k,2}(\mathbb{R}^2)$ and thereby it is a skew projection in $\mathbb{L}_2(\mathbb{R}^2)$. We obtain a connected curve parametrized by γ where smoothness of the projection increases with $\gamma > 0$.

We are mainly interested in the case where the features are obtained by α-derivatives within the scale space image u of the original image f, i.e. $\psi_k(\mathbf{x}) = (\tau_{\mathbf{b}_k} D^{\mathbf{n}_k} K_{s_k}^\alpha)(\mathbf{x}) = D^{\mathbf{n}_k} K_{s_k}^\alpha(\mathbf{x} - \mathbf{b}_k)$ for some multi-index $\mathbf{n}_k$, some position $\mathbf{b}_k \in \mathbb{R}^d$ and some scale s_k. In this case we can analytically compute the Grammian matrix (and thereby analytically compute the solution $g = P_V^{ext} f$):

$$G_{kj} = (\kappa_k, \kappa_j)_{S_{\mathbb{L}_2(\mathbb{R}^2), -|\Delta|^\alpha}} = (\mathcal{R}^{-2} \psi_k, \mathcal{R}^{-2} \psi_j)_{S_{\mathbb{L}_2(\mathbb{R}^2), -|\Delta|^\alpha}} = (\mathcal{R}^{-1} \psi_k, \mathcal{R}^{-1} \psi_j)_{\mathbb{L}_2(\mathbb{R}^2)}$$

$$= (\tau_{\mathbf{b}_k} D^{\mathbf{n}_k} K_{s_k + (s/2)}^\alpha, \tau_{\mathbf{b}_j} D^{\mathbf{n}_j} K_{s_j + (s/2)}^\alpha)_{\mathbb{L}_2(\mathbb{R}^2)} = \left(K_{s_j + s_k + s}^\alpha\right)^{(\mathbf{n}_k + \mathbf{n}_j)} (\mathbf{b}_k - \mathbf{b}_j).$$

Important: Here again the features are preserved and the base functions are smoothed. But now the smoothing kernels are given by the α-kernels themselves rather than the reproducing kernels of the isotropic Sobolev-spaces in the previous corollary. So instead of Tikhonov-regularization we smooth according to ordinary α-scale spaces. The relation between these 2 extreme ways of smoothing is given by the Laplace transform with respect to the scale parameter

$$\mathcal{L}[s \mapsto K_s^\alpha](\gamma^{-2k}) = \gamma^{2k} R_{d=2}^{k,\gamma,0} \text{ for all } \gamma > 0, \text{ where } k = \alpha. \tag{17}$$

By interchanging the order of Laplace transformation and integration, it is not difficult to obtain an analytic formula for the Grammian matrix in Corollary 1 (and thereby analytic formulas for the orthogonal projection) for the cases where $\alpha = k$.

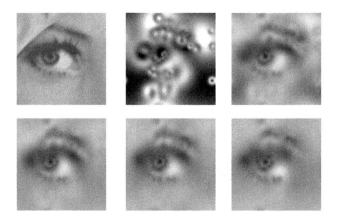

Fig. 2. Reconstruction from 31 top-points of "Lena's eye" with up to second order features only. The upper row shows the original image and reconstructions with $\gamma = 0$ and $\gamma = 5$. The second row shows reconstructions with $\gamma = 22$, $\gamma = 50$ and $\gamma = 250$. The first image in the second row shows the reconstruction with the lowest relative $\mathbb{L}_2$-error. For more details on evaluation we refer to our earlier work,[12],[13].

5 Flux-Features

Besides the regularizing effect of minimizing Sobolev norms there is another advantage of using Sobolev inner products: There exist several interesting features (such as grey-value fluxes) of images which can be constructed by means of Sobolev inner products, but which can not be constructed in the usual framework of $\mathbb{L}_2$-inner products. For example point evaluation $\delta_{\mathbf{a}}(f) = f(\mathbf{a})$ is a continuous linear functional on $\mathbb{H}_\gamma^{k,2}(\mathbb{R}^2)$, $k > 1$. As a result (by the Riesz representation Theorem) there exists reproducing kernels, see Appendix A, $R_{k,\gamma}^2 \in \mathbb{H}_\gamma^{k,2}(\mathbb{R}^2)$, $k > 1$ such that $\delta_{\mathbf{a}}(f) = f(\mathbf{a}) = (\tau_{\mathbf{a}} R_{k,\gamma}^2, f)$, which makes point evaluations linear features. This can not be done within the more familiar $\mathbb{L}_2(\mathbb{R}^2)$ space.

Another example of new possible linear features are so-called flux-features on images. They are given by the linear functionals

$$f \mapsto I_\Omega(f) = \int_{\partial\Omega} \frac{\partial f}{\partial n} \, d\sigma, \qquad f \in \mathbb{H}_\gamma^{2,2}(\mathbb{R}^2).$$

where Ω is a bounded region in $\mathbb{R}^2$, with surface measure $\mu(\Omega) < \infty$ with a orientable piecewise smooth boundary $\partial\Omega$ with outward normal $\mathbf{n}$. These linear functionals are continuous on $\mathbb{H}_\gamma^{k,2}(\mathbb{R}^2)$ if $k \geq 2$, which directly follows by Gauss divergence theorem and Cauchy-Schwarz: $|I_\Omega(f)| \leq |\int_\Omega \Delta f \mathrm{d}\mathbf{x}| \leq \mu(\Omega)\|f\|_{\mathbb{H}_\gamma^{2,2}(\mathbb{R}^2)}$. As a result there exist flux-kernels $\phi_{\Omega,k,\gamma}$ in $\mathbb{H}_\gamma^{k,2}(\mathbb{R}^2)$, $k \geq 2$, such that

$$I_\Omega(f) = (\phi_{\Omega,k,\gamma}, f)_{\mathbb{H}_\gamma^{k,2}(\mathbb{R}^2)}.$$

The Practical Reason for Flux Features: In the previous chapters we improved the top-point reconstruction by introducing spaces of Sobolev-type. The idea was to pick a smooth element within the metameric class of images with top-points at the same locations as the locations of the top-points of the scale space of the original image f, where a positive parameter controls the smoothness of this reconstruction. By increasing this parameter ($\gamma > 0$ in Corollary 1 or $s > 0$ in Corollary 2) this representant becomes smoother and thereby the number of extra top points of the scale space of this representant is reduced. Nevertheless, in practice there exist an upper bound to the parameter γ, since if the representant becomes too smooth, the contrasting areas (such as corners/edges) will vanish, which results in so-called "edge-leaking", cf.[12]. Therefore, we propose to reduce the number of extra top-points in the representant by means of extra features. Flux-features obtained by surfaces around critical paths in scale space are highly suitable for this purpose, as they describe how grey-value particles flow between extremal paths.

5.1   Definition and Implementation of Flux Features in Scale Space

Definition 3. *Let $s > 0$, $f \in \mathbf{L}_2(\mathbb{R}^2)$, with α-scale space representation $u_f^\alpha = K_s^\alpha * f$. Let Ω be a bounded region in $\mathbb{R}^2$ with an orientable piecewise smooth boundary $\partial\Omega$ with outward normal $\mathbf{n}$. Then we define the flux feature $I_\Omega^\alpha(f, s) =$*

$$\left. \frac{\partial}{\partial t} \int_\Omega u_f^\alpha(\mathbf{x}, t)\mathrm{d}\mathbf{x} \right|_{t=s}.$$

We notice that by means of Gauss' divergence theorem and changing the order of differentiation with respect to $s > 0$ and integration over Ω we can relate flow-vector fields $\mathbf{F}_\alpha u_f^\alpha(\cdot, s)$, recall (4), to flux-features

$$\begin{aligned}
I_\Omega^\alpha(f, s) &= \int_\Omega \frac{\partial}{\partial s} u_f^\alpha(\mathbf{x}, s) \, \mathrm{d}\mathbf{x} = \int_\Omega -(-\Delta)^\alpha u_f^\alpha(\mathbf{x}, s) \, \mathrm{d}\mathbf{x} = \int_\Omega \mathrm{div} \, \mathbf{F}_\alpha \, u_f^\alpha(\mathbf{x}, s) \, \mathrm{d}\mathbf{x} \\
&= \int_{\partial\Omega} \mathbf{F}_\alpha \, u_f^\alpha(\mathbf{x}, s) \cdot \mathbf{n}(\mathbf{x}) \, \mathrm{d}\sigma(\mathbf{x}),
\end{aligned}$$

$$(18)$$

Recall that $\mathbf{F}_1$ equals the gradient operator $\mathbf{F}_1 = \nabla$ and $\mathbf{F}_{\frac{1}{2}}$ equals the Riesz transform $\mathbf{F}_{\frac{1}{2}} = \mathbf{R}$. So, in case $\alpha = 1$ and in case $\alpha = 1/2$ we have

$$I_\Omega^1(f,s) = \int_{\partial\Omega} \frac{\partial u_f^1(\cdot,s)}{\partial n}\, d\sigma(\mathbf{x}) \qquad I_\Omega^{1/2}(f,s) = \int_{\partial\Omega} \mathbf{q}(\mathbf{x},s)\cdot\mathbf{n}(\mathbf{x})\, d\sigma(\mathbf{x}), \qquad (19)$$

where $\mathbf{q} = \mathbf{f}_s^{\frac{1}{2}} * f$ denotes the conjugate Poisson scale space.

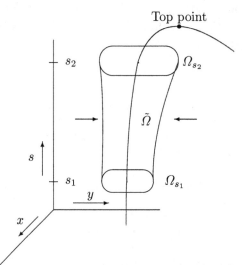

Grey-value flow of grey-value particles through surface $\partial\tilde{\Omega}$ around an extremal path in scale space

Definition 4. *Let* $\tilde{\Omega} = \{(\mathbf{x},s) \in \mathbb{R}^2 \times [0,\infty) \mid 0 \le s_1 \le s \le s_2, \mathbf{x} \in \Omega_s \subset \mathbb{R}^2\}$, *where for all* $s > 0$, Ω_s *is a bounded region in* $\mathbb{R}^2$, *with an orientable piecewise smooth boundary* $\partial\Omega$ *with outward normal* $\mathbf{n}$. *Suppose the lifetime of a grey-value particle through scale space is negatively exponentially distributed with expectation* μ^{-1}. *Then the grey-value flow trough* $\tilde{\Omega}$ *is given by*[6]

$$I_{\tilde{\Omega}}^{\alpha,\mu}(f) = \frac{1}{\mu}\int_{s_1}^{s_2} I_\Omega^\alpha(f,s)\, e^{-\mu s}\, ds. \qquad (20)$$

Notice that $\tilde{\Omega}$ need not be equal to $\Omega \times (s_1,s_2)$ as Ω_s may vary in $s > 0$. By straightforward computation and the Plancherel Theorem we have

$$I_\Omega^\alpha(f,s) = -((-\Delta)^\alpha u_f^\alpha(\cdot,s), 1_\Omega)_{\mathrm{L}_2(\mathbb{R}^2)} = -(\boldsymbol{\omega} \mapsto \|\boldsymbol{\omega}\|^{2\alpha}\hat{u}_f^\alpha(\boldsymbol{\omega},s), \widehat{1_\Omega})_{\mathrm{L}_2(\mathbb{R}^2)}$$

$$= (\boldsymbol{\omega} \mapsto \frac{1}{\sqrt{1+(\gamma\|\boldsymbol{\omega}\|)^{2k}}}\hat{f}(\boldsymbol{\omega}), \boldsymbol{\omega} \mapsto \frac{-\|\boldsymbol{\omega}\|^{2\alpha}e^{-s\|\boldsymbol{\omega}\|^{2\alpha}}}{\sqrt{1+(\gamma\|\boldsymbol{\omega}\|)^{2k}}}\widehat{1_\Omega}(\boldsymbol{\omega}))_{\mathrm{L}_2(\mathbb{R}^2\,;\,(1+\gamma\|\boldsymbol{\omega}\|^{2k})\,d\boldsymbol{\omega})}$$

$$= (\phi_{\Omega,k,\gamma}^{\alpha,s}, f)_{\mathbb{H}_\gamma^{k,2}(\mathbb{R}^2)}$$

$$\qquad (21)$$

---

[6] In case $\Omega_s = \Omega$, i.e. Ω_s does not change over scale, and $s_0 = 0$ and $s_1 \to \infty$ we obtain $\psi_{\Omega,k}^{\alpha,\mu} = \frac{1}{\mu}\mathcal{L}[s \mapsto \phi_{\Omega_s,k}^{\alpha,s}](\mu)$, where $\mathcal{L}$ denotes the well-known Laplace transform.

with $f \in \mathbb{L}_2(\mathbb{R}^2)$, $\alpha \in (0,1]$ and flux-kernel $\phi_{\Omega,k,\gamma}^{\alpha,s} = \mathcal{F}^{-1}[\hat{\phi}_{\Omega,k,\gamma}^{\alpha,s}] = \mathcal{F}^{-1}[\omega \mapsto \frac{-\|\omega\|^{2\alpha}e^{-s\|\omega\|^{2\alpha}}}{\sqrt{1+(\gamma\|\omega\|)^{2k}}}\widehat{1_\Omega}(\omega)]$. Notice that the substitution $k = 0$ in equality (21) yields $I_\Omega^\alpha(f,s) = (\phi_{\Omega,0}^{\alpha,s}, f)_{\mathbb{L}_2(\mathbb{R}^2)}$ only for $s > 0$. In case $s = 0$, where $u_f^\alpha(\cdot,0) = f$, we may write $I_\Omega^\alpha(f,0) = (\phi_{\Omega,k,\gamma}^{\alpha,0}, f)_{\mathbb{H}_\gamma^{k,2}(\mathbb{R}^2)}$ for $k \geq 2$. For $k = 0$ the inner product is not defined. It now follows that $I_\Omega^{\alpha,\mu}(f) = (\psi_{\Omega,k}^{\alpha,\mu}, f)_{\mathbb{H}_\gamma^{k,2}(\mathbb{R}^2)}$, where the netto flux kernel needed to compute $I_\Omega^{\alpha,\mu}(f)$ is simply given by $\psi_{\Omega,k}^{\alpha,\mu} = \frac{1}{\mu}\int_{s_0}^{s_1} \phi_{\Omega_s,k}^{\alpha,s}e^{-\mu s}ds$.

Finally we notice that $\phi_{\Omega_s,k,\gamma}^{\alpha,0} = \kappa_k * \phi_{\Omega,0}^{\alpha,s}$, where the flux-kernel $\phi_{\Omega_s,0}^{\alpha,s}$ is given by

$$\phi_{\Omega_s,0}^{\alpha,s} = \frac{\partial}{\partial s}K_s^\alpha * 1_\Omega = (\mathrm{div}\mathbf{F}_\alpha K_s^\alpha) * 1_{\Omega_s}. \tag{22}$$

The case where Ω_s equals an ellips: In case of the disk $\Omega_s = B_{0,a}$ there are two reasonable options, either the flux kernel is evaluated via the Fourier domain, which yields:

$$\phi_{B_{0,a},0}^{\alpha,s}(\mathbf{x}) = -a\int_0^\infty \rho^{2\alpha}J_1\left(\frac{\rho}{a}\right)J_0(\rho r)e^{-s\rho^{2\alpha}}\,d\rho, \qquad r = \|\mathbf{x}\|,$$

where we notice that $\mathcal{F}1_\Omega(\omega) = \frac{a J_1\left(\frac{\rho}{a}\right)}{\rho}$, $\|\omega\| = \rho$, or by means of (18), (19). In case $\alpha = 1$ we get

$$\phi_{\Omega,0}^{1,s}(\mathbf{y}) = \int_{\partial\Omega} \frac{\partial K_s^1(\mathbf{x}-\mathbf{y})}{\partial r}d\sigma_\mathbf{x}$$
$$= a\int_0^{2\pi}\left\{\cos\phi\left(\frac{y_1-a\cos\phi}{8\pi s^2}\right) + \sin\phi\left(\frac{y_2-a\sin\phi}{8\pi s^2}\right)\right\}e^{\frac{-(a\cos\phi-y_1)^2-(a\sin\phi-y_2)^2}{4s}}d\phi,$$

which is easily numerically approximated. Finally, we notice that the ellips-case $\Omega_s = E_{\theta(s),\lambda(s),a(s)} = \{\mathbf{x} \in \mathbb{R}^2 \mid \|L_{\lambda(s)}^{-1}R_{\theta(s)}^{-1}\mathbf{x}\|^2 = (a(s))^2\}$, $\theta(s) \in [0,2\pi)$, $\lambda(s) > 0$, $a(s) > 0$, recall (3), directly follows from the disk case by means of

$$\phi_{\Omega_s=E_{\theta(s),\lambda(s),a(s)},k}^{\alpha,s}(\mathbf{x}) = \phi_{B_{0,a},k}^{\alpha,s}(L_{\lambda(s)}^{-1}R_{\theta(s)}^{-1}\mathbf{x}), \qquad \mathbf{x} \in \mathbb{R}^d, s > 0.$$

6 Conclusion

The common (non)-linear reconstruction frameworks follow an Euler Lagrange minimization. If the Lagrangian (prior) is a norm induced by an inner product of a Hilbert space this Euler Lagrange minimization boils down to a simple orthogonal projection within the corresponding Hilbert space. This basic observation has been overlooked in image analysis for the cases where the Lagrangian equals a norm of Sobolev type resulting in iterative (non-linear) numerical methods, where we provide exact solutions. By means of Gelfand triples we consider two extreme cases (standard isotropic Sobolev spaces) and trajectory spaces. Although the reconstruction algorithm is slightly simpler for the trajectory space case, best results are obtained by minimizing isotropic Sobolev norms of low order, taking into account that in both cases smoothness of the reconstruction is tuned by a positive parameter. In our opinion a linear reconstruction should at least capture the topology (deep structure) of the scale space of the original image. Therefore we only consider linear features inspired by the deep structure of images. Besides top-points, the well-known scale space singularities, we introduce the concept of flux-features. They describe the transport of grey-value particles between extremal paths that lead to singular points in scale space. By including these features we provide another tool to minimize spurious top-points in the reconstruction image.

References

1. Duits, R., Florack, L., de Graaf, J., ter Haar Romeny, B.: On the axioms of scale space theory. Journal of Mathematical Imaging and Vision 20 (2004) 267298
2. Duits, R., Duits, M., van Almsick, M.: Invertible orientation scores as an application of generalized wavelet theory. Technical report, TUE, Eindhoven (2004) Technical Report 04-04, Biomedical Image and Analysis, Department of Biomedical Engineering, Eindhoven University of Technology.
3. Loog, M., Duistermaat, J.J., Florack, L.M.J.: On the behavior of spatial critical points under Gaussian blurring. a folklore theorem and scale-space constraints. [14] 183192
4. Kuijper, A., Florack, L.M.J.: Hierarchical pre-segmentation without prior knowledge. In: Proceedings of the 8th International Conference on Computer Vision (Vancouver, Canada, July 9 12, 2001), IEEE Computer Society Press (2001) 487493
5. Balmachnova, E., Florack, L., Platel, B., Kanters, F., ter Haar Romeny, B.: Stability of top-points in scale space. (Proceedings 5th Scale Space conference 2005) 6272
6. Felsberg, M., Duits, R., Florack, L.: The monogenic scale space on a bounded domain and its applications. Proceedings Scale Space Conference, Isle of Skye, UK. (2003) 209224
7. Nielsen, M., Lillholm, M.: What do features tell about images? [14] 3950
8. Lillholm, M., Nielsen, M., Griffin, L.D.: Feature-based image analysis. International Journal of Computer Vision 52 (2003) 7395
9. Kanters, B. Platel, L.M.J. Florack and B.M. ter Haar Romeny, F.: Image reconstruction from multiscale critical points. In Griffin, L., Lillholm, M., eds.: Scale Space Methods in Computer Vision, 4th International Conference, Scale Space 2003, Isle of Skye, UK, Springer (2003) 464478
10. Yosida, K.: Functional Analysis. Springer Verlag, Berlin, Heidelberg, New York (1980)
11. Robinson, D.: Elliptic Operators and Lie groups. Clarendon Press, Oxford, New York, Tokyo (1991)
12. Janssen, B., Kanters, F., Duits, R., Florack, L.M.J., ter Haar Romeny, B.M.: A linear image reconstruction framework based on sobolev type inner products. (To Appear in Proc. of the Scale Space Conference 2005)
13. Kanters, F., Lillholm, M., Duits, R., Janssen, B., Platel, B., Florack, L.M.J.: Image reconstruction from multiscale top points. (To appear at Proceedings 5th Scale Space Conference 2005)
14. Kerckhove, M., ed.: Scale-Space and Morphology in Computer Vision: Proceedings of the Third International Conference, Scale-Space 2001, Vancouver, Canada. Volume 2106 of Lecture Notes in Computer Science. Springer-Verlag, Berlin (2001)

A   The Reproducing Kernels $R^2_{k,\gamma}$ of the Sobolev Spaces $\mathbb{H}^{k,2}_\gamma(\mathbb{R}^2)$, $k > 1$.

In this section we compute the reproducing kernels $R^2_{k,\gamma}$ of the Sobolev spaces $\mathbb{H}^{k,2}_\gamma(\mathbb{R}^2)$, $k > 1$. They are needed in our reconstruction algorithms to relate $\mathbb{L}_2$-features to the Sobolev features on $\mathbb{H}^{k,2}_\gamma(\mathbb{R}^2)$, $k > 1$. Due to numerical limitations (sampling) the cases which are most practically relevant are $k = 0, 1, 2, 3, 4$. The (isotropic) functions $\mathbf{x} \mapsto R^2_{k,\gamma}(\mathbf{x})$, which are illustrated in figure 3 , are bounded iff $k > 1$, which coincides with the fact that $\mathbb{H}^{k,2}_\gamma(\mathbb{R}^2)$ is a functional Hilbert space iff $k > 1$.

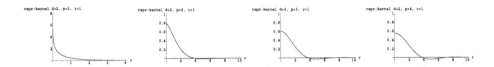

Fig. 3. Plots of the graphs of the functions $\|\mathbf{x}\| \mapsto R^2_{k,\gamma}(\mathbf{x})$, for $k = 1, 2, 3, 4$

Theorem 4. *The space $\mathbb{H}^{k,2}_\gamma(\mathbb{R}^d)$ is a reproducing kernel space iff $k > d/2$. The reproducing kernel (i.e. the Riesz-representant of the continuous point evaluation, $F(\boldsymbol{a}) = (R^d_{\gamma,k,a}, F)_{\mathbb{H}^{k,2}_\gamma(\mathbb{R}^d)})$ is then given by*

$$R^d_{\gamma,k,a}(\boldsymbol{x}) = \frac{1}{2\pi\gamma^{2k}}\mathcal{F}^{-1}\Big(\boldsymbol{\omega} \mapsto e^{i\boldsymbol{\omega}\cdot\boldsymbol{a}}\frac{1}{\gamma^{-2k}+\|\boldsymbol{\omega}\|^{2k}}\Big)(\boldsymbol{x})$$
$$= r^{-\frac{d-2}{2}}\frac{1}{2\pi}\int\limits_0^\infty \rho^{\frac{d}{2}} J_{\frac{d-2}{2}}(\rho r)\frac{1}{1+\gamma^{2k}\rho^{2k}}\,d\rho \ , \tag{23}$$

where $r = \|\boldsymbol{x} - \boldsymbol{a}\| > 0$, $\rho = \|\boldsymbol{\omega}\|$ and satisfies the following recursion: $R^d_{\gamma,2k,a} =$
$\frac{1}{2}\Big(R^d_{e^{\frac{i\pi}{4k}}\gamma,k,a} + R^d_{e^{\frac{-i\pi}{4k}}\gamma,k,a}\Big).$ *In case [7] $d = 2$ we have* $R^{d=2}_{\gamma,k,a}(\boldsymbol{x})$
$= \frac{1}{2\pi\gamma^2}G^{k+1,0}_{0,2k}\Big(\frac{\rho^{2k}}{\gamma^{2k}k^k} \mid \boldsymbol{a}_k\Big),$ *where $\boldsymbol{a}_k = \{a_{kj}\}^{2k}_{j=1} \in \mathbb{Q}^{2k}$ is given by $a_{kj} = \frac{j-1}{k}$*
for $1 \le j \le k$, $a_{k(k+1)} = \frac{k-1}{k}$ and $a_{kj} = a_{k(j-k-1)}$ for $k + 2 \le j \le 2k$.
In particular we have $R^{d=2}_{\gamma,k=1,a}(\boldsymbol{x}) = \frac{1}{2\pi\gamma^2}K_0\Big(\frac{r}{\gamma}\Big)$ and $R^{d=2}_{\gamma,k=2,a}(\boldsymbol{x}) = -\frac{1}{2\pi\gamma^2}\mathrm{kei}_0(r/\gamma)$,
with $r = \|\boldsymbol{x} - \boldsymbol{a}\|$

---

[7] Where we notice that J_μ is a Bessel function (first kind) of order μ and K_0 equals the well-known BesselK-function of order 0 and the Kelvin function $\mathrm{kei}_0(v) =$ $\frac{1}{2i}\Big(K_0\Big(e^{\frac{+i\pi}{4}}v\Big) - K_0\Big(e^{\frac{-i\pi}{4}}v\Big)\Big)$ and $G^{k+1,0}_{0,2k}$ denotes a Meyer-G function.

A Riemannian Framework for the Processing of Tensor-Valued Images

Pierre Fillard, Vincent Arsigny, Nicholas Ayache, and Xavier Pennec

INRIA Sophia Antipolis - Epidaure Project,
2004 Route des Lucioles BP 93,
06902 Sophia Antipolis Cedex, France
{Pierre.Fillard, Vincent.Arsigny, Nicholas.Ayache,
Xavier.Pennec}@Sophia.Inria.fr

Abstract. In this paper, we present a novel framework to carry out computations on tensors, i.e. symmetric positive definite matrices. We endow the space of tensors with an affine-invariant Riemannian metric, which leads to strong theoretical properties: The space of positive definite symmetric matrices is replaced by a regular and geodesically complete manifold without boundaries. Thus, tensors with non-positive eigenvalues are at an infinite distance of any positive definite matrix. Moreover, the tools of differential geometry apply and we generalize to tensors numerous algorithms that were reserved to vector spaces. The application of this framework to the processing of diffusion tensor images shows very promising results. We apply this framework to the processing of structure tensor images and show that it could help to extract low-level features thanks to the affine-invariance of our metric. However, the same affine-invariance causes the whole framework to be noise sensitive and we believe that the choice of a more adapted metric could significantly improve the robustness of the result.

1 Introduction

Symmetric positive definite matrices, or tensors, are widely used in image processing. They can either characterize the diffusion of water molecules as in diffusion tensor imaging (DTI) [1], or reveal structural information of an image (structure tensor) [2,3]. In this last application, tensors are used to detect singularities such as edges or corners in images. The structure tensor is classically obtained by a Gaussian smoothing of the tensor product of the gradient, or with a non-linear filtering as in [4], thus being naturally robust to noise. However, noisy images require a large amount of regularization to obtain a smooth structure tensor field in order to avoid being overwhelmed by outliers in features detection. By contrast, too much smoothing would completely wipe out small structures in images. To address this problem, one would prefer to preserve small structures in images by estimating structure tensors with a little smoothing and to regularize the noisy tensor field itself. This implies to be able to filter tensor images, and more generally to carry out computations with tensors.

O.F. Olsen et al. (Eds.): DSSCV 2005, LNCS 3753, pp. 112–123, 2005.

Working with tensors is arduous since the underlying space is a manifold that is not a vector space. While convex operations remain stable on the tensor space (e.g. the mean of a set of tensors is a tensor), one can quickly go out of the Euclidean boundaries with non-convex operations like a gradient descent. A critical consequence is that matrices with null or negative eigenvalues may appear and are problematic for most applications.

In this paper, we propose to apply a recently proposed Riemannian framework for tensors to the processing of structure tensor images. The limitations of the standard Euclidean calculus are completely overcome and the tensor space is replaced by a manifold with a regular structure. We show that it leads to very strong theoretical properties, such as the existence and uniqueness of the mean, and that most of the statistical tools as well as the algorithms that were until now reserved to vector space can be extended to tensors. The rest of the paper is organized as follows. In Sec. 2 we summarize the Riemannian framework for tensors. In Sec. 3, we extend the computations of classical image processing operators to tensors as well as more complex operations and we provide intrinsic numerical schemes for their implementation. In Sec. 4, we apply these tools on a structure tensor image. In particular, we perform an anisotropic smoothing and discuss about the potentiality of the method on this type of tensors.

2   A Riemannian Framework for Tensor Calculus

Much of the literature addresses tensor computing problems in the context of DTI regularization. In DTI, the Brownian motion of water is estimated by a MRI scanner at each position of the brain. This stochastic motion is characterized by its covariance matrix, which is called a diffusion tensor. Depending on the amount and direction of water diffusion, the tensor can be either cigar-shaped (region where the diffusion is restricted by oriented tissues), or a sphere (regions with free diffusion). As the MRI signal is corrupted with noise during acquisition, the resulting tensor field has to be filtered. To do so, the spectral decomposition of tensors is often exploited: [5] only processes the major eigenvector (eigenvector corresponding to the largest eigenvalue), leading to simple computations but a dramatical loss of information, while [6] independently regularizes the orthogonal matrices of eigenvectors and the eigenvalues. As the spectral decomposition is not unique, a preprocess step, where the eigenvectors are reoriented, is needed and is not trivial. More recently, differential geometric approaches have been developed to generalize the PCA to tensor data [7], for statistical segmentation of tensor images [8], for computing a geometric mean and an intrinsic anisotropy index [9], or as the basis of a full framework for Riemannian tensor calculus [10]. In this last work, we endow the space of tensors with an affine-invariant Riemannian metric to obtain results that are independent of the choice of the spatial coordinate system. Differential geometry tools allow to manipulate tensors while insuring the positive definiteness of the result. In this section, we present an overview of the affine-invariant metric for tensors.

2.1   An Affine-Invariant Riemannian Metric

We showed in [11] that choosing a Riemannian metric provides a powerful framework to generalize statistics and other operations to manifolds. We applied this concept to tensors and showed in [10] that it leads to interesting properties such as the existence and uniqueness of the (geometric) mean or the existence and uniqueness of the geodesic between two tensors. A complete description of the features of this framework can be found in [10] and is summarized below.

Let Σ be a point of the tensor space $Sym_+^*(n)$. The action of the linear group GL_n on $Sym_+^*(n)$ is:

$$\forall A \in GL_n, A \star \Sigma = A\Sigma A^T$$

Let us consider the standard matrix scalar product at the tangent space at identity $T_{I_d}M$:

$$\langle W_1|W_2 \rangle_{Id} \overset{def}{=} \mathrm{Tr}\left(W_1 W_2^T \right),$$

where W_1 and W_2 are elements of $T_{I_d}M$. As tangent spaces are vectorial spaces, W_1 and W_2 are called tangent vectors. They are simple symmetric matrix since the tensor space is a manifold included in the space of symmetric matrices $Sym(n)$.

An affine-invariant metric must verify: $< W_1|W_2 >_\Sigma = < A \star W_1|A \star W_2 >_{A \star \Sigma}$ for all $A \in GL_n$. This is verified in particular for $A = \Sigma^{-1/2}$, which allows us to write the scalar product at any point Σ from the product at $T_{I_d}M$:

$$\langle W_1|W_2 \rangle_\Sigma = \left\langle \Sigma^{-\frac{1}{2}} \star W_1 | \Sigma^{-\frac{1}{2}} \star W_2 \right\rangle_{Id} \tag{1}$$

$$= \mathrm{Tr}\left(\Sigma^{-\frac{1}{2}} W_1 \Sigma^{-1} W_2 \Sigma^{-\frac{1}{2}} \right) \tag{2}$$

Eq. 1 is an affine-invariant Riemannian metric. Actually, we only need the invariance by the linear group to obtain an affine-invariance since the translation is not taken into account in our applications (tensors are independent of their position on a grid).

As a general property on Riemannian manifolds, geodesics realize a local diffeomorphism, called the exponential map, from the tangent space at any point Σ to the manifold itself. This allows us to locally identify points of the manifold with tangent vectors. With the invariant metric of Eq. 1, we can show that this diffeomorphism is moreover global and is simply expressed with the matrix exponential:

$$\forall W \in T_\Sigma M, \quad \exp_\Sigma(W) = \Sigma^{\frac{1}{2}} \exp\left(\Sigma^{-\frac{1}{2}} W \Sigma^{-\frac{1}{2}} \right) \Sigma^{\frac{1}{2}} \tag{3}$$

$\exp_\Sigma(W)$ can be seen as the point of the manifold reached by the geodesic starting at Σ, with tangent vector W in a unit time step. Conversely, we can uniquely define the inverse mapping, the logarithmic map:

$$\log_\Sigma(\Lambda) = \Sigma^{\frac{1}{2}} \log\left(\Sigma^{-\frac{1}{2}} \Lambda \Sigma^{-\frac{1}{2}} \right) \Sigma^{\frac{1}{2}}. \tag{4}$$

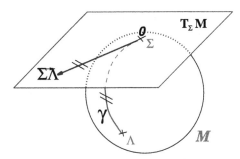

Fig. 1. Development of the geodesic γ linking Σ to Λ onto the tangent space $T_\Sigma M$. The geodesics starting at Σ are straight lines in $T_\Sigma M$ and the distance along them is conserved.

These diffeomorphisms turn any two points Σ and Λ of the manifold into the tangent vector $\overrightarrow{\Sigma\Lambda}$ such that the geodesic starting at Σ and with tangent vector $\overrightarrow{\Sigma\Lambda}$ reaches the point Λ in a unit step (Fig. 1).

These two diffeomorphisms are the key to the numerical implementation and generalization to manifolds of numerous algorithms that work on a vector space. Table 1 summarizes the basic operations of vector spaces and their Riemannian counterparts.

Geodesic marching: An important operator for solving partial differential equations (PDEs) is the gradient descent. It consists in following the opposite direction of the gradient of a criterion C we want to minimize for a short time step ε. In the tensor case, the Euclidean gradient descent scheme $\Sigma_{t+1} = \Sigma_t - \varepsilon \nabla C$ could easily lead out of the boundaries of the space and non-positive matrices may appear. The Euclidean scheme is advantageously replaced by the *geodesic marching scheme*: we follow the geodesic starting at Σ_t, with tangent vector $-\nabla C$ for a short time step: $\Sigma_{t+1} = \exp_{\Sigma_t}(-\varepsilon \nabla C)$. The exponential map insures that we always stay on the manifold: the result is guaranteed to be positive definite.

Table 1. Re-interpretation of the basic operations of vector spaces to Riemannian manifolds

Operation	Vector space	Riemannian manifold
Subtraction	$\overrightarrow{\Sigma\Lambda} = \Lambda - \Sigma$	$\overrightarrow{\Sigma\Lambda} = \log_\Sigma(\Lambda)$
Addition	$\Lambda = \Sigma + \overrightarrow{\Sigma\Lambda}$	$\Lambda = \exp_\Sigma(\overrightarrow{\Sigma\Lambda})$
Distance	$dist(\Sigma, \Lambda) = \|\overrightarrow{\Sigma\Lambda}\|$	$dist(\Sigma, \Lambda) = \|\overrightarrow{\Sigma\Lambda}\|_\Sigma$
Mean value	$\sum_i \overrightarrow{\bar{\Sigma}\Sigma_i} = 0$	$\sum_i \log_{\bar{\Sigma}}(\Sigma_i) = 0$
Gradient descent	$\Sigma_{t+\varepsilon} = \Sigma_t - \varepsilon \nabla C(\Sigma_t)$	$\Sigma_{t+\varepsilon} = \exp_{\Sigma_t}(-\varepsilon \nabla C(\Sigma_t))$
Linear (geodesic) interpolation	$\Sigma(t) = \Sigma_1 + t\,\overrightarrow{\Sigma_1\Sigma_2}$	$\Sigma(t) = \exp_{\Sigma_1}(t\,\overrightarrow{\Sigma_1\Sigma_2})$

In conclusion, the Riemannian framework gives a powerful alternative to the standard Euclidean calculus: classical operators are easily translated to tensors thanks to the combination of the logarithm and exponential maps and complex algorithms can be rewritten using these two diffeomorphisms. In the next section, we show that the classical image processing operators like gradient and Laplacian can be adapted to the Riemannian framework without much effort. More interestingly, we are able to achieve complex operations like anisotropic filtering directly on tensors, which was not possible with the standard Euclidean calculus.

3 Applications

In this section, we reinterpret various image processing operators in the Riemannian framework. First, we rewrite two classical operators of image processing (gradient and Laplacian) to tensor images, and second we describe more complex operations like multi-linear interpolation and anisotropic filtering.

3.1 Classical Image Processing Operators

In the following, we show that the gradient and Laplacian of a tensor field are easily expressed in our exponential chart, and we provide a practical numerical implementation of both operators.

Spatial Gradient of a Tensor Field. Basically, for a n-dimensional vector field $F(x)$ defined over $\mathbb{R}^d$, the spatial gradient in an orthonormal basis is: $\nabla F = [\partial_{x_1} F, \ldots, \partial_{x_d} F]^T$, where $\partial_{x_i} F$ is the directional derivative of F in the direction x_i. It can be approximated using a finite difference scheme: $\partial_{x_i} F(x) = (F(x + x_i) - F(x - x_i))/(2\|x_i\|)$.

For a tensor-valued image $\Sigma(x)$, we can proceed similarly except that the directional derivatives $\partial_{x_i}\Sigma$ are now tangent vectors of $T_{\Sigma(x)}M$. They can be approximated like above using finite differences in our exponential chart:

$$\partial_{x_i}\Sigma(x) \simeq \left(\overrightarrow{\Sigma(x)\Sigma(x + x_i)} - \overrightarrow{\Sigma(x)\Sigma(x - x_i)}\right)/(2\|x_i\|)$$

$$= \left(\log_{\Sigma(x)}\left(\Sigma(x + x_i)\right) - \log_{\Sigma(x)}\left(\Sigma(x - x_i)\right)\right)/(2\|x_i\|).$$

One must be careful to take the metric at point $\Sigma(x)$ into account when computing the norm of the gradient: $\|\nabla\Sigma(x)\|^2_{\Sigma(x)} = \sum_{i=1}^{d} \|\partial_{x_i}\Sigma(x)\|^2_{\Sigma(x)}$. Fig. 2 shows the difference between the Euclidean and Riemannian gradients. The Euclidean gradient (Fig. 2 middle) gives much more importance to tensors with large coefficients, and consequently its norm has higher values along the boundaries with the ventricles (a region characterized by large tensors), and lower values elsewhere. By contrast, the affine-invariant metric (Fig. 2 right) gives as much importance to variations of small tensors as to variations of large matrices. Consequently, the norm the Riemannian gradient is more regular.

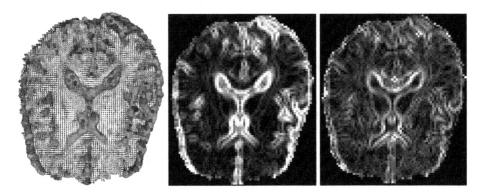

Fig. 2. Comparison of the norm of the Euclidean and Riemannian gradients of a tensor image. Left: A slice of a DTI tensor image. The color codes for the major eigenvectors of tensors: Red: left-right oriented tensor, blue: inferior-superior oriented tensor, green: posterior-anterior oriented tensor. Middle: Norm of the Euclidean gradient. Right: Norm of the Riemannian gradient. Remark how the Riemannian norm is more regular than the Euclidean norm.

Laplacian of a Tensor Field. For the numerical implementation of the Laplacian, one needs the second order derivatives. As for the gradient, we use the finite difference scheme to approximate the 2nd order derivative on a discrete grid: $\partial^2_{x_i} F(x) \simeq (F(x + x_i) - 2F(x) + F(x - x_i) / \|x_i\|^2$.
We proved in [10] that :

$$\partial^2_{x_i} \Sigma(x) = \left(\overrightarrow{\Sigma(x)\Sigma(x + x_i)} + \overrightarrow{\Sigma(x)\Sigma(x - x_i)} \right) / \|x_i\|^2$$

is a forth order approximation of the 2nd order directional derivative of $\Sigma(x)$ in the direction x_i. Finally, the manifold Laplacian (Laplace-Beltrami operator) of a tensor field is simply: $\Delta\Sigma(x) = \sum_{i=1}^d \partial^2_{x_i} \Sigma(x)$.

3.2   Interpolation and Filtering of Tensor Fields

Interpolation. Interpolation is one of the most important task in image processing. A simple operation is the interpolation between two tensors Σ_1 and Σ_2. The classical Euclidean calculus gives us the formulation: $\Sigma(t) = (1-t)\Sigma_1 + t\Sigma_2$. With our Riemannian framework, it consists in following the geodesic joining the two tensors: $\Sigma(t) = \exp_{\Sigma_1}(t\overrightarrow{\Sigma_1\Sigma_2})$.

For multi-linear interpolation, e.g. bi or trilinear interpolation on a regular 2D or 3D grid, the formulation is not trivial. One has to go through the computation of a weighted mean with classical bi- or trilinear coefficients calculated on a grid. With the standard Euclidean framework, the weighted mean of a set of tensors is: $\Sigma = (\sum_{i=1}^N \omega_i \Sigma_i)/\sum_{i=1}^N \omega_i$. In our Riemannian framework, one needs to go back to the Frechet definition of the mean, i.e. the minimum (if it exists) of the square distance to each tensor:

$$\bar{\Sigma} = \min_{\Sigma} \sum_{i=1}^{N} \text{dist}^2 \left(\Sigma, \Sigma_i \right)$$

In the case of the tensor space provided with the affine-invariant metric, the manifold has a non-positive curvature, so that the mean exists and is unique. However, because of the curvature, the Frechet formulation does not have an explicit solution. Instead, one has to minimize it through a Newton gradient descent and the estimation of the mean at time $t+1$ is given by:

$$\bar{\Sigma}_{t+1} = \exp_{\bar{\Sigma}_t} \left(\frac{\sum_{i=1}^{N} w_i \log_{\bar{\Sigma}_t}(\Sigma_i)}{\sum_{i=1}^{N} w_i} \right)$$

which consists in expressing each tensor in the tangent space at the current estimation of the mean with the logarithmic map, then going back to the manifold with the exponential map, and to reiterate the process. The existence and uniqueness of the mean guarantees the process to converge. In practice, the convergence of the iterative process is geometric and the mean value is reached after 5 to 10 iterations. In [10], we propose an extension of several statistical operations to tensors.

Anisotropic Filtering. In practice, we would like to filter a tensor image within homogeneous regions but not across the boundaries. The basic idea introduced by [12] is to penalize the smoothing in the directions where the magnitude of the gradient is high. This can be achieved through the minimization of the ϕ-functional:

$$C(\Sigma) = \frac{1}{2} \int_{\Omega} \phi \left(\|\nabla \Sigma(x)\|_{\Sigma(x)} \right) dx. \tag{5}$$

By choosing an adequate ϕ-function, one can give to the regularization an isotropic or anisotropic behavior [13]. In our experiments, we use $\phi(s) = 2\sqrt{1 + s^2/\kappa^2} - 2$, as proposed in [5]. The main difference with a classical Euclidean calculation is that we have to take the curvature into account by using the Laplace-Beltrami operator, and by expressing directional derivatives in the correct tangent space. After differentiation of Eq. 5, one obtains :

$$\nabla C(\Sigma) = -\frac{\phi(\|\nabla \Sigma\|_{\Sigma(x)})}{\|\nabla \Sigma\|_{\Sigma(x)}} \Delta \Sigma - \sum_{i=1}^{d} \partial_{x_i} \phi(\|\nabla \Sigma\|_{\Sigma(x)}) \partial_{x_i} \Sigma$$

Thanks to the numerical scheme of the gradient and Laplacian operators (Sec. 3.1) combined with the geodesic marching, we are able to perform a gradient descent to minimize criterion (5):

$$\Sigma_{t+1}(x) = \exp_{\Sigma_t(x)} \left(-\varepsilon \nabla C \left(\Sigma_t(x) \right) \right) \tag{6}$$

Fig. 3 shows the effect of the anisotropic regularization on a slice of DTI. The parameters for the regularization are: $\kappa = 0.05$, $\varepsilon = 0.1$ and 100 iterations (total diffusion time: 10). The boundaries with the ventricles are conserved while the interior is correctly regularized. Moreover, at the top of the ventricles lies a fiber tract delimited with cigar-shaped tensors, which are also very well preserved.

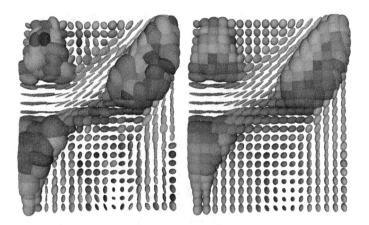

Fig. 3. Anisotropic regularization of a slice of DTI. Parameters: $\kappa = 0.05$, $\varepsilon = 0.1$, iterations: 100 (diffusion time = 10). Left: Raw data. Right: Anisotropic filtering in the Riemannian framework. The boundary of the ventricles (region with large tensors) is well preserved. Remark that the left-right oriented tensors (in red) that are delineating a fiber tract are also conserved. The color code is the same as in Fig. 2.

4   Applications to Structure Tensor Images

The structure tensor has become a useful tool for the analysis of features in images. It is used in edges and corners detection [2], texture analysis [14,15], filtering [16], and even medical image registration [17]. We show in this section how to apply our previously presented Riemannian framework to process structure tensor-valued images. In particular, we perform an anisotropic smoothing of the structure tensor field to enhance it, which could improve the quality of features detection.

4.1   The Structure Tensor

Let I be an image defined on a domain of $\mathbb{R}^d$. The structure tensor is based on the gradient of I: $\nabla I = (\partial_1 I, \ldots, \partial_d I)^T$, where each directional derivative $\partial_i I$ can be computed with a finite difference scheme or by filtering with a first order derivative of a Gaussian. The structure tensor S_σ can be defined as:

$$S_\sigma = G_\sigma * \left(\nabla I \nabla I^T \right)$$

with G_σ being a Gaussian of standard deviation σ. The variance σ controls the smoothness of the resulting tensor field. The noisier the image is, the higher σ must be to obtain a smooth field, but small structures may be wiped out. By contrast, smaller values of σ can help to extract low level features in images, but the resulting structure tensor image may be noisy. Consequently, one would like to perform an anisotropic filtering of the structure tensor field obtained with a low σ, in order to regularize homogeneous regions while preserving the boundaries with low-level features. In the following, we first compute the Riemannian

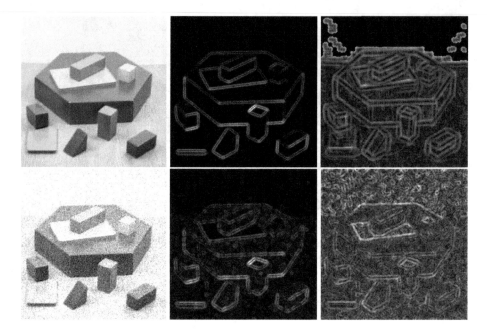

Fig. 4. Euclidean gradient versus Riemannian gradient. Top row: Original image (left), norm of the Euclidean (middle) and Riemannian (right) gradients. Bottom row: Noisy image (a Gaussian noise of variance 0.01 was added) (left), norm of the Euclidean (middle) and Riemannian (right) gradients.

gradient of a structure tensor image and compare it to the classical Euclidean gradient. Then, we perform an anisotropic filtering and discuss about the results.

4.2   Gradient of a Structure Tensor Image

Following the numerical scheme of Sec. 3.1, we computed the gradient norm of a structure tensor image obtained with a σ of 1.0 (Fig. 4 left is the original image). Then, we compared it to the Euclidean gradient. We also added noise in the original image to evaluate the robustness of both gradients. Results of comparisons are shown in Fig. 4.

First, we can notice that with the affine-invariant metric, outliers appear in the image background (Fig. 4 top right). This is intensified when adding noise (Fig. 4 bottom right): we see that the background is made with artefacts due to variations of small tensors that result from noise. Indeed, small tensors have as much importance as large ones because of the affine-invariance of the metric. Consequently, the Riemannian gradient of a variation of small tensors or large tensors will be identical. By contrast, the Euclidean gradient remains much less sensitive to tensors with small coefficients, and consequently only the main features are revealed (Fig. 4 bottom right and left).

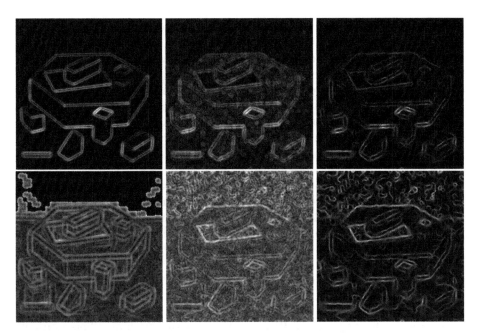

Fig. 5. Anisotropic filtering of a noisy structure tensor image. Diffusion parameters: $\kappa = 0.02$, $\varepsilon = 0.1$ and 500 iterations. Top row: From left to right: Original Euclidean gradient, Euclidean gradient with noise, Euclidean gradient after regularization. Bottom row: From left to right: Original Riemannian gradient, Riemannian gradient with noise, Riemannian gradient after regularization.

Second, details that are not present in the Euclidean norm appear in the Riemannian gradient: this is the case, for example, of low-contrasted edges in the original image. This also results from the affine-invariance of the metric.

To conclude, the Riemannian framework can reveal lower structural information such as low contrasted edges but is highly sensitive to small variation in the tensor image, and thus suffers from a lack of robustness.

Let us now investigate how the anisotropic filtering scheme can restore the noisy structure tensor image.

4.3   Anisotropic Filtering of a Structure Tensor Image

We applied the anisotropic filtering scheme of Sec. 3.2 on the noisy structure tensor image of Fig. 4 bottom left. We used the following parameters: $\kappa = 0.02$, $\varepsilon = 0.1$ and 500 iterations (total diffusion time: 50). Results are presented in Fig. 5.

The affine-invariance causes the variations of small tensors to be highly contrasted in the norm of the Riemannian gradient and thus to be preserved during the filtering process. Figures 5 bottom illustrate this behavior: the top of the original noisy image (middle image) is filled with artefacts that were preserved during the smoothing (right image). Taking the Euclidean norm (Fig. 5 top right) removes the artefacts in the image background. Homogeneous regions are smoother while edges are correctly conserved. However, some artefacts in the background that were expected to disappear are still present and the strength of most of the relevant edges is lower than in the affine-invariant case.

In conclusion, the affine-invariant metric that is well suited for DTI, or more generally for covariance matrices, seems not to be applicable directly to structure tensor images. The affine-invariance gives an identical role to small tensors versus large ones. Thus, while it allows to extract low-level features, it suffers from a lack of robustness.

However, the Riemannian framework we present in this paper is "parameterized" by the metric. The choice of the metric is crucial and determines the properties of the framework. The affine-invariance does not seem to be the best choice for structure tensor images, but a more adapted metric could significantly improve the results.

5   Discussion

We present in this paper a full Riemannian framework with an affine-invariant metric that allows to perform computations on tensors while insuring the result to be positive definite, which is often a critical issue as in DTI. While this framework is perfectly adapted to the processing of tensors representing covariance matrices, the affine-invariant metric does not appear to be the best suited choice for the processing of structure tensor images. In this case, the limitation comes from the affine-invariance which gives an identical influence to small and large tensors. Thus, an anisotropic smoothing will preserve the artefacts that are caused by variations of small tensors composing homogeneous regions. Beyond this limitation, the goal of this paper is to show that the choice of a Riemannian metric leads to a powerful framework which allows to extend classical vector space algorithms to manifolds thanks to the tools of differential geometry. One interesting track would be to specify what are the basic axioms that the structure tensor needs to satisfy and to derive the corresponding metric.

References

1. P. Basser, J. Mattiello, and D. Le Bihan. MR diffusion tensor spectroscopy and imaging. *Biophysical Journal*, 66:259–267, 1994.
2. W. Förstner and E. Glüch. A fast operator for detection and precise location of distinct points, corners and centers of circular features. In *ISPRS*, pages 281–305. Interlaken, June 1987.
3. J. Bigün and G. H. Granlund. Optimal orientation detection of linear symmetry. In *First International Conference on Computer Vision*, pages 433–438. IEEE Computer Society Press, June 1987.
4. T. Brox, J. Weickert, B. Burgeth, and P. Mrázek. Nonlinear structure tensors. Technical report, Saarland University, October 2004.

5. O. Coulon, D. Alexander, and S. Arridge. Diffusion tensor magnetic resonance image regularization. *Medical Image Analysis*, 8(1):47–67, 2004.
6. D. Tschumperlé and R. Deriche. Orthonormal vector sets regularization with PDE's and applications. *Int. J. of Computer Vision (IJCV)*, 50(3):237–252, 2002.
7. P.T. Fletcher and S.C. Joshi. Principal geodesic analysis on symmetric spaces: Statistics of diffusion tensors. In *Proc. of CVAMIA and MMBIA Workshops, Prague, Czech Republic, May 15, 2004*, LNCS 3117, pages 87–98. Springer, 2004.
8. C. Lenglet, M. Rousson, R. Deriche, and O. Faugeras. Statistics on multivariate normal distributions: A geometric approach and its application to diffusion tensor MRI. Research Report 5242, INRIA, 2004.
9. P. Batchelor, M. Moakher, D. Atkinson, F. Calamante, and A. Connelly. A rigorous framework for diffusion tensor calculus. *Mag. Res. in Med.*, 53:221–225, 2005.
10. X. Pennec, P. Fillard, and N. Ayache. A Riemannian framework for tensor computing. *International Journal of Computer Vision*, 2005. To appear (accepted for publication).
11. X. Pennec. Probabilities and Statistics on Riemannian Manifolds: A Geometric approach. Research Report 5093, INRIA, January 2004. submitted to Int. Journal of Mathematical Imaging and Vision.
12. P. Perona and J. Malik. Scale-space and edge detection using anisotropic filtering. *IEEE Trans. Pattern Analysis and Machine Intelligence (PAMI)*, pages 629–639, 1990.
13. G. Aubert and P. Kornprobst. *Mathematical Problems in Image Processing*. Springer.
14. J. Bigün, G. H. Granlund, and J. Wiklund. Multidimensional orientation estimation with applications to texture analysis and optical flow. *IEEE Transactions on pattern Analysis and Machine Intelligence*, 13(8):775–790, August 1991.
15. A. R. Rao and B. G. Schunck. Computing oriented texture fields. *CVGIP: Graphical Models and Image Processing*, 53:157–185, 1991.
16. J. Weickert. Coherence-enhancing diffusion filtering. *IJCV*, 31(2/3):111–127, April 1999.
17. R. Stefanescu. *Parallel nonlinear registration of medical images with a priori information on anatomy and pathology*. PhD thesis, Nice-Sophia Antipolis University, 2005.

From Stochastic Completion Fields to Tensor Voting

Markus van Almsick, Remco Duits,
Erik Franken, and Bart ter Haar Romeny

Technische Universiteit Eindhoven, 5600MB Eindhoven, The Netherlands
M.v.Almsick@tue.nl, B.M.terhaarRomeny@tue.nl
http://www.bmi2.bmt.tue.nl/image-analysis

Abstract. Several image processing algorithms imitate the lateral interaction of neurons in the visual striate cortex V1 to account for the correlations along contours and lines. Here we focus on two methodologies: *tensor voting* by Guy and Medioni, and *stochastic completion fields* by Mumford, Williams and Jacobs. The objective of this article is to compare these two methods and to place them into a common mathematical framework. As a consequence we obtain a sound stochastic foundation of *tensor voting*, a new tensor voting field, and an analytic approximation of the stochastic completion kernel.

1 Introduction

Blurring an image has the benefit of reducing noise and smoothing the data. The major negative side effect is the loss of image features at lower scale. To maintain contours and lines, one can resort to anisotropic or directed diffusion [7,8]. Here one applies an anisotropic or directed diffusion kernel on isotropic image features like luminosity. The methodologies *tensor voting* [1,2] and *stochastic completion fields* [3,12,4] go one step further. They apply directed diffusion to directed image features.

Tensor voting and *stochastic completion fields* operate in different spaces, on different objects, with different diffusion kernels. Our objective is to find the relations between these mathematical constructs and to compare the open as well as the hidden assumptions of both methodologies in 2D. We begin with the mathematical description of directed features in the theory of *stochastic completion fields*. Here the directed features are points in an orientation bundle. We then explain how tensors of *tensor voting* relate to a subspace of the Fourier transformed orientation bundle. In the subsequent section we derive the Fokker-Planck equation of the stochastic completion kernel relying only on simple stochastic considerations and on symmetry requirements, and give an approximate analytic solution for the stochastic completion kernel. Utilizing the relation between tensor fields and orientation bundles, we convert the analytic solution of the stochastic completion kernel into the corresponding tensor voting field. A comparison of this new tensor voting field with the original voting field postulated by Guy and Medioni will demonstrate the differences between the two methodologies.

O.F. Olsen et al. (Eds.): DSSCV 2005, LNCS 3753, pp. 124–134, 2005.

2   Orientation Bundles of Directed Receptive Fields

Image features like edges, lines, contours and patterns are usually extracted from a 2 dimensional image $f(\mathbf{x})$ via linear filters $\psi(\mathbf{x})$, which model the receptive fields in biological visual systems. To ensure invariance under Euclidean transformations (translations and rotations), these filters have to be applied at all locations in an image domain Ω and in all orientations. This leads to the following convolution that renders a response function $\mathcal{W}_\Psi$ in a 3 dimensional space, the orientation bundle [1] of translations $\mathbf{b}$ and rotations α.

$$\mathcal{W}_\Psi[f(\mathbf{x})](\alpha, \mathbf{b}) \;=\; \int_\Omega \Psi\big(\mathbf{R}_\alpha^{-1}(\mathbf{b} - \mathbf{x})\big)\, f(\mathbf{x})\, d\mathbf{x}\;. \tag{1}$$

where $\mathbf{R}_\alpha^{-1}$ denotes the rotation matrix in 2 dimensions. The difference between a regular convolution and equation (1) is the kernel rotation in addition to the kernel translation. We therefore address the transformation properties of $\Psi(\mathbf{x})$ under rotation and turn to polar coordinates r and ϕ to facilitate the matter. Note, that a Fourier transformation in ϕ decomposes the linear kernel[2] $\tilde{\Psi}(r, \phi)$ into steerable components $\tilde{\psi}_m(r)e^{im\phi}$.

$$\tilde{\Psi}(r, \phi) \;=\; \sum_{m=-\infty}^{\infty} \tilde{\psi}_m(r)\, e^{i\,m\,\phi}\;, \tag{2}$$

$$\text{with } \tilde{\psi}_m(r) \;:=\; \frac{1}{2\pi} \int_{-\pi}^{\pi} \tilde{\Psi}(r, \phi)\, e^{-i\,m\,\phi}\, d\phi\;.$$

These m-modes $\tilde{\psi}_m(r)$ are the components of $\tilde{\Psi}(r, \phi)$ in irreducible, rotation-invariant subspaces. Hence, a rotation of $\tilde{\Psi}(r, \phi)$ by α is achieved by multiplying each m-component with a complex phases $e^{-i\,m\,\alpha}$.

$$\Psi\big(\mathbf{R}_\alpha^{-1}\mathbf{x}\big) \;=\; \tilde{\Psi}(r, \phi - \alpha) \;=\; \sum_{m=-\infty}^{\infty} \tilde{\psi}_m(r)\, e^{i\,m\,(\phi - \alpha)} \;=\; \sum_{m=-\infty}^{\infty} e^{-i\,m\,\alpha}\, \tilde{\psi}_m(r)\, e^{i\,m\,\phi}.$$

The decomposition (2) of the kernel Ψ helps to rewrite equation (1) as an ordinary convolution.

$$\mathcal{W}_\Psi\left[f(\mathbf{x})\right](\alpha, \mathbf{b}) \;=\; \sum_{m=-\infty}^{\infty} e^{-im\alpha} \int_\Omega \Psi_m(\mathbf{b} - \mathbf{x})\, f(\mathbf{x})d\mathbf{x}\;. \tag{3}$$

With an edge or line detecting kernel $\Psi(\mathbf{x})$ we can now generate an orientation bundle from any image. The best known example is probably the convolution

---

[1] The correct mathematical term should be *the function space on the orientation bundle*. Points, or rather δ-functions in the orientation bundle are positions with a direction in the original image. For invertible orientation bundles, see [9].

[2] We distinguish functions in polar coordinates and their counter parts in cartesian coordinates by a '~'. Hence, $\tilde{\Psi}(r, \phi) := \Psi(r\cos\phi, r\sin\phi)$.

with the x and y-component of a Gaussian gradient filter. This example triggers two remarks. Equation (3) is only beneficial, if one may truncate the sum at practical lower and upper bounds for m. However, why consider an orientation bundle with an extra α-dimension, if just a few m-modes may contain all the necessary information? The latter objection brings us to the representation of oriented features by tensors of rank 2.

3   Tensors

The decomposition of kernels that rotate like vectors gives rise to two components: $\Psi_x(\mathbf{x}) = (\Psi_1(\mathbf{x}) + i\Psi_{-1}(\mathbf{x}))/2$ and $\Psi_y(\mathbf{x}) = i(\Psi_1(\mathbf{x}) - i\Psi_{-1}(\mathbf{x}))/2$. A Gaussian Hessian filter $\Psi_A(\mathbf{a})$, a typical line or ridge detector, rotates like a symmetric 2×2-matrix. The response $A(\mathbf{b}) = \int \Psi_A(\mathbf{b} - \mathbf{x})f(\mathbf{x})d\mathbf{x}$ of such a filter has the same rotational properties and decomposes into three m-modes A_{-2}, A_0 and A_2.

$$\begin{pmatrix} A_{-2} \\ A_0 \\ A_2 \end{pmatrix} = \begin{pmatrix} 1 & -2i & -1 \\ 1 & 0 & 1 \\ 1 & 2i & -1 \end{pmatrix} \cdot \begin{pmatrix} A_{xx} \\ A_{xy} \\ A_{yy} \end{pmatrix} \quad , \text{ where } \quad \mathbf{A} = \begin{pmatrix} A_{xx} & A_{xy} \\ A_{xy} & A_{yy} \end{pmatrix} , \quad (4)$$

which again simplifies rotations tremendously.

$$\mathbf{R}_\alpha \begin{pmatrix} A_{xx} & A_{xy} \\ A_{xy} & A_{yy} \end{pmatrix} \mathbf{R}_\alpha^T \quad \Longleftrightarrow \quad \begin{pmatrix} e^{-2i\alpha} A_{-2} \\ A_0 \\ e^{2i\alpha} A_2 \end{pmatrix} \quad (5)$$

Medioni and Guy consider only signals of directed receptive fields or filter kernels that rotate like symmetric, semi-positive definite 2×2-matrices $\mathbf{A}$ (or 2-rank tensors). These matrices can be interpreted as ellipses (or ellipsoids in 3D) as depicted in figure 1. The eigenvectors of $\mathbf{A}$ constitute the major axes

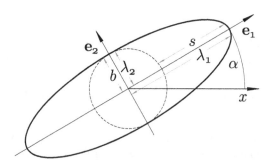

Fig. 1. shows the ellipse that represents a symmetric, semi-positive definite 2×2-matrix (or tensor of rank 2). $\mathbf{e}_1$ and $\mathbf{e}_2$ denote the two eigenvectors of the matrix. λ_1 and λ_2 are the eigenvalues. b is the *ballness* measure and $s = \lambda_1 - \lambda_2$ is giving the *stickness*. Angle α is the orientation of the ellipse with respect to the $\hat{\mathbf{x}}$-axis.

of the ellipse and the positive eigenvalues $\lambda_{1,2}$ determine the length of these axes. In *tensor voting* the isotropic portion of the ellipse is called *ballness* and the anisotropic remainder *stickness*. The direction of the major axis α is the direction of the *stickness*.

The characteristics of matrix $\mathbf{A}$ are determined by

$$\lambda_{1,2} = \frac{1}{2}\operatorname{tr}(\mathbf{A}) \pm \sqrt{\frac{1}{4}\operatorname{tr}^2(\mathbf{A}) - \det(\mathbf{A})}$$

$$\alpha = \arccos(\hat{\mathbf{e}}_1 \cdot \hat{\mathbf{x}}) = \arg(A_{xx} - A_{yy} + 2iA_{xy}),$$

and the notions of *tensor voting* are given by

$$\text{ballness} \quad b := \lambda_2,$$
$$\text{stickness} \quad s := \lambda_1 - \lambda_2.$$

These *tensor voting* characteristics are easily expressed in m-modes.

$$\text{ballness} \quad b := \frac{1}{2}\left(A_0 - \sqrt{A_{-2}A_2}\right) \tag{6}$$

$$\text{stickness} \quad s := \sqrt{A_{-2}A_2} \tag{7}$$

$$\text{stickness angle} \quad \alpha := \frac{1}{2}\arg(A_2) \tag{8}$$

Obviously, traditional *tensor voting* only considers modes with $|m| = 2$ and $m = 0$. These modes relate to the *stickness* and *ballness* measures and can be obtained from an orientation bundle $\mathcal{W}_{\Psi_A}$ by performing a Fourier transformation in α.

Transformation of orientation bundle $\mathcal{W}_{\Psi_A}$ into tensor A:

$$A_m(\mathbf{b}) = \frac{1}{2\pi}\int_{-\pi}^{\pi} e^{im\alpha}\,\mathcal{W}_{\Psi_A}\left[f(\mathbf{x})\right](\alpha, \mathbf{b})\,d\alpha. \tag{9}$$

Vice versa, one can utilize equation (3) to generate an orientation bundle from tensor field $A(\mathbf{b})$.

Transformation of tensor A into orientation bundle $\mathcal{W}_{\Psi_A}$:

$$\mathcal{W}_{\Psi_A}\left[f(\mathbf{x})\right](\alpha, \mathbf{b}) = \sum_{m=-2,0,2} e^{-im\alpha}A_m(\mathbf{b}). \tag{10}$$

Now, that we can convert tensors into orientation bundles and back, we are all set to proceed to the oriented diffusion process.

4   Casting a Stochastic Vote

The purpose of *stochastic completion fields* and *tensor voting* is the distribution of directional edge and line measurements along the axis of their orientation to fill or bridge gaps in contours and lines due to sparse data, noise, or occlusion. *Stochastic completion fields* rely on an elaborate diffusion kernel that acts on an orientation bundle and diffuses measurements $\mathcal{W}_\Psi\left[f(\mathbf{x})\right](\alpha, \mathbf{b})$ in and along α. The diffusion kernel is derived from a stochastic model of line or edge extrapo- lation, hence the name. In *tensor voting* one imitates the diffusion process via a voting field, that casts tensor-votes around each *stick* or *ball*-measurement.

We compare these two methods by first deriving the stochastic completion kernel and an analytic approximation thereof. Given the analytic approximation we will generate the corresponding tensor voting field and compare Medioni's *ad hoc* fundamental voting field with the stochastic version. We thereby gain a direct comparison between stochastic completion kernels and tensor voting fields.

Both, *tensor voting* and *stochastic completion fields* are based on the as- sumption, that directed image features are due to edges, contours or lines in the underlying image. Starting point is therefore a model that generates the trajectories of edges, contours or lines.

The process of extending a line or contour is not a deterministic but a stochas- tic process in the state space of line-/edge-segments. Mandatory properties of line-/edge-segments are position and direction. Optional properties are scale or curvature. We limit our focus on the mandatory line-features that are already present in the orientation bundle: position vector $\mathbf{b}$ and direction α. Assuming that the process of drawing a line or contour is independent of the line-/contour- history we end up with a Markov process in the orientation bundle. The general form of such a stochastic process is

$$\partial_t \begin{pmatrix} \mathbf{b}(t) \\ \alpha(t) \end{pmatrix} = \mathbf{a}(\mathbf{b}(t), \alpha(t)) + \mathbf{B}(\mathbf{b}(t), \alpha(t)) \cdot \boldsymbol{\eta}(t) . \tag{11}$$

The trajectory $(\mathbf{b}(t), \alpha(t))$ in position and direction is parameterized by *drawing* time t. The vector-valued function $\mathbf{a}(\mathbf{b}(t), \alpha(t))$ is the drift term that describes the deterministic part of the line evolution. Matrix-valued function $\mathbf{B}(\mathbf{b}(t), \alpha(t)))$ binds the random vector-variable $\boldsymbol{\eta}(t)$ to the process, determining the coupling and correlation of the process to a source of uncorrelated noise of mean 0, which models the randomness in line propagation.

Due to the randomness involved, it is appropriate to investigate the proba- bilistic measure $p(\mathbf{b}, \alpha, t|\mathbf{b}_0, \alpha_0, t_0)$ of the trajectory, which denotes the prob- ability of finding a line segment at time t in position $\mathbf{b}$ with orientation α given that at time t_0 the line was going through or started at position $\mathbf{b}_0$ in direction α_0. Stochastic calculus[10] enables us to transcribe the Markov pro- cess (11) into the corresponding Fokker-Planck equation (12), a partial differen- tial equation for $p(\mathbf{b}, \alpha, t|\mathbf{b}_0, \alpha_0, t_0)$ with initial condition $p(\mathbf{b}, \alpha, t_0|\mathbf{b}_0, \alpha_0, t_0) = \delta(\mathbf{b} - \mathbf{b}_0)\,\delta(\alpha - \alpha_0)$, Dirichlet boundary condition in $\mathbf{b}$ and periodic boundaries in α.

$$\partial_t\, p(\mathbf{b}, \alpha, t|\mathbf{b}_0, \alpha_0, t_0) = \mathcal{L}(\mathbf{b}(t), \alpha(t))\, p(\mathbf{b}, \alpha, t|\mathbf{b}_0, \alpha_0, t_0) , \tag{12}$$

with the differential operator $\mathcal{L}(\mathbf{b}(t), \alpha(t))$ given by

$$\mathcal{L}(\mathbf{b}(t), \alpha(t)) = -\sum_{j=\{x,y,\alpha\}} \partial_j [\mathbf{a}(\mathbf{b}(t), \alpha(t))]_j \, p(\mathbf{b}, \alpha, t | \mathbf{b}_0, \alpha_0, t_0)$$

$$+ \frac{1}{2} \sum_{j,k=\{x,y,\alpha\}} \partial_j \partial_k \left[\underbrace{\mathbf{B}(\mathbf{b}(t), \alpha(t)) \cdot \mathbf{B}^T(\mathbf{b}(t), \alpha(t))}_{\mathbf{D}(\mathbf{b}(t), \alpha(t))} \right]_{jk} p(\mathbf{b}, \alpha, t | \mathbf{b}_0, \alpha_0, t_0) .$$

The first sum of $\mathcal{L}(\mathbf{b}(t), \alpha(t))$ moves the probability distribution according to the deterministic drift term $\mathbf{a}(\mathbf{b}(t), \alpha(t))$. The second sum is the diffusion term with diffusion tensor $\mathbf{D}(\mathbf{b}(t), \alpha(t))$, which is due to the random pertubations by $\boldsymbol{\eta}(t)$.

Furthermore, we add a *killing* term $-\lambda p(\mathbf{b}, \alpha, t | \mathbf{b}_0, \alpha_0, t_0)$ to $\mathcal{L}(\mathbf{b}(t), \alpha(t))$, to model the chance that a line terminates. Again, if the probability of termination is line history independent, the line decay needs to be exponential, which is ensured by decay constant λ.

$$\partial_t \, p(\mathbf{b}, \alpha, t | \mathbf{b}_0, \alpha_0, t_0) = \mathcal{L}(\mathbf{b}(t), \alpha(t)) \, p(\mathbf{b}, \alpha, t | \mathbf{b}_0, \alpha_0, t_0) - \lambda \, p(\mathbf{b}, \alpha, t | \mathbf{b}_0, \alpha_0, t_0) , \tag{13}$$

The differential time-translation operator $e^{\tau \partial_t}$ takes the probability $p(\mathbf{b}, \alpha, t | \mathbf{b}_0, \alpha_0, t_0)$ at time t and renders $p(\mathbf{b}, \alpha, t + \tau | \mathbf{b}_0, \alpha_0, t_0)$ at a later time $t + \tau$. According to (13) we can substitute $\mathcal{L}(\mathbf{b}(t), \alpha(t)) - \lambda \mathcal{I}$ into the time-translation operator and obtain

$$p(\mathbf{b}, \alpha, t + \tau | \mathbf{b}_0, \alpha_0, t_0) = e^{\tau(\mathcal{L}(\mathbf{b}(t), \alpha(t)) - \lambda \mathcal{I})} p(\mathbf{b}, \alpha, t | \mathbf{b}_0, \alpha_0, t_0) . \tag{14}$$

We are not interested in the drawing process as such, but in the result, the drawn line or contour. Hence, we need to integrate over time t. The Green's operator $\mathcal{G} = \int_0^\infty e^{\tau(\mathcal{L}(\mathbf{b}(t), \alpha(t)) - \lambda \mathcal{I})} d\tau$ will consequently generate the marginal $p(\mathbf{b}, \alpha) := \int_{t_0}^\infty p(\mathbf{b}, \alpha, \tau | \mathbf{b}_0, \alpha_0, t_0) d\tau$, the drawn line, given the initial probability distribution at time t_0.

$$\mathcal{G} = \int_0^\infty e^{\tau(\mathcal{L} - \lambda \mathcal{I})} d\tau = (\mathcal{L} - \lambda I)^{-1} e^{\tau(\mathcal{L} - \lambda I)} \Big|_0^\infty = -(\mathcal{L} - \lambda \mathcal{I})^{-1} . \tag{15}$$

Instead of applying $\mathcal{G}$ to the initial probability $\delta(\mathbf{b} - \mathbf{b}_0) \, \delta(\alpha - \alpha_0)$, we use $\mathcal{G}^{-1}$ as a constraint to solve for $p(\mathbf{b}, \alpha)$

$$\mathcal{G}^{-1} p(\mathbf{b}, \alpha) = -(\mathcal{L} - \lambda \mathcal{I}) p(\mathbf{b}, \alpha) = \delta(\mathbf{b} - \mathbf{b}_0) \, \delta(\alpha - \alpha_0) . \tag{16}$$

Operator $\mathcal{L}$ is a function of drift and diffusion terms $\mathbf{a}(\mathbf{b}(t), \alpha(t))$ and $\mathbf{D}(\mathbf{b}(t), \alpha(t))$. We can obtain specific drift and diffusion functions by demanding invariance under translation and shift-twist-transformation in the orientation bundle. These transformations are the analog of translation and rotation in the underlying image. We ensure the invariance under translation and shift-twist-transformation by requiring operator $\mathcal{L}$ to commute with the infinitesimal generators of translation $\mathcal{T}_\mathbf{b} = \partial_\mathbf{b}$ and the shift-twist operation $\mathcal{S}_\alpha = -x \, \partial_y + y \, \partial_x + \partial_\alpha$.

Setting the commutation relations[3] $[\mathcal{L}, \mathcal{T}_\mathbf{b}]$ and $[\mathcal{L}, \mathcal{S}_\alpha]$ to 0 results in a set of ordinary differential equations for $\mathbf{a}(\mathbf{b}(t), \alpha(t))$ and $\mathbf{D}(\mathbf{b}(t), \alpha(t))$. The solutions depend on 9 constants $a_\parallel$, $a_\perp$, and a_α, as well as $D_{\parallel\parallel}$, $D_{\perp\perp}$, $D_{\alpha\alpha}$, $D_{\parallel\perp}$, $D_{\parallel\alpha}$, $D_{\perp\alpha}$ and have the form

$$a_x(\alpha(t)) = a_\parallel \, \cos(\alpha(t)) - a_\perp \, \sin(\alpha(t))$$
$$a_y(\alpha(t)) = a_\perp \, \cos(\alpha(t)) + a_\parallel \, \sin(\alpha(t))$$
$$a_\alpha(\alpha(t)) = a_\alpha$$
$$D_{xx}(\alpha(t)) = \frac{1}{2}(D_{\parallel\parallel} + D_{\perp\perp}) + \frac{1}{2}(D_{\parallel\parallel} - D_{\perp\perp}) \cos(2\alpha(t)) - D_{\parallel\perp} \sin(2\alpha(t))$$
$$D_{yy}(\alpha(t)) = \frac{1}{2}(D_{\parallel\parallel} + D_{\perp\perp}) + \frac{1}{2}(D_{\perp\perp} - D_{\parallel\parallel}) \cos(2\alpha(t)) + D_{\parallel\perp} \sin(2\alpha(t))$$
$$D_{xy}(\alpha(t)) = D_{\parallel\perp} \cos(2\alpha(t)) + \frac{1}{2}(D_{\parallel\parallel} - D_{\perp\perp}) \sin(2\alpha(t))$$
$$D_{x\alpha}(\alpha(t)) = D_{\parallel\alpha} \, \cos(\alpha(t)) - D_{\perp\alpha} \, \sin(\alpha(t))$$
$$D_{y\alpha}(\alpha(t)) = D_{\perp\alpha} \, \cos(\alpha(t)) + D_{\parallel\alpha} \, \sin(\alpha(t))$$
$$D_{\alpha\alpha}(\alpha(t)) = D_{\alpha\alpha} \,.$$

Not all constant values are admissible, meaningful, or of any consequence to the line model. The velocity with which the stochastic line or contour is drawn does not change its appearance. The norm of xy-projection of the drift term can therefor be set to unit speed. $\sqrt{a_\parallel^2 + a_\perp^2} = \sqrt{a_x^2 + a_y^2} = 1$ reduces the set of parameters by one. The ratio between $a_\parallel$ and $a_\perp$ determines the initial direction of the line with respect to α. Contours and edges progress orthogonally to their α-aligned gradient, so that $a_\parallel = 0$ and $a_\perp = 1$. Lines, however, with their major eigenvector of the Hessian aligned along α, comply with $a_\parallel = 1$ and $a_\perp = 0$. An angular drift a_α makes the line turn. The resulting curvature of the line is $\kappa = a_\alpha/\sqrt{a_x^2 + a_y^2}$. Since we do not consider curvature in our model, we assume $\kappa = 0$. To ensure a smooth line, one may only introduce noise to the line direction α, not to the line-position, which would only blur it. Thus, only $D_{\alpha\alpha} =: \sigma^2$ may be unequal 0, and we finally arrive, with these few assumptions, at the stochastic process considered by Jacobs, Thornber, Zweck, and Wang [4,5,6] in the theory of completion fields.

$$\partial_t p = (\mathcal{L} - \lambda \mathcal{I}) \, p \quad, \text{ where } (\mathcal{L} - \lambda \mathcal{I}) \; = \; -\cos\alpha \, \partial_x - \sin\alpha \, \partial_y + \frac{\sigma^2}{2} \partial_\alpha^2 - \lambda \,. \quad (17)$$

One can solve equation (17) with several numerical methods, which unfortunately are ill-suited for comparison with *tensor voting*, where we have an analytic formula for the voting field. To circumvent this difficulty we consider an approximation. First we rewrite (17) in cylindric coordinates $r = |\mathbf{b}|$, $\phi = \angle(\mathbf{b})$, and α.

$$(\mathcal{L} - \lambda \mathcal{I}) \; = \; -\cos(\alpha - \phi) \, \partial_r - \frac{\sin(\alpha - \phi)}{r} \partial_\phi + \frac{\sigma^2}{2} \partial_\alpha^2 - \lambda \,. \quad (18)$$

---

[3] $[\mathcal{A}, \mathcal{B}] := \mathcal{A}\mathcal{B} - \mathcal{B}\mathcal{A}$.

The initial line or contour propagation starts with $\phi = \alpha$ and it is thus safe to assume, that $|\alpha - \phi|$ is small within a certain vicinity, so that we can approximate $\cos(\alpha - \phi)$ by 1 and $\sin(\alpha - \phi)$ by $(\alpha - \phi)$. For $|\alpha| \ll \pi$ we can also relax the periodic boundary conditions and treat them as Dirichlet boundary conditions at infinity. Then, inspired by [3] we obtain an analytic solution for the Green's function, good enough for most practical purposes.

Stochastic voting field in an orientation bundle:

$$p(r, \phi, \alpha) = \frac{\sqrt{3}}{\pi (\sigma r)^2} e^{-\lambda r - \frac{(2\alpha - 3\phi)^2 + 3\phi^2}{2\sigma^2 r}} . \tag{19}$$

The versatility of this diffusion kernel in an orientation bundle has been shown in the applications of *stochastic completion fields* and the benefits of the above analytic solution will be the subject of a forthcoming article. Here we show the relation between (19) and the fundamental tensor voting field.

5   Voting with Tensors

With Green's function $p(r, \phi, \alpha)$ we can cast scalar votes to the surrounding of a line response in an orientation bundle. Medioni et al circumvent the construct of an orientation bundle by casting not scalar but tensorial votes directly in an image. Inspired by Gestalt laws, they assume that contours or lines run along circular trajectories of constant curvature (see figure 2), that the probability for a line decreases proportional to $e^{-s^2/\tilde{\sigma}^2}$ with s denoting the length of the line, and that lines with large curvatures κ are suppressed likewise by $e^{-c\kappa^2/\tilde{\sigma}^2}$. Hence, in cylindric coordinates the resulting weight of a cocircular tensor vote casted by a tensor with stickness α aligned along $\phi = 0$ is

$$p_{TV}(r, \phi,) \; \propto \; e^{-\frac{s^2 + c\kappa^2}{\sigma^2}} \quad, \text{ where } \quad s = \frac{\phi}{2} r \, \csc \frac{\phi}{2} \text{ and } \kappa = \frac{2}{r} \sin \frac{\phi}{2} . \tag{20}$$

For the normalization of $p_{TV}(r, \phi)$ and for the comparison with the stochastic completion kernel we consider the same linear approximation as applied to equation (18). Thus, for small $|\phi|$ we can write $s = r$ and $\kappa = \phi/r$. In this approximation the normalized, fundamental tensor voting field is

Fundamental tensor voting field approximation:

$$p_{TV}(r, \phi) = \frac{\sqrt{c}}{\sqrt{\pi}\, \tilde{\sigma}\, r} e^{-\frac{1}{\sigma^2}\left(r^2 + c\left(\frac{\phi}{r}\right)^2\right)} e^{4i\phi} , \tag{21}$$

where we added $e^{4i\phi}$ to encode the direction $\alpha = 2\phi$ of the tensorial vote in the complex phase according to (8), so that equation (21) displays the $(m = 2)$-mode of the tensor field. Hence, *stickness* is $|p_{S,TV}(r, \phi)|$ and the *stickness angle* is given by $\arg(p_{S,TV}(r, \phi))$. .

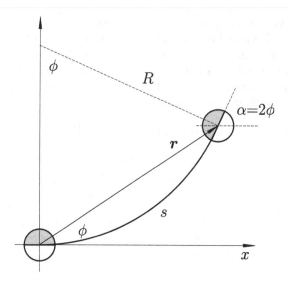

Fig. 2. shows the cocircular line model of *tensor voting*. A tensor aligned along the x-axis at the origin casts a vote at position $\mathbf{r}$ and polar angle ϕ. The orientation α of the tensorial vote is determined by the circular line segment that is uniquely determined by the origin, the alignment of the original tensor along-x and voting position $\mathbf{r}$. The weight of the vote depends on the curvature $\kappa = 1/R$ and the length of the circular line segment s.

6   Not all Voting Systems Are Created Equal

To relate the tensor voting field $p_{TV}(r, \phi)$ and the stochastic completion kernel $p(r, \phi, \alpha)$, we have to bring the latter from the orientation bundle into the image plane. To do so, we take an initial *stick*-tensor response, convert it to an orientation bundle with (10), apply the stochastic completion kernel (19) and bring the result back via equation (9). However, with this straight forward approach we overlook a hidden step in the *tensor voting* methodology. Even though *stick*-tensors exhibit an angular response of $e^{\pm 2i\alpha}$, the tensor voting field is only applied along a single α-direction, the direction of maximum response. This amounts to an angular thinning process in the orientation bundle of the initial *stick*-tensor, which will render just two delta spike at α and $\alpha + \pi$. So we only have to apply the stochastic completion kernel (19) onto the initial response $(\delta(\alpha) + \delta(\alpha - \pi))\delta(\mathbf{b})$ and convert the result to a tensor field via (9). The stochastic version of a tensor voting field in its $(m = 2)$-mode is

Stochastic tensor voting field approximation:

$$p_S(r, \phi) = \int_{-\infty}^{\infty} p(r, \phi, \alpha)\, e^{2i\,\alpha}\, d\alpha = \sqrt{\frac{3}{2\pi\, r^3 \sigma^2}}\; e^{-\frac{3\phi^2}{2r\sigma^2} - \frac{r\sigma^2}{2}}\; e^{-\lambda r}\; e^{3i\phi}\;. \quad (22)$$

One can observe three differences between the stochastic and the tensor voting kernel. In radius r the decay rate is $e^{-\lambda r}$ for p_S and $e^{-r^2/\tilde{\sigma}^2}$ for p_{TV}. The angular width of the stochastic kernel grows with $\sqrt{r}$, whereas the width of the tensor voting kernel increases with r. And finally, the stochastic trajectories are not cocircular. α is $3\phi/2$ and not 2ϕ as required by Medioni's model. Both kernels are displayed in figure 3.

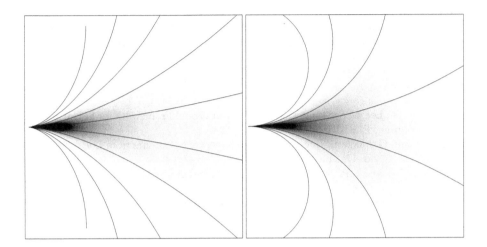

Fig. 3. The left shows a density plot of the stochastic completion kernel $p_S(r, \phi)$ for $\sigma = 1/2$ and $\lambda = 2$ in the range of r from 0 to 1. The tensor voting kernel $p_{TV}(r, \phi)$ is depicted on the right with $\tilde{\sigma} = 1/2$ and $c = 1/2$. Note that the tensor voting kernel widens more than the stochastic counter part. Each kernel is superimposed by of set of trajectories along $\alpha = 2\phi/3$ on the left and $\alpha = 2\phi$ on the right side.

As a last remark we like to point out that the stochastic completion kernel $p(r, \phi, \alpha)$ and the tensor voting fields $p_{TV}(r, \phi)$ and $p_S(r, \phi)$ can be decomposed into m-modes to facilitate their rotation in ϕ [11]. In the case of the stochastic tensor voting field we obtain

$$p_S(r, \phi) = \sum_{m=-\infty}^{\infty} \frac{1}{2\pi r} e^{-\lambda r} e^{-\frac{\sigma^2 r}{6}((m-3)^2+3)} e^{i m \phi} . \tag{23}$$

A truncation of the sum of m-modes amounts to a relaxation of the angular thinning process in α. Having some control over the angular thinning process may even be considered beneficial and has the advantage of a steerable voting field.

7   Conclusion

We have shown the relation between *stochastic completion fields* and the *tensor voting* paradigm. Starting with an arbitrary Markov process for the evolution of lines and edges, we have show that only a limited number of constants determine a shift-twist invariant stochastic process in an orientation bundle. The stochastic completion field falls into this category. We have given an analytic approximation for the Green's function of the stochastic process. Projecting the $(m = 2)$-mode of the analytic Green's function into the image plane, we generated the stochastic version of a tensor voting field. A comparison between the conventional tensor voting field and the stochastic version has shown, that the cocircular line model may be inappropriate. It leads to less directed voting fields. This difference may only have a small practical impact, but we have given *tensor voting* a mathematical underpinning based on stochastic assumptions.

References

1. Medioni, G., Lee, M.S., Tang, C.K.: A Computational Framework for Segmentation and Grouping. ELSEVIER, Amsterdam (2000)
2. G. Guy and G. Medioni, Inferring Global Perceptual Contours from Local Features, IJCV, vol 20, no. 1/2, pp. 113-133, 1996.
3. K. Thornber and L.R. Williams, Analytic Solution of Stochastic Completion Field, BioCyber, vol 75,1996, pp. 141-151.
4. L. Williams and D. Jacobs. Stochastic completion fields: A neural model of illusory contour shape and salience. Neural Computation, 9(4):837858, 1997.
5. L. Williams and D. Jacobs. Local parallel computation of stochastic completion fields. Neural Computation, 9(4):859881, 1997.
6. J. Zweck and L. R. Williams. Euclidean group invariant computation of stochastic completion fields using shiftable-twistable functions. In Proc. of the 6th European Conference on Computer Vision, Dublin, Ireland, 2000.
7. P. Perona and J. Malik, "Scale-space and edge detection using anisotropic diffusion", IEEE Tr. on Pattern Analysis and Machine Intelligence, vol. 12, pp. 629-639, July 1990.
8. J. Weickert, "Theoretical foundation of anisotropic diffusion in image processing", Computing, Suppl. 11, pp. 221-236, 1996.
9. R. Duits, M. van Almsick, M. Duits, E. Franken, L.M.J. Florack, , "Image Processing via Shift-twist Invariant Operations on Orientation Bundle Functions", 7th International Conference on Pattern Recognition and Image Analysis: New Information Technologies, St. Petersburg, pp. 193-196, October 2004.
10. F. Klebaner, "Introduction to Stochastic Calculus with Applications", World Scientific, 1998, or any other introductory textbook on stochastic calculus.
11. E. Franken, M. van Almsick, P. Rongen, L. Florack, B, ter Haar Romeny, Steerable tensor voting, IPMI 2005 (submitted)
12. D. Mumford, Elastica and computer vision, in Algebraic Geometry and Its Applications (Chandrajit Bajaj, Ed.), Springer-Verlag, New York, 1994

Deep Structure from a Geometric Point of View*

Luc Florack

Eindhoven University of Technology, Department of Biomedical Engineering,
Den Dolech 2, NL-5600 MB Eindhoven, The Netherlands
`L.M.J.Florack@tue.nl`
`http://www.bmi2.bmt.tue.nl/image-analysis/people/lflorack`

Abstract. The geometry of "empty" scale space is investigated. By virtue of the proposed geometric axioms the generating PDE, the linear isotropic heat equation, can be presented in covariant, or geometrical form. The postulate of a metric for scale space cannot be upheld, as it is incompatible with the generating equation. Two familiar instances of scale spaces consistent with the geometric axioms are considered by way of example, viz. classical, homogeneous scale space, and foveal scale space.

Keywords: Scale space geometry, homogeneous scale space, foveal scale space, deep structure.

1 Introduction

It is well-known that a Gaussian scale space representation of a static image f is generated by the isotropic heat equation [1]:

$$\frac{\partial u}{\partial t} = \Delta u \qquad (x;t) \in \mathbb{R}^n \times \mathbb{R}^+. \tag{1}$$

Under very mild conditions this PDE admits a closed-form solution, $u(x;t) = (f * \phi_t)(x;t)$. The Green's function ϕ_t is a normalized Gaussian of width $\sigma = \sqrt{2t}$. The solution is unique and smooth with respect to $(x;t) \in \mathbb{R}^n \times \mathbb{R}^+$, and analytical with respect to $x \in \mathbb{R}^n$ for each $t \in \mathbb{R}^+$ [2].

The term "deep structure" (proposed by Koenderink in his seminal paper [1]) has been introduced to distinguish genuinely multi-scale image descriptions from conventional descriptions in which spatial methods are applied scale-wise ("superficial structure"). Existing approaches towards the investigation of deep structure are almost invariably of a *topological* nature, based on Morse theory and singularity or catastrophe theory specifically adapted to be applicable to the solutions of the heat equation, cf. the work by Koenderink, Damon, Florack, and Kuijper [3,4,5,6,7,8]. Here I propose to investigate deep structure from a *geometric* vantage point. This is a relatively unexplored research direction.

---

* This work is part of the DSSCV project supported by the IST Program of the European Union (IST-2001-35443). The Netherlands Organisation for Scientific Research (NWO) is gratefully acknowledged for financial support.

O.F. Olsen et al. (Eds.): DSSCV 2005, LNCS 3753, pp. 135–145, 2005.

Eberly was one of the first to address the issue of geometry of "empty" scale space, i.e. the geometry of the (x, t)-domain regardless of the particular image realization, by postulating a Riemannian structure [9,10], cf. the appendix for a summary. This type of geometry is problematic, however. One conceptual problem is that the metric proposed by Eberly is not unambiguously defined, as it depends on an essentially arbitrary constant $\rho > 0$. As a result, distances in scale space are essentially arbitrary as well, and one might wonder why one would want to introduce a distance concept in the first place. Although one could fix the value of ρ once and for all in a heuristic, task dependent way, cf. Van Wijk and Nuij's application [11], a more serious conceptual problem remains: If scale space were indeed a metric space, the PDE of Eq. (1) should admit a *covariant formulation* in terms of covariant derivatives (or affine connection) compatible with the metric. (Compatibility entails that the metric should be "covariantly constant". Details and proofs can be found in Misner, Thorne and Wheeler [12].) Put differently, it should be possible to reformulate Eq. (1) in a *geometrically meaningful* way. No such formulation exists, however [12]. Heuristically this can be appreciated by noticing that the Laplace-Beltrami operator (i.e. the Laplacean in a general metric space) induced by any (nonsingular) metric always involves second order scale derivatives, which do not occur in the generating equation.

Below I propose a scale space geometry compatible with Eq. (1). The analogy with heat diffusion suggests a parallel with classical spacetime, with time and scale formally identified. Classical spacetime has been studied from a geometrical point of view by Cartan [13], but not until the geometry of relativistic spacetime had been established. Indeed, classical spacetime geometry is more intricate than its relativistic counterpart. Spivak's account [14] is a valuable resource for readers with a mathematical inclination. In his monograph Koenderink explains the significance of basic geometrical concepts, such as "vectors", "covectors", "multivectors", "multiforms", "metrics" and "covariant derivatives", via intuitive explanations and illustrations [15]. For the epistemological formulation I have based myself on this, and on retrospective accounts of Cartan's early work by Friedman [16], Glymour [17], and Misner, Thorne and Wheeler [12].

The motivation for considering empty scale space geometry is the scientific interest in *image induced geometries* inspired by specific scalar, color, or tensor image processing tasks, cf. the work by Kimmel, Sochen, Malladi, Lenglet, Deriche, and Faugeras, a.o. [18,19,20,21]. The PDE approach by Weickert is in the same spirit [22,23], as are to some extent most of the PDE approaches in image processing [24]. It is a natural assertion that if one gradually weakens the coupling of multiscale geometry and image structure, the geometry of empty scale space is the skeleton that should remain in the limit. If one wants to benefit from the potential power of perturbative techniques for analysing image induced geometries (cf. Feynman diagrammatic techniques in field theories, approximations in general relativity based on weak gravitational sources, or perturbative approaches in the theory of nonlinar PDEs), one needs to understand the "classical" limit of vanishing coupling strength.

An additional motivation is that the analysis of geometric axioms of linear scale space, once these have been synthetically established, may reveal hitherto unknown and potentially interesting instances of multiscale image representations.

2   Theory

Let M denote the scale space continuum. I postulate the following geometrical objects on M, respectively its tangent and cotangent spaces $V \in TM$ and $V^* \in T^*M$ (at any implicitly defined point in scale space): (i) an affine connection D, whose Riemann-Christoffel curvature tensor is R, acting on $V^* \times V \times V \times V$, (ii) a covector field $\omega \in V^*$, (iii) a symmetric tensor field h acting on $V^* \times V^*$, and (iv) a vector field $v \in V$. These are subject to the following constraints:

$$R = 0 \tag{2}$$
$$D_x \omega = 0 \tag{3}$$
$$D_x h = 0 \tag{4}$$
$$h(\omega, \xi) = 0 \tag{5}$$
$$D_x v = 0 \tag{6}$$
$$\omega(v) = 1 \tag{7}$$

for all $x \in V$ and $\xi \in V^*$. Alternatively, in terms of their components relative to a coordinate basis (summation convention applies):

$$R^i{}_{jkl} = 0 \tag{8}$$
$$\omega_{i;j} = 0 \tag{9}$$
$$h^{ij}{}_{;k} = 0 \tag{10}$$
$$h^{ij}\omega_i = 0 \tag{11}$$
$$v^i{}_{;j} = 0 \tag{12}$$
$$\omega_i v^i = 1 \tag{13}$$

A semicolon preceding an index i indicates covariant differentiation with respect to the coordinate x^i, $i = 0, \ldots, n$. Index value 0 refers to scale, index values in the range $1, \ldots, n$ denote spatial components. Recall that the components of the affine connection are given by the symbols $\Gamma^k{}_{ij}$:

$$D_{\partial/\partial x^j} \frac{\partial}{\partial x^i} = \Gamma^k{}_{ij} \frac{\partial}{\partial x^k}. \tag{14}$$

The components of the Riemann-Christoffel curvature tensor can be expressed in terms of the symbols $\Gamma^k{}_{ij}$ and their first order partial derivatives:

$$R^i{}_{jkl} = \frac{\partial \Gamma^i{}_{jl}}{\partial x^k} - \frac{\partial \Gamma^i{}_{jk}}{\partial x^l} + \Gamma^m{}_{jl}\Gamma^i{}_{mk} - \Gamma^m{}_{jk}\Gamma^i{}_{ml}. \tag{15}$$

Recall that if $\Gamma^k{}_{ij}$ and $\overline{\Gamma}^k{}_{ij}$ are the components of the affine connection in x^i, respectively y^i coordinates, then

$$\overline{\Gamma}^k{}_{ij} = \frac{\partial y^k}{\partial x^n}\frac{\partial x^l}{\partial y^i}\frac{\partial x^m}{\partial y^j}\Gamma^n{}_{lm} + \frac{\partial y^k}{\partial x^n}\frac{\partial^2 x^n}{\partial y^i \partial y^j}. \tag{16}$$

Affine transformations apparently induce homogeneous transformations. Thus any two "inertial" systems (in which, by definition, the components vanish identically) are related by such a transformation.

Eqs. (2–7), respectively Eqs. (8–13), establish the geometry of empty scale space; no image is involved at this stage. It should be appreciated that these axioms are, to a large extent, synthetical by nature. They can only be justified in retrospection by their consistency with (at least) established linear scale space theory, notably by their capability to geometrize the generating PDE, Eq. (1). In the next few sections I briefly discuss the intuitive significance of the geometric axioms introduced above, without claiming rigor. It is well beyond the scope of this brief treatise to be self-contained with respect to the geometric jargon employed. The interested reader is referred to the geometry literature, *loc. cit.*, and the references therein.

2.1 Flat Scale-Space

Eq. (2), or Eq. (8), expresses the fact that scale space is flat, i.e. has a flat connection. It can be shown that this is equivalent to the existence of a (local) coordinate chart in scale space such that the components $\Gamma^k{}_{ij}$ of the connection vanish identically. I will refer to such coordinates as "canonical coordinates".

The reason for choosing scale space to be flat is the common practice to describe it in terms of a single coordinate system, usually Cartesian spatial coordinates and logarithmic scale. As noted above this implies a flat geometry. In this paper I will not elaborate on curved geometries for empty scale space, but I stress that flatness is a choice made merely for the sake of simplicity. Intrinsic curvature of the scale space manifold is a possibility to be investigated. Of course, a non-vanishing intrinsic curvature will have to be consistent with one's assumptions about the scale space domain, such as homogeneity and/or isotropy. (The nature of intrinsic curvature induced by Eberly's metric is consistent in this respect.)

2.2 Absolute Scale

The evolution parameter t in Eq. (1) is a measure of scale in the sense of inverse resolution at which the image is resolved. One can formally identify scale in scale space theory with time in classical spacetime physics, e.g. by reinterpreting u as a temperature function, with initial distribution f, subject to heat diffusion in a homogeneous, isotropic medium. Thus the notion of "absolute time" in classical physics formally corresponds to *absolute scale* in the present context.

Absolute scale is brought in via the unit scale covector ω acting on the tangent spaces of the scale space manifold. The covector field ω is needed in order to subdivide the $(n + 1)$-dimensional tangent spaces V so as to account for the special role of the scale dimension. A vector $x \in V$ is called *scalelike* if $\omega(x) \neq 0$, otherwise it is *spacelike*. This induces a stratification of scale space into spatial slices labelled by their corresponding scale parameter.

Eq. (3), or Eq. (9), states that the covector field ω is "covariantly constant", and thus compatible with the flat connection. I will henceforth consider only the case of a closed 1-form

$$\omega = d\Omega(t) \quad \text{with } \Omega'(t) > 0 \text{ for all } t > 0. \tag{17}$$

A legitimate choice of scale parametrization is $\Omega(t) = t$, the scalar field that measures absolute scale corresponding to the evolution time t in Eq. (1) up to an arbitrary offset. The arbitrariness of the offset is removed by considering the differential form $d\Omega(t)$ instead of $\Omega(t)$ itself. Below we will consider other (in some sense more natural) choices of scale parametrization.

2.3   Absolute Space

If we wish to be able to tell whether two fiducial markers in scale space are "at the same place" we need to distinguish between spatial and scale directions, and to compare relative spatial positions despite scale differences (*absolute space*). This can be done by introducing a family of non-intersecting geodesics that intersect each fixed-scale plane transversally. If each point is assigned a unique geodesic we can say that the two markers are indeed at the same place just in case they lie on the same geodesic.

Dual to the unit scale covector $\omega \in V^*$ is the unit scale vector $v \in V$ defined by Eq. (7), or Eq. (13). It is a scalelike vector (recall Section 2.2) tangent to a geodesic at every point of the scale space manifold. This follows from Eq. (6), or Eq. (12). Eq. (17) implies that

$$v = \frac{1}{\Omega'(t)} \frac{\partial}{\partial t}. \tag{18}$$

Spacelike vectors can be obtained by projection onto the n-dimensional spacelike subspace of V: if $x \in V$ is any vector, then $x - \omega(x)v$ is spacelike. Likewise we may say that a covector $\xi \in V^*$ is scalelike if $\xi(v) \neq 0$, otherwise it is spacelike. In particular, the covector $\xi - \xi(v)\omega$ is spacelike.

2.4   Euclidean Space

We need a principle to derive a Euclidean metric for each n-dimensional fixed-scale plane in $(n + 1)$-dimensional scale space. As Friedman points out, it is better to proceed via a detour, and consider a symmetric bilinear operator h on the *cotangent* space, i.e. acting on $V^* \times V^*$ instead of a metric-like object on $V \times V$. This is the operator h defined through Eqs. (4–5), or Eqs. (10–11). The first of these equations expresses compatibility of the flat connection with the Euclidean spatial metric defined within each fixed-scale plane (a replica of

Euclidean n-space). The second one shows that h is singular in the sense that it effectively operates on the spacelike components of its arguments.

To see how a genuine metric on the spacelike subspaces of the tangent space arises, consider the operator

$$\flat : V^* \longrightarrow V_0 \subset V : \alpha \mapsto \flat\alpha \overset{\text{def}}{=} h(\alpha, \,.\,) \,.$$

(In tensor component notation one refers to this operation as "index raising".) It converts an arbitrary covector into a vector, but note that it is many-to-one as a result of the singular nature of h: if $\alpha' = \alpha + \kappa\omega$ for some $\kappa \in \mathbb{R}$, then $\flat\alpha' = \flat\alpha$, i.e. the $\flat$-operator discards any scalelike component, $\flat\omega = 0 \in V$. The n-dimensional spacelike subspace of V is denoted by V_0.

A metric $g : V_0 \times V_0$ can now be defined as follows:

$$g : V_0 \times V_0 \longrightarrow \mathbb{R} : (x_0, y_0) \mapsto h(\xi, \eta) \,, \tag{19}$$

in which $x_0 = \flat\xi$ and $y_0 = \flat\eta$. The metric makes sense only on spacelike vectors, since $\omega(\flat\xi) = 0$ for all $\xi \in V^*$. This identity ensures that although the definition is ambiguous with respect to the choices of ξ and η, no confusion is likely to arise.

There is a kind of reverse to the $\flat$ operator, but it is only defined between the spacelike subspaces of V and V^* ("index lowering"):

$$\sharp : V_0 \longrightarrow V_0^* \subset V^* : x_0 \mapsto \sharp x_0 \overset{\text{def}}{=} g(x_0, \,.\,) \,.$$

Note that $\flat \circ \sharp = \text{id}\,(V_0 \longrightarrow V_0)$, the identity map on V_0, whereas $\sharp \circ \flat = \pi(V^* \longrightarrow V_0^*)$, the projection onto the spatial subspace of V^*.

2.5   Homogeneous Scale Space Images

With the help of the previous geometrical concepts it is possible to write the PDE for a scale space image, Eq. (1), into covariant form:

$$D_v u = \text{div}\,\nabla u \,, \tag{20}$$

in which $D_v u = vu = du(v)$, $\text{div}\,x$ denotes the scale space divergence of the vector $x \in V$, and $\nabla u = \flat du$, i.e. the *spatial* gradient, a spacelike vector. Note that we do need both the unit scale vector v dual to the unit scale covector ω so as to obtain a scale (or rather, scalelike) derivative on the left hand side of Eq. (20), as well as the singular "dual metric" h so as to prevent a second order scale derivative from showing up on the right hand side. Since $x \in V_0$ implies $\text{div}\,x \in V_0$, a spatial gradient allows us to construct a *spatial* Laplacean, exactly as required.

In terms of an arbitrary coordinate system we have (a colon/semicolon preceding a subscript denotes a partial/covariant derivative w.r.t. the corresponding coordinate, respectively):

$$v^i u_{;i} = h^{ij} u_{;ij} \,. \tag{21}$$

Alternatively,

$$v^i u_{,i} = \|g\|^{-\frac{1}{2}} \left(\|g\|^{\frac{1}{2}} h^{ij} u_{,j} \right)_{,i} , \qquad (22)$$

in which $\|g\| = \det g$, the determinant of the *spatial* metric induced by h as defined by Eq. (19).

If we use Cartesian spatial coordinates and logarithmic scale as canonical coordinates, with

$$v = \frac{\partial}{\partial \tau} \quad \text{and} \quad \omega = d\tau , \qquad (23)$$

with scale parametrization $\sigma = \sqrt{2t} = e^\tau$ (i.e. $\Omega'(t) = 1/(2t)$, recall Eq. (17)), and if we set the spatial metric to be Euclidean, say

$$h^{ij} = \begin{bmatrix} 0_{1\times 1} & 0_{1\times n} \\ 0_{n\times 1} & \sigma^2 I_{n\times n} \end{bmatrix}_{0 \le i,j \le n} , \qquad (24)$$

then Eqs. (21–22) take the familiar form of Eq. (1):

$$\frac{\partial u}{\partial \tau} = \sigma^2 \Delta u , \qquad (25)$$

in which the Laplacean assumes the standard form as a sum of pure second order spatial derivatives.

Eberly's metric corresponds to a dual metric tensor given by

$$h^{ij} = \begin{bmatrix} \rho^2 & 0_{1\times n} \\ 0_{n\times 1} & \sigma^2 I_{n\times n} \end{bmatrix}_{0 \le i,j \le n} . \qquad (26)$$

The non-vanishing scale component induces a second order scale derivative in the Laplace-Beltrami operator in whatever coordinate system, e.g. in canonical coordinates we obtain

$$\frac{\partial u}{\partial \tau} = \rho^2 \frac{\partial^2 u}{\partial \tau^2} + \sigma^2 \Delta u , \qquad (27)$$

Consistency with Eq. (1) requires that we take the singular limit $\rho \longrightarrow 0$.

2.6   Foveal Scale Space Images

The field equations Eqs. (2–7), or (8–13), admit nontrivial solutions if we adopt a different choice of canonical coordinates. A relevant case is that of a foveal system, whereby homogeneity is dropped in return for the ability to sample a small region of interest around some preferred point with enhanced resolution, i.e. a fovea. For simplicity I consider the case of $n = 2$ spatial dimensions.

Let us consider Cartesian spatial coordinates $(x, y) \in \mathbb{R}^2$ and absolute scale $\sigma \in \mathbb{R}^+$, and circumvent the difficulties of non-Riemannian geometry by postulating a regularized (dual) metric of the form

$$h^{ij}_\epsilon \sim \begin{bmatrix} \epsilon^2 \sigma^2 & 0 & 0 \\ 0 & x^2 + y^2 & 0 \\ 0 & 0 & x^2 + y^2 \end{bmatrix}_{0 \le i,j \le 2} \quad \text{or} \quad h^\epsilon_{ij} \sim \begin{bmatrix} \dfrac{1}{\epsilon^2 \sigma^2} & 0 & 0 \\ 0 & \dfrac{1}{x^2 + y^2} & 0 \\ 0 & 0 & \dfrac{1}{x^2 + y^2} \end{bmatrix}_{0 \le i,j \le 2} ,$$

with $\epsilon > 0$ constant. Then we can use the well-known result that there exists a unique connection compatible with the metric, or, equivalently, with the dual metric, i.e. with Eq. (4) or Eq. (10), viz.

$$\Gamma^k{}_{ij} = \frac{1}{2} h_\epsilon^{kl} \left(\frac{\partial h^\epsilon_{jl}}{\partial x^i} + \frac{\partial h^\epsilon_{il}}{\partial x^j} - \frac{\partial h^\epsilon_{ij}}{\partial x^l} \right). \tag{28}$$

A straightforward computation yields

$$\Gamma^0_{00} = -\frac{1}{\sigma}$$

$$\Gamma^1_{11} = -\frac{x}{x^2 + y^2}$$

$$\Gamma^1_{21} = -\frac{y}{x^2 + y^2}$$

$$\Gamma^1_{12} = -\frac{y}{x^2 + y^2}$$

$$\Gamma^1_{22} = \frac{x}{x^2 + y^2}$$

$$\Gamma^2_{11} = \frac{y}{x^2 + y^2}$$

$$\Gamma^2_{12} = -\frac{x}{x^2 + y^2}$$

$$\Gamma^2_{21} = -\frac{x}{x^2 + y^2}$$

$$\Gamma^2_{22} = -\frac{y}{x^2 + y^2}$$

and all other Γ^i_{jk} vanish. Notice that none of these depend on ϵ, so these symbols are consistent with the non-Riemannian limit $\epsilon \longrightarrow 0$ (but unlike with the regularized case not necessarily unique). Apparently the coordinates (x, y, σ) are not canonical coordinates. Canonical coordinates can be obtained by setting the left hand side of Eq. (16) equal to zero. Let us identify $(x^0, x^1, x^2) \hat{=} (\sigma, x, y)$ and $(y^0, y^1, y^2) \hat{=} (\tau, \rho, \phi)$, such that

$$(\sigma, x, y) = (e^\tau, e^\rho \cos\phi, e^\rho \sin\phi). \tag{29}$$

The corresponding Jacobian matrices, expressed in x^i coordinates (i and j are row and column index respectively), are

$$\frac{\partial x^i}{\partial y^j} = \begin{bmatrix} \sigma & 0 & 0 \\ 0 & x & -y \\ 0 & y & x \end{bmatrix}_{0 \leq i,j \leq 2} \quad \text{respectively} \quad \frac{\partial y^i}{\partial x^j} = \begin{bmatrix} \dfrac{1}{\sigma} & 0 & 0 \\ 0 & \dfrac{x}{x^2 + y^2} & \dfrac{y}{x^2 + y^2} \\ 0 & -\dfrac{y}{x^2 + y^2} & \dfrac{x}{x^2 + y^2} \end{bmatrix}_{0 \leq i,j \leq 2}. \tag{30}$$

Furthermore

$$\frac{\partial^2 x^0}{\partial y^i \partial y^j} = \begin{bmatrix} \sigma & 0 & 0 \\ 0 & 0 & 0 \\ 0 & 0 & 0 \end{bmatrix}_{0 \le i,j \le 2} , \quad \frac{\partial^2 x^1}{\partial y^i \partial y^j} = \begin{bmatrix} 0 & 0 & 0 \\ 0 & x & -y \\ 0 & -y & -x \end{bmatrix}_{0 \le i,j \le 2} \quad \text{and} \quad \frac{\partial^2 x^2}{\partial y^i \partial y^j} = \begin{bmatrix} 0 & 0 & 0 \\ 0 & y & x \\ 0 & x & -y \end{bmatrix}_{0 \le i,j \le 2} . \tag{31}$$

With the help of these matrices, a tedious but straightforward computation shows that, indeed, all $\overline{\Gamma}^k{}_{ij}$ in Eq. (16) vanish identically. Thus (τ, ρ, ϕ) are canonical coordinates. These coincide with the familiar *logarithmic scale* parameter, respectively the *log-polar spatial coordinates* normally used to describe human cortical magnification due to foveation. This same result, by the way, can be obtained by an alternative method based on a spatial metric transform [25].

A subtle complication that has been glossed over here is the singularity at $(x, y) = (0, 0)$. For this case it is tacitly understood that Eqs. (2–7) or Eqs. (8–13) hold *almost everywhere*.

3   Summary and Conclusion

Scale-space cannot be endowed with a Riemannian metric. Its geometry is akin to Newtonian spacetime geometry as described by Cartan [13], with scale and time formally identified.

Various scale space theories fit naturally in the geometric framework of this paper, such as the standard formulation of homogeneous scale space, and the foveal scale space incorporating the inhomogeneous retinocortical mapping resulting from eccentricity dependent visual receptive field sizes ("log-polar scale space"). These scale space instances are singled out by postulating canonical coordinatisations consistent with the proposed geometric axioms. In practice canonical coordinates are the natural ones to use for discrete sampling on a regular grid. This depends on application as demonstrated.

References

1. Koenderink, J.J.: The structure of images. Biological Cybernetics **50** (1984) 363–370
2. Colton, D.: Partial Differential Equations. Random House, New York (1988)
3. Koenderink, J.J.: A hitherto unnoticed singularity of scale-space. IEEE Transactions on Pattern Analysis and Machine Intelligence **11** (1989) 1222–1224
4. Damon, J.: Local Morse theory for solutions to the heat equation and Gaussian blurring. Journal of Differential Equations **115** (1995) 368–401
5. Florack, L., Kuijper, A.: The topological structure of scale-space images. Journal of Mathematical Imaging and Vision **12** (2000) 65–79
6. Kuijper, A., Florack, L.M.J., Viergever, M.A.: Scale space hierarchy. Journal of Mathematical Imaging and Vision **18** (2003) 169–189
7. Kuijper, A., Florack, L.M.J.: The hierarchical structure of images. IEEE Transactions on Image Processing **12** (2003) 1067–1079

8. Kuijper, A., Florack, L.M.J.: The relevance of non-generic events in scale space models. International Journal of Computer Vision **57** (2004) 67–84
9. Eberly, D.: A differential geometric approach to anisotropic diffusion. [24] 371–392
10. Eberly, D.: Ridges in Image and Data Analysis. Volume 7 of Computational Imaging and Vision Series. Kluwer Academic Publishers, Dordrecht, The Netherlands (1996)
11. Wijk, J.J., Nuij, W.A.A.: Smooth and efficient zooming and panning. In Munzner, T., North, S., eds.: Proceedings of the IEEE Symposium on Information Visualization (InfoVis'2003), IEEE Computer Society Press (2003) 15–22 Best paper award.
12. Misner, C.W., Thorne, K.S., Wheeler, J.A.: Gravitation. Freeman, San Francisco (1973)
13. Cartan, É.: Sur les variétés à connexion affine et la théorie de la relativité generalisée (première partie). Ann. École Norm. Sup. **40** (1923) 325–412
14. Spivak, M.: Differential Geometry. Volume 1–5. Publish or Perish, Berkeley (1975)
15. Koenderink, J.J.: Solid Shape. MIT Press, Cambridge (1990)
16. Friedman, M.: Foundations of Space-Time Theories: Relativistic Physics and Philosophy of Science. Princeton University Press, Princeton (1983)
17. Glymour, C.: The epistemology of geometry. In Boyd, R., Gasper, P., Trout, J.D., eds.: The Philosophy of Science. MIT Press, Cambridge, Massachusetts and London, England (1991) 485–500
18. Kimmel, R., Sochen, N.A.: Geometric-variational approach for color image enhancement and segmentation. In Nielsen, M., Johansen, P., Olsen, O.F., Weickert, J., eds.: Scale-Space Theories in Computer Vision: Proceedings of the Second International Conference, Scale-Space'99, Corfu, Greece. Volume 1682 of Lecture Notes in Computer Science., Berlin, Springer-Verlag (1999) 294–305
19. Kimmel, R., Sochen, N.A., Malladi, R.: From high energy physics to low level vision. In Haar Romeny, B.M.t., Florack, L.M.J., Koenderink, J.J., Viergever, M.A., eds.: Scale-Space Theory in Computer Vision: Proceedings of the First International Conference, Scale-Space'97, Utrecht, The Netherlands. Volume 1252 of Lecture Notes in Computer Science. Springer-Verlag, Berlin (1997) 236–247
20. Lenglet, C., Deriche, R., Faugeras, O.: Inferring white matter geometry from diffusion tensor MRI: Application to connectivity mapping. In Pajdla, T., Matas, J., eds.: Proceedings of the Eighth European Conference on Computer Vision (Prague, Czech Republic, May 2004). Volume 3021–3024 of Lecture Notes in Computer Science., Berlin, Springer-Verlag (2004) 127–140
21. Sochen, N.A.: Stochastic processes in vision: From Langevin to Beltrami. In: Proceedings of the 8th International Conference on Computer Vision (Vancouver, Canada, July 9–12, 2001), IEEE Computer Society Press (2001) 288–293
22. Weickert, J.A.: Anisotropic Diffusion in Image Processing. ECMI Series. Teubner, Stuttgart (1998)
23. Weickert, J.A.: Coherence-enhancing diffusion filtering. International Journal of Computer Vision **31** (1999) 111–127
24. Haar Romeny, B.M.t., ed.: Geometry-Driven Diffusion in Computer Vision. Volume 1 of Computational Imaging and Vision Series. Kluwer Academic Publishers, Dordrecht (1994)
25. Florack, L.M.J.: A geometric model for cortical magnification. In Lee, S.W., Bülthoff, H.H., Poggio, T., eds.: Biologically Motivated Computer Vision: Proceedings of the First IEEE International Workshop, BMCV 2000 (Seoul, Korea, May 2000). Volume 1811 of Lecture Notes in Computer Science., Berlin, Springer-Verlag (2000) 574–583

26. Benedetti, R., Petronio, C.: Lectures on Hyperbolic Geometry. Springer-Verlag, Berlin (1987)
27. Fenchel, W.: Elementary Geometry in Hyperbolic Space. Volume 11 of Studies in Mathematics. Walter de Gruyter, Berlin (1989)

A   Eberly's Riemannian Scale-Space

Eberly [9,10] proposed to endow scale space with a Riemannian geometry. In this case the geometric object of interest is the scale space metric tensor, G. It is well known that there exists a unique affine connection compatible with a Riemannian metric. The Riemann-Christoffel curvature tensor thus follows from the metric.

More specifically, the metric proposed by Eberly depends on a parameter $\rho > 0$ that weighs the relative importance of spatial and scale measurements. The metric is given by

$$G = \frac{1}{2t} \left(\sum_{k=1}^{n} dx^k \otimes dx^k + \frac{1}{2\rho^2 t} dt \otimes dt \right),$$

inducing a constant negative Riemannian curvature $K = -\rho^2$. Riemannian curvature is defined for two independent 2-surface tangent vectors $a, b \in V$ as

$$K(a, b) = \frac{R(\sharp a, b, a, b)}{(a \cdot a)(b \cdot b) - (a \cdot b)^2},$$

in which $\sharp x = G(x, .)$. Note that $K(a, b)$ remains the same if a and b are replaced by linear combinations.

The Riemannian geometry corresponding to the case $K = -1$ is known as *hyperbolic geometry*. For details the reader is referred to existing literature [26,27]. For application in the context of linear scale space theory, *cf.* Eberly's accounts [9,10].

Maximum Likely Scale Estimation

Marco Loog[1], Kim Steenstrup Pedersen[1], and Bo Markussen[2]

[1] Image Analysis Group, Department of Innovation,
IT University of Copenhagen, Denmark
{marco, kimstp}@itu.dk
[2] Department of Computer Science,
University of Copenhagen, Denmark
boma@diku.dk

Abstract. A maximum likelihood local scale estimation principle is presented. An actual implementation of the estimation principle uses second order moments of multiple measurements at a fixed location in the image. These measurements consist of Gaussian derivatives possibly taken at several scales and/or having different derivative orders.

Although the principle is applicable to a wide variety of image models, the main focus here is on the Brownian model and its use for scale selection in natural images. Furthermore, in the examples provided, the simplifying assumption is made that the behavior of the measurements is completely characterized by all moments up to second order.

1 Introduction

The problem of scale estimation, or selection, is considered from a probabilistic perspective. For a given image a local scale estimation principle based on maximum likelihood is presented.

The basic idea is that, assuming a particular image model, an expression for the second order moments of measurements in an image can be derived for every scale. Such measurements can consist of, for example, a certain n-jet at a location or intensity measurements at several scales. Given an actual image and assuming that it is a realization of this image model, the local likelihood can be determined for every scale. The scale at which the likelihood becomes maximal is then taken to be the local scale at this point.

In what follows, a general maximum likelihood approach to this problem is formalized. Subsequently, assuming that the local image measurements consist of Gaussian filters, or derivatives thereof, a general expression for the second order moments under a 2-dimensional Brownian image model is given and, in addition, it is assumed that the filter responses can be described adequately by means of knowledge about the central moments of second order.

Following this formulation of the Brownian scale selection principle, two specific cases are illustrated more extensively, i.e., the case where scale is to be estimated from the n-jet and the case where a local estimation is based on a

O.F. Olsen et al. (Eds.): DSSCV 2005, LNCS 3753, pp. 146–156, 2005.

Gaussian filtering over several scales. Some illustrative examples on artificial Brownian images are provided.

Finally, the relation of the scale estimation principle with other scale selection mechanisms is shortly discussed.

2   Maximum Likelihood Scale Estimation

Let $F_x^1, F_x^2, \ldots F_x^k$ be a collection of k filters at a location x. Often, these filters are linear and typically assume the form of an inner product, i.e., for every $i \in \{1, \ldots, k\}$, there is a function f_x^i defined on the domain of images such that

$$F_x^i[L] = \langle L, f_x^i \rangle$$

for an image L. $F_x := (F_x^1, F_x^2, \ldots F_x^k)^{\mathrm{t}}$, i.e., the k-dimensional vector of measurement apertures.

Given a particular image model for every scale s, a k-dimensional distribution p_s of the filter responses coming from F_x can be determined. The maximum likelihood estimate for the scale at a specific location x, denoted by $\hat{s}(x)$, is then given by

$$\hat{s}(x) = \operatorname*{argmax}_{s \in (0, \infty)} \mathsf{p}_s\left(F_x[L]\right),$$

where the image L is assumed to be a realization of the image model under consideration and $F_x[L]$ is the vector with filter responses at the location x in the image L.

3   Brownian Image Model

The specific 2-dimensional model that is considered in more detail is the Brownian image model [1] (see also [2]). This model is the least committed, scale invariant image model that adequately represents the first and second order structure in natural images.

Using this model, restricting the types of measurement types to Gaussian filters and their derivatives, and making the simplifying assumption that the measurement behavior is fully specified by its second order structure, a more explicit expression of local likelihood over scale is given.

For a zero-mean Brownian model at scale s—having zero-scale power spectrum $\beta/\|\omega\|^2$, one can derive an analytic expression for the second central moment $\mathsf{C}_{mn}^{\sigma\tau}(s)$ (i.e., the covariance) of the responses of the Gaussian derivative filters $G_{m_1 n_1}^\sigma$ and $G_{m_2 n_2}^\tau$ at a position x. In this, $m_1 n_1$ and $m_2 n_2$ indicate the order of derivation for both filters.

In [1] a special instance of this covariance is derived. In the case considered there, one has that $\sigma = \tau$ and $s = 0$, and the covariance is given by

$$\mathsf{C}_{mn}^\sigma = (-1)^{\frac{m+n}{2} + m_2 + n_2} \frac{\beta m! n!}{2\pi\sigma^{m+n} 2^{m+n}(n+m)\frac{m}{2}! \frac{n}{2}!},$$

if both $m = m_1 + m_2$ and $n = n_1 + n_2$ are even. Otherwise, $C^\sigma_{mn} = 0$. From the derivation in [1], it then readily follows that in our case, if both $m = m_1 + m_2$ and $n = n_1 + n_2$ are even, the covariance is given by

$$C^{\sigma\tau}_{mn}(s) = (-1)^{\frac{m+n}{2}+m_2+n_2} \frac{\beta m! n!}{2\pi \left(\sqrt{\frac{\sigma^2}{2} + \frac{\tau^2}{2} + s^2}\right)^{m+n} 2^{m+n}(n+m)\frac{m}{2}!\frac{n}{2}!},$$

and again, $C^{\sigma\tau}_{mn}(s)$ equals zero otherwise. See [2] for more details.

A problem with the forgoing analytic expression for the covariance is that the parameter β is not known a priori. The influence of this parameter on the eventual maximum likelihood estimation of the scale, is related to changing image intensities by a certain multiplicative factor, and it can have a considerable impact. Our scale estimate should, of course, be invariant under intensity scaling and, therefore, intensities should be normalized in an explicit or implicit manner. Our choice is to take care of this implicitly by normalizing the covariance matrix used in the experiments: After determining the initial entries of the covariance matrix, say $C'(s)$, the final matrix $C(s)$ is a scaled version of $C'(s)$ such that $\det C(s) = 1$, i.e.,

$$C(s) = \frac{C'(s)}{\sqrt[k]{\det C'(s)}},$$

where k is the number of filter outputs based on which the estimation takes place. It should be noted that this normalization also has an effect on the dependence of C on s.

Because the scale estimation is based on (up to) second order structure and all zeroth orders equal zero, and because $\det C(s) = 1$ for all $s \in (0, \infty)$, determining the maximum likely scale boils down to taking the scale which gives the smallest Mahalanobis distance $F_x[L]^t C^{-1} F_x[L]$ for a feature vector $F_x[L]$, i.e., for the maximum likely scale $\hat{s}$ at position x, it holds that

$$\hat{s}(x) = \underset{s \in (0,\infty)}{\operatorname{argmin}} F_x[L]^t C^{-1}(s) F_x[L].$$

The scale estimations performed in the next section are based on this expression.

4   Illustrative Examples

This section chiefly provides a pictorial (over)view of the performance of the proposed scale selection procedure. For this purpose, three artificial noise images are generated (see Figure 1), all derived from the same initial, i.i.d., 256×256, Gaussian noise image. The first one is a Brownian image observed at scale $s = 8$. A Brownian image is a Gaussian random function for which the increments $B(x + \Delta x) - B(x)$ are independently, identically, and normally distributed with a variance proportional to the length of Δx.

The second one is a Brownian image observed at a scale that is varying in the x-coordinate: At the left and right border the scale is 2, while the scale

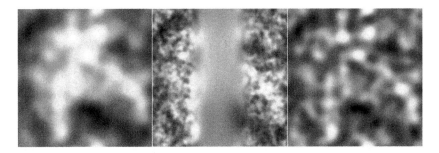

Fig. 1. On the left is the Brownian image observed at scale 8. The middle figure depicts the space-varying Brownian image. On the right is the image obtained by observing Gaussian i.i.d. noise at scale 8.

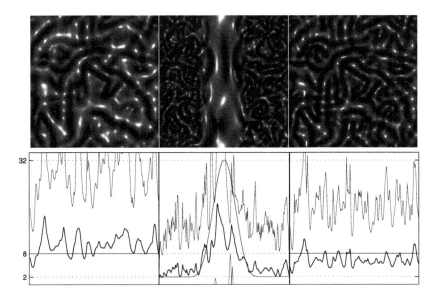

Fig. 2. Scale estimation based on the 2-jet at scale 4. The mean and standard deviation of the estimates for the constant Brownian image (on the left) are 10.4 and 10.1, respectively.

in the middle is $\sqrt{2^2 + 32^2} \approx 32.1$; the measurement scale follows a Gaussian profile along the x-direction. The third one, is the initial Gaussian noise image but then, like the Brownian image, observed at scale 8.

On these three images, local scale estimations are performed using nine different feature sets (behind the feature description, in parenthesis, is the number of filters and the figure in which the corresponding image containing the estimates is displayed):

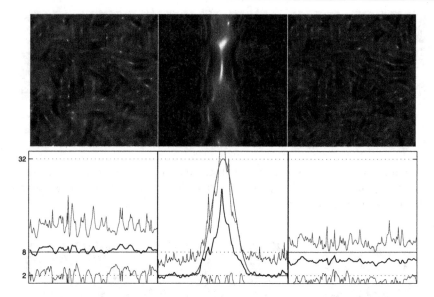

Fig. 3. Scale estimation based on the 3-jet at scale 4. The mean and standard deviation of the estimates for the constant Brownian image (on the left) are 8.6 and 3.5, respectively.

1. the 2-jet at scale 4   (5 dimensions, Figure 2),
2. the 3-jet at scale 4   (9 dimensions, Figure 3),
3. the 4-jet at scale 2   (14 dimensions, Figure 4),
4. the 4-jet at scale 4   (14 dimensions, Figure 5),
5. the 4-jet at scale 8   (14 dimensions, Figure 6),
6. the 4-jet at scale 16   (14 dimensions, Figure 7),
7. the 5-jet at scale 4   (20 dimensions, Figure 8),
8. three 2-jets at scales 2, 4, and 8   (15 dimensions, Figure 9),
9. three 2-jets at scales 4, 8, and 16   (15 dimensions, Figure 10).

We note that in our setting an n-jet does not include the zeroth order measurement, because it does not contain any information about the image structure necessary to perform an adequate scale estimation.

The Figures 2 to 10 show the outcome of the scale estimation procedure on all three images in Figure 1 based on the nine different filter collections. The lighter the color that is displayed, the larger the estimated scale (with white the largest scale and black the smallest). In every figure, colors in the three images are scaled relative to each other. In the caption, the mean and the standard deviation of the estimated scales for the constant scale Brownian image is given.

Directly below every scale estimate image is a 1-dimensional plot that gives the average of the estimated scale in the y-direction in the image directly above it. The thin black lines give an indication of the variance around the mean and

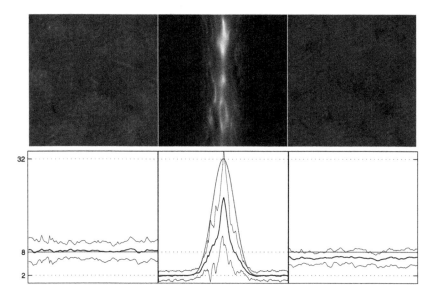

Fig. 4. Scale estimation based on the 4-jet at scale 2. The mean and standard deviation of the estimates for the constant Brownian image (on the left) are 8.3 and 1.3, respectively.

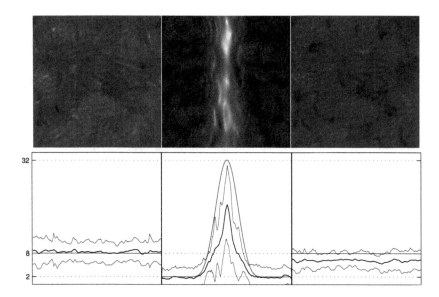

Fig. 5. Scale estimation based on the 4-jet at scale 4. The mean and standard deviation of the estimates for the constant Brownian image (on the left) are 8.4 and 1.5, respectively.

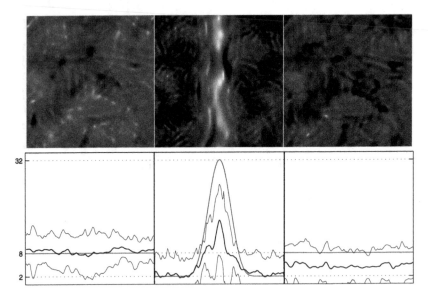

Fig. 6. Scale estimation based on the 4-jet at scale 8. The mean and standard deviation of the estimates for the constant Brownian image (on the left) are 8.5 and 2.3, respectively.

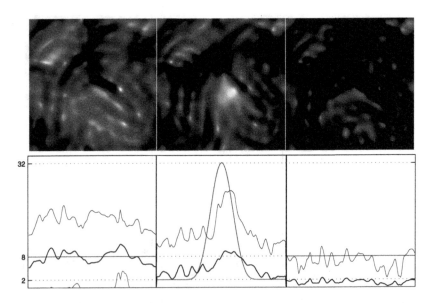

Fig. 7. Scale estimation based on the 4-jet at scale 16. The mean and standard deviation of the estimates for the constant Brownian image (on the left) are 7.9 and 5.0, respectively.

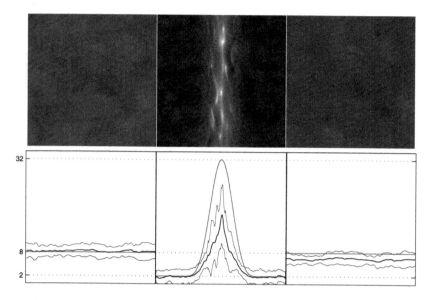

Fig. 8. Scale estimation based on the 5-jet at scale 4. The mean and standard deviation of the estimates for the constant Brownian image (on the left) are 8.3 and 0.9, respectively.

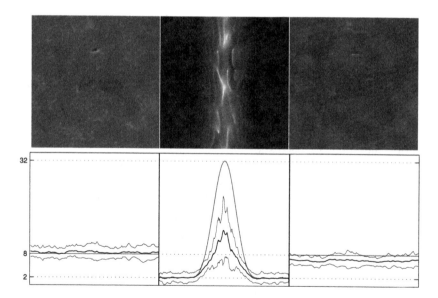

Fig. 9. Scale estimation based on the 2-jets at scales 2, 4, and 8. The mean and standard deviation of the estimates for the constant Brownian image (on the left) are 8.4 and 0.8, respectively.

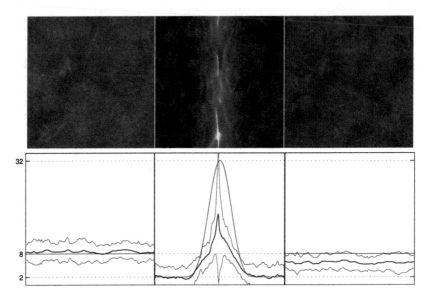

Fig. 10. Scale estimation based on the 2-jets at scale 4, 8, and 16. The mean and standard deviation of the estimates for the constant Brownian image (on the left) are 8.5 and 1.3, respectively.

are plotted at twice the standard deviation from the mean. For comparison, the real observation scale is shown in the same plot in red/gray.

From Figures 4 to 7, and Figures 9 and 10, one of the first observations that can be made is that increasing the scale leads to increased variance of the scale estimate. This behavior may be explained by the fact that the (co)variance for higher-order derivatives for increasing scale decreases rapidly and therefore measurement errors or instabilities in these observations have a large impact on the final estimate (note that the inverse of the covariance matrix C is used in calculating the Mahalanobis distance).

Although not apparent from the experiments, it is also to be expected that for very small scale, say around the inner scale, filter outputs are so unreliable that scale estimates will break down, resulting in a large variance.

From Figures 2, 3, 5, and 8, among others, it is clear that the number of filters used in the estimations has a large influence: The more filters that are used the more accurate the estimates. Of course, due to, for example, numerical limitations, this increase of precision will only be observed up to a certain maximum number of features. One weakness of the estimation procedure is that the inverse of the analytical covariance matrix is needed and inverting it may become unstable at a certain point. However, considering the special structure of the matrix, it may turn out to be possible to give an analytic expression for the inverse as well.

Generally, the average scale estimate for the constant Brownian image is quite close to the actual scale of the underlying process. Remarkably, though, is that it is more often overestimated than underestimated. This is partly because the inner scale does not appear in the expression for the analytic covariance. However, it is hard to judge, based on the illustrations presented, whether or not the consistent overestimation can be explained completely by this.

For the blurred Gaussian image the mean scale seems slightly bit more variable than for the Brownian image, and the variance might be a bit lower on average. What is most notable, however, is that the actual observation scale is rather consistently underestimated. A simple explanation for this may be that, although the constant Brownian and the constant Gaussian have the same scale, a Brownian image is intrinsically more blurred, and as such at a higher scale, than a Gaussian noise image. The reason for this is that the power spectrum of Brownian noise drops of like $1/f^2$, while the spectrum for Gaussian noise is flat.

Severe underestimation of the scale is also an issue for all of the filter choices in the Brownian image with spatially varying scale. Here part of the problem is that the size of the filters, based on which the estimation is carried out, is relatively large compared to the part of the image in which it actually takes on a particular scale. E.g. the smaller the scale used to compute the several 4-jets is the higher the peak in the y-averaged estimate. This part in the image, having largest scale, is for one part underestimated, because surrounding image parts are of lower scale. The scale 2 parts, for example, are relatively large and flat, and, indeed, the scale is predicted quite adequately in these areas. What we cannot explain is why the underestimation takes such severe form. Possibly, there is a bias towards small scale structures originating from the estimation process.

5   Discussion and Conclusions

A general local scale estimation procedure employing feature-based maximum likelihood estimation has been proposed and demonstrated to work quite well in certain settings for particular collections of filters. The specific instance of the general framework we considered provides an estimate of the local scale assuming the image to be from an underlying Brownian image model at a specific scale. Here, only artificial images have been experimented with and the actual performance, and interpretation of the outcome, on, for example, natural images has not been studied yet and is considered for future research.

A well-known, methodology for scale selection, which can be considered to be directly related to scale estimation, has been proposed by Lindeberg [3]. In [4], a similar selection scheme based on a fractional Brownian image model drew the connection between the fraction parameter and the intrinsic scale of the feature to be detected. Majer's dissertation [5] provides a very general scale selection framework based on a stochastic mechanism.

One of the most notable differences between the previous schemes and the scheme proposed here is that, in principle, the former are employed in combination with a specific feature detection task, whereas the current approach allows for a scale estimate irrespective of actual features to be detected. Therefore the scheme proposed here could be considered a way to obtain a local estimate of the *intrinsic* scale of the image. Especially References [4] and [5] could provide valuable clues on how to relate task-dependent and generic scale estimation schemes.

An interesting related remark, suggested in part by an appraiser of some of our preliminary work done on this subject, is that an approach similar to the one presented here might be directly applicable to generic feature detection. The basic underlying idea is that one could look at the actual likelihood at every position and find the positions in which the likelihood is small. The low likelihood indicates that the features measured do not fit the global underlying model well and therefore indicates a point of interest. Further considerations may, more directly, relate particular choices for such likelihood schemes to some of the known scale selection schemes. It would be interesting to see under what assumptions for the maximum likelihood model, it is possible to mimic the feature specific scale selection methods of Lindeberg [3].

Finally, although their focus is on determining a global estimate, a somewhat related approach to scale estimation may be found in [6]. In this, the authors derive a closed-form maximum likelihood estimate of scale for a broad class of Markov random field models. It is not directly clear how this relates to our jet-based estimation principle, however the global scale estimate in [6] should have a direct interpretation in terms of an averaging over certain local estimates such as can be determined in our framework.

References

1. Pedersen, K.S.: Properties of brownian image models in scale-space. In Griffin, L.D., Lillholm, M., eds.: Scale Space Methods in Computer Vision: Proceedings of the 4th Scale-Space conference. LNCS 2695, Isle of Skye, Scotland (2003) 281–296
2. Markussen, B., Pedersen, K.S., Loog, M.: A scale invariant covariance structure on jet space. In: Proceeding of the DSSCV, International Workshop on Deep Structure, Singularities and Computer Vision. LNCS, Maastricht, The Netherlands (2005) somewhere in these proceedings
3. Lindeberg, T.: Feature detection with automatic scale selection. International Journal of Computer Vision **30** (1998) 79–116
4. Pedersen, K.S., Nielsen, M.: The Hausdorff dimension and scale-space normalisation of natural images. Journal of Visual Communication and Image Representation **11** (2000) 266–277
5. Majer, P.: A Statistical Approach to Feature Detection and Scale Selection in Images. PhD thesis, University of Göttingen (2000)
6. Bouman, C.A., Sauer, K.: Maximum likelihood scale estimation for a class of Markov random fields. In: Proceedings of ICASSP '94. IEEE International Conference on Acoustics, Speech and Signal Processing, IEEE (1994) 537–540

Adaptive Trees and Pose Identification from External Contours of Polyhedra

Yannick L. Kergosien

Université de Cergy-Pontoise, Département d'Informatique,
196 rue des Rabats, F-92160 Antony, France
yannick.kergosien@libertysurf.fr

Abstract. We first describe two stochastic algorithms which build trees in high dimensional Euclidean spaces with some adaptation to the geometry of a chosen target subset. The second one produces search trees and is used to approximately identify in real time the pose of a polyhedron from its external contour. A search tree is first grown in a space of shapes of plane curves which are a set of precomputed polygonal outlines of the polyhedron. The tree is then used to find in real time a best match to the outline of the polyhedron in the current pose. Analyzing the deformation of the curves along the tree thus built, shows progressive differentiation from a simple convex root shape to the various possible external contours, and the tree organizes the complex set of shapes into a more comprehensible object.

1   Introduction

For many years Biology has mostly imported its models from human Technology, but as it addresses more complex problems, Technology borrows more of its solutions from Biological organisms. The tree algorithms we present here were first studied as abstractions or models of some biological phenomena like angiogenesis or artificial neural networks [3]. As such they have a more concrete and geometric flavor than the usual tree structures used in computer science. We now test their possible technological utility applying them to a classical Vision problem with important industrial and medical applications. The problem is to find the pose of a known polyhedron from the outline of its apparent contour. It is motivated by such fields as Robotics, Computer Assisted Surgery, Augmented Reality, and all sorts of tracking and recognition problems. Of course a lot of work has already been done in this area and, considering that the algorithms described are members of a family only starting to be studied, we shall only test the relevance of the approach and emphasize the versatility of the algorithm, which can be readily adapted to other problems. These trees also have aspects relating to shape description and the multi-resolution paradigm that might be of interest to the participants of this conference. We shall first describe the algorithms as a way to build geometric objects which grow like vessels toward an organ or tumor in familiar spaces, then turn to trees in spaces of shapes of plane curves, then address the vision problem and how to implement a solution, and finally comment on some multi-resolution aspects of the tree built.

O.F. Olsen et al. (Eds.): DSSCV 2005, LNCS 3753, pp. 157–168, 2005.

2 Adaptive Trees

For the moment we shall describe the tree algorithms in a Euclidean space, like $I\!R^n$, and will generalize only when needed for shape spaces. To explain our vocabulary, we can think of them as growing a vascular branching network from a seed toward a subset called the target, which stands like an organ or tumor to be reached in all of its parts. The tree algorithms start from a point (we call it the seed, it can also be a finite set of points) in a Euclidean space and grows a tree toward a subset (we call it the target), in the same space. It is a stochastic algorithm where points are repeatedly drawn from the target with a given probability distribution. We use uniform distributions on regular targets, but one can also start from a probability distribution in $I\!R^n$ and define the target as the support of it. The initial state of the tree is the seed, and each step adds a single point to the tree (we call this operation : accretion), with some connectivity data which gives it the structure of a tree. It is convenient to describe two variants of the algorithm.

2.1 First Algorithm

Start with a finite set R_0 as the initial network.

The rules for accretion in the first algorithm are, at the i-th step, after a point a_i has been randomly draw from the target:

1. Find the point b_i of the tree R_{i-1} closest to a_i,
2. Build the point for accretion as the barycenter $b_i' = \epsilon.a_i + (1 - \epsilon).b_i$, with a small positive ϵ so that the accretion will take place close to the network (we fix ϵ from the beginning, and the algorithm is not very sensitive to it).
3. Set $R_i = R_{i-1} \cup \{b_i'\}$. We say that accretion of b_i' took place at b_i. The points b_i' and b_i are declared to be neighbors.

This first set of rules leads to adaptive branching of the tree and some convergence properties of the tree toward general target sets have already been proved [5], namely that any neighborhood of a target point will in probability be eventually entered by the network (uniformly if the target is compact).

To understand why branching occurs, observe (fig. 1) that when the network gets close enough to the target, the target is seen from some points of the network with an angle exceeding $\pi/2$. It is then possible to accrete successively two points on the same point of the network, leading to branching (other cases are possible). The phenomenon of abortive bifurcations also occurs: observe on figure 1 that the first branching follows some small "spines" or "thorns" on the network. These spines are really branchings, but they were followed by some competition among the two branches, leading to the death of one of them, i.e., the other branch grew enough to be closer to any point of the target than any point of the first branch, thus irreversibly inhibiting the growth of it. That phenomenon has been analyzed in [5]: such competition leads to unstable "abortive" branchings when far enough from the target, but branching becomes stable when closer to the target, leaving both branches alive. The repetition of changes in the structure

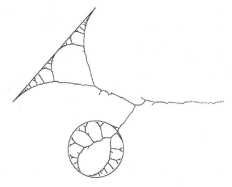

Fig. 1. Growing a tree to a line segment and a circle with the first algorithm. Abortive branchings can be observed.

of the dynamical systems governing the evolution of branches can be related to R. Thom's notion of a generalized catastrophe [12] to describe adaptive branching morphologies.

The behavior of the network toward complex or multiple targets is somewhat reminiscent of our vascular metaphor, as shown (fig. 1), showing convergence of the network to the target.

The complexity of the algorithm depends heavily on the search for a closest point at step 1 of the algorithm. At any time most points in the network are inactive since for any point of the target there is a point in the network which is closer than them. Such inactivation is irreversible, and a garbage collection, removing inactive points from the list of points to be tested, is highly desirable when possible. However such pruning algorithms require simple target geometries, which hinders pratical performance in the general case.

The dependence of the complexity on the dimension of the ambient space involves only computing the distance, so the algorithm can easily be run toward targets in high dimensional spaces (e.g., $I\!R^{200}$, as in the case of plane curves).

2.2   Second Algorithm

In order to get a tree which can be used for searches, and also to improve performance by enabling a fast search for nearest points in the network, we modify the set of rules, adding a rule to be used at branching steps. This rule irreversibly assigns a portion of the target to each of the future subtrees arising from the bifurcation, thus preventing abortive branchings and speeding up the search for a closest point at each step of the algorithm.

Rules. During the evolution, the space will be divided into more and more disjoint regions, starting with the whole space as a single region, and a region will be split when some branching occurs in it (the bird eye's view of fig.2 shows the nesting of regions). Each region will have its own seed and sub-target when created, and it will grow a network of its own. We take as a rule (Rule 0) that the intersection of the target and a region is that region's sub-target.

For a network, we shall call tips the points which have one neighbor, and branching points the points which have three neighbors. The seed is considered to have a neighbor from the start, even if that neighbor is not part of the region network; thus the seed is a tip before any accretion and becomes a branching point when two points are accreted to it.

At any time the total network is the union of all these regions'networks and of some archived points to keep a global tree starting from the first seed.

The rules for region splitting and network growing are now stated.

1. Start with the space as the only region, a single point as its seed, and the target as its sub-target.

Repeat:

2. Draw a random point from the target, determine to which region it belongs (call D that region).

3. Perform accretion on the network of D, according to the rules of the first algorithm.

4 Splitting rule: If branching occurs in D's network, that is if the accretion did not take place at the last point accreted in D, thus creating a branching point (with the special rules mentioned for the seed), then keep the two points accreted on the branching point, call them s_1 and s_2. Archive the points between the seed and the branching point and discard the others. Split D into D_1 and D_2 with D_1 defined as the subset of points of D which are closer to s_1 than to s_2, and D_2 being the subset of points of D which are closer to s_2 than to s_1. Make s_1 the seed of D_1 and s_2 the seed of D_2. The sub-target is split according to rule 0.

There should be some rule, deterministic or stochastic, for ties in distance comparisons. However some settings make such rules unnecessary, e.g., assuming that the intersection of the target with any hyperplane has null measure (such hypothesis can be supported by genericity arguments for some cases of manifolds with uniform probability). We shall make that assumption and disregard ties as almost surely absent. Rules for stopping the process are up to the user, e.g., number of points accreted, or number of regions, or some quantitative criterion related to the distance from the network to the target.

This algorithm is very efficient even on complex targets. The search at step 2 uses a binary search tree which in our experiments had satisfactory balancing. The rest of the search is done in the region's network which has small size. We maintain two trees. The binary search tree to rapidly locate a target point only stores the seeds of the regions (or pointers to them). Another tree stores the first seed and all the accreted points; it is used for the final parts of searches and also serves as an archive of the whole network.

Experimental Behavior. Experiments with this second algorithm show behaviors similar to the first one on many targets. Compare for instance figure 1

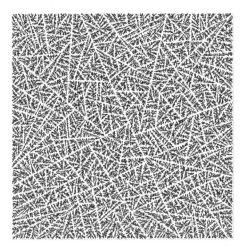

Fig. 2. From a seed not in the target's plane, evolution toward a square target with the second algorithm. What is shown is the projection of the network onto the target's plane. Notice the nesting of regions and the linear separatrices.

and figure 3 obtained for the same target with the two algorithms. Some differences must however be noticed. There are no abortive branchings for the second algorithm, which is one of its built-in properties, since branching leads to some irreversible splitting of the target and to no further competition between the networks of the corresponding subregions. Also the angle of the first branching is smaller with the second algorithm since no abortive bifurcation delays it. In this way the first algorithm adapts better to the target, producing a shorter network. The difference can be more dramatic for very uneven probability measures with light weighted portions of the target that manifest themselves late: late targets can access the closest part of the grown net with the first algorithm, whereas with the second one they have to address the current set of subnetwork, a possibly sub-optimal behavior.

Some target geometries are definitely bad for the second algorithm (fig. 4). When some parts of the target are "hidden" by other ones, the network needs to get very close to some target parts in order to reach other ones, and this produces region splitting adapted to some parts but not desirable for other parts, and still irreversible. This leads to the parallel growing of many branches, clearly an undesirable behavior. The first algorithm, on the contrary, can restart a network to a further target from a single tip. That difficult situation is only attenuated when parts of the targets are not strictly hidden by other one. In figure 5 we use the same projection representation as in figure 2. The target is made of two equal circles and a line segment lying in $I\!R^2$, with a seed in $I\!R^3$ not contained in the target's plane. Observe that the network toward the circle on the left side is perturbed by the separatrices caused by the nearby line segment.

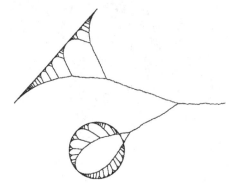

Fig. 3. Growing a tree with the second algorithm to the same target as in fig. 1

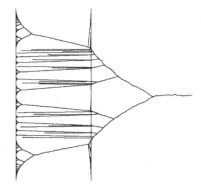

Fig. 4. Second algorithm, with two target segments: traversing the first part of the target sets up irreversible corridors constraining the adaptation to the second part

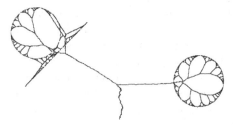

Fig. 5. From a seed not in the target's plane, evolution toward two circles and a segment (projection of the network on the target's plane). Approaching the segment interferes with the evolution toward the circle besides it.

Theoretical Considerations. The convergence results obtained for the first algorithm do not apply to the second one, and some of the experimental cases we showed should make us careful. Here we only outline our present directions of research. It must first be kept in mind that many variants of these algorithms exist, and that exploring them could be as rewarding as concentrating on a single particular one. For instance, it is easy to change the splitting rule so as to replace the separating hyperplane by one which splits the target better in some cases (we tried one that bisects the angle between the accreted points; this can be achieved by modifying the two seed points and still keeping the rest of the algorithm unaltered). One can also delay the splitting while collecting some rough statistics on the points drawn.

In the direction of some convergence results, we shall distinguish two kinds of problems. Proving convergence results with finite (meaning: not infinitesimal) ϵ leads to probability questions. For instance one can use the theory of branching processes to study situations like figure 4. On the other hand, one can study the limit of the process when ϵ tends to 0, possibly with some restrictions on the target, such as being contained in a hyperplane which does not contain the seed. Still being relevant to the behavior of algorithms, questions of that second type rely more on deterministic and geometric tools, and explicit deterministic limit processes can be found for some targets.

3   Growing Search Trees in Spaces of Curve Shapes

In order to retrieve the pose of a known polyhedron from the shape of its external contour, we need to search a a set of shapes of plane curves for that one closest to the shape of a given contour. We are thus going to grow a search tree using the second algorithm in a set of curve shapes. The formalism of section 2 has to be slightly modified, but we do it in a way that also permits growing a tree according to algorithm 1, and keep the formal convergence results in that case.

We are really interested in comparing shapes, i.e., we identify all polygonal plane curves which differ only by a plane displacement (rotation and translation). A shape is a set of such equivalent curves, even if it can be coded by one of its representative curves. Shape spaces have been studied by statisticians [2]. In order to extend our algorithms to it, the set of shapes needs a distance and an equivalent of our barycenter construction.

3.1   Computing the Distance

Two curve shapes c_1, c_2 being given each by a representative curve (C_1 and C_2), we compute a distance $d(c_1, c_2)$. Each curve C_i ($i \in \{1, 2\}$) is parameterized, i.e., it is given by a continuous mapping $\sigma_i : S^1 \to I\!\!R^2$ (assumed to be bijective) where S^1 is the unit circle, and we assume that the parameter is proportional to the curvilinear abscissa measured from $\sigma_i(0)$. For any phase $\phi \in [0, 2\pi]$ and any plane displacement T we can compute the quantity $d_{\phi,T}(\sigma_1, \sigma_2)$ equal to the square root of the average of $\|T(\sigma_2(t + \phi)) - \sigma_1(t)\|^2$ over $t \in [0, 2\pi]$ (where the norm is the Euclidean norm in $\mathbb{R}^2$). We take as the distance $d(c_1, c_2)$ the minimum of $d_{\phi,T}(\sigma_1, \sigma_2)$ over all possible values of T and all possible values of ϕ. Practically, the average is approximated using sampling, only a finite number of values of ϕ are tried, and there are classical formulas from Procrustes's methods [7](using singular value decomposition) to find directly the minima over T.

3.2   Computing a Shape for Accretion

Once a target shape a has been randomly drawn and the closest network shape b has been found (in the relevant region if we apply the second algorithm), we need to compute the shape to be accreted. Any member of its class is adequate. We note $\overline{\epsilon.a + (1 - \epsilon).b}$ the shape we are to find. We might want the following property to be enforced:

$$d(a, \overline{\epsilon.a + (1 - \epsilon).b}) = (1 - \epsilon).d(a, b)$$

the reason being that this permits to use with no modification the proof of the convergence theorem in the case of the first algorithm and obtain a similar result for a tree in the space of curve shapes (there is however some latitude to still get convergence with an approximate relation). An approximate solution is the following: After we computed the distance between a shape a in the target and a shape b in the network, these shapes being represented by the parameterized curves A and B respectively (with associated mappings σ_A and σ_B), we know the special $\hat{\phi}$ and $\hat{T}$ which permit to reach the minimum of $d_{\phi,T}(\sigma_2, \sigma_1)$ (here we prefer that order, even if it gives the same value to the distance). In other words, we know how to position two curves representing the two shapes and how to build a bijection between them for a best match. We just interpolate the curves in these positions using the given bijection, to get a curve C parameterized by:

$$\sigma_C : t \mapsto \epsilon.\hat{T}(\sigma_A(t + \hat{\phi}) + (1 - \epsilon).\sigma_B(t)$$

With these two modifications, we can apply either the first algorithm or the second one to grow trees in spaces of curve shapes. For the Vision problem we need a search tree and thus only use algorithm 2.

4   Application: Pose Identification from Outline of Polyhedra

We now test our second algorithm on a Vision problem. To cite [8] : "One of the classic problems in model-based vision is the estimation of the pose (i.e., the location and orientation) of a 3D object with respect to a scene described by sensory data (2D images or 3D range data)". In Medical Imaging and Computer Assisted Surgery for instance, anatomy-based registration tasks have to solve instances of that problem. Much work has of course been done in that field. Most of the early methods have used some iterative minimization of a functional, with good final results in terms of precision but with problems to find a good initial position and avoid local minima. This is where several methods can co-operate, and tree based methods, many of them using Breiman's Classification ad Regression Trees [1], are getting popular [10] [9]. We must also mention the vast topic of neural networks, among which Kohonen's Self Organizing Maps [6] where used for the identification of articulated models [11], an extension of the pose identification problem. As an apology for the algorithm we present, let us notice that most of the mentioned methods need either a lot of preprocessing, or the choice of several critical parameters, functionals, criteria, and often combine several methods or classifiers.

Here we take as our only data the outline of the polyhedron seen with an un-known pose. The method extends to a smooth surface. Scene analysis often uses other clues such as lighting and texture, but some X-Ray based registration prob-lems have comparable restricted input [8], using like in standard radiographic interpretation the singular curves of the projection of smooth contrast surfaces along the X-rays [4], or only part of them. Our data are simulated, i.e., com-puted from a model of the scene. We first choose a polyhedron (here a randomly perturbed piece of a discretized solid torus). That polyhedron now being per-fectly known, we can compute, for each pose of it, the curve of the outline of its projection on a fixed plane (we take an orthogonal projection), which figures its external contour as seen by a remote observer. We only keep the outline to get a single curve whatever the pose. The problem is: given an outline curve, retrieve a pose of the polyhedron (at least one of them if there are several solutions) which gives the same (or nearly the same) outline curve on the specified projection.

We take as our target the set of outlines possibly observed for the given polyhedron. It is a small subset of the set of all the possible curve shapes which we take as the ambient space. Each shape is stored by a member curve. To grow a search tree according to the second algorithm, we randomly draw rotations of the polyhedron around its center of mass, and for each of them we compute the outline, getting a point of the target. The density on the target is thus induced from a uniform probability measure on the set of rotation matrices. We set the seed equal to an ellipse and grow the tree from it, using the accretion rules already described. For each point of the network we keep, besides its representative curve, a record of the rotation matrix which produced the target curve involved in its accretion. The seed and representative curves of the tree are stored as polygons with a fixed number of vertices large enough to compute the distance accurately and to permit adaptation to the curves of the target. That tree is computed offline and stored to be used later in the demonstration part.

To test the ability of the search tree, we use a window and mouse and in-teractively control the position of an instance of the polyhedron. Each time the pose changes (we achieve real time) the outline is computed and sent to an independent part of the program which searches the tree already stored. That search produces the curve representing the shape which fits best the shape of the outline curve, together with the angle of the plane rotation used for the fit. Composing that plane rotation with the 3D rotation matrix stored with the best fitting curve gives a rotation matrix estimating the pose to be found. The poly-

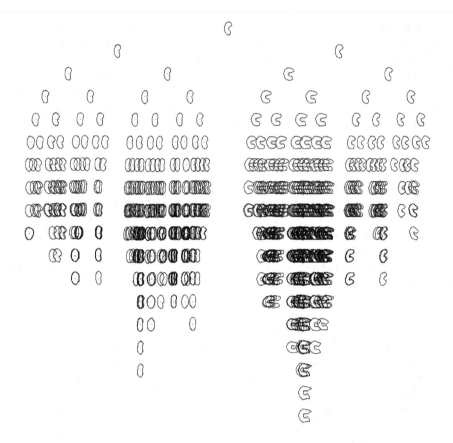

Fig. 6. The binary tree grown on outline curves of a polyhedron (inner nodes only), represented with some overlap. The curves correspond to branching points of the tree grown with the second algorithm.

hedron is simultaneously displayed with that estimated pose in a second window for visual assessment. A third window displays the outline curve and the fitted tree curve to further evaluate the method. On a portable computer (Pentium M, 1.8 GHz), five minutes permitted to grow a tree (fig. 6) with 430 leaves (average height : 10.05), after 5000 accretions ($\epsilon = 0.07$, 100 vertices per curve). That tree can then be used to recognize approximately, in real time, the poses of the same polyhedron from the outlines of its projections, as demonstrable in an interactive presentation. Allowing longer growing times leads to larger trees and better precision.

5   Relations to Multi-resolution Methods

The shapes of the curves corresponding to the points used for accretions can be monitored as the tree grows. The shapes can be seen (fig. 6 and fig. 7) to

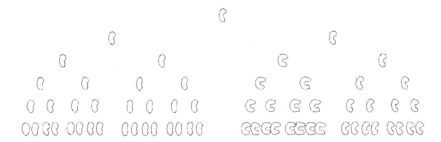

Fig. 7. First layers of the tree grown on outline curves of a polyhedron. The curves correspond to branching points of the tree. Observe the progressive shape differentiation from the root to the leaves.

progressively differentiate, starting from shapes close to that of the seed, toward the various possible shapes in the target, i.e., the different possible outline shapes of the polyhedron. These transformations look as a kind of reverse blurring and call for a comparison with deep structure methods and other multi-resolution procedures.

Shape differentiation of curves is observed for both algorithms but comparisons with blurring are probably easier with the second one. Going from the root to one of the leaves, the evolution of the curve associated to the points of that path in the tree is approximated (in the limit of a small epsilon) by the effect of a vector field along the curve, averaging at each point of the curve the displacement needed to reach the corresponding point on different curves of the target once matched to it. After each branching, the set of curves averaged to build the field along the current curve is split: it is the subset of the target to which the current curve is assigned. Such averages on smaller and smaller disjoint sets become more diverse with their respective sub-targets getting more homogeneous. This leads to better matching and to the differentiation of the curves. The reverse path can thus be compared to a combination of interpolation (involving the target) and some repeated local averaging on the target.

Applying these ideas to Image Analysis is a challenging program which can involve different levels of complexity. A single image can be taken as a target to build a tree towards it (a small ϵ making the tree more deterministic), but trees can also target directly volumetric data or more general sets of images.

6   Conclusions and Prospects

An algorithm derived from abstract biological modeling (branching in general spaces) could be used to address a concrete problem with very few changes. Its modest performance in this first application has to be balanced with the generality of it, since the only parts of the code specific to the problem addressed were the distance function and the interpolation procedure. The same algorithm permits so search a set of smooth curves like the sectional curves of a complex bone through all its intersecting planes [5]. There are also very few parameters to choose as the results are not very sensitive to ϵ. Its low complexity might make it or variants of it candidates for quick data exploration, dimensionality reduction, or visualization, e.g., in the processing of genomic or biometric data.

References

1. Breiman L., Friedman J. H., Ohlsen R. A., Stone C. J. : Classification and regression trees. Wadsworth, Belmont, 1984.
2. Kendall, D.G. : Shape manifolds, Procrustean metrics, and complex projective spaces. Bull. London Math. Soc. **16** (1984), 81–121.
3. Kergosien, Y. L. : Adaptive ramification and abortive concepts. Neural networks from models to applications (NEURO'88), I.D.S.E.T., Paris, 1988, pp. 439–449.
4. Kergosien, Y. L. : Generic sign systems in Medical Imaging. IEEE Comput. Graph. Appl., **11** (5) (sept. 1991), 46–65.
5. Kergosien, Y.: Adaptive branching in Epigenesis and Evolution. C. R. Biologies **326** (May 2003) 477–485.
6. Kohonen, T. : Self-organizing maps, Springer, Berlin, 1997.
7. Krzanowski, W. J. : Principles of multivariate analysis. Oxford Univ. Press, Oxford, 1988.
8. Lavallée, S., Szeliski, R., Brunie, L. : Anatomy-based registration of three-dimensional medical images, range images, X-ray projections, and threer- dimensional models using octree splines. Computer Integrated Surgery, Taylor, R. H., Lavallée, S., Burdea, G., Mosges, R., MIT Press, Cambridge MA, 1996, pp. 115–143.
9. Lockton, R., Fitzgibbon, A. W.: Real-time gesture recognition using deterministic boosting, Proceedings of the British Machine Vision Conference, 2002.
10. Nayar, S.K., Nene, S.A., Murase, H. : Real-time 100 object recognition system, IEEE International Conference on Robotics and Automation, vol.3of4 pp.2321–2325, 1996
11. Nölker, C., Ritter, H.: Parametrized SOMs for Hand Posture Reconstruction, S. I. Amari, C.L. Giles, M. Gori, and V. Piuri eds., Proceedings IJCNN2000.
12. Thom, R. : Stabilité structurelle et morphogénèse: essai d'une théorie générale des modèles, Benjamin, Reading, 1972.

Exploiting Deep Structure*

Arjan Kuijper

Image Group, IT-University of Copenhagen,
Rued Langgaardsvej 7, DK-2300 Copenhagen, Denmark

Abstract. Blurring an image with a Gaussian of width σ and considering σ as an extra dimension, extends the image to an Gaussian scale space ($\mathcal{GSS}$) image. In this $\mathcal{GSS}$-image the iso-intensity manifolds behave in an nicely pre-determined manner. As a result of that, the $\mathcal{GSS}$-image directly generates a hierarchy in the form of a binary ordered rooted tree, that can be used for segmentation, indexing, recognition and retrieval. Understanding the geometry of the manifolds allows fast methods to derive the hierarchy. In this paper we discuss the relevant geometric properties of $\mathcal{GSS}$ images, as well as their implications for algorithms used for the tree extraction. Examples show the applicability and increased speed of the proposed method compared to traditional ones.

1 Introduction

When images are considered, they are always considered at some scale. Often the focus is on single pixels - the so-called inner scale - in case of enhancement. However, at the same time also intermediate structures - scales - are relevant, since it is important to know if either noise or 'relevant data' is enhanced. This simple example illustrates the need of multi-scale image processing.

Since there exists a huge pile of possible multi-scale methods, it makes sense to restrict to those that have a firm mathematical and reasonable axiomatic basis. In the first group so-called test-functions are found, that transfer the discrete data into the continuous domain [16]. In the latter group we prefer those axioms stating that 'we know nothing of the image' [5]. At the intersection of both, one finds the well-known Gaussian filter.

When an image is blurred with a Gaussian filter, the scale (the width, or variance of the filter) needs to be chosen. The Gaussian scale space paradigm [2,6] states in contrast that *no* scale should be chosen in advance. The $(n)-$ dimensional image is thus extended to an $(n + 1)-$dimensional Gaussian scale space ($\mathcal{GSS}$) image.

Many results on the deep structure - the complete structure - of $\mathcal{GSS}$ images are reported, albeit that most results describe local situations, like neighbourhoods of point-events like so-called catastrophe points [1] or saddle points [3,10,11].

---

* This work is part of the DSSCV project supported by the IST Programme of the European Union (IST-2001-35443). WWW home page: `http://www.itu.dk/Internet/sw1953.asp`

O.F. Olsen et al. (Eds.): DSSCV 2005, LNCS 3753, pp. 169–180, 2005.

Recently, novel results were reported in the use of $\mathcal{GSS}$ images. They contain a hierarchical structure that can be used for a so-called pre-segmentation [11], a topological segmentation of the image based on its extrema. Furthermore, a binary ordered rooted tree can be extracted that represents the hierarchy [12]. A drawback of the extraction procedure as described in these papers, is their need for $(n + 1)$–D region extraction. Since $\mathcal{GSS}$ images can be complicated, the procedure is computationally expensive. Currently, these methods are in the state of evaluating their relevance with respect to image indexing and retrieval, as presented in [7].

In this paper we discuss the global geometrical structure of $\mathcal{GSS}$ images, bridging the local events and the hierarchical tree structure and yielding a faster method to derive the latter based on the former, using the geometry of iso-manifolds in the $\mathcal{GSS}$ image.

2   Background

In this section we briefly review Gaussian scale space, its deep structure and the hierarchy in the $\mathcal{GSS}$ image. For more details we refer to the literature mentioned in this section.

2.1   Scale Space

Let $L(\mathbf{x})$ be an image with $\mathbf{x}$ an n-dimensional spatial variable (point) and L the intensity measured at the point. In order to transfer the discrete image to the continuous domain, so-called test functions [16] are needed. Among those functions, we choose that one that satisfies the constraints that it has no pre-ferred orientation, size, location, and no memory. Finally, the function needs to be separable for computational purposes [5]. As a result, one ends up with the Gaussian filter [6,14]. Consequently, the *Gaussian scale space image* $L(\mathbf{x}; t)$ is defined as the convolution of L with a Gaussian:

$$L(\mathbf{x}; t) = \int_{R^n} \frac{1}{\sqrt{4\pi t}^n} e^{-\frac{|\mathbf{x}-\mathbf{y}|^2}{4t}} L(\mathbf{y}) \, d\mathbf{y}$$

As one can verify, the Gaussian scale space image satisfies the diffusion equation: $\partial_t L(\mathbf{x}; t) = \Delta L(\mathbf{x}; t)$ and $\lim_{t \downarrow 0} L(\mathbf{x}; t) = L(\mathbf{x})$. This is the result of an other axiom: causality, as suggested by Koenderink [9]. It boils down from the assumption that moving upwards in the $\mathcal{GSS}$ image no spurious details are cre-ated, and thus implies that no new level lines are created. However, it is possible that locally an extremum and a saddle are pair-wise created [1].

Generally, when blurring, structure disappears due to the pair-wise annihila-tion of a pair of critical points. This concept automatically leads to the definition of *critical curves*: one-dimensional strings through the $\mathcal{GSS}$ image that satisfy $\nabla_x L(\mathbf{x}; t_i) = 0$ for each fixed t_i. Note that this is just a formal definition linking critical points over scale. The linking respects the type of critical point (max-imum, saddle, minimum), and, as Damon showed [1], at so-called catastrophe points a saddle part and a extremum part meet. These points are the local extrema of the critical curve with respect to scale in the $\mathcal{GSS}$ image.

The critical points of the $\mathcal{GSS}$ image itself are always (scale space) saddle points [3,10,11]. At these points the spatial and the scale derivative are zero. The latter implies that the Laplacian is zero, given the diffusion equation.

2.2   Hierarchy

The concept of scale space saddles takes a prominent place in the hierarchical structure proposed by Kuijper and Florack [11,12]. Two distinct iso-manifolds (manifolds with the same intensity throughout the $\mathcal{GSS}$ image) are connected at these saddles. Each critical curve can be related to a manifold, vice versa, and each annihilating extremum can be related to a scale space saddle. So the saddle relates two different critical curves, while both curves have a different maximal scale location (the annihilation point). The first disappearing curve causes its related manifold to be called *critical*.

In [11] a difference in the hierarchy based on the scale location of the disappearance of a critical curve related to the critical manifold is advocated, whereas in [12] the focus is changed to the location of the scale space saddle in the $\mathcal{GSS}$ image. The manifold that was nameless is called *dual* in that paper. An example is given in Figure 1. The left image shows two manifolds joining at the scale space saddle. The critical curve through it also intersects the right manifold. At the top of the curve an annihilation takes place involving the saddle part (left, through the scale space saddle) and an extremum part (right, intersecting the manifold at its top). Therefore, the right manifolds is called *critical*. Consequently, the left manifold is called *dual*. Note that this manifold is also intersected at the top by an (other) critical curve. The right image shows the corresponding tree structure. The scale space saddle SSS is a node with two children: the critical curve determined by critical manifold, edge C and the critical curve determined by the dual manifold, edge D. The edge to its parent P is formed by the critical curve determined by dual manifold. The parent is either the root, or another scale space saddle. In the latter case is the edge either labeled C or D.

3   Geometry

In this section we describe the global structure of iso-manifolds in $\mathcal{GSS}$ and relate it to the scale space saddles, as well as the hierarchical structure. We will focus on 2D images and 3D $\mathcal{GSS}$ images for visualization purposes, but the results hold in arbitrary dimension.

3.1   Manifolds

From the definition of a $\mathcal{GSS}$ image itself it is clear that 'all things blur away'. As proven by Loog et al. [15], if the image is padded with zeros (it has infinite support), all critical points stay within the original image (the hull), while at

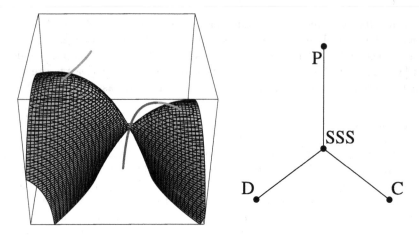

Fig. 1. a) A critical and a dual manifold joined at a scale space saddle. b) Building block of the tree structure.

some scale only one extremum remains. Theoretically, at infinite scale all intensities have spread out equally over the image with infinite support, i.e. the average intensity converges to zero. The importance of this result is that there is a scale at which there is only one extremum left in the blurred image.

At this scale in the blurred image, the isophotes form closed curves that can be traced downwards, while the single point forming the extremum forms the top of a dome-shape. What is within this dome cannot be reached given this blurred image [9].

Alternatively, given an arbitrary $n - D$ iso-manifold in the $(n + 1) - D$ $\mathcal{GSS}$ image, if it intersects an extremum it must intersect it at the top of a local dome (the maximal scale at which the manifold locally exists). Obviously, the manifold can have multiple local tops, although they are located at different scales - just like an arbitrary 1D function generically has extrema with different values. Furthermore, in the $\mathcal{GSS}$ image there is exactly one global top: at that scale the manifold is reduced to an extremum and when scale is increased the manifold disappears.

Consequently, in the $\mathcal{GSS}$ image all iso-manifolds are only open at the original image. So for $n = 2$, all $1 - D$ isophotes in the original $2 - D$ image converge at some scale to circles and disappear when increasing scale. Note that this does not have to happen immediately, as pointed out by Lifshitz and Pizer [13]. They reported the change in curves from non-intersecting to intersecting. This is due to the global structure of iso-manifolds in the neighbourhood of scale space saddles, as will be shown in the next section.

Finally - but perhaps most important, it should be noted that the causality principle states the there are no new level lines - isophotes created when increasing scale. This implies that in the $\mathcal{GSS}$ image it is impossible that an iso-manifold is completely closed (i.e. closed from below). It must have an open end towards the original image. As a result, each isophote at some scale is present in the original image and the critical points in the $\mathcal{GSS}$ image are saddle points. So it remains to investigate the global structure of iso-manifolds through these points.

3.2   Saddles

At spatial saddle points, generically two parts of a manifold are joined or split [3]. For example, one can think of a pair of trousers (join) or the two humps of a camel (split). More special are the scale space saddle, at which two parts have one contact in one point - at least locally [11].

However, only local information of the scale space saddle environment is insufficient: The two parts having contact may be indeed two iso-manifolds that do not share any other common point(s), but they may as well be one and the same manifold. If the latter case applied, the saddle is called 'void' according to [11]. This paper gives a closed definition to distinguish between the two cases, essential to build the hierarchy.

3.3   Contact at Saddles

The first item to be addressed is the contact at a scale space saddle. It is commonly said that two manifolds are touching, but this might give the wrong impression. Since the scale space saddle is also a spatial saddle, the isophote in the blurred image through the (scale space) saddle is self-intersecting. This intersection is transversal - there is a non-zero angle between the crossing parts. The two parts bounded by the isophote have a peak and are not isomorphic to a circle. So instead of two spheres touching at the scale space saddle, there are two peaks joined at a single point, see Figure 1a. The manifolds with a small difference in intensity divide in two cases. The first case yields (locally) two manifolds that do not (locally) intersect. The second case consists of one manifold that is tunnel-shaped around the scale space saddle.

3.4   Global Structure at Saddles

The second item to take into account is the types of critical curves involved. When two distinct manifolds are considered, there are two critical curves that intersect the manifolds at their tops. These critical curves can be either of the same type (both containing either minima or maxima), or of different type (one containing a minimum and one containing a maximum). Visualization of both types can be made easier when regarding the blurred image and the isophote through the (scale space) saddle.

Type 1: same types of critical points. If both curves have the same type, the (scale space) saddle is placed 'in between' both extrema: a 'common' eight-figure appears. In the $\mathcal{GSS}$ image the two iso-intensity manifolds are two juxtaposed peaky kissing domes, the result of two locally dome-like shapes approaching each other, see Figure 2a.

Type 2: different types of critical points. In case of an scale space saddle joining a maximum and a minimum curve, on extremum, say the minimum, is placed in between the saddle and the other extremum (thus being the maximum). This relates to a wrapped eight-figure, where one part lies inside the other. In the $\mathcal{GSS}$ image the minimum-related part of the manifold kisses the outside part of the maximum-related part of the manifold, see Figure 2b.

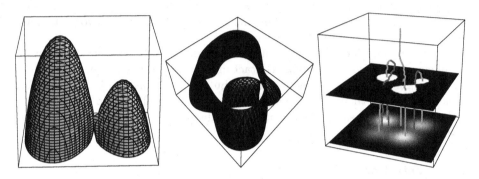

Fig. 2. a) Extrema are of the same type: two juxtaposed domes. b) Extrema are of different types: one dome inside the other. c) What will be the geometry of the dual and critical manifolds?

4   Avoiding 3D Region Growing

Once having obtained the critical curves, the scale space saddles and their relations, there are two major time–consuming things to do (see also Figure 2c).

Firstly, it needs to be determined how the manifolds are shaped at the original image. This is non-trivial, since the manifold may be 'trousers-like', giving rise to (at least) two distinct isophotes in the original image. So a global investigation is needed to find the correct form of the dual manifold. This is depicted in Figure 3. The left images show an intersection of the $\mathcal{GSS}$ image in the (x, t) plane, with x such that the two scale space saddles (the dots) are in the intersection plane. The continuous curves show the dual and critical manifolds (with D and C labels), the dashed curves represents the critical curves (with extremum e and saddle s branches), and the horizontal dashed line is the image at a scale with a scale space saddle (on s_2). The resulting tree structures are shown on the right. Both scaled images contain regions around the extrema e_1, e_2, and e_3. The latter is part of the critical manifold, but for the dual manifold one can see that the top row image has only e_2 as dual part, while the bottom row image has also the e_1 as part of the dual manifold.

Secondly, it needs to be determined what the top of the dual manifold is, or, in another way, to which other critical curve the saddle is related. This is essential for the linking in the tree. In [12] the authors propose a 3D-region growing with the scale space saddle as seed point. This clearly solves the problem, but the

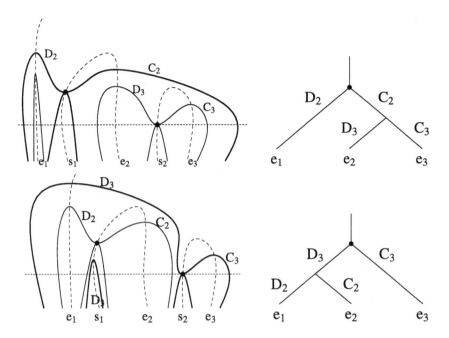

Fig. 3. Two scenarios with the same image thresholded at the intensity of the scale space saddle. See text for details.

shape of manifolds may make this a very time-consuming method. We propose a different method to overcome these problems.

4.1   Top-Finding

To find the top of the dual manifold, it suffices in most cases to find the extrema in the blurred image that are encapsulated by the isophote through the (scale space) saddle. Since the saddle is connected to one extremum in a critical curve, it is clear which of the two areas contribute to the inner part critical manifold. Taking the other part, one finds at least one extremum. If there are multiple extrema, then their intensities along the critical curve are known. So also the intensity of the scale space saddle is located on at least some of these curves. Then it suffices to take the extremum with that intensity that has the highest scale value, i.e. the one located highest in scale. This is the top of the dual dome and the extremum belongs to the critical curve related to that related to the critical manifold. This is the case in Figure 3, top row. The isophote contains the extrema e_3 and e_2. Since the first one vanishes with branch s_2 (containing the scale space saddle), it is part of the critical manifold. The latter extremum has an intensity equal to that of the scale space saddle, where it intersects the dual manifold.

It may happen that the curve doesn't contain the intensity. Then it is involved in a second scale space saddle elsewhere. Then the same procedure is taken for this extremum and the curves link to the dual manifold determined by the last scale space saddle This is the case in Figure 3, bottom row. The isophote contains (again) the extrema e_3 and e_2. Since the first one vanishes with branch s_2 (containing the scale space saddle), it is part of the critical manifold. The latter extremum doesn't have an intensity equal to that of the scale space saddle, but vanishes before it can intersect the manifold determined by the intensity of the scale space saddle. It therefore is a critical manifold, linked by its scale space saddle to extremum branch e_1, being the dual part. Therefore also e_3 is to be linked to this branch. Branch e_1 intersects both manifolds given by e_2 and e_3. The ordering follows by the intensities of these manifolds.

This is sufficient to derive the tree structure, since critical curves can only escape manifolds through their tops. To find the segments (bounded by isophotes) in the image related to each critical and dual manifold, one needs to follow the next procedure.

4.2   Region Shrinking / Sub-tree Selections

Given the root of the tree (the remaining extremum in the $\mathcal{GSS}$ image), one also has its intensity. Since this forms the top of some dome in the $\mathcal{GSS}$ image that has an open end at the original image, one can just trace from the boundary of the original image padded with zeros (containing being thus the 'isophote' with value zero) inwardly until the desired intensity is reached. Note that this cannot cause the isophote to be spilt, since all extrema but the remaining one are located within this region[1].

While going down in scale, one finds at one moment the first node, the scale space saddle at which a critical manifold was connected to the remaining extremum. This relates to shrinking the isophote in the original image to the first isophote(s) with the intensity of the scale space saddle. This time, splitting of isophotes in the dual part is possible due to the 'trousers' event. In the critical manifold part, there is exactly one isophote. Obviously, inside the isophote another isophote with the same intensity may occur due to the presence of other extrema.

The simple procedure is justified by the causality principle, regarded downwardly in scale: no level lines (isophotes) disappear.

From the tree point of view, this is just selecting the left sub-tree at a node being the dual manifold, and the right sub-tree as the critical manifold. Returning to Figure 3 again, the top row tree simply gives for e_2 the region around e_1 as dual and the regions around e_2 and e_3 as critical, since the top node defines the left and right sub-trees. For e_3 it is just e_2 as dual and e_3 as critical. The bottom row tree gives a different result. Now for e_2, e_1 is the dual part and e_2 the critical part, while for e_3 the dual part is obtained by e_1 and e_2.

---

[1] We consider generic images, so binary images are excluded. All non-generic images can be made generic by adding infinitesimal perturbations.

5 Examples

In this section we elaborate on the presented method based on the images given in Figure 4. The blob image is obtained by adding up four Gaussian blobs with

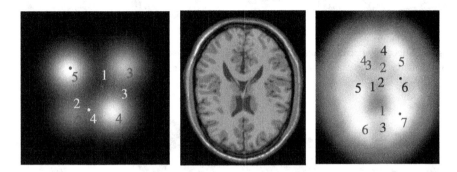

Fig. 4. Testimages a) artificail blob image with labels on critical points. b) MR image c) MR image at scale 8.37 with labels on critical points.

different intensities. In this way numerical calculations can be verified analytically. For computation, the function is sampled into a $81x81$ image with 80 scales logarithmically sampled. The MR image has dimensions $217x181$. Since it contains over 4000 critical points, as starting image the one at scale 8.37, shown in Figure 4c, is taken. For this image 89 scales are computed. These images were also used in [12], but that paper provides the dual and critical manifolds obtained by the 3D region growing method.

For the blob image the critical curves and the image thresholded at the intensity of the scale space saddles are shown in Figure 5. To verify the final results, Figure 6 shows the manifolds through the scales space saddles.

Comparing both figures, it is clear that the image at the scale of the scale space saddle (Figure 5) doesn't contain sufficient information. For extremum e_2 the extrema e_3, e_4, and e_5 are in the dual part (b), while for extremum e_3 only e_4 is in the dual part (c) - while there is a part of e_5 visible. For e_5 both e_3 and e_4 are in the dual part (d) - and e_3 isn't even present anymore at this scale. This is not obvious at all from Figure 5, but it is clear given the complete manifolds (Figure 6) .

However, the top-finding procedure returns e_4 as critical curve intersecting the dual manifold at the top in all cases. Next, when building the tree, the scale space saddles are ordered in their intensities. Tracing downwardly from the root, firstly the extremum e_1 is found generating a critical manifold. Note that this is a situation of different types of extrema (Figure 2b). Secondly, e_2 is split off, next e_5, and finally e_3.

The region shrinking procedure then finds the sequence shown in the top row of Figure 7. Here black regions denote the parts belonging to the critical

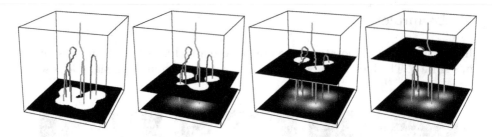

Fig. 5. Successive scale space saddles as scale increases with the intensity threshold at the intensity of the scale space saddle. a) e_1 b) e_2 c) e_3 d) e_5.

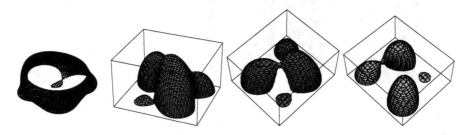

Fig. 6. Manifolds in $\mathcal{GSS}$ with the intensities of the scale space saddles, sorted on the intensities of the scale space saddles. a) e_1 b) e_2 c) e_5 d) e_3.

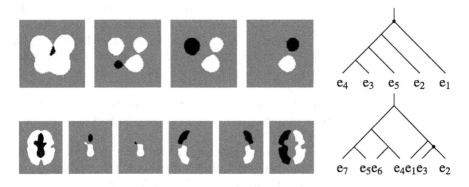

Fig. 7. Regions and trees for the blob (top row) and MR image (bottom) found by the shrinking / sub-tree search method. Black: critical, White: Dual.

manifold, while white regions denote the parts belonging to the dual manifold. Firstly the minimum e_1 is found (top left): a black region within the white (the wrapped eight figure). Secondly, within the white regions the shrinking takes place and e_2 is found as critical (top right), while the parts around the other maxima are part of the dual manifold. These two images still relate to the top rows of the Figures 5 and 6.

The next one that is found is extremum e_5 (bottom left) with e_3 and e_4 as part of the duals. Although this is clear from Figure 6 bottom left, it contradicts the intuition suggested by Figure 5 bottom right. This again warns that scale space is not trivial at all.

Note that these results are identical to the "ground truth" as given in [12]. This holds also for the MR image results, the bottom row of Figure 7. Here the images are derived from the sub-tree search. For example, the first image obtained $C(e_1)$ as the union of regions around e_1, e_2, and e_3, and $D(e_1)$ as the union of regions around e_4, e_5, e_6, and e_7, since the scale space saddle related to e_1 is the top node in the tree (see also [12]). This scale space saddle is of type 2, combining different types of critical points.

The main computational gain is given in Table 1. Although the running times are given for non-optimized code, the differences are clear.

Table 1. Running times of the 2D and 3D region grow algorithms in seconds

extremum	blobs				MRI					
	1	2	3	5	4	6	5	3	1	2
2D	0.470	0.311	0.280	0.291	1.021	0.601	0.551	0.721	0.371	0.721
3D	54.178	61.729	37.614	54.999	2360.1	649.183	731.281	354.98	238.694	522.01

6   Summary and Conclusions

In this paper we discussed the geometry of manifolds in Gaussian scale space images. We clarified the local behaviour at the scale space saddles and distinguished between two essentially different kinds of interactions of manifolds at scale space saddles. Furthermore we showed what the global structure of manifolds in $\mathcal{GSS}$ images looks like and how it can be used.

This links the known local events in Gaussian scale space with the global hierarchy and segmentation method proposed in [11,12]. This method relies on an $(n+1)$−dimensional region growing procedure to find relevant structures (i.e. the geometry of certain manifolds) and can be heavily time consuming.

Using the presented investigation of the geometry of $\mathcal{GSS}$ images, a region growing algorithm in the full $\mathcal{GSS}$ image in order to find the tree structure, can be avoided. It suffices to do a region growing on the scaled image only, in combination with a linear search along critical curves to find the hierarchy tree. Furthermore, a locally $(n-1)$−dimensional manifold shrinking in the original image, or (equivalently) a sub-tree search and region expanding around the found leaves, suffices to derive the segmentation of the image.

The presented examples showed the much faster running times to derive the tree structures and segmentations. Therefore the algorithms get a significantly less complexity, enabling faster use in image recognition and comparison as presented in e.g. [7].

References

1. J. Damon. Local Morse theory for solutions to the heat equation and Gaussian blurring. *Journal of Differential Equations*, 115(2):386–401, 1995.
2. L. M. J. Florack. *Image Structure*, volume 10 of *Computational Imaging and Vision Series*. Kluwer Academic Publishers, Dordrecht, The Netherlands, 1997.
3. L. D. Griffin and A. Colchester. Superficial and deep structure in linear diffusion scale space: Isophotes, critical points and separatrices. *Image and Vision Computing*, 13(7):543–557, September 1995.
4. L.D. Griffin and M. Lillholm, editors. *Scale Space Methods in Computer Vision*, volume 2695 of *Lecture Notes in Computer Science*. Springer -Verlag, Berlin Heidelberg, 2003.
5. B. M. ter Haar Romeny. *Front-end vision and multi-scale image analysis*, volume 27 of *Computational Imaging and Vision Series*. Kluwer Academic Publishers, Dordrecht, The Netherlands, 2003.
6. T. Iijima. On the Gaussian scale-space. *IEICE Japan, Trans. D*, E86-D(7):1162–1164, 2003.
7. F. Kanters, B. Platel, L. M. J. Florack, and B.M. ter Haar Romeny. Content based image retrieval using multiscale top points. In *Griffin and Lillholm [4]*, pages 33–43, 2003.
8. M. Kerckhove, editor. *Scale-Space and Morphology in Computer Vision*, volume 2106 of *Lecture Notes in Computer Science*. Springer -Verlag, Berlin Heidelberg, 2001.
9. J. J. Koenderink. The structure of images. *Biological Cybernetics*, 50:363–370, 1984.
10. J. J. Koenderink. A hitherto unnoticed singularity of scale-space. *IEEE Transactions on Pattern Analysis and Machine Intelligence*, 11(11):1222–1224, 1989.
11. A. Kuijper and L. M. J. Florack. Hierarchical pre-segmentation without prior knowledge. In *Proceedings of the 8th International Conference on Computer Vision (Vancouver, Canada, July 9–12, 2001)*, pages 487–493, 2001.
12. A. Kuijper and L.M.J. Florack. The hierarchical structure of images. *IEEE Transactions on Image Processing*, 12(9):1067–1079, 2003.
13. L. M. Lifshitz and S. M. Pizer. A multiresolution hierarchical approach to image segmentation based on intensity extrema. *IEEE Transactions on Pattern Analysis and Machine Intelligence*, 12(6):529–540, 1990.
14. T. Lindeberg. *Scale-Space Theory in Computer Vision*. The Kluwer International Series in Engineering and Computer Science. Kluwer Academic Publishers, 1994.
15. M. Loog, J. J. Duistermaat, and L. M. J. Florack. On the behavior of spatial critical points under Gaussian blurring, a folklore theorem and scale-space constraints. In *Kerckhove [8]*, pages 183–192, 2001.
16. L. Schwartz. *Théorie des Distributions*, volume I, II of *Actualités scientifiques et industrielles; 1091,1122*. Publications de l'Institut de Mathématique de l'Université de Strasbourg, Paris, 1950–1951.

Scale-Space Hierarchy of Singularities

Tomoya Sakai and Atsushi Imiya

Institute of Media and Information Technology, Chiba University, Japan
{tsakai, imiya}@faculty.chiba-u.jp

Abstract. This paper clarifies the nature of hierarchical relationships among singularities in the Gaussian scale-space. The hierarchy of the singular points is essentially provided by 'stationary curves' and flux curves of 'figure field'. They are defined, respectively, as the trajectories of stationary points across scale, and as the gradient field of the scale-space image at fixed scale. The figure field also reveals an important fact that a stationary point at infinity is involved in catastrophe events of local minimum points. These mathematical properties define the scale-space hierarchy, which is qualitatively described as a tree.

1 Introduction

The aim of this paper is to clarify the hierarchical structure of image by mathematical statements in scale space. The scale space treats images at all levels of resolution, simultaneously. The resolution of the image governs accuracy and cost of quantitative estimations in the computer vision, such as motion detection, reconstruction of objects, etc. Therefore, we require a priori knowledge of necessary and sufficient resolution to employ the quantitative estimations. In other words, the scale selection problem is inevitable.

The scale-space hierarchy is one of the important qualitative properties of image, which provides us with hierarchical approach to the scale selection problem. We focus on the hierarchical structure implied by the Gaussian scale-space in this paper. We firstly review the Gaussian scale-space theory to present the importance of some concepts: stationary curves, figure field, and a local minimum point at infinity. Secondly, we propose the scale-space tree which describes non-heuristic hierarchical structure of image. We also present temporal segmentation of motion image as a potential application of the proposed scale-space tree.

2 Theory

2.1 Gaussian Scale-Space

The Gaussian scale-space analysis of images goes back to Iijima [1,2,3,4,5], who introduced the Gaussian convolution as the fundamental transformation of images based on the following axioms: (i) nonnegative intensity, (ii) linearity, (iii) scale invariance and closedness under affine transformations, (iv) semigroup

O.F. Olsen et al. (Eds.): DSSCV 2005, LNCS 3753, pp. 181–192, 2005.

property, and (v) rotational invariance. In 1983, Witkin published a paper on scale-space filtering, and pointed out the importance of the Gaussian filtering in image processing [6].

We define the Gaussian scale-space image as follows.

Definition 1. *The Gaussian scale-space image $f(x, \tau)$, $(x, \tau) \in (\overline{\mathbb{R}}^N, \overline{\mathbb{R}}^+)$, is the convolution of the N-dimensional original image $f(x) \geq 0$ with the isotropic Gaussian kernel $G(x, \tau)$:*

$$f(x, \tau) = G * f, \quad G(x, \tau) = \frac{1}{\sqrt{4\pi\tau}^N} \exp\left(-\frac{|x|^2}{4\tau}\right). \tag{1}$$

Here $\overline{\mathbb{R}}^N$ denotes N-dimensional extended real space, which includes a point at infinity.

Note that the Gaussian scale-space is defined in compactified real scale-space in this paper. The point at infinity plays an important role in deriving consistent scale-space hierarchy.

In 1984, Koenderink suggested the mathematical equivalence between the Gaussian filtering and the linear diffusion equation, or the partial differential equation of the parabolic type [7].

Proposition 1. *The Gaussian scale-space image $f(x, \tau)$ satisfies the linear diffusion equation*

$$\partial_\tau f = \Delta f. \tag{2}$$

In advance of the above arguments, Iijima derived the linear diffusion equation from physical principles regarding the scale-space image $f(x, \tau)$ as an energy density distribution [3]. On the analogy of the energy density flow, Iijima defined the *figure field* or the vector field of the *figure flow*.

Definition 2. *The figure field F is defined as the negative of the spatial gradient vector field of the scale-space image:*

$$F = -\nabla f(x, \tau). \tag{3}$$

Definition 3. *The figure flow curve is the directional flux curve of the figure field.*

Since the figure field is considered as the current density flow of image intensity, the figure field satisfies the continuity equation.

Proposition 2. *The figure field F satisfies the following differential equation.*

$$\partial_\tau f + \nabla^\top F = 0. \tag{4}$$

Proof. Equation (4) is directly obtained from (2) and (3). □

The following proposition is the conservation law of image intensity.

Proposition 3. *Let $S \subset \overline{\mathbb{R}}^{N-1}$ denote a simple closed supersurface which encircles an arbitrary volume $V \subset \overline{\mathbb{R}}^N$. The net outward flux of the figure field crossing S is the rate of total loss of image intensity in V with respect to the scale.*

Proof. Set $\boldsymbol{n}$ to be the unit normal vector to S. From (2), (3) and the Gauss theorem, the net outward flux is calculated as

$$\int_S \boldsymbol{F}^\top \boldsymbol{n} dS = -\int_S \nabla f^\top \boldsymbol{n} dS = -\int_V \nabla^\top \nabla f dV = -\partial_\tau \int_V f dV. \qquad (5)$$

The last notation in (5) states the derivative of total loss of image intensity in V with respect to the scale τ. $\qquad \square$

Equation (5) is the integral form equivalent to (4).

2.2 Stationary Points

A remarkable feature of the image at fixed scale is a set of stationary points of $f(\boldsymbol{x}, \tau)$. The stationary points are defined as follows.

Definition 4. *The stationary points are defined as the points where the spatial gradient vanishes:*

$$\{\boldsymbol{x} \mid \nabla f(\boldsymbol{x}, \tau) = \boldsymbol{0}\}. \qquad (6)$$

The stationary points of N-dimensional ($N > 1$) scale-space images are classified into three types; local maximum points, local minimum points and saddle points. At the regular points where the determinant of the Hessian matrix of $f(\boldsymbol{x}, \tau)$ is non-zero, the types of stationary points can be discriminated by the second derivative of $f(\boldsymbol{x}, \tau)$, that is, the second derivative test. Since the directional derivative of $f(\boldsymbol{x}, \tau)$ in the direction of a unit vector $\boldsymbol{n}$ is calculated as

$$d_n f = \boldsymbol{n}^\top \nabla f, \qquad (7)$$

the second directional derivative of $f(\boldsymbol{x}, \tau)$ can be written in the quadratic form,

$$d_n^2 f = \boldsymbol{n}^\top \nabla (\boldsymbol{n}^\top \nabla f) = \boldsymbol{n}^\top \boldsymbol{H} \boldsymbol{n}, \qquad (8)$$

where $\boldsymbol{H} = \nabla \nabla^\top f$ is the Hessian matrix. Equation (8) implies that the maximum and minimum values of the second directional derivative $d_n^2 f$ are the maximum and minimum eigenvalues $\lambda_{\max}$ and $\lambda_{\min}$ of $\boldsymbol{H}$, respectively.

$$\lambda_{\min} \le d_n^2 f \le \lambda_{\max}. \qquad (9)$$

The eigenvalues of $\boldsymbol{H}$ and corresponding eigenvectors are called the principal curvatures and the principal directions, respectively. The principal curvatures are obtained by the second directional derivation in the principal directions. The function $f(\boldsymbol{x}, \tau)$ is said to be convex if the second directional derivative $d_n^2 f$ is positive for any direction of $\boldsymbol{n}$. Analogously, $f(\boldsymbol{x}, \tau)$ is concave for negative $d_n^2 f$.

The local maximum (minimum) points are the stationary points at the concave (convex) points. That is, $\lambda_{\min} > 0$ at the local minimum points and $\lambda_{\max} < 0$ at the local maximum points. The other stationary points are classified as the saddle points.

Since the scale-space image $f(x, \tau)$ is a superposition of the Gaussian function, the local maxima and minima are representatives of dominant parts of bright objects and cavities in the image, respectively. In the sense of the current density flow of image intensity, the local maxima and local minima are sources and drains of the flow, respectively. The local maxima and local minima are start-points and end-points of the figure flow curves. It is trivial that $F = -\nabla f \neq 0$ at any point x in the vicinity of an extremum, and we can draw a figure flow curve which passes through the point x in the direction of F unless x is the extremum itself.

We also recognise the existence of a stationary point at infinity.

Proposition 4. *A point at infinity is a local minimum.*

We can visualise the point at infinity with the stereographic projection. Figure 1 illustrates the one-to-one correspondence between the space x and the Riemann sphere under the stereographic projection. We see that any small displacement from the point at infinity (the pole N) increases the image intensity at corresponding point in the image. The local minimum point at infinity can be regarded as a representative of the dark background of the positive image. Since the scale-space image $f(x, \tau)$ is positive, the point at infinity is a drain of the figure flow from the whole region of the image.

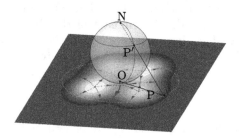

Fig. 1. Stereographic projection onto the Riemann sphere. The pole N corresponds to the point at infinity, which can be regarded as a local minimum point.

The saddle points appear on ridge-like and trough-like structures in two-dimensional images. According to the sign of the Laplacian $\Delta f(x, \tau)$, we can distinguish the saddle points as the ridge-like ($\Delta f < 0$), trough-like ($\Delta f > 0$), and balanced saddle ($\Delta f = 0$) [11]. The balanced-saddle is also known as scale-space saddle [12].

2.3   Stationary Curves

The *stationary curves* are of great importance to the investigation of the scale-space hierarchy.

Definition 5. *The stationary curves are the trajectories of stationary points in the scale space.*

The stationary curves are also classified as local maximum curves, saddle curves, and local minimum curves according to the second directional derivation in the same fashion as the classification of stationary points.

One of the local maximum curves is connected to the one remaining local maximum point at the coarsest scale. We call this local maximum curve "trunk curve". It is also notable that the local minimum point at infinity resides at any scale. That is, the collection of local minimum points at infinity can be regarded as the local minimum curve at infinity.

Generally, the sign of the Laplacian depends on the sum of eigenvalues of the Hessian matrix.

$$\Delta f = \text{tr} \boldsymbol{H} = \text{tr}(\boldsymbol{V \Lambda V}^\top) = \sum_i \lambda_i, \tag{10}$$

where $\boldsymbol{V}$ is the square matrix whose column vectors are eigenvectors of $\boldsymbol{H}$, and $\boldsymbol{\Lambda}$ is the diagonal matrix of eigenvalues λ_i. Since the sum of the eigenvalues is negative (positive) at the local maximum (minimum) points, the image intensities on the local maximum (minimum) curves decrease (increase) with increasing scale. By the same token, the image intensities on the saddle curves with negative (positive) Laplacian decrease (increase) with increasing scale. For two-dimensional images, the image intensities on the saddle curves composed of the ridge-like (trough-like) saddle points decrease (increase) with increasing scale.

The stationary curve is described as a one-dimensional manifold $\boldsymbol{x}(\tau)$ in the scale space. Zhao and Iijima [8] showed that the stationary curves are the solutions to the system of differential equations.

Proposition 5. *The stationary curves are the solutions to the equation*

$$\boldsymbol{H}\dot{\boldsymbol{x}} = -\nabla \Delta f, \tag{11}$$

where the dot indicates ordinary differentiation with respect to scale τ.

Proof. From the total differential equation of $f(\boldsymbol{x}, \tau)$ at the stationary points $\{\boldsymbol{x}(\tau) | \nabla f = \boldsymbol{0}\}$, we have

$$\boldsymbol{H}\dot{\boldsymbol{x}} + \nabla \partial_\tau f = \boldsymbol{0}. \tag{12}$$

Substituting (2) into (12), we can derive (11).   □

The endpoints of the stationary curves are the singular points where $\det \boldsymbol{H} = \prod_i \lambda_i = 0$, that is, at least one of the eigenvalues is zero. This property implies that the local maximum/minimum curve and saddle curve share the singular point as their endpoint. Note that the stationary points necessarily have the Laplacian Δf with a same sign at the singular point.

Proposition 6. *The maximum (minimum) curve and the saddle curve with negative (positive) Laplacian can share a singular point as their endpoint.*

This property was suggested by Griffin *et al.* [11] for two-dimensional images; a ridge-like saddle point cannot annihilate with a minimum point, and a trough-like saddle point cannot annihilate with a maximum point.

3 Hierarchy

In this section, we consider connectivity of the stationary points across scale and at fixed scale. We firstly discuss that the stationary curves imply the hierarchical relationships across scale. The stationary curves, however, does not completely clarify the scale-space hierarchy. Therefore, it is essential to study the connectivity at fixed scale. We show that the annihilation point is connected to a nonsingular stationary point at the annihilation scale. Such a nonsingular point can be found by tracing a unique figure flow curve from the annihilation point in *zero principal curvature direction*. Secondly, we introduce the *local minimum point at infinity* in order to define consistently the scale-space hierarchy. Finally, we propose the scale-space tree which explicitly describes the hierarchy.

3.1 Connectivity Across Scale

As the scale parameter increases, the image is simplified and the features of the image are reduced. The number of stationary points in the diffused image $f(\boldsymbol{x}, \tau)$ decreases when the different types of stationary points meet and annihilated at the singular point, and only one maximum point remains at the coarsest scale.

The behaviour of stationary points is described as the stationary curves in the scale space. Since the saddle points are always involved in the annihilations and creations of the stationary points [11,12], the different types of stationary curves share the singular point as their endpoint. Some singular points are connected by the stationary curves to the other singular points in higher scale. Therefore, the stationary curves imply the hierarchical relationships among singular points across scale.

In order to express this implicit hierarchy as a tree, we regard the singular points as nodes of the tree. The leaves of the tree are the stationary points at the finest scale. The branches of the tree represent the connections between the stationary points and singular points. However, the singular point at which the stationary points are annihilated does not always have the connection by the stationary curve to the singular point in higher scale.

3.2 Connectivity at Fixed Scale

In the previous section, we introduce the equation of stationary curve. Equation (11) gives the instantaneous velocity of the stationary points in the space with respect to the scale. Transforming the coordinates into the principal axis coordinates of $\boldsymbol{H}$, we obtain from (11)

$$\dot{\boldsymbol{p}}(\tau) = -\boldsymbol{\Lambda}^{-1}\nabla_p \Delta f, \tag{13}$$

where $\boldsymbol{p}(\tau) = \boldsymbol{V}^{\top}\boldsymbol{x}(\tau)$, and $\nabla_p = \boldsymbol{V}^{\top}\nabla$ is the gradient operator in the principal axis coordinates.

Equation (13) shows that the third derivatives are weighted by the reciprocal eigenvalues of $\boldsymbol{H}$. Recall that we have the zero eigenvalue at the singular point.

This indicates that the velocity component corresponding to the zero principal curvature becomes infinite at the singular point. In other words, the velocity of the stationary point is infinite in the direction of the zero principal curvature at the annihilation scale.

It has been shown that Fold catastrophes describe generic annihilation events [14,15,16]. In the principal axis coordinates, the annihilation event is modelled as

$$f(\boldsymbol{p}, \tau) = p_1^3 + 6p_1\tau + \sum_{i=2}^{N} \gamma_i(p_i + 2\tau). \tag{14}$$

where $\sum_{i=2}^{N} \gamma_i \neq 0$ and $\forall \gamma_i \neq 0$. For N-dimensional ($N > 1$) images, it suffices to consider the events in two-dimensional case

$$f(p_1, p_2, \tau) = p_1^3 + 6p_1\tau + \gamma(p_2^2 + 2\tau). \tag{15}$$

This model of scale-space image $f(p_1, p_2, \tau)$ has a local maximum point and a saddle point if $\tau < 0$ and $\gamma < 0$. These two stationary points meet at the origin at $\tau = 0$. The parameterised stationary curves are obtained from (13) and (15) as

$$\boldsymbol{p}(\tau) = (\pm\sqrt{-2\tau}, 0)^\top, \tag{16}$$

where the upper and lower signs correspond to the saddle curve and local maximum curve, respectively. The principal curvatures (λ_1, λ_2) are $(\sqrt{-2\tau}, 2\gamma)$ on the saddle curve and $(-\sqrt{-2\tau}, 2\gamma)$ on the local maximum curve. Therefore, the zero principal curvature direction at the annihilation scale $\tau = 0$ is in the p_1-axis.

Another significant aspect of the annihilation event is evolution of the figure field. Noting that $\nabla_p = \boldsymbol{V}^\top\nabla$, it follows from (3) and (15) that

$$\boldsymbol{F} = -(3p_1^2 + 6\tau, 2\gamma p_2)^\top. \tag{17}$$

A family of figure flow curves $p_2 = C(p_1)$ is derived from the differential equation,

$$\frac{dp_2}{dp_1} = \frac{\partial_{p_2} f}{\partial_{p_1} f}. \tag{18}$$

The solution to (18) for $f(p_1, p_2, \tau)$ is

$$p_2 = \begin{cases} A \left| \dfrac{p_1 - \sqrt{-2\tau}}{p_1 + \sqrt{-2\tau}} \right|^{\frac{\gamma}{3\sqrt{-2\tau}}} & (\tau < 0) \\[2ex] A \exp\left(-\dfrac{2\gamma}{3p_1}\right) & (\tau = 0) \\[2ex] A \exp\left(\dfrac{2\gamma}{3\sqrt{2\tau}} \tan^{-1}\dfrac{p_1}{\sqrt{2\tau}}\right) & (\tau > 0) \end{cases} \tag{19}$$

Figure 2 plots the figure flow curves before ($\tau < 0$), after ($\tau > 0$), and at ($\tau = 0$) the annihilation event of the local maximum point M and the saddle point S. The annihilation point P is called a shoe point because of the shape of the surface [11,13]. The shoe point has outward figure flow curves, but only one

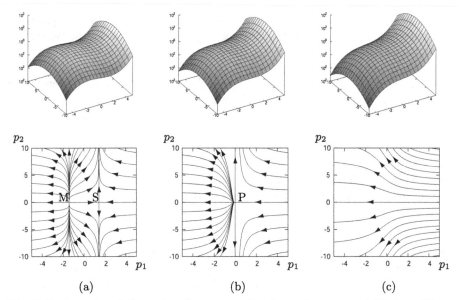

Fig. 2. Surface plot of $f(p_1, p_2)$ and corresponding figure flow curves (a) before, (b) at, and (c) after the Fold catastrophe event

inward figure flow curve is found. Here we call it "anti-directional figure flow curve". We clearly see that the anti-directional figure flow curve coincides with the zero principal curvature direction, that is, p_1-axis.

Let us observe the anti-directional figure flow curve in a global region of image at the annihilation scale. Figure 3(a) illustrates the annihilation of local maximum and saddle. The anti-directional figure flow curve reaches the shoe point P along the "instep" of the shoe. The anti-directional figure flow curve connects the shoe point P to another maximum point Q as the source of the flow. Therefore, the maximum point Q can be considered as the parent node of the annihilation point P. Since the ridge-like saddle point appears between the local maximum points, the anti-directional figure flow curve always connects the annihilation point of one local maximum to the other local maximum.

3.3   Connectivity to the Point at Infinity

The generic annihilation events of local minimum point and the saddle point can be also described as the Fold catastrophes when we take $\gamma > 0$ in (15). It can be deduced that the stationary point as the parent of annihilation point of the local minimum and trough-like saddle is always the minimum point.

However, we cannot always identify the stationary point as the parent of annihilation point in the finite domain of image. Figure 3(b) shows such a case of the annihilation event. The annihilation point P in Fig. 3(b) has inward figure flow curves, but only one outward figure flow curve is found as the anti-directional figure flow curve. The outward figure flow curve reaches the boundary of the region of image.

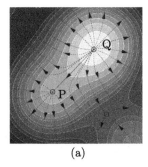 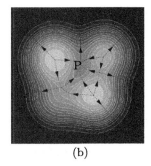

(a) (b)

Fig. 3. Figure flow around annihilation points. (a) The shoe point. The anti-directional figure flow (solid line) penetrates into the shoe point P, which leads to a maximum point Q as the source of the flow. (b) An annihilation point P of a local minimum point and a saddle point. The anti-directional figure flow (solid curve) from P does not have a drain in the region.

This example suggests that the annihilation point like this case is linked to a drain of whole image intensity, that is, a local minimum point at infinity. Since the image $f(x, \tau)$ is defined in the infinite domain, all of the outward figure flow curves from the whole region of the image, including the anti-directional figure flow curve, are considered to converge at the local minimum point at infinity.

Furthermore, we presume that the local minimum point at infinity is annihilated with one remaining maximum point at infinite scale. At the infinite scale, the scale-space image $f(x, \tau)$ is completely flat and no stationary point is found. This concept allows us to connect the remaining maximum curve to the local minimum curve at infinity.

Consequently, the annihilation points of the maximum points are linked to the other local maximum points via anti-directional figure flow curves at the annihilation scales. The annihilation points of the minimum points are linked to the other local minimum points including a local minimum point at infinity. When we observe the stationary point with decreasing scale from the coarsest scale, a first local minimum point is generically linked to the local minimum point at infinity.

3.4   Scale-Space Tree

The hierarchical relationships among the annihilation points are described as a tree. The root of the tree is a virtual annihilation point of the local minimum point at infinity and the remaining maximum point at infinite scale. The nodes of the tree are annihilation points. Stationary points which are connected to the annihilation points by the anti-directional figure flow curves are also selected as the nodes of the tree. Some nodes may be the points at infinity. The leaves of the tree are the stationary points at the finest scale, including the local minimum point at infinity. The branches indicate the connections between the nodes by the stationary curves across scale and the anti-directional figure flow curves at fixed scale. Thus, the figure field and stationary curves define the scale-space hierarchy.

4 Application

We demonstrate the classification of two-dimensional images, using a rotating box sequence [17]. The sequence consists of 29 frame images, in which the box with rectangular faces rotates from left to right. Since the frame images display the dark box in bright background, we analyse negative images of the original frame images. The scale-space tree is constructed for each frame image. Note that we omit some branches which do not concern any topological changes of the tree throughout the sequence.

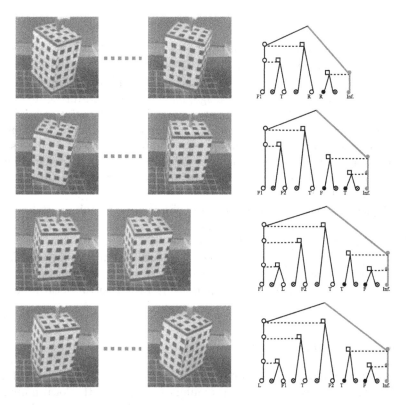

Fig. 4. Groups of images and corresponding scale-space trees of rotating box. The first row: the 1st to 11th frames, the second row: the 12th to 19th frames, the third row: the 20th and 21st frames, and the fourth row: the 22nd to 29th frames. The open circle, filled circle and crossed circle indicate local maximum, local minimum, and saddle point. Inf. indicates the local minimum at infinity.

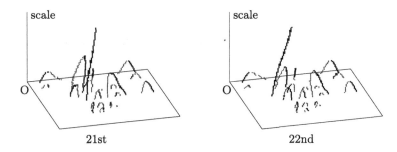

Fig. 5. Switch of the trunk curve between the 21st and 22nd frames. The stationary curves are plotted in (x, y, τ) scale space, where O indicates the top-left of the image.

Figure 4 shows the frame images and resulting scale-space trees. The image sequence is segmented into four groups of frames according to three major transitions of the tree observed in coarse scale. In the first transition, nodes of the annihilation points of extrema R corresponding to the right face of the box disappear from the tree at 11th frame. Instead, a new local minimum F, T and a local maximum F2 uprise in the front face and top face of the box. A local minimum L representing dark pieces in the left face appears in the second transition at 20th frame. The front face of the box is dominant in the 12th to 19th frame images. The third transition is a switch of local maximum curves between the 21st and 22nd frames. The trunk curve switches the connection from the local maximum point in the front face to that in the left face, see Fig. 5. This indicates the shift of weight center of image intensity due to the appearance of the left face.

As a result, temporal segmentation of the motion image of the rotating box is achieved based on the scale-space hierarchy. In this experiment, several levels of scale-space tree are enough to detect the critical frames of the appearance/disappearance of faces, and the transition of dominant part of the box in the motion image.

5   Conclusions

We showed that the stationary curves across scale and the figure field at fixed scale define the scale-space hierarchy. The scale-space tree has two types of nodes: the annihilation points and additional local extrema. The local extrema selected as the nodes are linked to the annihilation points by the anti-directional figure flow curves, of which directions coincide with the zero principal curvature directions at the annihilation points. A local minimum point at infinity can be involved in the annihilation events of local minimum point. The point at infinity is connected to a remaining maximum point at infinite scale.

The scale-space tree is a powerful tool to classify the images. We demonstrated temporal segmentation of motion image as a potential application. The sequence of images is segmented into groups based on the hierarchical structures of frame images. This temporal segmentation scheme is non-heuristic, non-model-based, and is performed without any quantitative estimation such as edge extraction, motion estimation, etc.

References

1. Iijima, T., *Basic theory on the normalization of pattern (in case of typical one-dimensional pattern)*, Bulletin of Electro-technical Laboratory, 26, 368-388, 1962 (in Japanese).
2. Iijima, T., *Basic theory on the normalization of two-dimensional visual pattern*, Studies on Information and Control, Pattern Recognition Issue, IEICE Japan, 1, 15-22, 1963 (in Japanese).
3. Iijima, T., *Basic equation of figure and observational transformations*, IEICE Japan, Trans. C., 54-C, 37-38, 1971.
4. Iijima, T., *Pattern Recognition*, Corona Pub. Co. Ltd., Tokyo, 1973 (in Japanese).
5. Iijima, T., *The Fundamental Theory of Visual Information: The Foundation of the Pattern Recognition Problem*, Corona Pub. Co. Ltd., Tokyo, 1999.
6. Witkin, A.P., *Scale space filtering*, Proc. of 8th IJCAI, 1019-1022, 1983.
7. Koenderink,.J. J., *The structure of images*, Biological Cybernetics, 50, 363-370, 1984.
8. Zhao, N.-Y., Iijima, T., *Theory on the method of determination of view-point and field of vision during observation and measurement of figure*, IEICE Japan, Trans. D., J68-D, 508-514, 1985 (in Japanese).
9. Zhao, N.-Y., Iijima, T., *A theory of feature extraction by the tree of stable view-points.* IEICE Japan, Trans. D., J68-D, 1125-1135, 1985 (in Japanese).
10. Weickert, J., Ishikawa, S., Imiya, A., *Linear Scale-Space has First been Proposed in Japan*, Journal of Mathematical Imaging and Vision, 10, 237-252, 1999.
11. Griffin, L. D., Colchester, A., *Superficial and deep structure in linear diffusion scale space: Isophotes, critical points and separatrices*, Image and Vision Computing, 13, 7, pp. 543-557, 1995.
12. Kuijper, A., Florack, L.M.J., Viergever, M.A., *Scale Space Hierarchy*, Journal of Mathematical Imaging and Vision, 18-2, 169-189, 2003.
13. Olsen, O.F., Nielsen, M., *Generic events for the gradient squared with application to multi-scale segmentation*, LNCS, 1252, 101-112, 1997.
14. Kuijper, A., *The deep structure of Gaussian scale-space images*, PhD thesis, Utrecht University, 2002.
15. Damon, J., *Local Morse Theory for Solutions to the Heat Equation and Gaussian Blurring*, Journal of Differentia Equations, 115, 368-401, 1995.
16. Damon, J., *Generic Properties of Solutions to Partial Differential Equations*, Arch. Rational Mech. Anal., 140, 353-403, 1997.
17. Computer Vision Laboratory at UMass, http://vis-www.cs.umass.edu/vislib /Motion/box/images.html

Computing 3D Symmetry Sets; A Case Study*

Arjan Kuijper and Ole Fogh Olsen

Image Group, IT-University of Copenhagen,
Rued Langgaardsvej 7, DK-2300 Copenhagen, Denmark

Abstract. In this paper we discuss the implementation of methods to derive 3D Symmetry Sets, given a parameterized shape, as well as an unorganized point cloud. It presents a geometric method to derive the Symmetry Set, that is an extension of the one given in [6]. Although the mathematics is a simple extension of the 2D case, the visualization, numerical computations and their stability are much more complicated. An example is given by means of an ellipsoid. In this example the Symmetry Set can be computed exactly and results can be compared to the ground truth.

1 Introduction

Although there has been no publication on 3D Symmetry Sets (yet), there has been published quite a lot of work on deriving and presenting the Medial Axis in 3D. Most of the geometrical approaches that incorporate knowledge of possible and allowed transitions is due to Leymarie proposing a method to derive the Medial Axis in 3D [8,7,9], as well as Kimia and Giblin, who give a formal classification of the Medial Axis points [3] and transitions [2] Also Voronoi diagrams to detect the skeleton, in combination with ridges for additional information, have been reported [4].

In this work we consider shapes in 3D. These shapes are considered to be closed 2D manifolds that allow a parameterization for the purpose of computing the Symmetry Set by the standard definition introduced by Bruce, Giblin and Gibson [1].

Let $L(x, y, z) = 0$ define implicitly a shape. Then its Gaussian surface curvature K and Mean surface curvature H (Koenderink, [5], p. 515) are given by

$$K = \frac{L_x^2 L_{yy} L_{zz} + L_y^2 L_{xx} L_{zz} + L_z^2 L_{xx} L_{yy}}{(L_x^2 + L_y^2 + L_z^2)^2}$$
$$H = \frac{L_x^2 (L_{yy} + L_{zz}) + L_y^2 (L_{xx} + L_{zz}) + L_z^2 (L_{xx} + L_{yy})}{2(L_x^2 + L_y^2 + L_z^2)^{\frac{3}{2}}}$$

and the minimal and maximal curvatures follow from

$$\kappa_{max} = H + \sqrt{H^2 - K}$$
$$\kappa_{min} = H - \sqrt{H^2 - K}$$

* This work is part of the DSSCV project supported by the IST Programme of the European Union (IST-2001-35443). WWW home page: http://www.itu.dk/Internet/sw1953.asp

O.F. Olsen et al. (Eds.): DSSCV 2005, LNCS 3753, pp. 193–204, 2005.

At umbilic points [10] , the two principal curvatures coincide and $H^2 = K$. These points are generically isolated points. Also both evolutes intersect at these points. All other intersections of the two evolutes are due to different points of the shape.

On the shape, ridges can be identified, defined as those points with locally extremal curvature in one principal direction.

Since there are two distinct curvatures, we can assign to each point the points $\mathcal{S} + \mathcal{N}/\kappa_{min}$ and $\mathcal{S} + \mathcal{N}/\kappa_{max}$, where $\mathcal{N}$ is the unit normal vector. They define two evolutes, representing the maximal and the minimal curvatures.

2 Ellipsoid

Since 3D Medial Axes are hard to compute and visualize, the forecast for these tasks on the Symmetry Set is bad. In order to get at least the visualization as clear as possible, we investigate a simple shape that allows an exact computation, viz. an ellipsoid. Although it is still very artificial, it is the first shape (next to the "degenerated sphere) that gives a non-trivial Symmetry Set. In (x, y, z) coordinates, define a generic ellipsoid by

$$L(x, y, z) = \frac{x^2}{a^2} + \frac{y^2}{b^2} + \frac{z^2}{c^2} = 1,$$

with $a > b > c > 0$. The ellipsoid had its endpoints at $\pm(a, 0, 0)$, $\pm(0, b, 0)$, and $\pm(0, 0, c)$. An example with $(a, b, c) = (6, 3, 2)$ is given in Figure 1.

The ridges of the ellipsoid occur at $x = 0$, $y = 0$, and $z = 0$. In Figure 1 they are visible as the curves. They intersect pair wise at the poles (bright blobs). Note that the apparently triple intersection is due to projection.

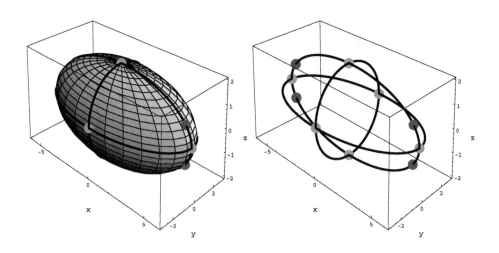

Fig. 1. An ellipsoid with ridges and special points (see text)

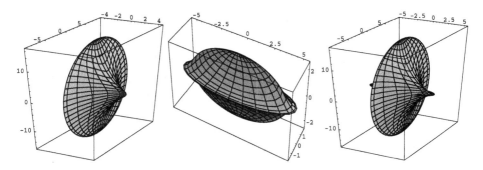

Fig. 2. The evolutes for the ellipsoid. From left to right: depending on the maximal curvature, the minimal curvature, and both (intersecting) evolutes.

The ellipsoid has four umbilic points [10] at $(\pm a \cos \phi, 0, c \sin \phi)$ with ϕ the solutions of $a^2 \sin^2 \phi + c^2 \cos^2 \phi = b^2$. In Figure 1 they are visible as the dark blobs.

Its Gaussian surface curvature K, Mean surface curvature H, and the minimal and maximal curvatures follow directly from the previous section.

So to each point we can assign the points $S + \mathcal{N}/\kappa_{min}$ and $S + \mathcal{N}/\kappa_{max}$, defining two evolutes. They are shown in Figure 2. Note that they intersect, as shown in the right plot. The umbilic points lie on the intersection curves.

2.1   Implicit Surface: (x, y, z) Data

In the remainder, let $a = 6, b = 3, c = 2$. Then $\mathcal{N}(x, y, z) = (x, 4y, 9z)(x^2 + 16y^2 + 81z^2)^{-1/2}$ and locations of the SS are found at $(x, y, z) - r\mathcal{N}$. Since the shape is symmetric, the locations are at the $x = 0$, $y = 0$, and $z = 0$ ovoids.

Then for r the values $r_{x=0} = (x^2 + 16y^2 + 81z^2)^{1/2}$, $r_{y=0} = \frac{1}{4}(x^2 + 16y^2 + 81z^2)^{1/2}$, and $r_{z=0} = \frac{1}{9}(x^2 + 16y^2 + 81z^2)^{1/2}$ are found, with the SS ovoids $p_{x=0}$, $p_{y=0}$, and $p_{z=0}$.

The first ovoid, $p_{x=0} = (0, -3y, -8z)$, is given by $(16y)^2 + (9z)^2 = (144)^2$, with its extremal positions $\pm(0, 9, 0)$ and $\pm(0, 0, 16)$

The second one, $p_{y=0} = (3x/4, 0, -5z/4)$, is given by $(5x)^2 + (9z)^2 = (45/2)^2$, with its extremal positions $\pm(\frac{9}{2}, 0, 0)$ and $\pm(0, 0, \frac{5}{2})$

The third one, $p_{z=0} = (8x/9, 5y/9, 0)$, is given by $(5x)^2 + (16y)^2 = (80/3)^2$, with its extremal positions $\pm(\frac{16}{3}, 0, 0)$ and $\pm(0, \frac{5}{3}, 0)$.

This is visualized in Figure 3. The left image shows the ovoids. The bright point mark the positions of the pole-related points, while the dark points the umbilic related point represent. The lines are due to the ridges forming the boundaries of the ovoids - the A_3 curves- and the intersections of ovoids - A_1^2/A_1^2 lines. The origin is an $A_1^2/A_1^2/A_1^2$ point, while the intersection with the A_3 curves result in $A_1 A_3$ points. They are also shown in the middle image. The right image shows a close-up, where it can be seen that the umbilic related points are indeed on the curves. The umbilic points are found to be at $\phi = \pm \arccos(\pm \frac{3}{8}\sqrt{6})$, at the points $(\pm \frac{9}{4}\sqrt{6}, 0, \pm \frac{1}{4}\sqrt{10})$.

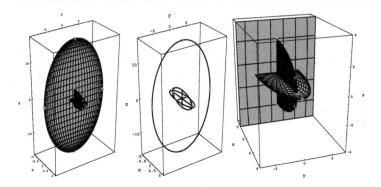

Fig. 3. Left: symmetry set ovoids with special points and curves. Middle: The special curves and special points. Right: Close-up of the symmetry set ovoids with special points and curves.

The evolutes intersect at the umbilic point. They also form the boundary of the Symmetry Set ovoids in the cusp-curves (just as the 2D Symmetry Set is bounded in the cusp-point of the evolute). At the umbilic point the two evolutes interchange their task in bounding the Symmetry Set ovoid that intersects the shape with its boundary. The other two ovoids have boundaries either completely inside (in this case the Medial Axis ovoid), or completely outside the shape.

In this simple case the pre-symmetry set can be computed exactly, and is given by the sets of points (x, y, z) combined with $(-x, y, z),(x, -y, z)$, and $(x, y, -z)$.

2.2   Parameterisation - s, t Data

A parameterisation of $L(x, y, t)$ is given by $(6 \sin s \cos t, 3 \cos s \cos t, 2 \sin t)$, with $s \in [-\pi, \pi[$ and $t \in [-\frac{\pi}{2}, \frac{\pi}{2}[$. The extremal positions are obtained for $(s, t) = ((s, -\frac{\pi}{2}), (s, \frac{\pi}{2}), (0, 0), (\pi, 0), (\frac{\pi}{2}, 0)), (-\frac{\pi}{2}, 0)$ which relate to $(x, y, z) = ((0, 0, -2), (0, 0, 2), (0, 3, 0), (0, -3, 0), (6, 0, 0), (-6, 0, 0))$, respectively.

Note that for $t = \pm\frac{\pi}{2}$ the two poles are obtained. There all s values coincide. Ridge lines - A_3 curves of the SS - are found on the boundary of each ellipse. The symmetry set ovoids are given by

$\qquad p_{x=0} = (0, -3y, -8z)$, so $(x, y, z) = (0, -9 \cos s \cos t, -16 \sin t)$,
$\qquad p_{y=0} = (3x/4, 0, -5z/4)$, so $(x, y, z) = (\frac{9}{2} \sin s \cos t, 0, -\frac{5}{2} \sin t)$, and
$\qquad p_{z=0} = (8x/9, 5y/9, 0)$, so $(x, y, z) = (\frac{16}{3} \sin s \cos t, \frac{5}{3} \cos s \cos t, 0)$.

The curvatures along the ridges are shown in Figure 4. The intersection of the two curvatures in the middle graph is due to the umbilic points. The curvatures coincide for $(s, t) = (\pm\frac{1}{2}\pi, \pm \arccos(\pm\frac{3}{8}\sqrt{6}))$. These D_4^+ points are on the boundary of $p_{y=0}$. They do not affect the ellipse, although the minimal curvature (bounding the Symmetry Set) has a non-differential point there.

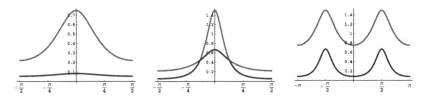

Fig. 4. Curvatures along ridges. a) $x = 0$, b) $y = 0$, c) $z = 0$.

2.3 Pre-symmetry Set Surfaces

For the pre-Symmetry Set we find the sets
$(s, t, -s, t)$ (for $(x, y, z) = (-x, y, z)$),
$(s, t, \|\pi - s\|_\pi, t)$ (for $(x, y, z) = (x, -y, z)$), and
$(s, t, s, -t)$ (for $(x, y, z) = (x, y, -z)$).
The axes of symmetry in the pre-symmetry set are, respectively,
$s = 0, \pi$ i.e. $(x, y, z) = (0, \pm 3\cos t, 2\sin t)$, the ridge in the $x = 0$ ovoid,
$s = \pm \pi/2$ i.e. $(x, y, z) = (\pm 6 \cos t, 0, 2\sin t)$, the ridge in the $y = 0$ ovoid, and
$t = 0$ i.e. $(x, y, z) = (6\sin s, 3\cos s, 0)$, the ridge in the $z = 0$ ovoid.

Therefore the ridge lines in the pre-Symmetry Set are formed by the curves
$(0, t, 0, t)$, (π, t, π, t), $(\pi/2, t, \pi/2, t)$, $(-\pi/2, t, -\pi/2, t)$, and $(s, 0, s, 0)$.

Intersections take place at $(s, t, -s, t) = (s, t, s, -t)$, so $s = 0, \pi$ and $t = 0$ due
to boundary conditions of s and t. Therefore intersections occur at $(s, t) = (0, 0)$,
i.e. $(x, y, t) = (0, 3, 0)$, and $(s, t) = (\pi, 0)$, i.e. $(x, y, t) = (0, -3, 0)$. This implies
that they occur at the extremal points on the y-axis. This intersection implies
$(-x, y, z) = (x, y, -z)$, so $(x, y, z) = (0, y, z]$ is expected, with $y = \pm 3$: the
intersection of the two ridges in the $x = 0$ and $z = 0$ ovoids.

$(s, t, s, -t) = (s, t, \|\pi - s\|_\pi, t)$, so $s = \pm \pi/2$ and $t = 0$. Then $(s, t) = (-\pi/2, 0)$, i.e. $(x, y, t) = (-6, 0, 0)$, and $(s, t) = (\pi/2, 0)$, i.e. $(x, y, t) = (6, 0, 0)$.
This implies that they occur at the extremal points on the x-axis.

$(s, t, -s, t) = (s, t, \|\pi - s\|_\pi, t)$, so $t = \pm \pi/2$. Then $(s, t) = (s, -\pi/2)$, i.e.
$(x, y, t) = (0, 0, -2)$, and $(s, t) = (s, \pi/2)$, i.e. $(x, y, t) = (0, 0, 2)$. This implies
that they occur at the extremal points on the z-axis, the poles.

Therefore, intersections of the pre-symmetry set surfaces occur at the extremal values of the ellipsoid.

3 Computation

In the following sections we present three different ways to compute the 3D
symmetry set of the ellipsoid. The 3D symmetry set is defined similarly to the
2D case: the closure of centers of spheres tangent to the shape at at least two
points. The radius r and the center of the sphere are given by

$$p_i - rN_i = p_j \pm rN_j \tag{1}$$

3.1   Exact Computation

For the exact computation, we take the parameterised ellipsoid and get a set of data points by choosing $s = \frac{\pi}{20} + i\frac{\pi}{10}$, $i = 0, 1, \ldots, 19$, and $t = -\frac{\pi}{2} + \frac{\pi}{40} + j\frac{\pi}{20}$, $j = 0, 1, \ldots, 19$. So there are 20 x 20 data points, see Figure 5a. Note that the poles and ridges are not taken into the parameterisation.

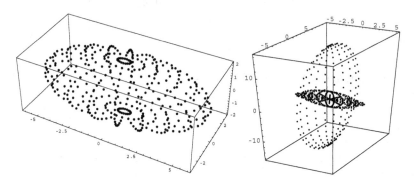

Fig. 5. a) Selected points. b) Symmetry Set.

Next, the pre-SS is *constructed* by choosing the sets $(s, t, -s, t)$, $(s, t, \|\pi - s\|_\pi, t)$, and $(s, t, s, -t)$. The corresponding SS is derived from the 3D extension of the 2D algorithm presented in [6]. It solves equation 1 exactly by construction of the pre-SS.

The results are shown in Figure 5b. The separate ovoids are visualized in Figure 6.

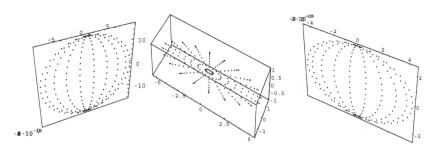

Fig. 6. 3 distinct ovoids of the Symmetry Set

As a check of the correctness of the solution, we verify that the minimum absolute value of each triple (x, y, z) that is found as an SS point, is "close enough" to zero: note that the SS points form filled ellipses in the $x = 0$, $y = 0$, or $z = 0$ ovoids. This graph is shown in Figure 7. It is within machine precision,

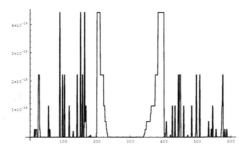

Fig. 7. Minimum absolute value of each SS triple (x, y, z), ideally equal to zero

$O(10^{-16})$. Note that 600 points (200 in each ovoid) are found. The algorithm generates 3 x 20 x 20 = 1200 points, but half of them occur double due to symmetry.

3.2   Extension of the 2D Zero-Crossings Algorithm

If the pre-SS needs to be computed from the data points and their normal vectors, similar equations hold as in the 2D case for the zero-crossings algorithm if the shape is (s, t)-parameterized and p_1 is short notation for $p(s_1, t_1)$:

$$(p_1 - p_2).(N_i \pm N_j) = 0$$
$$(p_1 - p_2).(N_i \times N_j) = 0 \qquad (2)$$

The second constraint is new in 3D and rises from the fact that the line $(N_i \times N_j)$ is the intersection of the two normal ovoids. This line is given by $(N_{y1}N_{z2} - N_{y2}N_{z1}, -N_{x1}N_{z2} + N_{x2}N_{z1}, N_{x1}N_{y2} - N_{x2}N_{y1})$.

As in the 2D case, the Anti Symmetry Set points should be removed from this set. These points satisfy the fact that their tangent planes are parallel. Equivalently, the normal vectors are aligned. Consequently, the normal at the first point is perpendicular to the tangent plane at the second plane. This plane is computed as follows. Let $v_1 = N_1 = (a, b, c)$. Then two vectors are sought that satisfy $v_1.v_2 = 0$, $v_1.v_3 = 0$, and $v_2.v_3 = 0$. One combination satisfying these constraints is the set $v_2 = (-2bc, ac, ab)$ and $v_3 = (ab^2 - ac^2, -a^2b - 2bc^2, a^2c + 2b^2c)$.

So the ASS is found as the intersection of the solutions of

$$(N_{x1}, N_{y1}, N_{z1}).(2N_{y2}N_{z2}, N_{x2}N_{z2}, N_{x2}N_{y2}) = 0$$
$$(N_{x1}, N_{y1}, N_{z1}).(N_{x2}N_{y2}^2 - N_{x2}N_{z2}^2, -N_{x2}^2N_{y2} - 2N_{y2}N_{z2}^2, N_{x2}^2N_{z2} + 2N_{y2}^2N_{z2}) = 0 \qquad (3)$$

Note that the pre-SS space is a 4D space. The zero-crossings are obtained by taking changes in the signs of the equations above in all four directions.

Calculation of the pre-SS and SS. To compute the pre-SS, one should be careful. If the data is constructed as in the previous section, one enters exact

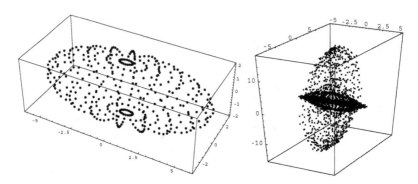

Fig. 8. a) Selected points. b) Symmetry Set.

solutions of the positions of zero-crossings. This is non-generic in general, and the algorithm, detecting only full sign-changes, will fail to find these points. So additional infinitesimal noise should be added to generate a generic parameterized point cloud. Noise is taken in the order of $O(10^{-5})$ and affects both the positions - so points may be slightly off-ellipse, and normal vectorss - so they are not calculated at the right position and do not have exactly unit length. The point cloud, Figure 8a, looks similar to the unperturbed cloud.

In this case with 400 data points computational time is reaching the limits of being acceptable. It takes the algorithm 8.4 seconds to find 24216 points for the first zero-crossing, and 11.4 seconds to find 55556 points for the second zero-crossing, yielding 8210 points on the intersection. Next, it takes 7.4 seconds to find 73359 points for the first ASS zero-crossing, and 11.2 seconds to find 63226 points for the second ASS zero-crossing, yielding 30104 ASS points as intersection. The complement of both intersection results gives 5438 SS-solutions, but since the pre-SS is symmetric, in total 2719 SS-points are found. The resulting symmetry set is shown in Figure 8b.

Next, the points in the three ovoids are shown in Figure 9. This is a view of the SS along each of the three axes, while the plot area is restricted to $(-.1, .1)$.

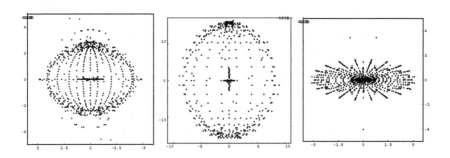

Fig. 9. 3 distinct ovoids of the Symmetry Set

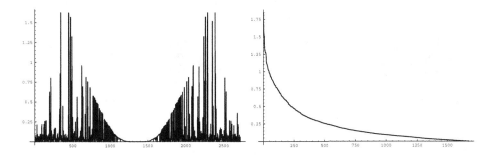

Fig. 10. Minimum absolute value (unsorted and sorted) of each SS triple (x, y, z), ideally equal to zero

As one can see there are some outliers. This is verified by the minimum absolute value of each triple (x, y, z) that is found as an SS point. These minimal values-graph is shown in Figure 10. The left image indicates some symmetry that is indeed present due to the algorithm

The largest value is caused by the point $(-2.16, -1.62, -2.74)$. It resembles to points at $p_1 = (-4.94, 1.26, .7653)$ and $p_2 = (-3.92, 1.96, 7654)$. Apparently, their z values are close. We have $\|p_1 - p_2\| = 1.24$, $\|N_1 - N_2\| = 0.257$, $\|N_1 + N_2\| = 1.98$, $\|N_1 \times N_2\| = .255$. For the two zero-crossing values we find values $(p_1 - p_2).(N_1 + N_2) = .02$ and $(p_1 - p_2).(N_1 \times N_2) = .13$, normalized they are .007 and .43, respectively. Apparently they are found of zero crossings, but due to the relatively flatness of the shape their positions cause a large error in the position.

Outliers. Lets look into ASS points more detailed. Consider the tangent circle for a point $p_1 = (x, y, z)$ with corresponding normal $N_1 = (N_x, N_y, N_z)$. We have as SS point, say, $p_2 = (-x, y, z)$ with corresponding normal $N_2 = (-N_x, N_y, N_z)$, and as an ASS point, say, $p_3 = (-x, -y, z)$ with corresponding normal $N_3 = (-N_x, -N_y, N_z)$.

Now $p_1 - p_2 = (2x, 0, 0)$, $N_1 - N_2 = (2N_x, 0, 0)$, $N_1 + N_2 = (0, 2N_y, 2N_z)$, $N_1 \times N_2 = (0, -2N_x N_y, 2N_y N_x)$. So $(p_1 - p_2).(N_1 + N_2) = 0$ and $(p_1 - p_2).(N_1 \times N_2) = 0$.

Also $p_1 - p_3 = (2x, 2y, 0)$, $N_1 - N_3 = (2N_x, 2N_y, 0)$, $N_1 + N_3 = (0, 0, 2N_z)$, $N_1 \times N_3 = (2N_y N_z, -2N_x N_z, 0)$. So $(p_1 - p_3).(N_1 + N_3) = 0$ and $(p_1 - p_3).(N_1 \times N_3) = 4N_z(xN_y - yN_x)$ which may become (close to) zero for certain combinations of points, especially when two points are nearby. If this is the case, the two normal vectors are almost pointing into the same direction and the norm of their sum is close to 2, and subtracting yields almost 0. So as an extra check one can remove these point combinations.

So, experiment 1: require that $\|N_1 - N_2\| > \epsilon \geq 0$. For $\epsilon = .25$, 1926 SS points are left. However, the point mentioned above is still part of the SS. For $\epsilon = .5$, 2912 SS points are left. The maximal minimum values are significantly lower. See Figure 11a,b.

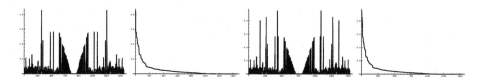

Fig. 11. a) min norm constraint. b) Idem, sorted. c) max norm constraint. d) Idem, sorted.

Experiment 2: require that $\|N_1 + N_2\| < \epsilon \leq 2$. For $\epsilon = 1.98$ 1906 SS points are left. Also in this case, the point mentioned above is still part of the SS. For $\epsilon = 1.95$ 3066 SS points are left. The maximal minimum values are again significantly lower. See Figure 11c,d.

Apparently subtracting is less sensitive. Furthermore, setting this norm seems to affect the large SS-ellipse. This makes sense, since it depends on the parts of the shape that are most flat, requires longest radii and have (thus) normal vectors that are close to each other.

Another constraint may be requiring that the normalised inner product values of the vectors found as zero-crossings, is small. Set it to .2 for both, in combination with $\|N_1 - N_2\| > .5$, gives 994 points with maximum minimal error value .55. This opens possibilities to the next approach.

3.3   Symmetry Sets from Point Clouds

Apparently, the parameterisation causes problems, especially at the north and south poles, but also at points in flat regions. To overcome these problems, extra constraints can be added. What one does in that case, is not looking for zero-crossings explicitly, but pairs of points that are close enough to be considered as zero crossings. As zero-crossings require a parameterization, the "close enough" approach can be considered as parameterless.

It is therefore worth the effort to investigate what these constraints would do on a random point set. That is, given an arbitrary set of points p_i on the ellipse with unit normal vectors N_i, select each combination satisfying

$$(p_1 - p_2).(N_1 + N_2) < \delta_1$$
$$(p_1 - p_2).(N_1 \times N_2) < \delta_2 \qquad (4)$$
$$\|N_1 - N_2\| > \epsilon$$

and define this set as the Symmetry Set.

This approach has been taken in the following. A random point set on the ellipsoid is taken in the (x, y, z) space, see Figure 12. A selection in the (s, t) space yields a similar cloud, although more points are close to the north and south poles. One can see that the large ovoid is least detailed, as expected. Since the normal vectors are known by definition, regularization is not needed and the Symmetry Set can be computed directly. With 1000 points, 10191 Symmetry Set points are found in 150 seconds. Limiting to 500 points, 2573 points are found

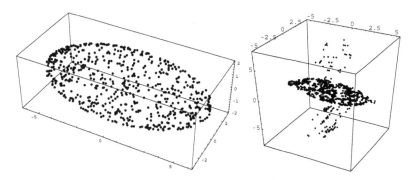

Fig. 12. a) Randomly selected points. b) Symmetry Set.

in 37 seconds. For the latter we set $\delta_1 = .1$, $\delta_2 = .75$, and $\epsilon = 1.95$, yielding 1599 points.

The deviation from the ovoids is in the order of the previous calculations, see Figure 13. Of course, more tuning of the parameters δ_1, δ_2, and ϵ may improve the performance.

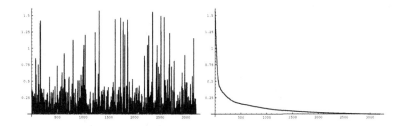

Fig. 13. Minimum absolute value of each SS triple - random point cloud

4 Conclusions and Perspectives

For shapes in 3D, the Symmetry Set can be computed using a simple extension of the approach taken in the 2D case. Although this is an almost trivial extension, numerical problems arise earlier than in the 2D case. Since the algorithms imply computation of the pre-Symmetry Set, the complexity of the algorithm prohibits large data sets. A refinement of the shape in adding more data points is therefore not possible.

The zero crossings method used requires a parameterisation. Since additional parameters / thresholds are needed to avoid numerical instabilities, the parameterization may as well be ignored and the method works on unordered point clouds. In the example given the normal vectors were known a priori, but if they need to be estimated by means of some kind of regularisation, (large) errors may be introduced. This needs more experiments.

Next, the visualization of the Symmetry Set in 3D is hard. It cannot be avoided by using the pre-Symmetry Set, since this set lives in a 4D space, albeit that the set itself contains only 2D manifolds. The use of this set and some of the mathematical properties may reveal interesting and useful starting points. For instance, in 2D curves in the pre-SS do not intersect, while in 3D they do.

References

1. J. W. Bruce, P. J. Giblin, and C. Gibson. Symmetry sets. *Proceedings of the Royal Society of Edinburgh*, 101(A):163–186, 1985.
2. P. J. Giblin and B. B. Kimia. Transitions of the 3D medial axis under a one-parameter family of deformations. In *Proceedings of the 7th European Conference on Computer Vision (2002)*, pages 718–734, 2002. LNCS 2351.
3. P. J. Giblin and B. B. Kimia. A formal classification of the 3D medial axis points and their local geometry. *IEEE Transactions on Pattern Analysis and Machine Intelligence*, 26(2):238–251, 2004.
4. M. Hisada, A. G. Belyaev, and T. L. Kunii. Towards a singularity-based shape language: ridges, ravines, and skeletons for polygonal surfaces. *Soft Computing*, 7(1):45–52, 2002.
5. J. J. Koenderink. *Solid Shape*. MIT Press, Cambridge, Massachusetts, 1990.
6. A. Kuijper, O.F. Olsen, P.J. Giblin, Ph. Bille, and M. Nielsen. From a 2D shape to a string structure using the symmetry set. In *Proceedings of the 8th European Conference on Computer Vision - ECCV 2004, Part II (Prague, Czech Republic, May 11-14, 2004)*, volume II, pages 313–326, 2004. LNCS 3022.
7. F. Leymarie. *3D Shape Representation via Shock Flows*. PhD thesis, Division of Enginering., Brown University, Providence, RI, 02912, 2003.
8. F. Leymarie and B.B. Kimia. The shock scaffold for representing 3D shapes. In *Proceedings International Workshop on Visual Form*, volume 2059, pages 216–228, 2001. LNCS 2059.
9. F. Leymarie and B.B. Kimia. Computation of the shock scaffold for unorganized point clouds in 3D. In *Proceedings IEEE Computer Society Conference on Computer Vision and Pattern Recognition (CVPR'03)*, volume 1, pages 821–827, 2003.
10. Ian Porteous. *Geometric Differentiation - for the intelligence of curves and surfaces*. Cambridge University Press, Cambridge, UK, 1994. 301 pages.

Irradiation Orientation from Obliquely Viewed Texture

Sylvia C. Pont and Jan J. Koenderink

Helmholtz Institute, Utrecht University

Abstract. We studied image texture due to the shading of corrugated (3D textured) surfaces, which are Lambertian on the micro scale. Our theory applies to physically canonical cases of isotropic Gaussian random surfaces, under collimated illumination. In this investigation we analyze effects of oblique viewing, extending our theory which applied to normal viewing conditions only [5]. The theory for normal views predicts the structure tensors from either the gradient or the Hessian of the image intensity and allows for inferences of the orientation of irradiation of the surface. Even for surfaces that are not at all Gaussian, the BRDF [10] far from Lambertian, with vignetting and multiple scattering present, such inferences of the orientation of irradiation were accurate up to a few degrees. In this paper we derive predictions for oblique viewing conditions, for which the inferences of the irradiation orientation will deviate from the veridical value in a systematic manner, depending on the viewing and illumination directions. Theoretical predictions are compared with empirical data, for rendered and for real rough surfaces, and found to be in good agreement. We discuss issues of scale selection and robustness.

1   Introduction

In this paper, we present a practical result of application of first/second order scale space theory. In images of natural scenes, image texture due to the illumination of rough (three-dimensionally corrugated) surfaces provides us with cues about the illumination [2,4,8]. We showed that for frontally viewed rough surfaces, the second order image intensity structure of the texture (a statistical description) depends directly on the tangential component of the light vector [5]. We were able to infer the orientation of the irradiation of the surface on the basis of the structure tensors from either the gradient or the Hessian of the image intensity. Interestingly, human observer performance was similar to the results of our computer vision algorithm [6]. This theory was based on rather restrictive assumptions (locally Lambertian [7] isotropic random Gaussian surfaces under collimated illumination in normal view) and effects of shadowing, occlusions, and multiple scattering were neglected. Still, for textures from the Curet database [3], irradiation orientations were recovered empirically with an accuracy of a few degrees. In this paper, we extend our theory with oblique viewing conditions, and we test our theory for Gaussian surfaces.

O.F. Olsen et al. (Eds.): DSSCV 2005, LNCS 3753, pp. 205–210, 2005.

2   Theory

For an in-depth treatment of the statistics of the illuminance distribution for stationary, isotropic, random Gaussian surfaces with shallow relief, Lambertian reflectance [7] and constant albedo, illuminated obliquely with a collimated beam of radiation, and viewed frontally, see [5]. Consider a collimated beam from the direction $\mathbf{j} = \cos\vartheta(\cos\varphi\mathbf{e_x} + \sin\varphi\mathbf{e_y}) + \sin\vartheta\mathbf{e_z}$, where $\mathbf{e_z} = \mathbf{n}$ the local surface normal whereas $\mathbf{e_{x,y}}$ span the tangent plane. Because we assume isotropic corrugations the direction of $\mathbf{e_x}$ has to be assigned arbitrarily. Derivation of the squared gradient and Hessian, applying the theories of Longuet-Higgins [9] and of Berry and Hannay [1], leads to the fact that both the squared gradient $\mathbf{G_2}$ and the Hessian $\mathbf{H_2}$ are equal to the symmetric matrix

$$\mathbf{S} = \frac{M_{2n}}{8}\cot^2\vartheta\begin{pmatrix} 2 + \cos 2\varphi & \sin 2\varphi \\ \sin 2\varphi & 2 - \cos 2\varphi \end{pmatrix},$$

with $n = 2$ for $\mathbf{G_2}$ and $n = 3$ for $\mathbf{H_2}$. The factor of proportionality depends upon the particular circular moments M_{2n} that characterize the surface texture, $i.e.$, on the particular autocorrelation function of the heights. The angular dependence itself is quite independent of the circular moments. The eigenvectors of $\mathbf{S}$ are $\{\cos\varphi, \sin\varphi\}$ (it points in (or away from) the direction of illumination) with eigenvalue 3 and $\{\cos(\varphi + \pi/2), \sin(\varphi + \pi/2)\}$ with eigenvalue 1. The confidence is $c = (\lambda_1^2 - \lambda_2^2)/(\lambda_1^2 + \lambda_2^2) = 0.8$, indicating a rather strong orientational bias.

If the surfaces are viewed from an oblique angle instead of frontally, the 3D texture will be affected by foreshortening and local occlusions. We study the effect of foreshortening theoretically; effects of local occlusions will be studied empirically in future research, but will be neglected in our theoretical shallow relief approach. Let φ denote the azimuth of the direction of illumination in the unforeshortened view. Assume that the X-direction suffers a perspective foreshortening by a factor $\cos\mu$ (viewing angle μ). Then each differentiation by x scales the matrix element by $\cos\mu$. Thus the average Hessian becomes:

$$\mathbf{M} = \frac{M_{2n}}{8}\cot^2\vartheta\begin{pmatrix} (2 + \cos 2\varphi)/\cos^2\mu & \sin 2\varphi/\cos\mu \\ \sin 2\varphi/\cos\mu & 2 - \cos 2\varphi \end{pmatrix},$$

If we apply our algorithm straightforward and estimate the irradiance orientation on the basis of the structure tensors from either the gradient or the Hessian of the image intensity we will find an "estimated orientation of incidence":

$$\psi = 1/\arctan\left(\frac{\cos\mu}{2}\frac{1}{\sin 2\varphi}\left(-2 + \cos 2\varphi + \frac{2 + \cos 2\varphi}{\cos^2\mu} + \sqrt{\frac{-12}{\cos^2\mu} + (2 + \frac{2}{\cos^2\mu} + \cos 2\varphi\tan^2\mu)^2}\right)\right),$$

from the eigenvectors of $\mathbf{M}$ (ψ reduces to φ for $\mu = 0$). The confidence can be estimated from the eigenvalues of $\mathbf{M}$, following the definition of c as shown above. The resulting formula is rather unwieldy and therefore not shown.

3 Predictions and Test

Figure 1 shows graphs of predictions of uncorrected estimates of the irradiance orientation (left) and the corresponding confidence levels (right), as a function of the viewing angle μ, for actual irradiance orientations $\varphi = -90°, -85°, ..., 90°$. It is clear that if our original algorithm would be applied without accounting for oblique viewing angles, the results will generally deviate from the veridical irradiation orientation and from the confidence level 0.8. The orientation deviations are larger for more oblique viewing directions and for larger differences between the foreshortening direction and the actual irradiance orientation. The confidence shows "false" high levels which can be as large as 1. The solution behaves critically around 55°. For angles smaller than 55° we expect that the

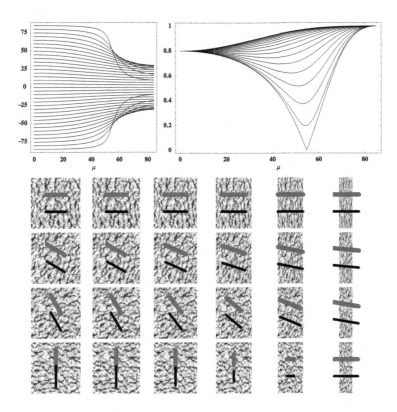

Fig. 1. Top: Graphs of the uncorrected predictions of irradiance orientation estimates (left) and the corresponding confidence levels (right), as a function of the viewing angle μ, for actual irradiance orientations $\varphi = -90°, -85°, ..., 90°$. Bottom: Photographs of Gaussian surfaces which were illuminated from angles of $0°, 30°, 60°, 90°$ (top to bottom) and foreshortened for angles of $\mu = 0°, 15°, ..., 75°$ (left to right). The orientations of the bars represent predictions ψ (in black) and calculations on the basis of the Hessian (in grey). The bar lengths were scaled according to the confidence level.

Fig. 2. An illustration of the issue of scale selection with regard to 3D resolution or shape. The photograph shows textures at two different scales: the macro scale of the balls and the meso scale of the rough finish of the balls. The illumination came from the left. If we choose a scale for the differential operator which is just smaller than the dimensions of the balls and which is much larger than the dimensions of the rough finish of the balls, we find irradiance orientation estimates in accordance with the global irradiance orientation (above right). If we choose the width of the differential operator to be smaller than the dimensions of the roughness on the balls, we find that the irradiance orientation estimates represent the illuminance flow over the balls. Those flow patterns radiate out from the point at which the illumination hits the surface head-on.

orientation estimates can be corrected, using estimates of μ. For viewing angles larger than $55°$ there are no unique solutions on the basis of orientation only.

Figure 1 shows Gaussian textures, illuminated from angles of $0°, 30°, 60°, 90°$ (top to bottom) and foreshortened for angles of $\mu = 0°, 15°, ..., 75°$ (left to right). The orientations of the black and grey bars show predictions ψ and calculations on the basis of the Hessian. The bar lengths were scaled according to the confidence level. It is clear that the predictions and the data are in good agreement. The scales of the Gaussian derivatives and of the area over which the averaging was done were selected according to the following procedure. The scale of the Gaussian derivative was selected to be similar to or smaller than the width of the smallest dipole structures in the textures. This resulted in a small range of numbers for the first scale. Next, we ran our algorithm for several values of the averaging/blurring kernel, resulting in several sets of estimates for the orientations and confidence levels. The data for the globally flat surfaces in Figure 1, were selected from those sets on the basis of maximalization of the median confidence level. Typically the choice of the width of the averaging/blurring kernel for the local estimates would depend on the "shape" or, in other words, 3D resolution; for an illustration see Figure 2. For the Gaussian textures in Figure 1 the complete data set showed that results were robust if the scale of the Gaussian derivative was smaller than the smallest dipole structures. However, if the derivative scale was just slightly larger, the images in the second last column and last rows the estimates depended very much on scale choice. In other words, estimates showed critical behavior around the singular point at $\mu = 55°$.

4   Discussion

The issue of scale selection needs further investigation, with special attention to the presence of multiple scales in foreshortened 3D textures. Currently we are testing our theory for real textures and we are investigating to what extent the effects of oblique viewing can be corrected for, using estimates of local surface orientation from texture. Finally, these studies will provide insight into the 3D texture gradients over 3D objects (illuminance flow [11] over solid, rough objects). These 3D texture gradients provide cues, which are complementary to shading cues, for shape and light field estimates.

Acknowledgments

This work was supported by the Netherlands Organisation for Scientific Research (NWO).

References

1. Berry, M. V., Hannay, J. H.: Umbilic points on Gaussian random surfaces. J.Phys.A: Math.Gen. **10** (1977) 1809–1821
2. Chantler, M., Schmidt, M., Petrou, M., McGunnigle, G.: The effect of illuminant rotation on texture filters: lissajous's ellipses. In: Heyden, A. et al (eds), ECCV2002, Springer, Heidelberg (2002) LNCS2352, 289–303
3. *Columbia–Utrecht Reflectance and Texture Database.* http://www.cs.columbia.edu/CAVE/curet
4. Knill, D.C.: Estimating illuminant direction and degree of surface relief. JOSA A **7** (1990) 759–775.
5. Koenderink, J.J., Pont, S.C.: Irradiation direction from texture. JOSA A **20 (10)** (2003) 1875–1882
6. Koenderink, J.J., van Doorn, A.J., Kappers, A.M.L., te Pas, S.F., Pont, S.C.: Illumination direction from texture shading. JOSA A **20 (6)** (2003) 987–995
7. Lambert, J.H.: Photometria Sive de Mensure de Gradibus Luminis, Colorum et Umbræ. Eberhard Klett, Augsburg (1760)
8. Lee, C.H., Rosenfeld, A.: Improved methods of estimating shape from shading using the light source coordinate system. Artif.Intell. **26** (1985) 125–143
9. Longuet-Higgins, M. S.: The statistical analysis of a random moving surface. Phil.Trans.R.Soc. A **249** (1956) 321-64
10. Nicodemus, F.E., Richmond, J.C., Hsia, J.J., Geometrical Considerations and Nomenclature for Reflectance (Natl.Bur.Stand., U.S., Monogr. 160, 1977)
11. Pont, S.C., Koenderink, J.J.: Surface illuminance flow. Second International Symposium on 3D data Processing, Visualization and Transmission (2004)

Using Top-Points as Interest Points for Image Matching

B. Platel, E. Balmachnova, L.M.J. Florack[*],
F.M.W. Kanters, and B.M. ter Haar Romeny

Technische Universiteit Eindhoven,
P.O. Box 513, 5600 MB Eindhoven,
The Netherlands

Abstract. We consider the use of so-called top-points for object retrieval. These points are based on scale-space and catastrophe theory, and are invariant under gray value scaling and offset as well as scale-Euclidean transformations. The differential properties and noise characteristics of these points are mathematically well understood. It is possible to retrieve the exact location of a top-point from any coarse estimation through a closed-form vector equation which only depends on local derivatives in the estimated point. All these properties make top-points highly suitable as anchor points for invariant matching schemes. In a set of examples we show the excellent performance of top-points in an object retrieval task.

1 Introduction

Local invariant features are useful for finding corresponding points between images when they are calculated at invariant interest points. The most popular interest points are Harris points [7], extrema in the normalized scale-space of the Laplacian of the image [10,11] or a combination of both [13]. For an overview of different interest points the reader is referred to [15].

We propose a novel, highly invariant type of interest point, based on scale-space and catastrophe theory. The mathematical properties and behavior of these so-called top-points are well understood. These interest points are invariant under gray value scaling and offset as well as arbitrary scale-Euclidean transformations. The noise behavior of top-points can be described in closed-form, which enables us to accurately predict the stability of the points. For tasks like matching or retrieval it is of decisive importance to take into account the (in)stability of the descriptive data.

For matching it is important that a set of distinctive local invariant features is available in the interest points. An overview of invariant features is given in [12]. The choice of invariant features taken in the top-points is free. Because of their simple and mathematically nice nature we have chosen to use a complete set of differential invariants up to third order [5,6] as invariant features. A similarity measure between these invariant feature vectors based on the noise behavior of the differential invariants is proposed.

A small set of examples will demonstrate the potential of our interest points.

---

[*] The Dutch Organization for Scientific Research (NWO) is gratefully acknowledged for financial support.

O.F. Olsen et al. (Eds.): DSSCV 2005, LNCS 3753, pp. 211–222, 2005.

2   Interest Points

We present an algorithm for finding interest points in Gaussian scale-space. As input we may use the original image, but we may also choose to use its Laplacian, or any other linear differential entity. The input for our algorithm will be referred to as $f(x, y)$.

2.1   Scale Space Approach

To find interest points that are invariant to zooming we have to observe the input function at all possible scales. Particularly suitable for calculating the scale space representation of the image (or any other linear differential entity of the image) is the Gaussian kernel [9]

$$\phi_\sigma(x, y) = \frac{1}{2\pi\sigma^2} e^{-\frac{1}{2}(x^2+y^2)/\sigma^2}. \tag{1}$$

The input function can now be calculated at any scale by convolution with the Gaussian

$$u(x, y, \sigma) = (\phi_\sigma * f)(x, y). \tag{2}$$

Derivatives of the input function can be calculated at any scale by

$$\mathcal{D}u(x, y, \sigma) = (\mathcal{D}\phi_\sigma * f)(x, y), \tag{3}$$

where $\mathcal{D}$ is any linear derivative operator with constant coefficients.

2.2   Catastrophe Theory

Critical points are points at any fixed scale at which the gradient vanishes. Catastrophe theory studies how such points change as certain control parameters change, in our case scale.

In the case of a generic 2D input function the catastrophes occurring in Gaussian scale space are creations and annihilations of critical points with opposite Hessian signature [2,4], i.e. extrema and saddles. The movement of critical points through scale induces critical paths. Each path consists of one (or multiple) saddle branch(es) and extremum branch(es). The point at which a creation or annihilation occurs is often referred to as a *top-point*[1]. A typical set of critical paths and top-points of an image is shown in Fig. 1. In a top-point the determinant of the Hessian of the input function becomes zero. If u denotes the image, a top-point is thus defined as a point for which

$$\begin{cases} u_x & = 0, \\ u_y & = 0, \\ u_{xx}u_{yy} - u_{xy}^2 & = 0. \end{cases} \tag{4}$$

The extrema of the normalized Laplacean scale space as introduced by Lindeberg [10], and used by Lowe [11] in his matching scheme, lie on the critical paths of the Laplacean image. Multiple of such extrema may exist on the extremum branch of a critical path, whereas there is only one top-point per annihilating extremum/saddle pair, Fig. 2a.

---

[1] This misnomer is reminiscent of the 1D case [8], in which only annihilations occur generically, so that a top-point is only found at the top of a critical path.

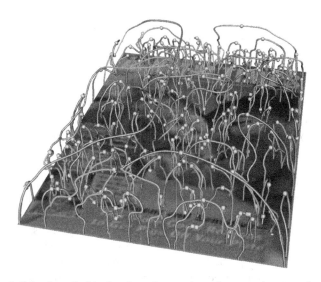

Fig. 1. Selection of critical paths and top-points of a magazine cover image

2.3 Invariance

Interest points are called invariant to transformation if they are preserved by the transformation. From their definition (4), it is apparent that top-points are invariant under gray value scaling and offset.

Suppose $\mathcal{G}$ is some group of affine spatial transformations, which acts on the function u as follows:

$$\tilde{u}(\tilde{x}, \tilde{y}, \tilde{\sigma}) = au(x, y, \sigma) + b, \qquad (5)$$

where

$$\begin{bmatrix} \tilde{x} \\ \tilde{y} \end{bmatrix} = \begin{bmatrix} a_{11} \ a_{12} \\ a_{21} \ a_{22} \end{bmatrix} \begin{bmatrix} x \\ y \end{bmatrix} + \begin{bmatrix} b_1 \\ b_2 \end{bmatrix},$$

and in which a and b depend on the parameters a_{ij}, b_i. A top-point of u is invariant under $\mathcal{G}$, since, in corresponding points,

$$\begin{cases} \tilde{u}_{\tilde{x}} &= a_{11}u_x + a_{12}u_y, \\ \tilde{u}_{\tilde{y}} &= a_{21}u_x + a_{22}u_y, \\ \tilde{u}_{\tilde{x}\tilde{x}}\tilde{u}_{\tilde{y}\tilde{y}} - \tilde{u}_{\tilde{x}\tilde{y}}^2 &= a^2(a_{11}a_{22} - a_{12}^2)^2(u_{xx}u_{yy} - u_{xy}^2), \end{cases} \qquad (6)$$

recall (4). This shows that top-points and critical paths are invariant under rigid transformations and zooming (i.e. the scale-Euclidean group).

2.4 Detection Versus Localization

Critical paths are detected by following critical points through scale. Top-points are found as local maxima or minima in scale on the critical paths.

The detection of top-points does not have to be exact, since, given an adequate initial guess, it is possible to refine their position such that (4) holds to any desired precision by a perturbative technique proposed by Florack and Kuijper [4]. This allows one to use a less accurate but fast detection algorithm.

2.5   Stability

The stability of a top-point can be expressed in terms of the variances of spatial and scale displacements induced by additive noise. Since top-points are generic entities in scale space, they cannot vanish or appear when the image is only slightly perturbed. We assume that the noise variance is "sufficiently small" in the sense that the induced dislocation of a top-point can be investigated by means of a perturbative approach. Given this assumption it can be shown that the displacement depends on derivatives up to fourth order evaluated at the top-point, and on the noise variance. For detailed formulas (and experimental verifications) the reader is referred to [1].

The advantage of this approach is that variances of scale space displacements can be predicted theoretically and in analytically closed-form on the basis of the local differential structure at a given top-point, cf. Fig. 2b for an illustration. The ability to predict the motion of top-points under noise is valuable when matching noisy data (e.g. one may want to disregard highly unstable top-points altogether).

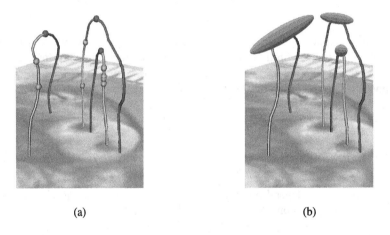

(a)   (b)

Fig. 2. a. A set of critical paths with corresponding top-points (topmost bullets), and extrema of the normalized Laplacian (remaining bullets). b. The ellipses capture the variances of the scale space displacement of each top-point under additive noise of known variance.

2.6   Repeatability

Schmid et al. [15] introduced the so-called repeatability criterion to evaluate the stability and accuracy of interest points and interest point detectors. The repeatability score for a given pair of images is computed as the ratio between the number of point-to-point correspondences and the minimum number of interest points detected in the images.

The perturbative technique proposed by Florack and Kuijper [4] mentioned in Sec. 2.4 is used to find a vector in each top-point of the unperturbed image, that points to the location of a top-point in the perturbed image. If this vector moves the top-point less than a distance of ϵ pixels we mark the point as a repeatable point (typically we set $\epsilon \approx 2$ pixels).

Experiments show the repeatability of top-points under image rotation (Fig. 3a) and additive Gaussian noise (Fig. 3b). Image rotation causes some top-points to be lost or created due to the resampling of the image. In the Gaussian noise experiment we demonstrate that by using the stability variances described in Sec. 2.5 the repeatability of the top-points can be increased. The top-points are ordered on their stability variances. From this list 100%, 66% and 50% of the most stable top-points are selected for the repeatability experiment respectively. From Fig. 3b it is apparent that discarding instable points increases the repeatability significantly. The high repeatability rate of the top-points enables us to match images under any angle of rotation and under high levels of noise.

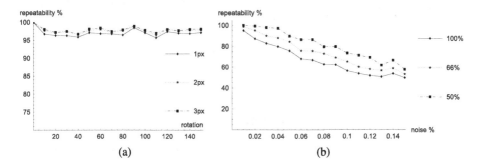

(a)   (b)

Fig. 3. a. The repeatability of top-points under image rotation, for distances ϵ=1, 2 and 3 pixels respectively. b. The repeatability of top-points under additive Gaussian noise, for 100%, 66% and 50% of the most stable top-points respectively ($\epsilon = 2$ pixels).

3   Matching Using Top-Points

For matching it is important that a set of distinctive local invariant features is available in the interest points. It is possible to use any set of invariant features in the top-points. Mikolajcyck and Schmid [12] give an overview of a number of such local descriptors.

3.1   Local Invariant Features

For our experiments we have used a complete set of differential invariants up to third order. The complete sets proposed by Florack et al. [6] are invariant to rigid transformations. By suitable scaling and normalization we obtain invariance to spatial zooming and intensity scaling as well, but the resulting system has the property that most low order invariants vanish identically at the top-points of the original (zeroth order) image, and thus do not qualify as distinctive features. Thus when considering top-points of the original image other distinctive features will have to be used. In [14] the embedding of a graph connecting top-points is used as a descriptor. This proved to be a suitable way of describing the global relationship between top-points of the original image. In this paper we use the image Laplacian as input function for our top-point detector. For this case the non-trivial, scaled and normalized differential invariants up to third order are collected into the column vector given by(7), in which summation convention applies:

$$
\begin{pmatrix}
\sigma\sqrt{u_i u_i / u} \\
\sigma u_{ii} / \sqrt{u_j u_j} \\
\sigma^2 u_{ij} u_{ij} / u_k u_k \\
\sigma u_i u_{ij} u_j / (u_k u_k)^{3/2} \\
\sigma^2 u_{ijk} u_i u_j u_k / (u_l u_l)^2 \\
\sigma^2 \varepsilon_{ij} u_{jkl} u_i u_k u_l / (u_m u_m)^2
\end{pmatrix}.
\tag{7}
$$

Here ε_{ij} is the completely antisymmetric epsilon tensor, normalized such that $\varepsilon_{12} = 1$. Note that the derivatives are extracted from the original, zeroth order image, but evaluated at the location of the top-points of the image Laplacian. This is, in particular, why the gradient magnitude in the denominator poses no difficulties, as it is generically nonzero at a top-point.

The resulting scheme (interest point plus differential feature vector) guarantees manifest invariance under the scale-Euclidean spatial transformation group, and under linear grey value rescalings.

4   Similarity Measure in the Feature Space

To investigate the stability of the feature vectors we use the same approach as described in Sec. 2.5 for the stability of top-points. This results in the covariance matrix Σ of which the elements depend on derivatives in the interest point up to third order. The uncertainty of the feature vector $\mathbf{x}_0$ can be modeled as a normal distribution with density function (8) (where $n = 6$).

$$
\rho(\mathbf{x}; \mathbf{x}_0) = \frac{1}{\sqrt{\det \Sigma_{\mathbf{x}_0} (2\pi)^{n/2}}} \exp[-\frac{1}{2}(\mathbf{x} - \mathbf{x}_0)^T \Sigma_{\mathbf{x}_0}^{-1}(\mathbf{x} - \mathbf{x}_0)]
\tag{8}
$$

We define our measure of similarity d between interest points $\mathbf{x}_0$ and $\mathbf{x}_1$ as $1-$the probability for point $\mathbf{x}_0$ to be inside the iso-probability contour of the density function going through $\mathbf{x}_1$. This is schematically demonstrated in Fig. 4a.

$$
d(\mathbf{x}_0, \mathbf{x}_1) = 1 - \int_\Omega \rho(\mathbf{y}; \mathbf{x}_0) d\mathbf{y} = \frac{\Gamma(R^2/2, \frac{n}{2})}{\Gamma(\frac{n}{2})}
\tag{9}
$$

The radius of the iso-probability contour and the region inside the contour are given by $R^2 = (\mathbf{x}_1 - \mathbf{x}_0)^T \Sigma_{\mathbf{x}_0}^{-1}(\mathbf{x}_1 - \mathbf{x}_0)$ and $\Omega = \{\mathbf{y} \mid (\mathbf{y} - \mathbf{x}_0)^T \Sigma_{\mathbf{x}_0}^{-1}(\mathbf{y} - \mathbf{x}_0) \leq R^2\}$ respectively. $\Gamma(x, n)$ is the incomplete gamma function given by $\Gamma(x, n) = \int_0^x e^{-y} y^{n-1} dy$ and the Euler gamma function $\Gamma(n) = \Gamma(\infty, n)$.

Similarity measure d always yields a number between 0 and 1, where 0 is not similar and 1 is very similar. This allows us to use a well defined threshold on the similarity of interest points, in order to decrease complexity of the matching algorithm without losing valuable data, as will be demonstrated in Sec. 5.

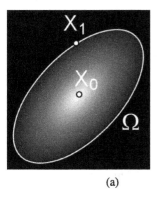
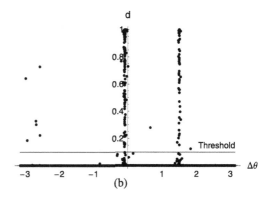

(a)   (b)

Fig. 4. a. Schematic 2D representation of the probability density function around interest point x_0 and the iso-probability contour going through x_1. b. Similarities d for corresponding interest points. Two clusters with the same angles $\Delta\sigma$ can be identified. Mismatched points have a similarity measure close to 0.

5   Matching

In our examples we consider an object-scene retrieval problem in which the scene may contain rotated, scaled, and occluded versions of a query object. This implies that we have a set of interest points and features belonging to the query object and a set belonging to the scene from which we try to retrieve the object.

Apart from the invariant feature vector we store the location (x, y, σ) and the gradient angle θ of each interest point. For each interest point of the object we find a corresponding interest point in the scene. Correspondence is obtained by finding the interest point with maximal similarity d (9), between their feature vectors. For each pair of corresponding object and scene interest points we calculate the difference in gradient angle ($\Delta\theta = \theta_{\text{scene}} - \theta_{\text{object}}$) and logarithmic scale ($\Delta\tau = \tau_{\text{scene}} - \tau_{\text{object}}$, with $\tau \propto \ln\sigma$). Thus every pair of corresponding interest points yields a coordinate pair $(\Delta\theta, \Delta\tau)$.

A scatter plot of all these pairs reveals clusters, as shown in Fig. 5a for an object-scene matching experiment where the scene contains two instances of the object with different rotation angles and zooming factors. Figure 4b shows the similarity measures for corresponding interest points. Two clusters of points with the same difference in angles $\Delta\theta$ can be identified. Corresponding points that do not have the correct angles (mismatched points) have a similarity measure close to 0. By applying a threshold on the similarity of $d > 0.1$ (the threshold value is not very critical) the clusters are cleaned up significantly (Fig. 5b), facilitating the clustering step of the algorithm.

The mean of each cluster yields a particular rotation and zooming needed to map the query object to a corresponding object in the scene.

We have used a shared-nearest-neighbor (SNN) approach to solve the clustering problem [3], but the bin-based approach as suggested by Lowe [11] can also be used for this task. By using the SNN approach the clusters with the highest densities are identified.

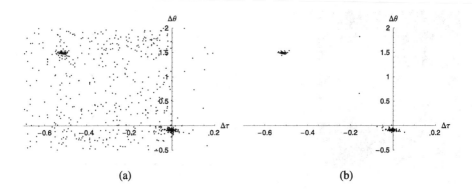

Fig. 5. a. Cluster of the differences in angles and scales $(\Delta\theta, \Delta\tau)$ of corresponding interest points. b. Same as in a. but now corresponding points with similarity measure $d < 0.1$ are discarded.

After clustering, the coordinate triple (x, y, σ) of each scene interest point belonging to a cluster is rotated and scaled according to the cluster's mean $(\overline{\Delta\theta}, \overline{\Delta\tau})$, so that the transformed triple (x_t, y_t, σ_t) matches the corresponding interest point in the query object:

$$\begin{pmatrix} x_t \\ y_t \\ \sigma_t \end{pmatrix} = e^{\overline{\Delta\tau}} \begin{pmatrix} \cos\overline{\Delta\theta} & -\sin\overline{\Delta\theta} & 0 \\ \sin\overline{\Delta\theta} & \cos\overline{\Delta\theta} & 0 \\ 0 & 0 & 1 \end{pmatrix} \begin{pmatrix} x \\ y \\ \sigma \end{pmatrix}. \tag{10}$$

Note that this step is independent of *where* the object is in the scene. After this step the difference in spatial positions of the query object's interest points and those in the clustered scene are calculated. One obtains a coordinate pair $(\Delta x, \Delta y)$ for each object/scene pair in the cluster. These coordinate pairs can be clustered in the same way as before, giving us the translation(s) of the object(s) in the scene. With this final step we have identified the location of the object in the scene. In particular we can now transform the outline of the query object according to the mean parameters $(\overline{\Delta\theta}, \overline{\Delta\tau}, \overline{\Delta x}, \overline{\Delta y})$, and project it onto the scene image.

The complete matching algorithm is summarized in algorithm 1.

Algorithm 1 Object retrieval algorithm

1: Detect the critical paths.
2: Extract the approximate locations of the top-points from the critical paths.
3: Refine the location of the top-points.
4: Calculate the feature vectors for the top-points.
5: Form pairs of corresponding object and scene top-points.
6: Cluster $(\Delta\theta, \Delta\tau)$ to solve for rotation and scaling.
7: Rotate and scale the scene top-points to match the object points.
8: Cluster $(\Delta x, \Delta y)$ to solve for translation.
9: Transform the outline of the query object by $(\overline{\Delta\theta}, \overline{\Delta\tau}, \overline{\Delta x}, \overline{\Delta y})$ and project it onto the scene.

---

6   Retrieval Examples

We have included some examples of an object retrieval task. We have a set of magazine covers (of size 200×140 pixels) and a scene (of size 400×350 pixels) containing a number of the magazines, distributed, rotated, scaled, and occluded.

The task is to retrieve a magazine from the scene image. For the query images we find approximately 500 top-points per query image (which may be pre-computed off-line). For the scene image we find approximately 3000 top-points.

Fig. 6. Matching interest points (white) of a query object and a scene containing two rotated, scaled and occluded versions of the object. Interest points that do not match are shown in grey.

Table 1. Transformation error. a, b and c represent the magazine covers in the left column of Fig. 7 respectively. The second column shows the number of matched interest points for each object in the scene. The third column shows the error made in rotation (degrees), zooming (factor) and translation (pixels).

	Size	Error in $(\overline{\Delta\theta}, e^{\overline{\Delta\tau}}, \overline{\Delta x}, \overline{\Delta y})$	
a.	218, 58	{0.1, 0.005, 0.1, 0.2},	{0.5, 0.001, 0.4, 0.5}
b.	21	{0.06, 0.002, 0.01, 0.8}	
c.	175, 15	{0.005, 0.005, 0.05, 0.5},	{0.006, 0.006, 0.2, 0.4}

We follow algorithm 1 and match the top-points of query magazine covers to the top-points in the scene. Such a match is demonstrated in Fig. 6.

Correct matches are found for all the magazine covers in the scene, even for the highly occluded ones. In Fig. 7 three retrieval tasks are demonstrated. The amount of correctly matched points and the errors made in the retrieved transformations compared to the ground truth are shown in Table 1.

Fig. 7. Combined results of matches to the query objects in the left column. Note that even the highly occluded magazine at the bottom is retrieved correctly.

The examples show that the interest points and features are indeed invariant under rotation and scaling, and that the algorithm is able to handle severe occlusions (in the example relative occlusions up to approximately 85% pose no difficulties).

Since our interest points are found in scale-space, the algorithm can also handle different kinds of grey-tone renderings of the image. We demonstrate this by using a coarse-grained dithering on the scene image. Even under these circumstances the algorithm was able to correctly retrieve the magazine covers by matching coarse scale interest points. An example of this is shown in Fig. 8.

Fig. 8. Successful retrieval of an object in a coarsely dithered scene image

7 Summary and Conclusions

We have introduced top-points as highly invariant interest points that are suitable for image matching. Top-points are versatile as they can be calculated for every generic function of the image.

We have pointed out that top-points are invariant under scale-Euclidean transformations as well as under gray value scaling and offset. The sensitivity of top-points to additive noise can be predicted analytically, which is useful when matching noisy images. Top-point localization does not have to be very accurate, since it is possible to refine its position using local differential image structure. This enables fast detection, without losing the exact location of the top-point.

As features for our interest points we use a feature vector consisting of only six normalized and scaled differential invariants. We have also introduced a similarity measure based on the noise behavior of our feature vectors. Thresholding on this similarity measure facilitates the clustering significantly. The conducted experiments show excellent performance with very little error in the localization of the objects in the scene.

Acknowledgement

This work is part of the DSSCV project supported by the IST Programme of the European Union (IST-2001-35443). We would like to thank M. Egmont-Petersen for his help on the clustering algorithm.

References

1. E. Balmachnova, L.M.J. Florack, B. Platel, F.M.W. Kanters, and B.M. ter Haar Romeny. Stability of top-points in scale space. In *Proceedings of the 5th international conference on Scale Space Methods in Computer Vision (Germany, April 2005)*, pages 62–72.
2. J. Damon. Local Morse theory for solutions to the heat equation and Gaussian blurring. *Journal of Differential Equations*, 115(2):368–401, January 1995.
3. L. Ertoz, M. Steinbach, and V Kumar. Finding clusters of different sizes, shapes, and densities in noisy, high dimensional data. In *Proc. of SIAM DM03 (2003)*.
4. L. Florack and A. Kuijper. The topological structure of scale-space images. *Journal of Mathematical Imaging and Vision*, 12(1):65–79, February 2000.
5. L. M. J. Florack, B. M. ter Haar Romeny, J. J. Koenderink, and M. A. Viergever. Scale and the differential structure of images. 10(6):376–388, July/August 1992.
6. L. M. J. Florack, B. M. ter Haar Romeny, J. J. Koenderink, and M. A. Viergever. Cartesian differential invariants in scale-space. *Journal of Mathematical Imaging and Vision*, 3(4):327–348, November 1993.
7. C. Harris and M Stephens. A combined corner and edge detector. In *Proc. 4th Alvey Vision Conf.*, pages 189–192, 1988.
8. P. Johansen, S. Skelboe, K. Grue, and J. D. Andersen. Representing signals by their top points in scale-space. In *Proceedings of the 8th International Conference on Pattern Recognition (Paris, France, October 1986)*, pages 215–217. IEEE Computer Society Press, 1986.
9. J. J. Koenderink. The structure of images. *Biological Cybernetics*, 50:363–370, 1984.
10. T. Lindeberg. Scale-space theory: A basic tool for analysing structures at different scales. *J. of Applied Statistics*, 21(2):224–270, 1994.
11. David G. Lowe. Distinctive image features from scale-invariant keypoints. *Int. J. Comput. Vision*, 60(2):91–110, 2004.
12. Krystian Mikolajczyk and Cordelia Schmid. A performance evaluation of local descriptors. Submitted to PAMI, 2004.
13. Krystian Mikolajczyk and Cordelia Schmid. Scale and affine invariant interest point detectors. *International Journal of Computer Vision*, 60(1):63–86, 2004.
14. B. Platel, M. Fatih Demirci, A. Shokoufandeh, L.M.J. Florack F.M.W. Kanters, and S.J. Dickinson. Discrete representation of top points via scale space tessellation. In *Proceedings of the 5th international conference on Scale Space Methods in Computer Vision (Germany, April 2005)*.
15. Cordelia Schmid, Roger Mohr, and Christian Bauckhage. Evaluation of interest point detectors. *Int. J. Comput. Vision*, 37(2):151–172, 2000.

Transitions of Multi-scale Singularity Trees

Kerawit Somchaipeng[1,2], Jon Sporring[2],
Sven Kreiborg[1], and Peter Johansen[2]

[1] 3D-Lab, School of Dentistry, Dept. of Pediatric Dentistry,
University of Copenhagen, Nørre Alle 20, DK-2200,
Copenhagen N, Denmark
[2] Dept. of Computer Science, University of Copenhagen,
Universitetsparken 1, DK-2100,
Copenhagen N, Denmark

Abstract. Multi-Scale Singularity Trees(MSSTs) [10] are multi-scale image descriptors aimed at representing the deep structures of images. Changes in images are directly translated to changes in the deep structures; therefore transitions in MSSTs. Because MSSTs can be used to represent the deep structure of images efficiently, it is important to investigate and understand their transitions and impacts. We present four kinds of MSST transitions and discuss the potential advantages of Saddle-Based MSSTs over Extrema-Based MSSTs. The study of MSST transitions presented in this paper is an important step towards the development of the image matching and indexing algorithms based on MSSTs.

1 Introduction

In scale-space theory [3,13,4], the relations between image structures at different scales is referred to as the deep structure [4,6]. Based on the scale-space theory and the singularity theory [12,2], the Extrema-Based and Saddle-Based Multi-Scale Singularity Trees(MSSTs) [10] representing the deep structure of images are constructed. Since MSSTs can be used to efficiently represent the deep structures of images, the investigation of their transitions as the images are smoothly changed is both theoretically interesting and crucially important for the development of algorithms based on MSSTs. In that way, different images can be related to each other through a series of transitions.

In this paper, we investigate the transitions of MSSTs by observing the changes of critical paths in scale-space images as the images are smoothly changed. Transitions of MSST are then derived and presented together with illustrative examples. Four kinds of transitions are presented, i.e. change of catastrophe-extremum/saddle position, change of catastrophe-catastrophe relation, change of catastrophe ordering, and change of extremum-catastrophe connection. We present each transition and discuss its impacts using a simple example. The potential advantages of the Saddle-Based MSSTs over the Extrema-Based MSSTs are also discussed and illustratively presented. Similar

O.F. Olsen et al. (Eds.): DSSCV 2005, LNCS 3753, pp. 223–233, 2005.

study of the transitions of the Pre-Symmetry Set has also done by one of our European Project partners [5].

2   Gaussian Scale-Space

The $N+1$ dimensional Gaussian scale-space, $L : \mathbb{R}^{N+1} \to \mathbb{R}$, of an N dimensional image, $I : \mathbb{R}^N \to \mathbb{R}$, is an ordered stack of images, where each image is a blurred version of the former [3,13,4]. The blurring is performed according to the diffusion equation,

$$\partial_t L = \nabla^2 L, \tag{1}$$

where $\partial_t L$ is the first partial-derivative of the image in the scale direction t, and ∇^2 is the spatial Laplacian operator, which in two dimensions reads $\partial_x^2 + \partial_y^2$. The Gaussian kernel is the Green's function of the heat diffusion equation, i.e.

$$L(\cdot; t) = I(\cdot) \otimes g(\cdot; t), \tag{2}$$

$$g(x; t) = \frac{1}{(4\pi t)^{N/2}} e^{-x^T x/(4t)}, \tag{3}$$

where $L(\cdot, t)$ is the image at scale t, $I(\cdot)$ is the original image, $\otimes$ is the convolution operator, $g(\cdot; t)$ is the Gaussian kernel at scale t, N is the dimensionality of the image I, and $t = \sigma^2/2$, using σ as the standard deviation of the Gaussian kernel.

3   Energy Functional and Energy Partitions

Given an image and a set of landmarks, we would like to partition the image into segments so that each segment contains exactly one landmark. Let $\Omega \subset \mathbb{R}^N$ be a compact connected domain. We define $I : \Omega \to \mathbb{R}^+$ as an image, and $e, x \in \Omega$ as a landmark and a point in the domain, respectively. Consider a set of continuous functions $\gamma : [0, P] \to \Omega$ for which $\gamma(0) = e$ and $\gamma(P) = x$. Write $\gamma \in \Gamma_{ex}$, where Γ_{ex} is the set of all possible paths in the domain connecting landmark e to point x, and where γ is parameterized using Euclidean arc-length. We define the energy $E_e(x)$ with respect to a landmark e evaluated at x as,

$$E_e(x) = \inf_{\gamma \in \Gamma_{ex}} \int_0^P \sqrt{(1 - \alpha) \mid \frac{d\gamma(p)}{dp} \mid^2 + \alpha \mid \frac{\partial I(\gamma(p))}{\partial p} \mid^2} \, dp, \tag{4}$$

where $\gamma \in [0, 1]$ is a tunable weighting parameter. Note that (4) is independent of the parameterization, e.g. integrating with respect to $q : [0, P] \to [0, P]$ we find:

$$
\begin{aligned}
E_e(x) &= \inf_{\gamma \in \Gamma_{ex}} \int_{p^{-1}(0)}^{p^{-1}(x)} \sqrt{(1-\alpha)\,|\,\frac{d\gamma(p(q))}{dp}\,|^2 + \alpha\,|\,\frac{\partial I(\gamma(p(q)))}{\partial p}\,|^2}\, dq \\
&= \inf_{\gamma \in \Gamma_{ex}} \int_{p^{-1}(0)}^{p^{-1}(x)} \sqrt{(1-\alpha)\,|\,\frac{d\gamma(p)}{dp}\cdot\frac{dp}{dq}\,|^2 + \alpha\,|\,\nabla I\cdot\frac{d\gamma(p)}{dp}\cdot\frac{dp}{dq}\,|^2}\, dq \\
&= \inf_{\gamma \in \Gamma_{ex}} \int_{p^{-1}(0)}^{p^{-1}(x)} \sqrt{(1-\alpha)\,|\,\frac{d\gamma(p)}{dp}\,|^2 + \alpha\,|\,\frac{\partial I(\gamma(p))}{\partial p}\,|^2\,\frac{dp}{dq}}\cdot dq \\
&= \inf_{\gamma \in \Gamma_{ex}} \int_{0}^{P} \sqrt{(1-\alpha)\,|\,\frac{d\gamma(p)}{dp}\,|^2 + \alpha\,|\,\frac{\partial I(\gamma(p))}{\partial p}\,|^2}\, dp .
\end{aligned}
\tag{5}
$$

Let $\mathcal{E} \subset \Omega$ be the set of all landmarks in the image. An image segment or an *energy partition* S_i associated with landmark $e_i \in \mathcal{E}$ is defined as the set of all points in the images, where the energy $E_{e_i}(x)$ is minimal,

$$
S_i = \{x \in \Omega | E_{e_i}(x) < E_{e_j}(x), \forall e_j \in \mathcal{E}, i \neq j\}.
\tag{6}
$$

An approximation of the energy map $E_{e_i} : \Omega \to \mathbb{R}^+$, which gives energy with respect to landmark e_i at every point in the image , can be efficiently calculated using the *Fast Marching Methods* [8]. The resulting energy map is an approximation because isophotes generally do not coincide with the sampling points in digital images. We are currently developing an energy map calculating algorithm specifically designed according to this requirement.

4   Multi-scale Singularity Trees

MSSTs are constructed by connecting annihilation catastrophes in the scale-space images.

In order to preseve the preferable tree structure of the MSSTs, creations and loops in scale-space images are systematically removed:

1. Creations occuring in a critical path that can be traced back up to the original image together with the corresponding annihilations are pairwise removed and the whole critical path is considered as the critical path that originates from the original image.
2. Creations immediately followed by annihilations creating loops together with the critical paths involved in the loops are completely ignored.

The connections between catastrophes are decided from the nesting of image segments defined by the energy functional and mathematical landmarks. Because of the natural pairwise interactions between critical points in the generic scale-space images [2] and the tree building scheme to be represented in the following, resulting MSSTs are always rooted ordered binary trees [10]. A MSST consists of nodes and their relations. Each MSST node has three components: (i) the *rightport* denoting the disappearing image segment, (ii) the *body* denoting the annihilation catastrophe where the nesting is decided, and (iii) the *leftport* denoting the image segment which immediately covers over the disappearing one. Because we choose landmarks such that exactly one landmark disappears at an annihilation catastrophe, and because there is exactly one image segment associated with each landmark, then exactly one image segment disappears at an annihilation catastrophe. This event creates nesting of image segments in scale-space and the linking in MSSTs.

A node $S_{left}C_{body}S_{right}$ is generated when an image segment S_{right} disappears at the catastrophe C_{body} inside an image segment S_{left} . The inclusion is easily determined by calculating the energy map with respect to the catastrophe C_{body}: the image segment S_{right} is nested inside the image segment S_{left}, if the energy evaluated at the landmark of S_{left} is minimal among all landmarks existing at that scale. MSSTs are built top-down starting from the top annihilation catastrophe at the coarsest scale. A new node $N_{new} : S_{new,left}C_{new,body}S_{new,right}$ is connected as the *leftchild* of a node $N_i : S_{i,left}C_{i,body}S_{i,right}$, if the node N_i does not have the leftchild and $S_{new,left} = S_{i,left}$, or as the *rightchild*, if the node N_i does not have the rightchild and $S_{new,left} = S_{i,right}$.

It can easily be seen that this process is deterministic. When a node is added, one connection point is closed while two new connection points are opened. Free ports are always unique.

4.1   Extrema-Based MSSTs

Assuming that critical paths, the paths of critical points in scale-spaces, and catastrophes have already been detected, the Extrema-Based MSST building algorithm is as follows:

1. Set the root of the tree as $BC_{\infty}E_{last}$, where B denotes the border of the image, E_{last} denotes the last extremum in scale, and C_{∞} denotes the virtual catastrophe at scale infinity, where the last extremum virtually disappears inside the image segment of the border.
2. At the highest unprocessed catastrophe C_{next}, calculate the energy map with respect to the catastrophe and create node $E_{cover}C_{next}E_{ann}$, where E_{ann} is the extremum that disappears at catastrophe C_{next}, and the energy evaluated at extremum E_{cover} is minimal among all extrema existing at that scale.
3. Link the new created node as the leftchild of a node in the tree that does not have the leftchild and where E_{cover} equals its leftport, or as the rightchild of a node in the tree that does not have the rightchild and where E_{cover} equals its rightport.
4. Repeat 2. until all catastrophe points are processed.

The schematic deep structure and its constructed Extrema-Based MSSTs are shown together in the left column of Fig. 1.

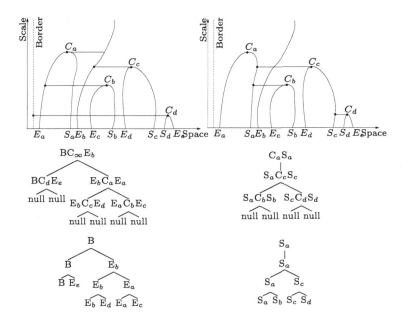

Fig. 1. The deep structure and its corresponding Extrema-Based MSST are shown in the first and the second rows of the left column, while the deep structure and its corresponding Saddle-Based MSST are shown in the first and the second rows of the right column, respectively. Es denote extrema, Ss denote saddles, and Cs denote catastrophes. Horizontal lines indicate the paths with minimal energies. The last row of the figure shows trees of extrema and saddles, presented for better interpretation.

4.2   Saddle-Based MSSTs

A similar procedure is applied to construct Saddle-Based MSSTs, however now we consider saddles for landmarks instead of extrema. The algorithm is as follows:

1. Set the root of the tree as $C_{top}S_{top}$, where the leftport is set to *null*, C_{top} denotes the highest catastrophe in scale, and S_{top} denotes the saddle that annihilates at catastrophe C_{top}.
2. At the highest unprocessed catastrophe C_{next} in scale, calculate the energy map with respect to the catastrophe and create node $S_{cover}C_{next}S_{ann}$, where S_{ann} is the saddle that disappears at catastrophe C_{next} and the energy evaluated at saddle S_{cover} is minimal among all saddles existing at that scale.
3. Link the new created node as the leftchild of a node in the tree that does not have the leftchild and S_{cover} equals its leftport or as the rightchild of a node in the tree that does not have the rightchild and S_{cover} equals its rightport.
4. Repeat 2. until all catastrophe points are processed.

Notice that since the virtual catastrophe C_{inf} is not relavent, Saddle-Based MSSTs always have one node less than those of Extrema-Based MSSTs of the same images. The deep structure and its constructed Saddle-Based MSST are shown together in the right column of Fig. 1.

5 Transitions of MSSTS

An experiment aimed at studying the possible transitions of MSSTs is carried out. A series of generated images of three stationary and one moving Gaussian blobs is used in the experiment. A few examples of the test images are shown in Fig. 2

Smooth changes of the test images are forced by smoothly changing the parameters used for generating the images. For each test image, a scale-space is computed, the critical paths and catastrophes are extracted and detected. Finally, the Extrema-Based and Saddle-Based MSST are constructed. Changes in the constructed MSSTs between neighbouring images are observed and carefully classified into categories. Four kinds of transitions can be observed, i.e. change of catastrophe-extremum/saddle position, change of catastrophe-catastrophe relation, change of catastrophe ordering, and change of extremum-catastrophe connection.

Fig. 2. Images of three stationary and one moving Gaussian blobs. A few images taken from the series of generated images used in the experiment.

5.1 Change of Catastrophe-Extremum/Saddle Position

The change of position transition is simple. It is caused by the movement of catastrophes due to the movements of extrema/saddles and/or changes in intensity values in the original image. Catastrophes may move as long as their ordering in scale is undisturbed. The transition produces no impacts on the topology of the MSST but only on the contents stored in the nodes. The change of catastrophe-extremum/saddle position transition is illustrated in Fig. 3.

5.2 Change of Catastrophe-Catastrophe Relation

When the nesting of image segments in scale changes, the parent-child relations in the Extrema-Based and Saddle-Based MSSTs will change accordingly. It results in the change of the leftport of the corresponding node and the movement of the node with its right-subtree to the new location. The left-subtree is then

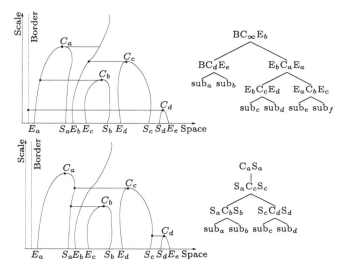

Fig. 3. The original deep structures and the corresponding Extrema-Based and Saddle-Based MSSTs before and after the change of position transition are shown in the top and bottom row respectively. No topological change of the MSSTs.

move up to replace the position of its moved parent. Insert the node together with its right-subtree at the new location according to the order of the catastrophe and its updated leftport. Finally, the replaced subtree is then reconnected as the left-subtree of the inserted node. The situation is illustrated as the transition from the MSSTs in Fig. 3 to the MSSTs in Fig. 4, where the node of C_b is changed from being nested inside E_a to being nested inside E_b in the Extrema-Based MSST and the node of C_b is changed from being nested inside S_a to being nested inside S_c in the Saddle-Based MSST. Note that the change of relation transition usually occurs simultaneously with the change of position transition.

5.3   Change of Catastrophe Ordering

The structure of MSSTs depends strongly on the ordering of the catastrophes in scale. If the ordering changes the structure of Extrema-Based and Saddle-Based MSSTs will change. If we only consider local reordering between two neighboring nodes in scale–larger changes of the ordering can be arrived by multiple local reordering, the situation is quite simple. Either:

1. *The two nodes do not posses parent-child relations:*
   The structure of the MSST is intact.
2. *The two nodes posses parent-leftchild relation:*
   Swap the locations of the two nodes thereby swap their parent-leftchild relations. Exchange the content of their leftports and finally reconnect the left-subtree of the moved-up leftchild (new parent) as the left-subtree of the moved-down parent (new leftchild). Their right-subtrees are left untouched.

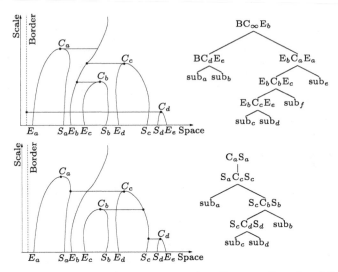

Fig. 4. The deep structures and the corresponding Extrema-Based and Saddle-Based MSSTs after the change of catastrophe-catastrophe relation transition are shown in the top and bottom row respectively

3. *The two nodes posses parent-rightchild relation:*
   Swap the locations of the two nodes thereby swap their parent-leftchild relations. Set the leftport of the moved-down parent (new rightchild) to that of the rightport of the moved-up rightchild (new parent). Reconnect the right-subtree and the left-subtree of the new parent as the left-subtree and the right-subtree of the new rightchild, respectively. Finally, update the leftport of the new parent and reconnect it at the new location, defined by its new leftport, followed by the procedure of the change of relation transition.

The first case of the change of ordering transition is simply reduced to a special kind of the change of position transition, where local reordering of catastrophes is allowed. The second case can be thought of as a combination of the change of position and the change of catastrophe ordering, while the third case is a combination of change of position, change of catastrophe-catastrophe relation, and change of catastrophe ordering that occurs simultaneously.

The change of ordering transition is illustrated as a transition from the MSSTs in Fig. 3 to the MSSTs in Fig. 5, where the neighboring nodes of C_a and C_c swap their ordering positions in scale.

5.4   Change of Extremum-Catastrophe Connection

The change of extremum-catastrophe connection is the swapping of extremal paths. This transition is only relavent to Extrema-Based MSSTs. The transition is the swapping of the right-ports and the whole right-subtrees of the two nodes involved. The change of extremum-catastrophe connection transition is

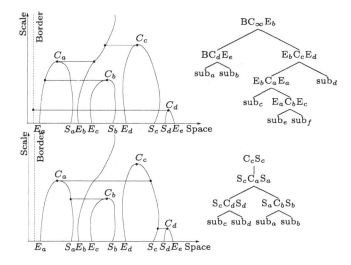

Fig. 5. The deep structures and the corresponding Extrema-Based and Saddle-Based MSSTs after the change of catastrophe ordering transition are shown in the top and bottom row respectively

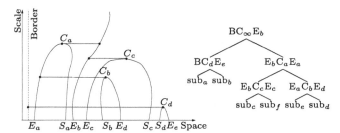

Fig. 6. The deep structure and Extrema-Based MSST after the change of extremum-catastrophe connection transition

illustrated as the transition from the Extrema-Based MSST in the top row of Fig. 3 to the Extrema-Based MSST in Fig. 6, where the catastrophe-extremum connections between E_c and C_b and between E_d and C_c swap.

6   Extrema-Based vs. Saddle-Based MSSTs

Critical points in generic images can be categorized into extrema and saddles by the eigenvalues of the Hessian matrix. With proper boundary conditions, e.g. zero-padding, the image in scale-space at scale infinity will posses only one extremum and no saddle [7].

Frequently, the positions of extrema, when are traced back from the catastrophes to the original image at scale zero, can change completely, even if only slight perturbation is imposed to the image. These jumps of positions are caused by the swapping of extremal paths connecting extrema and their catastrophes, and extremal paths that extends to higher scales. The swapping of extremal paths results in complex transitions on Extrema-Based MSSTs as described in the previous section. On the other hand, the swapping of extremal paths does not disturb the topology of Saddle-Based MSSTs at all since only saddle paths are considered. The situation comparing the stability of Extrema-Based and Saddle-Based MSSTs when the swapping of extremal paths occurs is illustrated in Fig. 7.

Nevertheless, Saddle-Based MSSTs do not fail to capture these changes of the original image, since the swapping of the extremal paths is simply transformed to simple movements of saddles and catastrophes on Saddle-Based MSSTs. The smaller and simpler set of transitions of Saddle-Based MSSTs is preferable and may lead to simpler, faster and easier to implement and understand algorithms based on MSSTs.

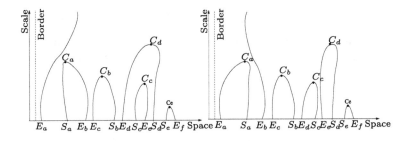

Fig. 7. The figure shows the deep structures of an image before and after imposing slight perturbation to the original image. Frequently, the extremal paths connecting extrema at different scales can be easily disturbed but the saddle paths can be considered stable.

7   Summary and Conclusions

This paper presents the set of possible transitions of the Extrema-Based and Saddle-Based Multi-Scale Singularity Trees. The transitions presented in this paper is a sufficient set of MSST transitions in a sense that all possible trees of the same number of nodes can be related to each other through series of transitions found in this set. However, we have not proved conclusively that the set is complete, since there might be other complex combinations of those transitions in the set that, generically, occur simultaneously.

The simplicity of Saddle-Based MSST transitions, in comparison with those of Extrema-Based MSSTs, is favorable. Because they are simpler, they are easier to be understood which allows us to be able to derive sensible estimates for their cost and simplifies further developments.

The study of transitions of Extrema-Based MSST presented in this paper is an important step towards the development of the image matching and indexing algorithms based on MSSTs and the Tree Edit Distance (TED) algorithms [1], where the difference or distance between two images is found as the minimum cost of a series of edit operations, derived in accordance with the MSST transitions, that transforms the MSST of one image into another.

Possible applications of MSSTs include image matching with MSSTs, multi-scale image pre-segmentation, sub-object extraction, hierarchical image retrieval in large image databases, etc. Recently, MSSTs also found applications in computer graphics [9].

Acknowledgements

his work is part of the DSSCV project sponsored by the IST Programme of the European Union (IST-2001-35443)

References

1. P. Bille. Report on Known Algorithm for Tree Matching. Technical report, Deliverable No.5, DSSCV, IST-2001-35443, 2003.
2. J. Damon. Local Morse Theory for Gaussian Blurred Functions. In Sporring et al. [11], chapter 11, pages 147–163.
3. T. Iijima. Basic theory on normalization of a pattern (in case of typical one-dimensional pattern). *Bulletin of Electrotechnical Laboratory*, 26:368–388, 1962. (in Japanese).
4. J. J. Koenderink. The Structure of Images. *Biological Cybernetics*, 50:363–370, 1984.
5. A. Kuijper and O. F. Olsen. Transitions of the Pre-Symmetry Set. In *Proceedings of the 17th Intl Conference on Pattern Recognition (ICPR'04)*, 2004.
6. T. Lindeberg. *Scale-Space Theory in Computer Vision*. The Kluwer International Series in Engineering and Computer Science. Kluwer Academic Publishers, Boston, USA, 1994.
7. M. Loog, J.J., Duistermaat, and L.M.J. Florack. On the Behavior of Spatial Critical Points under Gaussian Blurring. A Folklore Theorem and Scale-Space Constraints. In *Proceedings of the 3rd Intl Conference on Scale-Space 2001*, pages 183–192, July 2001.
8. J. A. Sethian. Fast Marching Methods. *SIAM Review*, 41(2):199–235, 1999.
9. K. Somchaipeng, K. Erleben, and J. Sporring. A Multi-Scale Singularity Bounding Volume Hierarchy. In *Proceedings of the 13th Intl Conference in Central Europe (WSCG'05)*, pages 179–186, January 2005.
10. K. Somchaipeng, J. Sporring, S. Kreiborg, and P. Johansen. Multi-Scale Singularity Trees: Soft-linked Scale-Space Hierarchies. In *Proceedings of the 5th Intl Conference on Scale-Space 2005*, pages 97 – 106, April 2005.
11. J. Sporring, M. Nielsen, L. Florack, and P. Johansen, editors. *Gaussian Scale-Space Theory*. Kluwer Academic Publishers, Dordrecht, The Netherlands, 1997.
12. J. Weickert, S. Ishikawa, and A. Imiya. Om the History of Gaussian Scale-Space Axiomatics. In Sporring et al. [11], chapter 4, pages 45–59.
13. A. P. Witkin. Scale–space filtering. In *Proc. 8th Int. Joint Conf. on Artificial Intelligence (IJCAI '83)*, volume 2, pages 1019–1022, Karlsruhe, Germany, August 1983.

A Comparison of the Deep Structure of
α-Scale Spaces*

Remco Duits, Frans Kanters, Luc Florack, and Bart ter Haar Romeny

Eindhoven University of Technology,
Den Dolech 2, NL-5600 MD Eindhoven, The Netherlands
{R.Duits, F.M.W.Kanters, L.M.J.Florack, B.M.terhaarRomeny}@tue.nl
http://www.bmi2.bmt.tue.nl/image-analysis/people/rduits

Abstract. We compare the topology and deep structure of alternative scale space representations, so called α-scale spaces, $1/2 \leq \alpha \leq 1$, which are subject to a *first order* pseudo partial differential equation on the upper half plane $\{(x, s) \in \mathbb{R}^d \times \mathbb{R} \mid s > 0\}$. In particular, the cases $\alpha = 1$ and $\alpha = 1/2$, which correspond to respectively Poisson scale space and Gaussian scale space, are considered. Poisson scale space is equivalent to harmonic extension to the upper half plane, inducing potential physics, whereas Gaussian scale space is generated by the diffusion equation on the upper half plane, inducing heat physics. Despite the continuous connection (by parameter $1/2 \leq \alpha \leq 1$) between these scale spaces and the similarity between their convolution convolution kernels, we show both theoretically and experimentally that there is a strong difference between the topology in the deep structure of these scale spaces.

Keywords: α-Scale Spaces, Deep structure, Morse Theory.

1 Introduction

In linear scale space theory one obtains a so-called α-scale space representation $u_f^\alpha : \mathbb{R}^d \times \mathbb{R}^+ \to \mathbb{R}$ of a grey value image image $f \in \mathbb{L}_2(\mathbb{R}^d)$ by means of a holomorphic semi group generated by $-(-\Delta)^\alpha$, $0 < \alpha \leq 1$, i.e. they satisfy the unique solutions of the pseudo differential evolution system

$$\begin{cases} u_s = -(-\Delta)^\alpha u \\ \lim_{s \downarrow 0} u(\cdot, s) = f(\cdot) \, , \end{cases} \tag{1}$$

The unique solutions of which are obtained by means of a convolution

$$u_f^\alpha(\mathbf{x}, s) = (K_s^\alpha * f)(\mathbf{x}), s > 0, \mathbf{x} \in \mathbb{R}^d, \tag{2}$$

where $K_s^\alpha = \mathcal{F}^{-1}[\boldsymbol{\omega} \mapsto e^{-s\|\boldsymbol{\omega}\|^{2\alpha}}]$. These isotropic linear scale space representations follow from a list of fundamental axioms, cf.[1] and the most common

---

* The Netherlands Organization for Scientific Research is gratefully acknowledged for financial support.

O.F. Olsen et al. (Eds.): DSSCV 2005, LNCS 3753, pp. 234–248, 2005.

cases are $\alpha = 1$ and $\alpha = \frac{1}{2}$ leading to respectively a diffusion system and $\alpha = \frac{1}{2}$ a potential problem on the upper space $s > 0$. In these cases the convolution kernel[1] equals respectively the Gaussian kernel and the Poisson kernel:

$$K_s^1(\mathbf{x}) = \frac{1}{(4\pi s)^{d/2}} e^{-\frac{\|\mathbf{x}\|^2}{4s}} \quad \text{and} \quad K_s^{\frac{1}{2}}(\mathbf{x}) = \frac{2}{\sigma_{d+1}} \frac{s}{(s^2 + \|\mathbf{x}\|^2)^{\frac{d+1}{2}}}. \quad (3)$$

With respect to Poisson scale space case we notice that the Laplacian factorizes in two important ways:

$$\Delta_{d+1} = \frac{\partial^2}{\partial s^2} + \Delta_d = \left(\frac{\partial}{\partial s} - \sqrt{-\Delta_d}\right)\left(\frac{\partial}{\partial s} + \sqrt{-\Delta_d}\right) \quad (4)$$

From this factorization it directly follows that (under the extra condition that $u(\cdot, s) \to 0$ uniformly as $s \to \infty$), that the case $\alpha = 1/2$ corresponds to harmonic extension to the upper plane, where we notice that $\left(\frac{\partial}{\partial s} + \sqrt{-\Delta_d}\right) u = 0 \Leftrightarrow u_s = -\sqrt{-\Delta_d}\, u$. Furthermore, we notice that α-scale spaces correspond to symmetric α-stable Levy-processes, that arise in the generalization of the Central Limit Theorem[2], [3] Chapter IX, 9.

An important geometrical quantity is the *grey-value flow* within an α scale space u_f^α of image f. This multi-scale vector field is given by

$$\mathbf{F}_\alpha[u_f^\alpha](\mathbf{x}, s) = (\mathbf{f}_s^\alpha * f)(\mathbf{x}), \quad (5)$$

where $\mathbf{f}_s^\alpha(\mathbf{x}) = \mathcal{F}^{-1}[\boldsymbol{\omega} \mapsto i\frac{1}{\|\boldsymbol{\omega}\|^{2(1-\alpha)}}\boldsymbol{\omega}\, e^{-s\|\boldsymbol{\omega}\|^{2\alpha}}](\mathbf{x})$. To this end we notice that

$$\frac{\partial}{\partial s}[u_f^\alpha] = -(-\Delta)^\alpha u_f^\alpha = \operatorname{div} \mathbf{F}_\alpha[u_f],$$

which is easily verified in the Fourier domain: $-\|\boldsymbol{\omega}\|^{2\alpha} = i\boldsymbol{\omega} \cdot i\frac{1}{\|\boldsymbol{\omega}\|^{2(1-\alpha)}}\boldsymbol{\omega}$. The grey-value flow tells us how the grey-value particles flow within the scale space representation and reveals the interaction between extremal paths in scale space. For the special case of a Gaussian scale space $\alpha = 1$ the grey-value flow is obtained by means of the gradient as we have

$$\mathbf{F}_{\alpha=1}[u_f](\mathbf{x}, s) = \nabla_{\mathbf{x}} u_f(\mathbf{x}, s)$$

and $\mathbf{f}_s^{\alpha=1} = \nabla_{\mathbf{x}} K_s^1(\mathbf{x})$. For the special case of a Poisson scale space $\alpha = \frac{1}{2}$ the grey value flow is obtained by means of the Riesz transform

$$\mathbf{F}_{\alpha=\frac{1}{2}}[u_f](\mathbf{x}, s) = \mathbf{R}_{\mathbf{x}} u_f(\mathbf{x}, s)$$

---

[1] For the other $\alpha \in (0, 1], \alpha \neq \frac{1}{2}, 1$ there do not exist closed form expressions in the spatial domain. Nevertheless, as is shown by Kanters et al.[2] α-kernels, with $\alpha \in [\frac{1}{2}, 1]$, can accurately be approximated by convex combinations of the Poisson and Gaussian kernel.

[2] In the central limit theorem sums of identically distributed (with finite variance) independent variables are considered. If the finite variance assumption is omitted the limiting distributions become α-kernel distributed.

and $\mathbf{f}_s^{\alpha=\frac{1}{2}}$ equals the vector-valued conjugate Poisson kernel:

$$\mathbf{f}_s^{\alpha=\frac{1}{2}}(\mathbf{x}) = \mathbf{R}_{\mathbf{x}} K_s^{1/2}(\mathbf{x}) = \mathbf{Q}_s(\mathbf{x}) = \frac{2}{\sigma_{d+1}} \frac{\mathbf{x}}{(s^2 + \|\mathbf{x}\|^2)^{\frac{d+1}{2}}}.$$

By extending a scale space with its flow, one obtains a vector scale space which equals the first order jet of a Gaussian scale space if $\alpha = 1$ and which equals the monogenic scale space, cf.[4], if $\alpha = 1/2$, which is most practical as it comes to phase based image processing. If one considers α-scale spaces on a bounded

	Poisson Scale Space	Gaussian Scale Space
Physics:	Potential Theory	Heat Physics
Generator:	$-\sqrt{-\Delta} = -\nabla \cdot \mathbf{R}$	$\Delta = \nabla \cdot \nabla$
Flow:	$\mathbf{R}(K_s^{\frac{1}{2}} * f)(\mathbf{x}) = (\mathbf{Q}_s * f)(\mathbf{x})$	$-\nabla(K_s^1 * f)(\mathbf{x})$
Extension	Monogenic S.S.	1st order jet
Derivatives:	Spherical Harmonics	Hermite-polynomials

Fig. 1. A short overview of the correspondence between Gaussian scale space and Poisson scale space

domain Ω with reflective Neumann boundary conditions $\frac{\partial u}{\partial n}\big|_{\partial\Omega} = 0$ (preferable over other boundary conditions, cf. [5]) then the connection becomes even more straight forward, as in this case the generators extend to a compact self-adjoint operator on $\mathbb{L}_2(\Omega)$. From this observation it follows that the (generators of the) α-scale spaces have a common orthonormal basis of eigen functions and the solutions are given by

$$u_{f,\Omega}^\alpha = \sum_{m,n} f_{mn} \, e^{-(-\lambda_{mn})^\alpha s}, \tag{6}$$

where $\Delta f_{mn} = \lambda_{mn} f_{mn}$ and $(f_{mn}, f_{m'n}) = \delta_{mm'}\delta_{nn'}$. For explicit computation of $\{f_{mn}, \lambda_{mn}\}$ and implementation of the bounded domain α-scale spaces for the special cases of the rectangle $[0, a] \times [0, b]$, $a, b > 0$ and the disk $B_{0,a}, a > 0$ we refer to [5], [6], where also (applications of) the Monogenic scale space on a bounded domain is considered. In the limiting case where the bounded domain fills the whole $\mathbb{R}^2$ the solutions (6) converge to convolutions with α-kernels. In the deep structure differences between the bounded and unbounded domain cases only show up at either high scales or close to the boundary at lower scales. In this article we will mainly consider α-scale spaces on a unbounded domain as they are much more suitable for local analysis on topology.

On the one hand the strong connection, see figure 1, between α-scale spaces is interesting as it smoothly relates methods using a Gaussian scale space, to methods using a Poisson scale space and visa versa. On the other hand the strong connection/similarity on (both the unbounded domain and bounded domain) α-scale spaces puts the question whether there is a relevant difference between them. From the practical field in image analysis, there is a slight indication that Poisson scale space (and its monogenic extension) is the optimal choice for phase based processing and texture analysis, but until now an in-depth well-founded comparison[3] has not been made.

In this article we approach this issue from a purely topological point of view, i.e. we investigate the differences (and analogies) between the deep structure of α-scale spaces, which appears to be rather different. In Section 2, we give a brief introduction to the deep-structure of α-scale spaces and show experimentally that the extremal curves continuously depend on α, if the scale in a α-scale space is re-scaled by $s \mapsto s^{\frac{1}{2\alpha}}$. Nevertheless, it quite often happens in images (provided they do not only include low frequencies) that in a Poisson scale space different extrema and saddles annihilate than extrema and saddles in its Gaussian counterpart. We give a non-artificial example of an image whose Gaussian scale space contains two creations, whereas its Poisson scale space contains no creations and similarly show the extremal paths in the rescaled α-scale spaces evolve as a function of $\alpha \in [\frac{1}{2}, 1]$. In Section 3 we both show theoretically and experimentally that creation events do occur in a 1D-Poisson scale space, whereas they do not occur in a 1D-Gaussian scale space. In Section we investigate the difference between α-scale spaces concerning causality, maximum principle and Koenderink's principle. In a Poisson scale space maxima can increase in value over scale, which is not possible in a Gaussian scale space.

2   Deep Structure

The topological structure in a scale space and in particular the change of topological structure of $u(\cdot, s)$ over $s > 0$, reflects the hierarchical structure of objects (like blobs) in an image. As the resolution increases extrema disappear until at finite scale $S > 0$ only one extremum is left, cf.[7]. Points in scale space where a saddle and extremum annihilate or points where an extremum and a saddle are created are called top-points. The set of top-points is given by

$$\{(\mathbf{x}, s) \mid (\det H_{\mathbf{x}} u(\cdot, s))(\mathbf{x}) = 0 \text{ and } (\nabla_{\mathbf{x}} u(\cdot, s))(\mathbf{x}) = \mathbf{0}\}.$$

At these points the topological structure changes. Other interesting points in scale space are scale space saddles[4], these are exactly those points were $\nabla_{\mathbf{x},s} u(\mathbf{x}, s) = (\mathbf{0}, 0)$. Although it is possible to construct a hierarchical tree-structure by means of these points , cf. [8].

The tangent vector $\partial_\beta(\mathbf{x}(\beta), s(\beta))$, with $s = \beta \det H_{\mathbf{x}} u$ of a critical path (moving with infinite speed through a top-point) in an alpha scale space ($\alpha \in (0, 1]$) is given by

$$\partial_\beta(\mathbf{x}(\beta), s(\beta)) = (-\tilde{H}_{\mathbf{x}} u \nabla_{\mathbf{x}} \partial_s u, \det H_{\mathbf{x}}(u)\beta),$$

---

[3] Such a comparison is difficult, regarding the fact that scale in a Poisson scale space has physical dimension length, whereas scale in the Gaussian scale space has physical dimension length squared.

[4] As is shown in [1], there do not exist interior extrema (with respect to scale and position) in α-scale spaces.

where $\frac{1}{\det(H_{\mathbf{x}}u)}\tilde{H}_{\mathbf{x}}u = (H_{\mathbf{x}}u)^{-1}$. This directly follows by application of the chain rule:

$$\partial_\beta(\nabla_{\mathbf{x}}u(\mathbf{x}(\beta), s(\beta))) = H_{\mathbf{x}}u(\mathbf{x}(\beta), s(\beta))\dot{\mathbf{x}}(\beta) + \nabla_{\mathbf{x}}u_s(\mathbf{x}(\beta), s(\beta))\frac{ds}{d\beta} = \mathbf{0}.$$

The curvature at a top-point (or catastrophe point) $(\mathbf{x}*, s*)$ along a critical curve is given by $\kappa(\mathbf{x}*, s*) = \frac{1}{\|\overline{\mathbf{w}}(\mathbf{x}*, s*)\|^2} \det M(\mathbf{x}*, s*)$, where

$$M(\mathbf{x}*, s*) = \begin{pmatrix} H_{\mathbf{x}}u & \partial_s(\nabla_{\mathbf{x}}u)^T \\ \nabla_{\mathbf{x}} \det H_{\mathbf{x}}u & \partial_s \det H_{\mathbf{x}}u \end{pmatrix}\Bigg|_{(\mathbf{x},s)=(\mathbf{x}*,s*)}, \qquad (7)$$

In case the curvature at a catastrophe point is negative, the catastrophe is an annihilation and if the curvature is positive, the catastrophe is a creation. For proof and definition of $\overline{\mathbf{w}}(\mathbf{x}*, s*)$ we refer to Florack et al.[9]. To this end we notice that Florack's derivation (only done for the case $\alpha = 1$) is straightforwardly generalized to the general case $\alpha \in (0, 1]$. The critical curves through α-scale

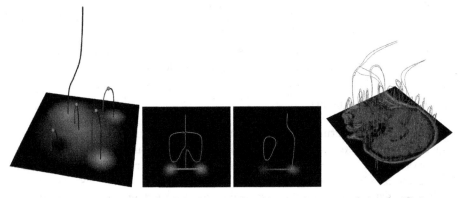

Fig. 2. Left: Illustration of annihilations in Gaussian scale space of simple 2D image. Middle: Illustration of creations in Gaussian scale space of simple 2D image. Right: Illustration of critical paths within Gaussian (in blue) and Poisson scale space (in red) of MRI-image of the brain.

spaces continuously depend on α, if scale is re-parameterized by $s \mapsto C * s^{1/(2\alpha)}$. Here the dimensionless constant $C > 0$ is still arbitrary and in our evaluations it is chosen to scale the last annihilation at a fixed length. Furthermore we notice that the physical dimension of the re-parameterized scale equals length for all $\alpha \in (0, 1]$. This continuous dependence is not surprising as the solutions (both on a bounded and unbounded domain) continuously depend on α, recall (2) and (6). However, in practice, it quite often happens that different extrema and saddles annihilate in α-scale spaces, because of bifurcations with respect to the deformation of the scale space parameterized by α. Top-points can be created and annihilated with increasing α. Although, not considered here, this may be a point for further investigation from a Morse-theoretical point of view, see figure 3.

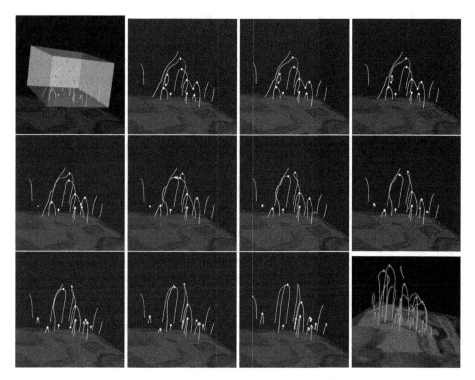

Fig. 3. The critical curves trough α scale spaces of some arbitrary 2D-grey-value image only plotted within a box $[s_1, s_2] \times [x_1, x_2]$, $s_1 < s_2$, $x_1 < x_2$. From top left to bottom right, $\alpha = 1$ (Gaussian scale space) down to $\alpha = 1/2$ Poisson scale space, $\alpha = 0.1, 0.95, 0.9, \ldots, 0.5$. Notice that in the case $\alpha = 1$ there are two creations (two crtical curves are bending below). In one of these cases (the closed loop) this creation is immediately followed by a annihilation of the same extremum and saddle. The critical curves continuously depend on α, but still for example at $\alpha \approx 0.75$ a (besides the bifurcation where the closed creation-annihilation-loop disappears) bifurcation arises where a scale space creation and annihilation meat eachother. The last figure in the bottom row clearly illustrates the large difference in topology (due to the bifurcations in α) within the Gaussian and Poisson scale space in a larger box within the same scale space.

3   Local Morse Theory for Gaussian Scale Space and Poisson Scale Space

In this subsection we give a short summary of the local Morse theory developed initially by James Damon,[10], for the diffusion equation and investigate how they translate to the case of the Poisson equation. It turns out that the generic topological changes in Poisson scale space correspond to the generic topological changes in Gaussian scale space. However, a fundamental difference between the frameworks, is that a Poisson scale space allows creations in scale spaces of 1D signals ($d = 1$), whereas in the Gaussian scale space the diffusion equation does not allow creations in scale space of a 1D signal. Although these creations in a 1D Poisson scale space are stable/generic in the mathematical sense, they do not seem to occur frequently in practical situations[5]. Nevertheless, we will show both analytic and representative numerical examples of 1D-Poisson scale spaces including creation events.

Damon[10] introduces the groups $G = \mathcal{H}$, with $\mathcal{H}$ the group of pairs (ϕ, c), with $\phi : \mathbb{R}^{d+1} \to \mathbb{R}$ and $c : \mathbb{R} \to \mathbb{R}$ diffeomorphisms, acting on the space of solutions of smooth functions $\mathcal{S}_\alpha$ satisfying the evolution equation $\frac{\partial u}{\partial s} = -(-\Delta)^\alpha u$, $\alpha \in (0, 1]$, (in particular α-scale spaces) the group action

$$g \cdot u(x, s) = u(\phi_1(\mathbf{x}, s), \phi_2(s)) + c(s) ,$$

where $g \in \mathcal{H}$, the group of pairs $(\mathbf{x}, s) \mapsto (\phi_1(\mathbf{x}, s), \phi_2(s))$, where $c, \phi_1 : \mathbb{R}^{d+1} \to \mathbb{R}^d$ and $\phi_2 : \mathbb{R}^+ \to \mathbb{R}^+$ are diffeomorphisms and where $\phi_2'(0) > 0$. Furthermore, Damon[10] introduces the group $G = \mathcal{IS}$, with $\mathcal{IS}$ the group of pairs (ϕ, ψ), with $\phi : \mathbb{R}^{d+1} \to \mathbb{R}$, $\psi : \mathbb{R}^2 \to \mathbb{R}$ diffeomorphisms of the forms $\phi(\mathbf{x}, s) = (\phi_1(x, s), \phi_2(s))$ and $\psi(y, t) = (\psi_1(y, t), t)$ with $\phi_2'(0) > 0$ and $\frac{\partial}{\partial y}\psi(0, 0) > 0$ and $\psi(0, t) = 0$, acting on $\mathcal{S}_\alpha$ by

$$g \cdot u(x, s) = \psi_1(u \circ \phi(\mathbf{x}, s), s) + c = \psi_1(u(\phi_1(\mathbf{x}, s), \phi_2(s)), s) .$$

By introducing these groups, he defines equivalence relations by means of

$$u \sim v \text{ iff there exists a } g \in G \text{ such that } u = g \cdot v, \tag{8}$$

i.e. two elements within $\mathcal{S}_\alpha$ are equivalent iff they lie on the same orbit, which yields $\mathcal{H}$ and $\mathcal{IS}$-equivalence depending on the choice of group (action).[6] However, here we follow an approach first formulated by J.C.van der Meer to singularity theory for the diffusion equation, which is similar to the case $G = \mathcal{IS}$ similar cf. [11]. In this approach the action of the group $G = \text{Diff}_d \times \text{Diff}_1$, with Diff_n the group of diffeomorphisms from $\mathbb{R}^d$ to itself, acting on images $f : \mathbb{R}^d \to \mathbb{R}$ is given by

$$(g \cdot f)(\mathbf{x}) = \psi \cdot f \cdot \phi^{-1}(\mathbf{x}), \qquad g = (\phi, \psi).$$

Notice that this group rather acts on the set of images, rather than on the space of double sided ($\tilde{u}_f = e^{-(-\sqrt{-\Delta})s}f, s \in \mathbb{R}$) scale spaces, which are to be considered as 1-parameter deformations on images.

Definition 1. *Let $f : \mathbb{R}^d \to \mathbb{R}$. A 1-parameter deformation(or unfolding[7]) of f is a continuous map $u : \mathbb{R}^d \times \mathbb{R}^1 \to \mathbb{R}$ such that $u(\boldsymbol{x}, \boldsymbol{0}) = f(\boldsymbol{x})$.*

---

[5] They do seem to occur more frequently in the conjugate Poisson scale space.

[6] Notice that with respect to $\mathcal{IS}$-equivalence, that the $\mathcal{IS}$-group action is rather similar to the $\mathcal{H}$-group, but the intensity may change over scale as well (by ψ_1) and the role of $s > 0$ is no longer distinguished, so that by the equivalence relation one keeps track of local changes of an iso-intensity surface as it undergoes a transition and the intensity level of that critical point.

[7] With unfolding one usually means the map $(\mathbf{x}, s) \mapsto (u(\mathbf{x}, s), s)$.

By considering 1-parameter deformations of the identity of the group G we obtain the group G_{un}, which acts on 1-parameter deformations of images (in particularly scale spaces) by means of

$$(\tilde{g} \cdot u)(\mathbf{x}, s) = \tilde{\psi}(u(\tilde{\phi}^{-1}(\mathbf{x}, s)), s) \ ,$$

where $\tilde{\psi}(y, 0) = \psi(y)$ and $\tilde{\phi}^{-1}(\mathbf{x}, 0) = (\phi^{-1}(\mathbf{x}), 0)$. Notice that $(\tilde{g} \cdot \tilde{u}_f)(\mathbf{x}, 0) = (g \cdot f)(\mathbf{x})$, for all $\tilde{g} \in G_{un}$ corresponding to a certain $g \in G$ for every $f \in \mathbb{L}_2(\mathbb{R}^2)$.

Definition 2. *Two deformations u, v are called $\tilde{G}$-equivalent if u lies within the obit of v, or more precisely, there exists a $\tilde{g} \in \tilde{G}$ such that $u \sim v \Leftrightarrow u = \tilde{g} \cdot v$.*

Definition 3. *A function $f : \mathbb{R}^d \rightarrow \mathbb{R}$ is G-stable if any deformation is G-equivalent to the constant deformation. A deformation u is $\tilde{G}$-stable[8] if any deformation of u is $\tilde{G}$ equivalent to the constant deformation.*

A function $f : \mathbb{R}^d \rightarrow \mathbb{R}$ is G-stable (or generic) iff the tangent space at f, $T_G(f)$ equals $\mathcal{E}_0$, the space of all smooth germs of functions at zero.

Lemma 1. *Thereby a double-sided scale space representation $\tilde{u}_f$ is $\tilde{G}$-stable iff either f is stable or the co-dimension of f in $\mathcal{E}_0$ equals 1, $dim(\mathcal{E}_0/T_G(f)) = 1$, and $\frac{\partial}{\partial s}\tilde{u}_f\big|_{\tau=0}$ generates the complement.*

However, we are merely interested in single sided scale spaces where scale is a strictly positive parameter, $s > 0$, as we do not want to include (ill-posed) deblurring.

This means that in the co-dimension one case we can only generate half [9] of the remainder in the tangent space.

This is the reason for a distinction between one-sided and two sided stability. In the case of two sided stability the function (or rather germ) f was already stable, whereas in the second case the co-dimension of f in $\mathcal{E}_0$ equals 1. For further details, see Van der Meer[11].

3.1   A Partition of Equivalence Classes of $\tilde{G}$-Stable Gaussian Deformations

The space of $\tilde{G}$-stable Gaussian Deformations $\mathcal{S}_{\alpha=1}$ can be partitioned into equivalence classes due to the equivalence relation given by (2). First we consider the case $d \geq 2$. Then the equivalence classes (germs) are represented by one of the following functions:

1. Two sided stable germs:
    (a) $u(\mathbf{x}, s) = x_1$, (submersion)

---

[8] The notion of stability can be rephrased as follows: A function u is stable if all functions that are close to u (in an appropriate topology) are $\tilde{G}$-equivalent to u.

[9] The sign of $\frac{\partial u}{\partial s}\big|_{s=0}$ relative to becomes relevant in the definition of $\tilde{G}$-equivalence.

(b) $2ds + \sum_{i=1}^{d} x_i^2$

(c) $\sum_{i=1}^{d} a_i x_i^2$, with $\sum_{i=1}^{d} a_i = 0$ all $a_i \neq 0$. (classified by the signs of a_i)

2. One sided stable germs:

   (a) $x_1^3 - 6 x_1(x_2^2 + s) + Q(x_2, \ldots, x_d, s)$, (creations of critical points),
   (b) $x_1^3 + 6s\, x_1 + Q(x_2, \ldots, x_d, s)$, (annihilations of critical points),

with $Q(\mathbf{x}, s) = \sum_{k=2}^{d} \epsilon_k(x_k^2 + 2s)$, with $\epsilon_k = \pm 1$ for $k = 2, \ldots, n$.

The two-sided stable germs are of less interest since in all of these cases $T_{\mathcal{G}}(f) = \mathcal{E}_0$ and thereby $T_{\mathcal{G}}(f) + \mathbb{R}^+ \left. \frac{\partial u}{\partial s} \right|_{s=0} = T_{\mathcal{G}}(f) = \mathcal{E}_0$. So here we have no bifurcations of the critical paths in scale space.

It follows from Lemma 1 that the only bifurcations the image f can undergo as a consequence of Gaussian blurring are given by singularities of co-dimension 1. The standard form of a co-dimension one function is given by

$$C_1(\mathbf{x}) = x_1^3 + \sum_{i=2}^{d} a_i x_i^2, a_i \neq 0, \tag{9}$$

with universal deformation $x_1^3 + t\, x_1 + \sum_{i=2}^{d} a_i x_i^2$. For $t > 0$ there are no critical points while for $t < 0$ there are two critical points, a saddle and an extremum. This is known as the cusp catastrophe [12].

The Gaussian deformation of C_1 is given by $(G_s * C_1)(\mathbf{x}) = x_1^3 + 6s\, x_1 - 2(\sum_{i=2}^{d} a_i)s + \sum_{i=2}^{d} a_i x_i^2$. This yields the germs describing the annihilation of critical points in a Gaussian scale space. Notice that the complement to the tangent space is spanned by the vector $\Delta C_1(\mathbf{x}) = 6\, x_1 \equiv x_1$.

Consider $C_2(\mathbf{x}) = x_1^3 - 6x_2^2 x_1 + \sum_{i=2}^{d} a_i x_i^2$. Although C_2 is equivalent to C_1 their Gaussian deformations are not one-sided equivalent: The Gaussian deformation of C_2 equals $G_s * C_2(\mathbf{x}) = x_1^3 - 6x_2^2 x_1 - 6x_1 s - 2(\sum_{i=2}^{d} a_i)s + \sum_{i=2}^{d} a_i x_i^2$, so now the complement to the tangent space is spanned by the vector $\Delta C_2(\mathbf{x}) = -6\, x_1 \equiv -x_1$.

The case $d = 1$ can be treated in an analogue matter, except for the annihilation germ, where no such x_2 is at hand. Creations can not occur in a Gaussian scale space. Recall, to this end that that the curvature at a catastrophe point $(\mathbf{x}*, s*)$ (u_{xx} and u_x vanish) equals $\kappa = \frac{1}{\|\mathbf{w}\|^2} \det M$, see (7). In $1D$ the matrix M is given by

$$M(\mathbf{x}*, s*) = \begin{pmatrix} u_{xx}(\mathbf{x}*, s*) & u_{xs}(\mathbf{x}*, s*) \\ u_{xxx}(\mathbf{x}*, s*) & u_{xxs}(\mathbf{x}*, s*) , \end{pmatrix}$$

and since $u_{xx}(\mathbf{x}*, s*) = 0$ it directly follows from

$$\det M(\mathbf{x}*, s*) = -u_{xs}(\mathbf{x}*, s*)u_{xxx}(\mathbf{x}*, s*) = -(u_{xxx}(\mathbf{x}*, s*))^2$$

that the curvature is always negative, allowing only annihilations and no creations. Notice that this argument does not hold in a Poisson scale space, where

$$\det M(\mathbf{x}*, s*) = u_{xs}(\mathbf{x}*, s*)u_{xxx}(\mathbf{x}*, s*) = -\frac{1}{2}[\frac{d}{ds}u_{xs}]^2(\mathbf{x}*, s*) = -\frac{1}{2}[\frac{d}{ds}v_{xx}]^2(\mathbf{x}*, s*),$$

where v denotes the conjugate Poisson scale space, is not a priori negative.

3.2 A Partition of $\mathcal{G}$-Stable Poisson Deformations

Following the same line as for the Gaussian case we obtain the following partition of $\tilde{G}$-stable Poisson Deformations:

1. Two sided stable germs:
   (a) $u(\mathbf{x}, s) = x_1$, (submersion)
   (b) $-2ds^2 + \sum_{i=1}^{d} x_i^2$
   (c) $\sum_{i=1}^{d} a_i x_i^2$, with $\sum_{i=1}^{d} a_i = 0$ all $a_i \neq 0$. (classified by the signs of a_i)
2. One sided stable germs:
   (a) $x_1^3 - 3s^2 x_1 - s\, x_1 + Q(x_2, \ldots, x_d, s)$, (creations of critical points),
   (b) $x_1^3 - 3s^2 x_1 + s\, x_1 + Q(x_2, \ldots, x_d, s)$, (annihilations of critical points),

with $Q(\mathbf{x}, s) = \sum_{k=2}^{d} \epsilon_k(x_k^2 - s^2)$, where $\epsilon_k = \pm 1$ for $k = 2, \ldots, d$.

The annihilation and creation germ are obtained by means of harmonic extension of the cusp catastrophe C_1 given by (9). To this end we notice that $\Re((x_1^3 \pm is)^3) = x_1^3 - 3s^2 x_1$. At this point it should be noticed that the Laplace operator factorizes in 2 different ways

$$\Delta_{d+1} = \frac{\partial^2}{\partial s^2} + \frac{\partial^2}{\partial x_1^2} + \Delta_{d-1} = \left(\frac{\partial}{\partial s} - \sqrt{-\Delta_d}\right)\left(\frac{\partial}{\partial s} + \sqrt{-\Delta_d}\right)$$
$$= \left(\frac{\partial}{\partial s} + i\frac{\partial}{\partial s}\right)\left(\frac{\partial}{\partial s} - i\frac{\partial}{\partial s}\right) + \Delta_{d-1},$$

As we already noticed, the first factorization tells us that upward harmonic extension of an image $f \in L_2(\mathbb{R}^d)$ under the additional requirement that the harmonic extension should uniformly vanish as $s \to \infty$ is equivalent to solving the first order pseudo differential evolution system (1) for $\alpha = 1/2$, leading to Poisson scale space. Here we only consider local behavior and do not have the additional requirement at hand. Therefore harmonic extension of the 1 cusp catastrophe (with co-dimension 1) is not sufficient. For example, a creation by harmonic extension could be due to a Poisson de-blurring.[10] More precisely, the Poisson deformation could in principle be obtained by means of the evolution generated by $+\sqrt{-\Delta}$ rather than $-\sqrt{-\Delta}$). At this point, in comparison to the Gaussian case, there arises a technical problem as the convolution of the cusp catastrophe with the Poisson kernel does not exist.

---

[10] Annihilations become creations if $s \mapsto -s$.

Therefore (as we are interested in local behavior only) we compute $(H_s^d *$ $g_{b,\varepsilon}^d)(\mathbf{x})$, where H_s^d denotes the d dimensional Poisson/Cauchy kernel and

$$g_{b,\varepsilon}^d(\mathbf{x}) = g_{b,\varepsilon}^1(x_1) = (x_1^3 + \varepsilon x_1)1_{[-b,b]}(x_1), \mathbf{x} = (x_1, \ldots, x_d),$$

where $\varepsilon = \pm 1$ and $1_{[-b,b]}(x_1) = 1$ if $|x_1| < b$ and 0 elsewhere. Some computation yields

$$\begin{aligned} (H_s^d * g_{b,\varepsilon}^d)(\mathbf{x}) &= (H_s^1 * g_{b,\varepsilon}^1)(x_1) \\ &= \tfrac{1}{2\pi} \left\{ 8\,x_1\,b\,s - 2(x_1^3 - 3x_1s^2 + \varepsilon x_1) \left[\arctan\left(\tfrac{x_1-b}{s}\right) - \arctan\left(\tfrac{x_1+b}{s}\right) \right] \right. \\ &\quad \left. -s(s^2 - 3x_1^2 + 2) \log \tfrac{(x_1-b)^2+s^2}{(x_1+b)^2+s^2} \right\}. \end{aligned}$$

If we now omit the order $O(b)$-term and take the limit $b \to \infty$ we indeed obtain the annihilation $(\varepsilon = 1)$ and creation $(\varepsilon = -1)$ germs $x_1^3 - 3\,x_1s^2 + \varepsilon x_1$, $\varepsilon = \pm 1$.

Further we notice that in contrast to the Gaussian case creations are $\mathcal{G}$-stable in the 1D-case $d = 1$. Notice that in the 1D-creation case the critical paths of the above germ are given by $x(s) = \pm\sqrt{s^2 + \tfrac{1}{3}s}$, $s > 0$, whereas the critical paths of the annihilation germ are given by $x(s) = \pm\sqrt{s^2 - \tfrac{1}{3}s}$, $s < 0$.

For a simple analytic example of a 1D-creation (at scale $s = 0$) in Poisson scale space, where the initial condition only consists of 3-delta spikes, see figure 4. To this end we notice that in stead of δ-spikes (which are distributions, not functions) one may as well take the step function $f = -1_{(-d,d)} + 1_{(a-d,a+d)} + C * 1_{(-b-d,-b+d)}$, with $a, b > 2 * d$ as initial condition. In this case the Poisson scale space can also be computed analytically and the scale space is given by

$$\begin{aligned} u_f^\alpha(x, s) &= \tfrac{1}{\pi} \left(\arctan\left(\tfrac{x-a+d}{s}\right) - \arctan\left(\tfrac{x-a-d}{s}\right) \right. \\ &\quad \left. - \arctan\left(\tfrac{x+d}{s}\right) + \arctan\left(\tfrac{x+d}{s}\right) + C \arctan\left(\tfrac{x+b+d}{s}\right) - C \arctan\left(\tfrac{x+b-d}{s}\right) \right), \end{aligned}$$

which also has five extrema at $s = 1/4$, for example at $\approx -1.50, 0.128, 0.304, 2.96$ and 4.00, if $a = 4$, $b = 1.5$, $d = 0.1$, $C = 25$. For a numerical example of a 1D-creation *within* (at a scale $s > 0$) Poisson scale space see figure 5.

4   Causality in Gaussian and Poisson Scale Space

Another difference the deeps structure between Gaussian scale space and other α-scale spaces $(\alpha \neq 1)$ is causality. There exists two types of causality, see Definition 4, the Gaussian scale space is the only α-scale space which satisfies strong causality.[11] To this end we refer to figure 7 and we note that it is already shown by Hummel[13] that strong causality is equivalent to the maximum principle, see Definition 5, which is well-known to hold for the diffusion system. The maximum principle follows directly follows by the Koenderink's principle that states that $u_s(\mathbf{x}, s)\Delta u(\mathbf{x}, s) > 0$ at spatial extrema, which only holds in a Gaussian scale space, and which guarantees that local extrema do not enhance.

---

[11] In [1] we have shown that all α-scale spaces satisfy weak causality.

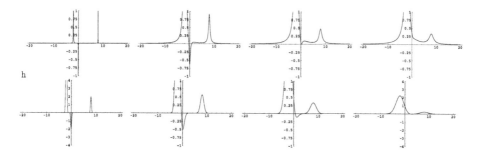

Fig. 4. Top Row: From left to right, slices of the Poisson scale space, $u_f^\alpha(\cdot, s)$, of a signal f consisting of only 3 δ-spikes, with analytic solution $u_s^{\alpha=1/2}(x) = K_s^{\alpha=1/2}(x - a) + K_s^{\alpha=1/2}(x) + c * K_s^{\alpha=1/2}(x + b)$, $a = 8, b = 2, c = 10$ at $s = 0.001$, $s = 0.05$, $s = 0.1$, $s = 0.15$. Bottom Row: Corresponding Gaussian scale space $u_s^{\alpha=1}(x) = K_s^{\alpha=1}(x - a) + K_s^{\alpha=1}(x) + c * K_s^{\alpha=1}(x + b)$, $s = (1/2)\sigma^2$ at $\sigma = 0.2$, $\sigma = 0.7$, $\sigma = 0.12$, $\sigma = 0.17$. This simple analytical example gives a clear illustration of a creation (3 singular points at $s = 0$ become 5 singular points at $s > 0$) in Poisson scale space at $s = 0$, whereas in the Gaussian scale space the number of extrema remains 3 as it should as creations can not occur in a 1D-Gaussian scale space. Notice that the extremum at $x \approx 1.5$ increases in value in the Poisson scale space, this is not possible in a Gaussian scale space, due to the Koenderinks principle, which is related to the difference in causality (and maximum principle) between Gaussian and Poisson scale space.

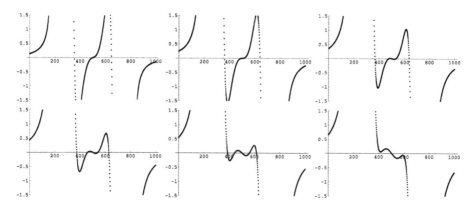

Fig. 5. Top down, left to right, slices of a numerical implementation of a 1D-Poisson scale space, $u_f^\alpha(\cdot, s)$, of a numerical signal f, with $s = 0, 0.4, 0.8, 1.2, 1.6., 2.0$. It is clearly seen that a creation event takes place at $(x, s) \approx (500, 0.5)$.

Definition 4. Weak Causality : *Any scale space isophote $u(\boldsymbol{x}, s) = \lambda$ is connected to the ground plane, i.e. it is connected to a point $u(\boldsymbol{x}, 0) = \lambda$.*
Strong Causality Constraint : *For every $s_1 \geq 0$ and $s_2 > 0$ with $s_2 > s_1$ the intersection of any connected component of an isophote within the domain $\{(\boldsymbol{x}, s) \in \mathbb{R}^d \times \mathbb{R}^+ \mid \boldsymbol{x} \in \mathbb{R}^d, s_1 \leq s < s_2\}$ with the plane $s = s_1$ should not be empty.*

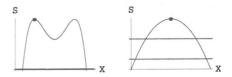

Fig. 6. Left: Weak causality, Right: Strong causality

Definition 5. *(Cylinder Maximum Principle.) Let Ω be a (arbitrary) bounded subset of $\mathbb{R}^d$ and $s_1 > 0$ such that u is continuous on $\overline{\Omega} \times [0, s_1]$, then u attains its maximum or minimum in say $(x, s) \in \overline{\Omega} \times [0, s_1]$. Either we must have $s = 0$ or $x \in \partial\Omega$.*

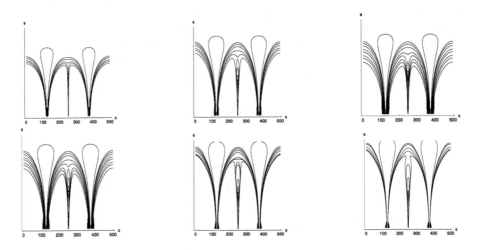

Fig. 7. Isophotes of various scale space representations of a signal consisting of 1 small delta spike between two larger delta spikes. Top row: $\alpha = 0.5$ (Poisson scale space), $\alpha = 0.6$, $\alpha = 0.7$, bottom row: $\alpha = 0.8$, $\alpha = 0.9$ and $\alpha = 1$ (Gaussian scale space). The α scale spaces are sampled according to $s_\alpha = e^{\alpha \tau_n}$, with equidistant τ_n. To this end we notice that both $(s_\alpha)^{\frac{1}{2\alpha}}$ and $\sqrt{s_1} = \sigma$ have dimension [Length]. The stretching of the isophotes as α increases is of no importance. The above figure shows that for each $\alpha \in (0, 1)$ there exist locally concave critical isophotes .

5   Conclusion

There exists a simple and strong connection between α-scale spaces and the corresponding vector scale spaces (and their flow fields). In particular between the case of Poisson scale space ($\alpha = 1/2$), where this vector scale space is the well-known Monogenic scale space, and the case of Gaussian scale space ($\alpha = 1$), where this vector scale space extension equals the first order jet, which is somewhat surprising concerning the different physics involved (respectively potential physics and heat physics). This raises the question whether these α-scale spaces are essentially different for multi-scale image analysis, as methods in one framework are easily translated to methods in the other frameworks. We approached this question only from a topological point of view and conclude that the deep structure of α-scale spaces, although continuously deformed by α, provided scale is properly re-parameterized, is rather different:

- Experiments on daily life images often show that different extrema and saddles annihilate in α-scale spaces. Moreover, creation events that take place in one scale space need not take place in the other.
- By applying morse theory on Poisson scale space and Gaussian scale space we deduce that creations are generic events in 1D-Poisson scale space (illustrated by both analytic and numerical examples), whereas they can not occur in Gaussian scale space.
- Isophotes through critical points do behave differently in Gaussian scale space than in the other α-scale spaces, where they behave similarly.

Acknowledgements

Special thanks to professor James Damon, Department of Mathematics at the University of North-Carolina, who pointed us to the fact that most results on singularity theory for the diffusion equation also applied to the Poisson equation. Furthermore the authors wish to thank to dr. J.C. van der Meer, Department of Mathematics Eindhoven University of Technology for his remarks on singularity theory.

References

1. Duits, R., Florack, L., de Graaf, J., ter Haar Romeny, B.: On the axioms of scale space theory. Journal of Mathematical Imaging and Vision 20 (2004) 267298
2. Kanters, F., Florack, L., Duits, R., Platel: α-scale space kernels in practice. In Geppener, Gurevich, N.Z.e.a., ed.: 7th International Conference on Pattern Recognition and Image Analysis, New Information Technologies, St.Petersburg (2004) 260263 Extended version is to appear in special issue of the International Journal for Pattern Recognition and Image Analysis MAIK NAUKA/Interperiodica, Publishing Moscow, 2005 Volume 15 number 2.
3. Feller, W.: An Introduction to Probability Theory and its Applications. Volume 2. John Wiley and sons, Inc., New York, London, Sydney (1966)
4. Felsberg, M.: Low-Level Image Processing with the Structure Multivector. PhD thesis, Institute of Computer Science and Applied Mathematics Christian-Albrechts-University of Kiel (2002)
5. Duits, R., Felsberg, M., Florack, L.: α scale spaces on a bounded domain. Proceedings Scale Space Conference, Isle of Skye,UK. (2003) 494510
6. Felsberg, M., Duits, R., Florack, L.: The monogenic scale space on a bounded domain and its applications. Proceedings Scale Space Conference, Isle of Skye, UK. (2003) 209224

7. Loog, M., Duistermaat, J.J., Florack, L.M.J.: On the behavior of spatial critical points under Gaussian blurring. a folklore theorem and scale-space constraints. In Kerckhove, M., ed.: Scale-Space and Morphology in Computer Vision: Proceedings of the Third International Conference, Scale-Space 2001, Vancouver, Canada. Volume 2106 of Lecture Notes in Computer Science. Springer-Verlag, Berlin (2001) 183192

8. Kuijper, A., Florack, L.M.J.: Hierarchical pre-segmentation without prior knowledge. In: Proceedings of the 8th International Conference on Computer Vision (Vancouver, Canada, July 9 12, 2001), IEEE Computer Society Press (2001) 487493

9. Florack, L., Kuijper, A.: The topological structure of scale-space images. Journal of Mathematical Imaging and Vision 12 (2000) 6579

10. Damon, J.: Local Morse theory for solutions to the heat equation and Gaussian blurring. Journal of Differential Equations 115 (1995) 368401

11. van der Meer, J.C.: A note on local morse theory in state-scale space and gaussian deformations. In preparation: Technical CASA-report , Department of Mathematics, University of Technology Eindhoven, http://www.win.tue.nl/casa/research/casareports/2005.html (2005)

12. Poston, T., Stewart, I.N.: Catastrophe Theory and its Applications. Pitman, London (1978)

13. Hummel, R., ed.: Proc. IEEE Comp. Soc. Conf. Computer Vision and Pattern Recognition, Miami Beach, IEEE (1986)

A Note on Local Morse Theory in Scale Space and Gaussian Deformations

Jan–Cees van der Meer

Faculteit Wiskunde en Informatica,
Technische Universiteit Eindhoven,
P.O.box 513, 5600 MB Eindhoven, The Netherlands
j.c.v.d.meer@tue.nl

Abstract. In this note we study the local behavior of singularities occurring in scale space under Gaussian blurring. Based on ideas from singularity theory for vector fields this is done by considering deformations or unfoldings. To deal with the special nature of the problem the concept of Gaussian deformation is introduced. Using singularity theory the stability of these deformations is considered. New concepts of one-sided stability and one-sided equivalence are introduced. This way a classification of stable singularities is obtained which agrees with those known in literature.

1 Introduction

In computer vision (see [6], [7]) the main problem is to identify and manipulate objects in a computer screen image. In general the image is given by a "pixel intensity" function. By embedding this function in a one-parameter family a scale-space representation is obtained, with the parameter representing the scale. The scale on which the image is considered is changed by applying "blurring". In most literature Gaussian blurring is considered. Starting with an intensity function $u_0(x)$ on $\mathbb{R}^n$ Gaussian blurring yields a family of intensity functions $u(x; \tau)$, where τ can be considered the scale parameter. When considering Gaussian blurring these functions have to satisfy the diffusion equation

$$\frac{\partial u}{\partial \tau} = \Delta u \,, \tag{1}$$

with $u(x, 0) = u_0(x)$, $u_0 : \mathbb{R}^n \to \mathbb{R} \in C^0(\mathbb{R}^n, \mathbb{R})$. In [5] it is shown that the axioms of scale space allow also blurring with respect to the operators $-(-\Delta)^\alpha$, $0 < \alpha < 1$. Through blurring a less detailed image is obtained by diffusion of the intensity function which is equivalent to considering a larger scale. This way the image can be blurred in such a way that it only contains the relevant information. At some stages one may however want to reconstruct parts of the image in more detail.

In the following we want to understand the behavior of the intensity functions, especially the qualitative changes the intensity functions will undergo when

O.F. Olsen et al. (Eds.): DSSCV 2005, LNCS 3753, pp. 249–258, 2005.

changing the scale parameter. We will at first restrict to the case of two dimensional images, where local qualitative changes will be studied. Local qualitative changes occur when a critical point of the intensity function changes its nature. If the intensity functions are required to be sufficiently differentiable one can interpret the level lines of the intensity function as integral curves of an Hamiltonian system or equipotential lines of a gradient vector field. The scale parameter can now be considered as a deformation parameter of some planar Hamiltonian system or gradient vector field. Consequently, the questions concerning the local behavior of critical points of smooth functions is similar to studying bifurcations of vector fields. The intensity functions are however parameter dependent in a particular way, i.e. the parameter is introduced by Gaussian blurring. To deal with this we introduce the new concept of semigroup deformations and show that this is the proper framework for studying bifurcations under Gaussian blurring. We will illustrate the theory by applying it to Gaussian deformations, that is, work with the semigroup generated by the Laplace operator. For semigroups generated by the operators $-(-\Delta)^{\alpha}$, $0 < \alpha < 1$, the theory should apply as well. Because in this case the computations will be somewhat more complicated this question will not be addressed in this paper. When considering the local behavior of critical points of smooth function on $\mathbb{R}^2$ we may assume the critical point to be at the origin. This can be obtained by allowing shifts or working modulo addition of constants. Also the gradient vanishes at the critical point and consequently the nature of the critical point is determined by the eigenvalues of the hessian. By Morse theory the generic critical points are centers and saddles. The idea taken from the study of singularities of vector fields is now to start from a (possibly non-generic) critical point, unfold the function and derive results concerning its stability. This way this paper provides an alternative way to obtain results concerning stable singularities in Gaussian scale space which can be found in [3] where a complete singularity theoretic treatment is given of Gaussian blurring. In a much more general context results are obtained in [4] for many other generalizations, including working wit other semigroups. Compared to the singularity theoretic approach in [3] we circumvent the problem of defining the right group of transformations by applying geometric arguments. These geometric arguments allow us to obtain the results concerning this special case in a straightforward way from the results known in singularity theory. The results obtained are in a slightly different form compared to Damon's. The origin of these differences lies in the fact that the underlying group of transformations is different from the ones chosen in [3] as we exploit full $\mathcal{A}$-equivalence.

2   Preliminaries on Stability, Deformations and Unfoldings

We will start with recalling some facts from singularity theory and/or bifurcation theory ([1,2,10]) in order to reveal the precise meaning of the terminology used.

Let $\mathcal{G}$ be a group of transformations acting on the space of functions. (or a local group at 0 acting on the space of germs of functions). For instance right-left action of origin preserving diffeomorphisms $\mathcal{G} = \mathcal{A} = \mathit{Diff}_n \times \mathit{Diff}_1$, with Diff_n the group of C^∞ diffeomorphisms from $\mathbb{R}^n$ to itself, acting by $g \cdot f(x) = \psi \circ f \circ \phi^{-1}(x)$, $g \in \mathcal{G}$, $\phi \in \mathit{Diff}_n$ and $\psi \in \mathit{Diff}_1$.

Also other groups can be chosen. To illustrate this we will give the groups used by Damon [3]. Damon [3] introduces $\mathcal{G} = \mathcal{H}$, with $\mathcal{H}$ the group of pairs (ϕ, c), $\phi \in \mathit{Diff}_{n+1}$ of the form $\phi(x,t) = (\phi_1(x,t), \phi_2(t))$ with $\phi_2'(0) > 0$ and $c \in \mathit{Diff}_1$, and acting by $g \cdot f(x,t) = f \circ \phi(x,t) + c(t)$. In addition $\mathcal{G} = \mathcal{IS}$ is introduced in [3], with $\mathcal{IS}$ the group of pairs (ϕ, ψ), $\phi \in \mathit{Diff}_{n+1}$ of the form $\phi(x,t) = (\phi_1(x,t), \phi_2(t))$ with $\phi_2'(0) > 0$ and $\psi \in \mathit{Diff}_2$ of the form $\psi(y,t) = (\psi_1(y,t), t)$ with $(\partial \psi_1 / \partial y)(0,0) > 0$ and $\psi_1(0,t) = 0$, and acting by $g \cdot f(x,t) = \psi_1(f \circ \phi(x,t), t) + c$. The groups $\mathcal{H}$ and $\mathcal{IS}$ should be considered as local groups of germs of diffeomorphisms at the origin acting on germs of functions. Damon describes $\mathcal{IS}$-equivalence as $\mathcal{A}$-equivalence of unfoldings preserving the target.

Note that Damon considers groups of diffeomorphisms on $\mathbb{R}^{n+1}$, that is, the parameter is included. In the sequel we will start with considering group actions of groups that do not depend on the scale parameter. The parameter will be introduced by unfolding and considering equivalence of unfoldings.

Taking the scale parameter t in $\mathcal{IS}$ equal to a constant this group reduce to to $\mathcal{A}$ with adding constants, i.e we obtain the group $\mathcal{IS}_c$ which is the group of triples (ϕ, ψ, c), $\phi \in \mathit{Diff}_n$, $\psi \in \mathit{Diff}_1$ with $(\partial \psi / \partial y)(0) > 0$ and $\psi(0) = 0$, c a constant, and acting by $g \cdot f(x) = \psi(f \circ \phi(x)) + c$.

Definition 1. *Two functions f, h from $\mathbb{R}^n$ to $\mathbb{R}$ are $\mathcal{G}$- **equivalent** if*

$$f = g \cdot h$$

for some $g \in \mathcal{G}$.

Note that the notion of equivalence depends on the choice of the group of transformations chosen.

Definition 2. *Let $f_0 : \mathbb{R}^n \to \mathbb{R}$. A **s-parameter unfolding** of f_0 is a map $f : \mathbb{R}^n \times \mathbb{R}^s \to \mathbb{R} \times \mathbb{R}^s$ such that*

i. $f(x,u) = (\tilde{f}(x,u), u)$, where $x \in \mathbb{R}^n$, $u \in \mathbb{R}^s$, $\tilde{f}(x,u) \in \mathbb{R}$, i.e. $\pi \circ f = \pi$, where $\pi : \mathbb{R}^n \times \mathbb{R}^s \to \mathbb{R}^s$ and $\pi : \mathbb{R} \times \mathbb{R}^s \to \mathbb{R}^s$ are the canonical projections.
ii. $f_0(x) = \tilde{f}(x,0)$.

In practice one often calls $\tilde{f}(x,u)$ an unfolding of f_0, although, if one wants to be precise $\tilde{f} : \mathbb{R}^n \times \mathbb{R}^s \to \mathbb{R}$ is actually a **deformation** of f_0. The **constant unfolding** is the unfolding f of f_0 with $\tilde{f}(x,u) = f_0(x)$.

When considering unfoldings of functions $f(x,u)$ we may also consider a group of transformations $\tilde{\mathcal{G}}$ consisting of unfoldings of $\mathcal{G}$ acting on these unfolded functions. A transformation $g(x,u) \in \tilde{\mathcal{G}}$ is an **unfolding of the identity** if $g(x,0) = id$. We denote the unfoldings of the identity by $\mathcal{G}_{un}$.

Let f be a s-parameter unfolding of f_0. Consider a map χ given by $\chi : v \to u = \chi(v)$, i.e. a transformation acting on the parameter space is considered. The **pull-back** of f by χ is the t-parameter unfolding

$$\chi^* f : \mathbb{R}^n \times \mathbb{R}^t \to \mathbb{R} \times \mathbb{R}^t; (x, v) \to (\tilde{f}(x, \chi(v)), v) .$$

Definition 3. *Two s-parameter unfoldings f and h of f_0 are **equivalent** if there exists a $g \in \mathcal{G}_{un}$ such that*

$$h = g \cdot f .$$

*An unfolding is **trivial** if it is equivalent to the constant unfolding. An unfolding f of f_0 is **universal** if every unfolding of f_0 is equivalent to $\chi^* f$ for some mapping χ.*

For $\mathcal{A}_{un}$ equivalence this means that

$$h = \psi \circ f \circ \varphi^{-1} \qquad (2)$$

with

$$\varphi : \mathbb{R}^{n+s} \to \mathbb{R}^{n+s}; (x,t) \to (\tilde{\varphi}(x,t), t) ,$$

and

$$\psi : \mathbb{R}^{1+s} \to \mathbb{R}^{1+s}; (y,t) \to (\tilde{\psi}(y,t), t) ,$$

where both $\tilde{\varphi}$ and $\tilde{\psi}$ are unfoldings of the identity, i.e. $\tilde{\varphi}(x,0) = x$ and $\tilde{\psi}(x,0) = x$.

Two arbitrary unfoldings f and h of f_0 are equivalent if h is $\mathcal{G}_{un}$ equivalent to $\chi^* f$ for some C^∞ map χ.

With abuse of language we wil say in the remainder of this paper that unfoldings f and h are $\mathcal{G}$-equivalent, where the action of the maps is as given above.

Like before a trivial or universal unfolding gives rise to a trivial or universal deformation.

Moreover

Definition 4. *A function f_0 is **stable** if any unfolding of f_0 is trivial.*

The notion of stability can be rephrased as follows. A function f_0 is stable if all functions that are close to f_0 (in an appropriate topology) are equivalent to f_0, i.e. are in the $\mathcal{G}$-group orbit through f_0. Stability is usually considered through the equivalent notion of infinitesimal stability, i.e. formulated in terms of the tangent space to the orbit. Let f_0 be in $\mathcal{E}_0$, the space of smooth germs of functions at zero. Let $T\mathcal{G}(f_0)$ denote the tangent space at f_0 to the $\mathcal{G}$-orbit through f_0.

Proposition 1. *$f_0 \in \mathcal{E}_0$ is **stable** if an only if $T\mathcal{G}(f_0) = \mathcal{E}_0$.*

Thus f_0 is stable if and only if the complement to the tangent space to the $\mathcal{G}$-orbit at f_0 is empty. If f_0 is not stable then define

Definition 5. *The **$\mathcal{G}$-codimension** of $f \in \mathcal{E}_0$ is*

$$d(f, \mathcal{G}) := dim\left(\mathcal{E}_0 / T\mathcal{G}(f)\right) .$$

If the co-dimension is non-zero the nontrivial deformations of f_0 can be found by unfolding f_0 in the directions which are in the complement to the tangent space. The tangent space can be given the form of a module of vector fields. Also describing the complement by a basis of vector fields X_i, we may consider the one-parameter groups e^{tX_i} acting on the space of functions. Then $f(x,t) = e^{tX_i}f_0(x)$ gives a deformation of f_0 in the direction of X_i with initial speed $X_i f_0$, where $X_i f_0$ is the derivative of f_0 along X_i. A deformation is a universal deformation if the unfolding directions span the complement to the tangent space to the orbit at f_0. Therefore a universal deformation is stable.

3 Deformations by Semi-groups

If the unfolding directions are prescribed to follow the orbit of a semigroup, for instance because the deformation is governed by some partial differential equation, we speak of a semigroup deformation. Let S_τ, $\tau > 0$ be a semigroup, then the semigroup deformation of f_0 is a function $f(x,\tau) = S_\tau f_0$, with $f : \mathbb{R}^n \times \mathbb{R}_+ \to \mathbb{R}$. By extending the domain of the parameter τ to $\mathbb{R}$ we obtain $F(x,\tau)$ with $F : \mathbb{R}^n \times \mathbb{R} \to \mathbb{R}$. We obtain the following theorem (cf [3] Lemma 4.5).

Theorem 1. $F(x,\tau)$ is $\mathcal{G}$-stable if and only if either f_0 is stable or $d(f_0,\mathcal{G})=1$ and $\frac{\partial S_\tau f_0}{\partial \tau}|_{\tau=0}$ generates the complement of $T_{\mathcal{G}}(f_0)$ in $\mathcal{E}_0$.

Proof. If f_0 is stable then any unfolding is trivial and hence stable. If f_0 is of co-dimension 1 then the unfolding $F(x,\tau)$ is stable if and only if it is universal.
□

In the above the notion of stability is used with respect to the full group action. A semigroup deformation, by definition, only exists for $\tau > 0$. That is, we have a **one-sided deformation**. As a consequence the initial speed $\frac{\partial S_\tau f_0}{\partial \tau}|_{\tau=0}$ of the deformation has to be taken with its direction. Therefore in the $\mathcal{G}$-codimension-one case we can at most obtain half of $\mathcal{E}_0$ because the diffeomorphisms acting on the deformation must respect the sign of τ. Consequently the deformation does not cover a full neighborhood of f_0 but only a halfspace. To cover the other half we need an other deformation, which, with respect to the full group, is equivalent to the previous one. The two are not equivalent if we restrict our group action to the proper halfspace and consider stability with respect to the restricted group action. To make this precise, if we have that $\mathbb{R}\{\frac{\partial S_\tau f_0}{\partial \tau}|_{\tau=0}\} + T_{\mathcal{G}}(f_0) = \mathcal{E}_0$ considered as modules, then $F(x,\tau)$ is a universal deformation. With $\mathbb{R}_+ = \{\tau \in \mathbb{R}|\tau > 0\}$ we obtain for a semigroup deformation $f(x,\tau) = S_\tau f_0$ the halfspace $\mathbb{R}_+\{\frac{\partial S_\tau f_0}{\partial \tau}|_{\tau=0}\} + T_{\mathcal{G}}(f_0)$ which is half of the tangent space if $F(x,\tau)$ is a nontrivial universal deformation.

Definition 6. *Two non-trivial one-parameter deformations* $h(x,\tau)$ *and* $g(x,\tau)$ *of* $f(x)$ *are one-sided* $\mathcal{G}$-*equivalent if they are* $\mathcal{G}$-*equivalent and*

$$\mathbb{R}_+\{\frac{\partial h}{\partial \tau}\Big|_{\tau=0}\} + T_{\mathcal{G}}(f) = \mathbb{R}_+\{\frac{\partial g}{\partial \tau}\Big|_{\tau=0}\} + T_{\mathcal{G}}(f) .$$

Now if f_0 and g_0 are $\mathcal{G}$-equivalent then also universal deformations f and g are equivalent. This need not be true for semigroup deformations because $\mathbb{R}_+\{\frac{\partial S_\tau f_0}{\partial \tau}|_{\tau=0}\} + T\mathcal{G}(f_0)$ and $\mathbb{R}_+\{\frac{\partial S_\tau g_0}{\partial \tau}|_{\tau=0}\} + T\mathcal{G}(g_0)$ need not be equivalent, i.e. diffeomorphic by a τ dependent map which respects the sign of τ.

Definition 7. *Two non-trivial semigroup deformations $S_\tau f_1$ and $S_\tau f_2$ are one-sided $\mathcal{G}$-equivalent if f_1 and f_2 are $\mathcal{G}$-equivalent, i.e. if there exists a $g \in \mathcal{G}$ such that $f_1 = g \cdot f_2$, and $S_\tau f_1$ and $g \cdot S_\tau f_2$ are on-sided $\mathcal{G}$-equivalent as one parameter deformations of f_1*

Here in $g \cdot S_\tau f_2$ the action of $g \in \mathcal{G}$ is on the x variable only. Consequently $g \cdot S_\tau f_2$ is an unfolding of $g.f_2$.

Definition 8. *A non-trivial semigroup deformation $S_\tau f_0$ is one-sided $\mathcal{G}$-stable if any semigroup deformation $S_\tau f_1$ such that $f_0 = g \cdot f_1$ for some $g \in \mathcal{G}$ and such that $\frac{\partial S_\tau f_0}{\partial \tau}(x,0)$ and $\frac{\partial g \cdot S_\tau f_1}{\partial \tau}(x,0)$ have the same sign as vectors in $\mathcal{E}_0$ is one-sided $\mathcal{G}$-equivalent to $S_\tau f_0$.*

Note that two one-sided stable semigroup deformations need not be one-sided equivalent. They might lie on different sides of the tangent space to the orbit through f_0.

For trivial deformations we have to adjust our definition.

Definition 9. *A trivial semigroup deformation $S_\tau f_0$ is two-sided $\mathcal{G}$-stable if f_0 is $\mathcal{G}$-stable.*

Note that in this case

$$\mathbb{R}_+\{\left.\frac{\partial S_\tau f_0}{\partial \tau}\right|_{\tau=0}\} + T\mathcal{G}(f_0) = T\mathcal{G}(f_0) = \mathcal{E}_0 \ .$$

Theorem 2.

(i) *If for a semigroup deformation $S_\tau f_0$, $F(x,\tau)$ is a non-trivial $\mathcal{G}$-stable deformation then $S_\tau f_0$, is one-sided $\mathcal{G}$-stable.*

(ii) *If for a semigroup deformation $S_\tau f_0$, $F(x,\tau)$ is a trivial $\mathcal{G}$-stable deformation then $S_\tau f_0$ is two-sided $\mathcal{G}$-stable.*

or phrased differently

Corollary 1. *If for a semigroup deformation $S_\tau f_0$, $F(x,\tau)$ is a non-trivial $\mathcal{G}$-universal deformation then $S_\tau f_0$, $\tau \in \mathbb{R}_+$, is one-sided $\mathcal{G}$-stable.*

Note that two one-sided stable semigroup deformations need not be one-sided equivalent. They might lie on different sides of the tangent space to the orbit through f_0.

4   Gaussian Deformations

In the case where one wants the deformation of f_0 to be a solution of the diffusion equation the deformation is completely prescribed by the diffusion equation giving $\frac{\partial u}{\partial \tau}$, that is, the direction in which one has to unfold is in fact given. The unfolding transformations are given by the semigroup $exp(\tau\Delta)$.

Definition 10. *Consider a function f_0. The one parameter deformations $f(x;\tau)$ of f_0 with the unfolding direction given by*

$$\frac{\partial u}{\partial \tau} = \Delta u ,$$

are

$$f(x,\tau) = exp(\tau\Delta)f_0 .$$

These deformations are called Gaussian deformations.

Note that $exp(\tau\Delta)$ is a holomorphic strongly continuous one-parameter semigroup, therefore its action on smooth functions is well defined. The Gaussian deformation can also be obtained by convolution with the Gaussian kernel.

The following theorem allows us to consider the notion of stability for such one-parameter semi-group deformations

Corollary 2. *$f(x,\tau) = exp(\tau\Delta)f_0$ is $\mathcal{G}$-stable if and only if either f_0 is stable or $d(f_0,\mathcal{G})=1$ and Δf_0 generates the complement of $T_\mathcal{G}(f_0)$ in $\mathcal{E}_0$.*

Thus the possible bifurcations f_0 can undergo as a consequence of Gaussian blurring are given by the singularities of co-dimension-1 for which $f(x,\tau) = exp(\tau\Delta)f_0$ is $\mathcal{G}$-stable.

Note that the constant and linear terms in f_0 do not influence the unfolding terms but linear terms and constant terms (i.e. depending only on t) can appear as unfolding terms. The linear terms in the deformation do influence the behavior of critical points. Therefore we will work modulo constant terms. Phrased differently we may include adding constant terms, which may be terms depending on t only, in the group action (compare the groups $\mathcal{H}$ and $\mathcal{IS}$ of Damon [3]). These constant terms change the intensity-level but not the qualitative behavior of the bifurcation.

If we consider $\mathcal{A}$-equivalence than the stable functions are the Morse-functions $a_1 x^2 + a_2 y^2$. The Gaussian deformations of these Morse-functions are $a_1 x^2 + a_2 y^2 + 2t(a_1 + a_2)$. These are trivial $\mathcal{A}$-deformations. That is the initial speeds belong to the tangent space to the $\mathcal{A}$-orbit through the function. They are stable. Because there is no initial speed transversal to the orbit we have two-sided stability.

The standard form of an $\mathcal{A}$-co-dimension one function is $y^3 + x^2$, with universal $\mathcal{A}$-deformation $y^3 + ty + x^2$. For $t > 0$ there are no critical points while for $t < 0$ there are two critical points, a saddle and a node. We have creation or annihilation of critical points depending on the sign of t. In terms of vector fields this is known as the saddle-node bifurcation [8]. In catastrophe theory it is the fold catastrophe [11].

Now this is an $\mathcal{A}$-deformation while we have to consider Gaussian deformations. The Gaussian deformation of $y^3 + x^2$ gives $y^3 + 6ty + x^2 + 2t$, $t > 0$. Because it is equivalent to the universal $\mathcal{A}$-deformation it is one-sided $\mathcal{A}$-stable. The complement to the tangent space is spanned by the vector y. Now the saddle-node bifurcation is in this case a saddle and a center which exist for $t < 0$ and join and disappear at $t = 0$. Thus restricting to $t > 0$ there is no structural change other then the critical point disappearing. Only by de-blurring, i.e. use $exp(-\tau\Delta)$, one sees that a saddle and a center are created. Thus blurring corresponds to annihilation.

In order to cover the codimension one case we need two one-sided $\mathcal{A}$-deformations obtained from semi-group deformations. Consider $y^3 - 6yx^2 + x^2$ which has $\mathcal{A}$-codimension one and is actually $\mathcal{A}$-equivalent to $y^3 + x^2$. Its universal $\mathcal{A}$-deformation is $y^3 - 6yx^2 + ty + x^2$ and its Gaussian deformation is $y^3 - 6yx^2 - 6ty + x^2 + 2t$. The complement to the tangent space is spanned by the vector $-y$. Thus we obtain the complementary one-sided $\mathcal{A}$-stable deformation. In terms of catastrophe theory the latter is a fold embedded in the elliptic umbilic. Again there is a saddle-node bifurcation. This time the saddle and center are created at $t = 0$.

More on catastrophe theory in the context of image analysis can be found in [9]

This classifies all the one-sided $\mathcal{A}$-stable Gaussian deformations. (cf [3] Theorem 3)

Theorem 3. *The $\mathcal{A}$-stable Gaussian deformations in $\mathbb{R}^2$ are listed in table 1.*

Table 1. $\mathcal{A}$-stable Gaussian deformations in $\mathbb{R}^2$

Initial function	Gaussian deformation	Stability type
$x^2 + y^2$	$x^2 + y^2 + 4t$	two-sided $\mathcal{A}$-stable
$x^2 - y^2$	$x^2 - y^2$	two-sided $\mathcal{A}$-stable
$y^3 + x^2$	$y^3 + 6ty + x^2 + 2t$	one-sided $\mathcal{A}$-stable
$y^3 - 6yx^2 + x^2$	$y^3 - 6yx^2 - 6ty + x^2 + 2t$	one-sided $\mathcal{A}$-stable

A straightforward generalization to higher dimensions is obtained by adding quadratic Morse functions in the additional variables (see [2]) .

Theorem 4. *The $\mathcal{A}$-stable Gaussian deformations in $\mathbb{R}^n$ are listed in table 2. Here Q is a quadratic function as in (i) but with variables x_i, $i > 1$, with $Q(t)$ its Gaussian deformation.*

If we considers functions $f(x, y)$ on $\mathbb{R}^2$ with a critical point at the origin and $f(0, 0) = 0$, then a normal form for the co-dimension 1 singularity is given by $y^3 + x^2$ which has universal deformation $y^3 + \lambda y^2 + x^2$. This universal deformation

Table 2. $\mathcal{A}$-stable Gaussian deformations in $\mathbb{R}^n$

$p = 1, \cdots, n$	Initial function	Gaussian deformation	Stability type
$(i)_p$	$\sum_{i=1}^{p} x_i^2 - \sum_{j=1}^{n-p} x_i^2$	$\sum_{i=1}^{p} x_i^2 - \sum_{j=1}^{n-p} x_i^2 + 2(2p-n)t$	two-sided $\mathcal{A}$-stable
$(ii)_p$	$x_1^3 + Q$	$x_1^3 + 6tx_1 + Q(t)$	one-sided $\mathcal{A}$-stable
$(iii)_p$	$x_1^3 - 6x_1x_i^2 + Q$	$x_1^3 - 6x_1x_i^2 - 6tx_1 + Q(t)$	one-sided $\mathcal{A}$-stable

describes the transcritical bifurcation ([8]). If one considers Gaussian blurring the question is wether this deformation is equivalent to a Gaussian deformation. Therefore take $y^3 + 6ty + x^2 + 2t$ and apply the shift $y = z + \sqrt{-2t}$ (or $y = z - \sqrt{-2t}$), we get $z^3 + 3\sqrt{-2t}z^2 + x^2 + g(t)$. An additional shift on the target puts the Gaussian deformation in the required form $z^3 + 3\sqrt{-2t}z^2 + x^2$. Thus for $t > 0$ we do not get any equivalence with (part of) the transcritical bifurcation. De-blurring gives $z^3 + 3\sqrt{2t}z^2 + x^2$. Thus we obtain the part of the transcritical bifurcation with $\lambda = 3\sqrt{2t} > 0$. We get equivalence of deformations but not for all values of the parameters. The mapping $\lambda^2 = 18t$ in parameter space reflects that the transcritical bifurcation is a folded fold. Note that using the shift $y = z - \sqrt{2t}$ gives the other half. However $z^3 + 3\sqrt{2t}z^2 + x^2$ and $z^3 - 3\sqrt{2t}z^2 - x^2$ are equivalent, so our equivalence class does not allow us to distinguish between the role of saddles and centers. Consequently both shifts $y = z + \sqrt{-2t}$ and $y = z - \sqrt{-2t}$ describe the same phenomena. In a similar fashion one can show that $y^3 - 6yx^2 - 6ty + x^2 + 2t$ is equivalent to half the transcritical bifurcation.

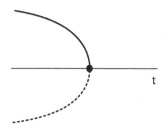

Fig. 1. Saddle-node bifurcation

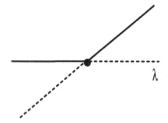

Fig. 2. Transcritical bifurcation

5 Conclusion

If we restrict to $\mathcal{A}$-equivalence and allow diffeomorphisms on the parameter space then combining all actions lead to

$$\tilde{\psi}_2(\psi_1(\tilde{f}(\tilde{\varphi}_3^{-1}(\varphi_1^{-1}(x), \varphi_2^{-1}(t)))),$$

with $\varphi_1 \in Diff_n$, $\varphi_2 \in Diff_1$, $\psi_1 \in Diff_1$, $\tilde{\varphi}_3$ and $\tilde{\psi}_2$ as in (2), which comes down to $\mathcal{A}$-equivalence of map germs $\mathbb{R}^n \times \mathbb{R} \to \mathbb{R} \times \mathbb{R}$. That is, unfoldings are also considered under right-left equivalence. The above approach was chosen to reveal the role of the directional preference invoked by the use of Gaussian deformations. It shows that one can actually take the singularity theoretic normal forms obtained for $\mathcal{A}$-equivalence and relate them to solutions of the diffusion equation. The above framework provides an alternative way to obtain the generic qualitative changes in Gaussian scale space in comparison to [3,4]. It indicates how to generalize to higher dimensions and how to deal with other operators than the Laplace-operator. Differences with the work of Damon occur because we exploit full $\mathcal{A}$-equivalence. This gives a larger group of transformations and therefore a less detailed classification. For instance there is no distinction between ellipses and circles. Furthermore working modulo constants makes it impossible to carefully keep track of the intensity levels.

Acknowledgement

I would like to thank Luc Florack for introducing me to this subject.

References

1. Arnold, V.I.: Singularities of Smooth Mappings ; Russian math. Suveys **23** (1968) 1–43
2. Arnold, V.I.: Normal forms for Functions near Degenerate Critical Points, the Weyl Groups of A_k, D_k, E_k and Lagrangian Singularities ; Funct. Anal. Appl. **6** (1972) 254–272
3. Damon, J. : Local Morse Theory for Solutions to the Heat Equation and Gaussian Blurring ; J. Diff. Eq. **115** (1995) 368–401
4. Damon, J. : Scale-Based Geometry of Nondifferentiable Functions, Measures, and Distributions, Parts I,II,III ; preprint Dept. of Math., University of North Carolina at Chapel Hill (2002)
5. Duits, R., Florack, L., De Graaf, J., and Ter Haar Romeny, B. : On the Axioms of Scale Space Theory ; J. of Math. Imaging and Vision **20** (2004) 267–298
6. Florack, L. and Koenderink, J. : A priori Scale in Classical Scalar and Density Fields ; preprint Univ. of Utrecht (1997)
   http://webdoc.sub.gwdg.de/ebook/ah/2000/techrep/CS-1997/1997-26.pdf
7. Florack, L. and Kuijper, A. : The Topological Structure of Scale-Space Images ; J. of Math. Imaging and Vision **12** (2000) 65–79
8. Guckenheimer, J. and Holmes, P. : Nonlinear Oscillations, Dynamical Systems and Bifurcations of Vector Fields, Springer-Verlag, New-York etc. (1983)
9. Kuijper, A. and Florack, L.J.M. : The Application of Catastrophe Theory to Image Analysis ; preprint Univ. of Utrecht (2001)
10. Martinet, J. : Singularities of Smooth Functions and Maps, London Math. Soc. Lect. Notes Series 58, Cambridge University Press, Cambridge (1982)
11. Poston, T. and Stewart, I. : Catastrophe Theory and Its Applications, Pitman, London (1978)

Author Index

Lecture Notes in Computer Science

For information about Vols. 1–3682

please contact your bookseller or Springer

Vol. 3726: L.T. Yang, O.F. Rana, B. Di Martino, J.J. Dongarra (Eds.), High Performance Computing and Communications. XXVI, 1116 pages. 2005.

Vol. 3725: D. Borrione, W. Paul (Eds.), Correct Hardware Design and Verification Methods. XII, 412 pages. 2005.

Vol. 3724: P. Fraigniaud (Ed.), Distributed Computing. XIV, 520 pages. 2005.

Vol. 3723: W. Zhao, S. Gong, X. Tang (Eds.), Analysis and Modelling of Faces and Gestures. XI, 4234 pages. 2005.

Vol. 3722: D. Van Hung, M. Wirsing (Eds.), Theoretical Aspects of Computing – ICTAC 2005. XIV, 614 pages. 2005.

Vol. 3721: A. Jorge, L. Torgo, P.B. Brazdil, R. Camacho, J. Gama (Eds.), Knowledge Discovery in Databases: PKDD 2005. XXIII, 719 pages. 2005. (Subseries LNAI).

Vol. 3720: J. Gama, R. Camacho, P.B. Brazdil, A. Jorge, L. Torgo (Eds.), Machine Learning: ECML 2005. XXIII, 769 pages. 2005. (Subseries LNAI).

Vol. 3719: M. Hobbs, A.M. Goscinski, W. Zhou (Eds.), Distributed and Parallel Computing. XI, 448 pages. 2005.

Vol. 3718: V.G. Ganzha, E.W. Mayr, E.V. Vorozhtsov (Eds.), Computer Algebra in Scientific Computing. XII, 502 pages. 2005.

Vol. 3717: B. Gramlich (Ed.), Frontiers of Combining Systems. X, 321 pages. 2005. (Subseries LNAI).

Vol. 3716: L. Delcambre, C. Kop, H.C. Mayr, J. Mylopoulos, Ó. Pastor (Eds.), Conceptual Modeling – ER 2005. XVI, 498 pages. 2005.

Vol. 3715: E. Dawson, S. Vaudenay (Eds.), Progress in Cryptology – Mycrypt 2005. XI, 329 pages. 2005.

Vol. 3714: J. H. Obbink, K. Pohl (Eds.), Software Product Lines. XIII, 235 pages. 2005.

Vol. 3713: L.C. Briand, C. Williams (Eds.), Model Driven Engineering Languages and Systems. XV, 722 pages. 2005.

Vol. 3712: R. Reussner, J. Mayer, J.A. Stafford, S. Overhage, S. Becker, P.J. Schroeder (Eds.), Quality of Software Architectures and Software Quality. XIII, 289 pages. 2005.

Vol. 3711: F. Kishino, Y. Kitamura, H. Kato, N. Nagata (Eds.), Entertainment Computing - ICEC 2005. XXIV, 540 pages. 2005.

Vol. 3710: M. Barni, I. Cox, T. Kalker, H.J. Kim (Eds.), Digital Watermarking. XII, 485 pages. 2005.

Vol. 3709: P. van Beek (Ed.), Principles and Practice of Constraint Programming - CP 2005. XX, 887 pages. 2005.

Vol. 3708: J. Blanc-Talon, W. Philips, D.C. Popescu, P. Scheunders (Eds.), Advanced Concepts for Intelligent Vision Systems. XXII, 725 pages. 2005.

Vol. 3707: D.A. Peled, Y.-K. Tsay (Eds.), Automated Technology for Verification and Analysis. XII, 506 pages. 2005.

Vol. 3706: H. Fuks, S. Lukosch, A.C. Salgado (Eds.), Groupware: Design, Implementation, and Use. XII, 378 pages. 2005.

Vol. 3704: M. De Gregorio, V. Di Maio, M. Frucci, C. Musio (Eds.), Brain, Vision, and Artificial Intelligence. XV, 556 pages. 2005.

Vol. 3703: F. Fages, S. Soliman (Eds.), Principles and Practice of Semantic Web Reasoning. VIII, 163 pages. 2005.

Vol. 3702: B. Beckert (Ed.), Automated Reasoning with Analytic Tableaux and Related Methods. XIII, 343 pages. 2005. (Subseries LNAI).

Vol. 3701: M. Coppo, E. Lodi, G. M. Pinna (Eds.), Theoretical Computer Science. XI, 411 pages. 2005.

Vol. 3700: J.F. Peters, A. Skowron (Eds.), Transactions on Rough Sets IV. X, 375 pages. 2005.

Vol. 3699: C.S. Calude, M.J. Dinneen, G. Păun, M. J. Pérez-Jiménez, G. Rozenberg (Eds.), Unconventional Computation. XI, 267 pages. 2005.

Vol. 3698: U. Furbach (Ed.), KI 2005: Advances in Artificial Intelligence. XIII, 409 pages. 2005. (Subseries LNAI).

Vol. 3697: W. Duch, J. Kacprzyk, E. Oja, S. Zadrożny (Eds.), Artificial Neural Networks: Formal Models and Their Applications – ICANN 2005, Part II. XXXII, 1045 pages. 2005.

Vol. 3696: W. Duch, J. Kacprzyk, E. Oja, S. Zadrożny (Eds.), Artificial Neural Networks: Biological Inspirations – ICANN 2005, Part I. XXXI, 703 pages. 2005.

Vol. 3695: M.R. Berthold, R.C. Glen, K. Diederichs, O. Kohlbacher, I. Fischer (Eds.), Computational Life Sciences. XI, 277 pages. 2005. (Subseries LNBI).

Vol. 3694: M. Malek, E. Nett, N. Suri (Eds.), Service Availability. VIII, 213 pages. 2005.

Vol. 3693: A.G. Cohn, D.M. Mark (Eds.), Spatial Information Theory. XII, 493 pages. 2005.

Vol. 3692: R. Casadio, G. Myers (Eds.), Algorithms in Bioinformatics. X, 436 pages. 2005. (Subseries LNBI).

Vol. 3691: A. Gagalowicz, W. Philips (Eds.), Computer Analysis of Images and Patterns. XIX, 865 pages. 2005.

Vol. 3690: M. Pěchouček, P. Petta, L.Z. Varga (Eds.), Multi-Agent Systems and Applications IV. XVII, 667 pages. 2005. (Subseries LNAI).

Vol. 3689: G.G. Lee, A. Yamada, H. Meng, S.H. Myaeng (Eds.), Information Retrieval Technology. XVII, 735 pages. 2005.

Vol. 3688: R. Winther, B.A. Gran, G. Dahll (Eds.), Computer Safety, Reliability, and Security. XI, 405 pages. 2005.

Vol. 3687: S. Singh, M. Singh, C. Apte, P. Perner (Eds.), Pattern Recognition and Image Analysis, Part II. XXV, 809 pages. 2005.

Vol. 3686: S. Singh, M. Singh, C. Apte, P. Perner (Eds.), Pattern Recognition and Data Mining, Part I. XXVI, 689 pages. 2005.

Vol. 3685: V. Gorodetsky, I. Kotenko, V.A. Skormin (Eds.), Computer Network Security. XIV, 480 pages. 2005.

Vol. 3684: R. Khosla, R.J. Howlett, L.C. Jain (Eds.), Knowledge-Based Intelligent Information and Engineering Systems, Part IV. LXXIX, 933 pages. 2005. (Subseries LNAI).

Vol. 3683: R. Khosla, R.J. Howlett, L.C. Jain (Eds.), Knowledge-Based Intelligent Information and Engineering Systems, Part III. LXXX, 1397 pages. 2005. (Subseries LNAI).